Downtown, Inc.

Downtown, Inc.
How America Rebuilds Cities

Bernard J. Frieden
Lynne B. Sagalyn

The MIT Press
Cambridge, Massachusetts
London, England

This book was set in Palatino by Achorn Graphic Services, Inc. and printed and bound in the United States of America.

Library of Congress Cataloging-in-Publication Data

Frieden, Bernard J.
    Downtown, Inc., how America rebuilds cities / Bernard J. Frieden and Lynne B. Sagalyn.
        P.   cm.
    Includes bibliographical references.
    ISBN 0-262-06128-7
    1. Urban renewal—United States. 2. Central business districts-
    -United States. I. Sagalyn, Lynne B. II. Title.
    HT175.F75 1989   89-36211
    307.3′42176′0973—dc20   CIP

To Elaine and Debbie
B. F.

To Emily and my parents
L. S.

Contents

Contents

Preface

One of the longest campaigns of local government has been the campaign to rebuild downtown. For more than thirty years starting in the early 1950s, big-city mayors and their allies struggled to salvage dying city centers. At first their false starts and flawed plans led to devastating, often brutal results in the urban renewal and highway programs. But by the 1970s they were working to repair the damage left from bulldozer days, and they were producing useful, attractive, and popular projects. By the 1980s the long-awaited revitalization of downtown was a reality in many cities and well under way in others.

The professionals who wrote about cities overlooked this turnaround; their books and articles were overwhelmingly critical and negative throughout the thirty-year period. Even while an unparalleled construction boom was gathering strength, most were still spelling out the reasons why efforts to rebuild downtown could not possibly succeed. When we searched for teaching material on how city officials and developers were building the new downtowns, the library was bare.

In 1983 we started work on case studies to use in class. Our hope was to learn how cities and developers went about planning and building specific projects and to get the essentials down on paper for students who intended to work at city development in the public or private sector. The projects that interested us most were the downtown retail centers springing up in dozens of cities, often regarded as the capstones of redevelopment. They were pivotal in changing the character of downtown. In contrast to earlier projects planned for an elite clientele, these were designed to draw large crowds of ordinary people. Built to compete against suburban shopping malls that had an iron grip on the retail market, they required elaborate city help to get started, and they demanded the fullest range of public and private strategies to deal with problems along the way. Whatever made these difficult projects feasible might explain what was working to stimulate downtown development in general.

We chose to study several types of retail projects in different parts of the country: Faneuil Hall Marketplace in Boston, Pike Place Market in Seattle, Town Square/Saint Paul Center in St. Paul, Plaza Pasadena, and Horton Plaza in San Diego. For a suburban benchmark case, we studied University Town Centre just outside San Diego.

Many public officials and private developers helped us with these case studies. First, we had to learn enough about shopping mall development to know which questions to ask. Our patient and good-humored tutor was Ernest Hahn, one of the most knowledgeable and experienced people in the business. He spent many hours explaining how his firm did their projects, and he encouraged his executives to brief us and to let us look over their shoulders. Others in the Hahn Company who were especially helpful include John Gilchrist, Daniel Felix, William Doyle, and Dale Nelson. Our friend Harry Newman encouraged us from the outset, guided us through the maze of retail development, and shared his enthusiasm for education through case studies. Norman Elkin of Urban Investment and Development Company, a leading downtown mall developer, was also generous in sharing information and insights with us over a period of several years.

Our chief tutors on the public side were Gerald Trimble, executive vice-president of San Diego's Centre City Development Corporation, and Joseph Coomes, one of the leading redevelopment attorneys in California. John Clise, of Seattle's Pike Place Preservation and Development Authority, was generous with his help and opened the files of his agency to us. A. Jerry Keyser provided advanced instruction on how projects work by tapping his special background as a consultant on the economics and finances of redevelopment.

We were fortunate to have the services of capable reseach associates who interviewed people, dug up background material, and wrote a case study of each project. Christie Baxter prepared the Town Square and University Town Centre cases, Jacques Gordon was responsible for Faneuil Hall and Horton Plaza, Nancy Fox for Pike Place Market, and Anita Landecker for Plaza Pasadena. They in turn owed much to people who had played major roles in each project and who agreed to be interviewed, often more than once. The main people interviewed for each project are cited in our annotated bibliography; we are grateful for their help.

Once we completed the teaching cases in 1984, we began to draw material from them to use in this book, and we broadened our research to other places and topics. Several colleagues in academia and in real estate gave us helpful advice, including Robert Fogelson, Gary Marx, Robert Weaver, James Rouse, Donald Schon, Carol Nichols, Martin Millspaugh, Jerome Lipp, Roy Drachman, and Raymond Nasher. Many people were generous in making available their own unpublished work or in leading us to data: John Avault, J. Thomas Black, Grady Clay, Sheldon Danziger, Margaret Dewar, Jameson Doig, Robert Duckworth, Samuel Ehrenhalt, Alex Ganz, Erwin Hargrove, Bennett Harrison, Arthur Johnson, Gideon Kanner, Judith Lidsky, Patricia Nicoson, Thierry Noyelle, John E. Petersen, Saskia Sassen-Koob, Susan Shick, Margaret Sowell, and Clarence Stone. On numerous occasions the International Council of Shopping Centers shared its wealth of information and experience with us; we are particularly indebted to Albert Sussman, John Riordan, John Chapman, and Margaret Hunter. We also want to acknowledge the good work of MIT research assistants David Birnbaum, Nicole Fagin, Mary Anne Knasas, Beverlee Seronick, and Rebecca Stevens.

We owe a special debt of gratitude to those who read a very long first draft of this book and made critical comments and suggestions: to Robert Wood, Martin Levin, and Robert Fogelson, whose detailed critiques were exceptionally helpful, and to Alan Altshuler, Barbara Ankeny, Jill Conway, Joseph Coomes, Lois Craig, Ned Eichler, John Gilchrist, David Grossman, Ernest Hahn, Bennett Harrison, Marshall Kaplan, Lisa Peattie, Martin Rein, Marian Shapiro, Lawrence Susskind, Judith Tendler, Gerald Trimble, Raymond Vernon, and Michael Wheeler.

We acknowledge with gratitude the financial support that made this book possible. The Ernest W. and Jean E. Hahn Foundation sponsored the preparation of teaching cases in retail development as a curriculum development project in the MIT Department of Urban Studies and Planning. An award from the Department of Housing and Urban Development's small grant program helped launch our research, and we are grateful to Donald Hovde and Feather O'Connor for encouraging us to submit a proposal. H. James Brown, director of the MIT–Harvard Joint Center for Housing Studies, provided office space and administrative help when we started. MIT sabbatical funds helped us to continue the work, together with support from the professorial chairs we have been honored to hold—the Class of 1942 Chair (Frieden) and the Class of 1922 Career Development Chair (Sagalyn). In addition, director James McKellar and research director Lawrence Bacow of the MIT Center for Real Estate Development filled gaps in our funding when we did the teaching cases and then again when we were completing the book. Rolf Engler did a superb job of managing our financial accounts and helping us to stretch available resources.

Our greatest debt is to our families—experts in shopping malls in their own right—for their encouragement, support, patience, and endurance during the many years we spent on research and writing.

Downtown, Inc.

1   A Bunch of Nobodies

In the summer of 1976, the year when cities and towns across the United States celebrated the country's two hundredth birthday, Boston staged a party for one of its own historic shrines. The templelike Quincy Market, centerpiece of three market buildings pointing from Faneuil Hall toward the waterfront, was ready for business after a four-year shutdown for reconstruction.

Opening day ceremonies reveled in the history of the place. Speakers unveiled a seven-foot stone honoring Josiah Quincy, the mayor who had dedicated the original market exactly 150 years earlier, as well as the current mayor, Kevin White. In front of the Greek Revival entrance with its classical columns, the Ancient and Honorable Artillery Company stood in formation sporting bright blue period uniforms while a brass band played "The Star-Spangled Banner." Mayor White called the occasion "truly an historical event, a rebirth." When the speeches were over, a functionary in a tricornered hat swung a handbell to open the market the way it was done in Josiah Quincy's time. Then White cut the ribbon, and developer James Rouse led a company of red-kilted Stuart Highlanders inside to pipe in the crowd for a champagne reception.

People who turned out for opening day found a place full of surprises and contradictions. The reconstruction had both preserved and changed Quincy Market: it was partly a cleaned-up gem of 1826 architecture, partly a contemporary shopping arcade. Work crews had stripped away 150 years of alterations—interior walls, add-on sheds, roof extensions—to reveal the original structure in its graceful simplicity. But they had also tampered with that historic building. They cut a hole in the first-floor ceiling to create a rotunda with a view up into the great dome above the second story. They took out the old multipaned windows and mounted large sheets of glass on pivots.

Where produce merchants had once put up canvas awnings to cover outside stalls, they built glass canopies with overhead sections that could slide down like garage doors in bad weather. And where wooden bins and tables once stood, they installed the latest stainless-steel showcases that displayed tempting wedges of cheese and pastry kept cool at eye level.

The renovation also made a feature of traditional, comfortable materials that would have found no place in a modern shopping mall: worn bricks, granite paving stones, rough wooden beams, weathered copper, stone pillars. Antique business signs embellished the rotunda, and glass panels with nineteenth-century etchings of fish and farm animals hung over the central aisle. Another old-fashioned touch came from wooden pushcarts: on opening day some forty of them were dotted around the market, operated by artists, weavers, jewelry makers, and others selling unusual handmade products.

Inside the antique shell of a building was a modern, efficient retail operation. At first glance it looked like one of the food courts that had just begun to pop up in suburban shopping malls, but there was a difference: the shopkeepers were independent Boston merchants rather than fast food franchise managers, and they sold top-quality, restaurant-grade delicacies. Their displays were a cornucopia of fresh fruits and vegetables, newly baked bread, prime steaks, imported cheeses, coffee beans, sausages, oysters, and ethnic specialties from bagels to wonton. The sight and smells of food dominated this shopping mall, sold from forty stands plus ten cafes and informal restaurants. There were also kitchenware shops and the pushcarts with carvings, pottery, stuffed toys, and other handicrafts. Unlike a shopping mall, there were no department stores and no big-ticket items. Even a starving customer would find it hard to spend more than twenty-five dollars in a visit, and most would buy snacks for less than ten dollars.

Few people in the opening day crowd knew why the market was organized this way. Its curious blend of historic setting and modern retailing was part of a deliberate strategy to merchandise history in the form of a unique shopping environment. The plan was for small, independent merchants peddling their wares aggressively to create a lively, colorful atmosphere that would draw customers away from the chain store blandness of suburban malls. To make sure tenants understood that they were to act like old-time shopkeepers, clauses in their leases ruled out such contemporary touches as canned music, shopping carts, and plastic wrappings.

Department stores were missing because there was no way to cram them into the tight spaces of the old market. National chains were missing partly by design and partly out of necessity. When Rouse's leasing agents had trouble finding enough capable independent merchants, they tried to persuade national retailers to locate branches there as well. But chain store executives accustomed to modern shopping malls took one look at the run-down Quincy Market with its basement awash at high tide and lost all interest in this strange venture.

The attractive glass canopies that fanned out from the market building were more than architectural flourishes. To cover the high cost of renovation, Rouse needed as much rentable floor space as possible, and the canopies overhead made room for two more aisles of shops and stands on the ground. The innovative pushcarts, soon widely imitated across the country, were also there to solve a practical problem. As the opening date approached, leasing was far behind schedule: "We have never opened a project that wasn't 80, 85, 90 percent leased," according to Rouse, "and six weeks before opening we were less than 50 percent leased." His managers urged him to put off the late summer opening rather than reveal an embarrassing amount of unleased space, but he was determined to get the market into operation before Labor Day. The problem was how to hide the empty stores. One of the leasing agents had interviewed about 900 artists and crafts people who had interesting products but could not afford to rent and furnish a store. Now she suggested choosing the best of these prospects and offering them a chance to lease pushcarts by the week for fifty dollars plus a percentage of their sales.

At the opening forty-three pushcarts artfully masked the dead spaces. They also added to the carnival atmosphere and made such a hit that management set aside a permanent place for them. Renting a pushcart soon became the way to set up a small business, with most vendors doing well enough to stay on for years and some moving eventually into full-sized stores. All this was the result of unleased space on opening day: "To face that disaster," Rouse acknowledged, "we . . . reinvented the pushcart and the one-week lease."[1]

Most people on opening day were in the dark about why this unusual market was built at all. Mayor White's prominence in the proceedings underscored the fact that city government had a major hand in it, but few people knew that the city was shelling out $12 million in public funds, nearly 30 percent of the total cost to redo the three market buildings next to Faneuil Hall. Fewer still understood the financial deal the city had struck with Rouse, turning over the entire property to him on a ninety-nine-year lease in exchange for a guaranteed minimum annual payment plus a share of project income from retail rents above that minimum.

City officials took the lead in organizing this venture, but they did not have a retail center in mind when they began. A dozen years earlier, redevelopment chief Edward Logue had decided to save the market buildings from demolition because of their architectural merit. After the wholesale meat and produce merchants had moved out to newer trucking terminals, the problem was to find some economic use for the place. There were vague plans for offices or apartments that could fit inside the obsolete shells and pay enough rent to preserve them. Meanwhile this was one of the most prominent sites in Boston—the first place visitors saw when they came out of the tunnel from the airport—and it was a civic embarrassment. To make matters worse, when Mayor White invited guests to his stunning office in the new City Hall, they looked through monumental windows and saw a crumbling market surrounded by delivery trucks and debris from the few remaining produce dealers. Every morning this scene of ruin and litter reminded White to do something to make it into a more fitting symbol of the new Boston he hoped to build.

While the city fathers were eager to save the market buildings any way they could, Cambridge architect Ben Thompson became intrigued with the charming but useless market complex and began to draw plans for a shopping mall based on the pageantry of food. He showed his plans to Logue, searched for a developer willing to build what he had in mind, and eventually found James Rouse in Maryland. A successful builder of suburban malls and an innovator who built the new community of Columbia between Baltimore and Washington, Rouse had the business skills to match Thompson's vision. For years he had wanted to build a shopping center in the heart of a big city, and he had confidence that it could be done. Further his company had the resources to give the city of Boston a solid guarantee of financial returns on its investment. The motivations of White, Thompson, and Rouse dovetailed remarkably well to produce a retail project for the Faneuil Hall markets.

There was more to the story behind Quincy Market, however. Boston, like other cities, was trying hard to rebuild downtown in order to climb out of a steep decline in its economy. Its first redevelopment projects, undertaken in the late 1950s and early 1960s, proved to be controversial and disappointing. Despite some achievements, such as Prudential Center, the outlook was still bleak. The public at large found little to like in big cities, and developers and investors were avoiding downtown in favor of the suburbs. The largest shopping center developer in the country, Edward DeBartolo, summed up the situation in 1973. "I wouldn't put a penny downtown," he told a reporter who asked about his business plans. "It's bad. . . . Face it, why should people come in? They don't want the hassle, they don't want the danger. . . . And the money: My God, you'd need fantastic government subsidies, amazing subsidies." "No individual or corporate setup," he maintained, "can make even a dent in these problems. So what do you do? Exactly what I'm doing: stay out in the country. That's the new downtown."[2]

Faced with these negative attitudes, big-city mayors like Kevin White were willing to take risks, to try new kinds of projects that might appeal to the public as well as demonstrate commercial success. A downtown retail center was a new idea and a risky one. If it worked, it might draw the crowds that would encourage developers and investors to come downtown.

While Boston was negotiating with Rouse, other cities were also trying to revive downtown retailing. Seattle was organizing to rebuild its Pike Place Market, St. Paul was carving out a site for its Town Square mall, and San Diego was studying the first plans for Horton Plaza. Maverick developers were responding to city invitations in several other parts of the country. In the West Ernest Hahn was the leading downtown retail developer, beginning with redevelopment projects in Hawthorne and other small California cities in the 1960s and moving on to Pasadena, Long Beach, and San Diego in the early 1970s. Rouse also began to specialize in downtown centers, venturing into Philadelphia, Baltimore, and Milwaukee even before the Faneuil Hall complex was finished. Another early developer in this field was Urban Investment and Development Company, whose Water Tower Place in Chicago opened the same year as Quincy Market. Several other downtown retail centers were already open, including Ghirardelli Square and the Cannery in San Francisco, lending credibility to proposals such as the one that Rouse and Thompson put forward.

The idea of reviving downtown retailing was in the air, but most people in the shopping center industry were skeptical, and mayors were hiding their own nervousness behind a facade of optimism. Quincy Market became an important test case. Its size, its visibility in a key location, and its unconventional character made it a project to watch. If it worked, there was hope for other old cities as well.

This project broke so many rules of retail development that even Rouse Company executives and the lenders who financed them worried about the outcome. To one leading Boston banker, the independent merchants Rouse counted on to drive this enterprise were "a bunch of nobodies"—in comparison, that is, with the moneyed national chains that dominated suburban malls. Parking was scandalously inadequate: a few hundred high-priced spaces next door and a large municipal garage ten minutes away by foot instead of the free, convenient, plentiful parking customers took for granted in the suburbs. The only air-conditioning in the food arcade came from an occasional harbor breeze blowing through an open window. Outside the once-congested streets between the three market buildings had been converted to attractive pedestrian plazas, but there was no shelter overhead against the sun, rain, or snow.

Boston bankers pondered all these handicaps and agonized so long over whether to underwrite a share of the construction loan that mayoral arm twisting was necessary to bring them into line. Even the mayor had doubts, however. Speaking at a preopening dinner, he cautioned not to expect early success. Turning to Rouse, he said: "Jim, I want you to stand firm and have faith in this market. It will take time for Boston to adopt it, but in the long run it will become part of the city."

Opening day was Thursday, August 26, a time of year when most people who had no business in town were likely to stay away to avoid the heat and the traffic. The weather forecast was for a humid day with the temperature in the eighties. The merchants were there early to set up shop, many having moved in only the day before. A moderate crowd turned out for the opening ceremonies at 11:00 in the morning, and then a huge second wave came pouring out of the financial district at lunch time. The crowd kept growing throughout the day, 100,000 strong according to police estimates. The public response was, according to the *New York Times*, "instant acceptance" as thousands wandered among the food stands and mingled with jugglers, magicians, puppeteers, acrobats, a steel band, and actors dressed as vegetables.

The crowds never stopped coming, even though Quincy Market was still one-fifth vacant on opening day and the other two market buildings would not open until 1977 and 1978. Ten million visitors came through during the first year of operations, equal to the gate count at Disneyland. With the crowds came record-breaking retail sales by the standards of Boston and most other cities. When the banks were wavering over whether to lend Rouse money, they figured his project would have to make up for its high development cost by producing an exceptional volume of sales—on the order of $150 per square foot, twice the prevailing figure in Boston stores and on a par with the most successful suburban malls. Quincy Market astounded almost everyone by producing sales of $233 per square foot in its first year, with the pushcarts doing best of all.

Faneuil Hall Marketplace, the three-building complex that included Quincy Market, soon became the first nationally recognized, popular success in the rebuilding of downtown. Its reputation spread quickly, signaling a long-awaited turnaround in the way Americans felt about cities and spawning dozens of similar retail projects across the country and beyond. Rebuilding the centers of cities was never as much of a struggle after the opening of Quincy Market as it had been before.

Legacy of the Big Stores

When mayors and their redevelopment chiefs looked to retail centers to revive their weak downtowns, they were returning to an old tradition. Retailing—and especially the department store as its key institution before the modern shopping mall—was the magnet that drew people to downtown and the glue that held it together.

The downtown that mayors were determined to rebuild was a product of the late nineteenth century and the rise of the department store. With the growth of city populations at the time, the establishment of large-scale manufacturing, and increases in personal income, there were more goods to sell and more people to buy them—if someone could figure out how to bring the people and goods together. The department store, with its wide selection and low prices, was the engine for mass merchandising. Starting as dry goods stores selling fabrics and ready-made clothing, department stores spread to the main cities of Western Europe and the United States by the last decades of the century.

These emporiums were community institutions as well as businesses. One of their functions was consumer education. For people just climbing into the middle class, shopping was a problem. Clothing and home furnishings were important for status, yet it was hard to know what to buy. Learning the value of products was not easy either since the specialty merchants who served the wealthy put no price tags on their displays and expected to bargain with their customers. To approach a milliner, cabinet-maker, or upholsterer without knowledge of products and prices could be embarrassing and costly. Department stores, in contrast, put their wares out on the floor, set the same price for everyone, and marked the prices clearly. Their elaborate displays were calculated to educate anxious shoppers in how to dress tastefully or how to furnish the parlor.

Department stores prospered by recognizing the changing place of women in society. By the mid-nineteenth century women were taking greater responsibility for managing family budgets and deciding on major purchases. Department store owners treated women as their major customers and tried to make them comfortable. They kept their stores clean, orderly, and hospitable. They offered special services designed for women, such as lounges, restaurants, reading and writing rooms, nurseries, and even club rooms. And they hired women for most sales jobs.

Department stores also succeeded by making shopping magnificent. Their buildings were often palatial in design, with interior grand courts, rotundas, columned galleries, chandeliers, thick carpets, and polished mahogany counters. Large windows and skylights brightened the shopping areas, window and floor displays were lavish, and the huge number of products in one place was like a world exposition where everything was for sale. In Zola's phrase of the time, the department store "democratized luxury."

The big stores also made shopping fun. A. T. Stewart, whose Marble Palace in New York was arguably the first department store in the United States, entertained his customers with organ music and fashion shows as early as the 1850s. R. H. Macy, Stewart's competitor, imported a mechanical singing bird from Europe that not only pleased the crowds but impressed even P. T. Barnum. Macy's Christmas window displays were famous by the 1880s. By 1907 Marshall Field in Chicago claimed to have more show windows and a bigger indoor Christmas tree than any other store in the world.

In the early days of flying the stores arranged rooftop landings, and Gimbel's sponsored an airplane race between its New York and Philadelphia branches. In the early days of radio Strawbridge and Clothier opened a radio station in its Philadelphia store. Jordan Marsh of Boston set up a giant wind machine and mounted a sailboat on a swiveling platform for sailing demonstrations. Wanamaker's raised department store restaurants to a new scale by equipping its Crystal Tea Room to serve 10,000 people at once. Gimbel's cleared its fourth floor for an indoor golf tournament. By the 1920s Hudson's in Detroit and Macy's in New York had organized Thanksgiving parades that became annual pageants. In staging their own promotional events, the department stores were adding color and theater to downtown.

The department stores changed downtown by opening it to women. Newly liberated from home and neighborhood, middle-class women began to spend hours in town on shopping trips. As the nearby sidewalks turned into busy promenades, other merchants opened businesses between the streetcar lines and the department stores. Soon long rows of specialty shops, restaurants, and variety stores created shopping thoroughfares around the big stores. By making streets better for women, these stores made downtown a cleaner, safer place for everyone.

By the turn of the century the heart of most big cities was a popular retail district in which department stores, specialty shops, restaurants, and entertainment places all complemented each other. The department stores stood out as huge enterprises: Macy's in New York with a staff of 3,000, Marshall Field in Chicago with more than 8,000, and Jordan Marsh in Boston the fourth largest employer in New England. They drew crowds that even modern retailers would envy, with Marshall Field recording as many as a quarter of a million customers in a day. New transportation technology—first the horsecar, then the electric trolley, and then the subway—made these department stores and retail districts possible by bringing together their mass market. Once the shopping areas were well established, they became the focal points of city transit systems. When department stores ran into trouble after World War II, citizens who enjoyed downtown and property owners who profited from it both had stakes in protecting them.

Nineteenth-century merchants also came up with an unusual retail layout that would eventually help bring people back to downtown. City streets in the center of Paris around 1800 were narrow, crowded with horse-drawn traffic, slippery from greasy cart axles, spattered with slop and mud, and had no sidewalks. These were no places for casual promenading or window shopping. As an alternative to dangerous and unpleasant streets, some ingenious merchants cut passageways through large buildings and filled them with booths or shops on either side.

These passageways were the early arcades, forerunners of the shopping mall. These narrow pedestrian promenades were shut off from the surrounding streets and closed to traffic. The more luxurious ones were fully enclosed, with skylights overhead. A few experimented with glass roofing and gaslights. One historian's account of the Paris arcades reads like the rationale for a mall of the 1980s: "It was not enough to save the pedestrian from the distress and anxiety of the street tumult; one had to attract him positively to the arcade. . . . It all depended on the ability to build an arcade as bright as an open space, warm in winter, cool in summer, always dry and never dirty and dusty."[3]

By the 1820s and 1830s arcades spread to London, Brussels, Glasgow, Milan, Philadelphia, and Providence (where the Weybosset Arcade, generally considered the oldest shopping mall in the United States, got a fresh start with a renovation by Ben Thompson in the 1970s). Architects made use of new iron and glass technology to build vaults and domes, letting in more light while spanning longer distances and covering wider passageways. Once established these arcades soon became more than shopping districts. Although managed privately and for profit, they turned into public promenades and civic gathering places distinguished by a high quality of design.

In time street improvements and sidewalk construction took away the original rationale for arcades, but people still liked them. Arcade building became a form of competition among cities searching for public settings to establish their status in the world. After Belgium won its independence in 1830, Brussels searched for an appropriate symbol of its role as capital and decided to build a monumental arcade. Milan built its renowned Galleria Vittorio Emanuele II to celebrate the unification of Italy, as well as to give the city a new center. These arcades were also tourist draws. Mark Twain, an early visitor to the Galleria in Milan, had this to say: "Blocks of new buildings . . . rich with decoration and graced with statues, the streets between . . . roofed over with glass at a great height, the pavements all of smooth and variegated marble, arranged in tasteful patterns—little tables all over these marble streets, people sitting at them, eating, drinking, or smoking—crowds of other people strolling by—such is the Arcade. I should like to live in it all my life."[4]

Twentieth-century historians found much to admire in these structures. Lewis Mumford singled out the glass-covered shopping arcade as the only specialized architectural form generated by commercial enterprise during the nineteenth century. He wrote with warmth that "the most magnificent is that great cruciform structure in Milan, a generous concourse, with its shops, its cafes, its restaurants." And he praised the original purpose of arcades: "These new structures had the special merit of taking shopping off the crowded street, with its confusion of vehicles and noise: an admirable example of functional planning."[5] This same logic would inspire cities and developers to build off-street retail centers in the 1970s.

Vanishing Crowds

The downtown of department stores, retail districts, and popular entertainment survived through the end of World War II, when a new set of circumstances in the United States began to tear it apart. After fifteen years of depression and war had stifled housing construction, the pent-up hunger for new homes was enormous. Defense workers who had banked their earnings during wartime shortages and returning veterans with their discharge pay were ready and willing to take out home mortgages. Thanks to New Deal efforts to revive the construction industry, they could get their home loans on very good terms. Federally insured mortgages asked for only a 10 percent down payment and a twenty-five-year payback at a low fixed rate of interest. Veterans could buy houses for nothing down and a thirty-year mortage at 4 percent. A new industry of merchant builders organized to meet the demand, and housing starts jumped from a level of 300,000 a year in the 1930s to 1 million in 1946 and 2 million by 1950.

The buying public looked mainly for single-family homes in uncrowded neighborhoods so children would have room to play. The best place for this kind of living was in the suburbs, where land was open and cheap and free from complicated building regulations. Once people were in the suburbs, they were outside the city transit network and had to use cars to get around. With inexpensive cars rolling off the Detroit assembly lines, gas cheap and abundant, income rising, and the first postwar highways under construction, it was easy enough to love the car and get along without public transportation.

While the housing choices and life-styles of the average family were shifting the centers of population from the cities to the suburbs, executives in industry were beginning to move their firms in the same direction. Truck deliveries were replacing railroad freight, and city streets were too congested for truck access and loading docks. At the same time new technologies for goods handling and assembly-line manufacturing favored buildings with long, horizontal spaces instead of the older multistory warehouses and factories. Industrialists who were ready to invest in new plants looked for sites with good highway connections, large parcels of land, and industrial zoning. They found these sites mainly in the suburbs. In the top forty metropolitan areas central cities lost an average of 26,000 manufacturing jobs between 1954 and 1963, and the central city share of manufacturing work slipped from two-thirds in the early 1950s to less than half by 1963.

As the postwar boom got under way, the pressures for suburban growth were overpowering. Even if central city officials had been fully aware of what was coming, nothing they could have done would have overcome the combined effects of economic recovery, life-style choices, new forms of mortgage finance, and changing industrial technology in time to make much of a difference. The circumstances that undermined central business districts were as complex and mutually reinforcing as those that had led to their creation.

The downtown shopping district was in trouble soon after the war. The first sign of change was a sharp drop in the number of people using public transportation, evidence of increasing car ownership and new travel patterns. The number of passengers on rail transit systems sank far below prewar levels—by 1955 to one-third the ridership of the 1930s. To make matters worse, the decline was concentrated in the off-peak hours when shoppers used to ride the buses and trains. The loss of transit riders meant that downtown retailers were cut off from their main source of customers, the middle-class neighborhoods now taking shape outside the city. They had another important group of customers among people who worked in town, but the loss of in-town jobs made this a shrinking market as well.

Retail executives with stores in the largest cities saw the results and began to act, opening branches in the suburbs and cutting their downtown operations. Wanamaker's, a fixture on lower Broadway for fifty years, closed its downtown store in the mid-1950s to go to the surburbs. Sears moved from New Haven into a suburban shopping center at about the same time. By the early 1960s department stores across the country were closing their doors downtown.

Many of the specialty stores that brought people into town were also closing. The prosperous establishments that had made attractive promenades along Market Street in Philadelphia and Tremont Street in Boston gave way to cheap costume jewelry stores, joke shops, and boarded-up storefronts. Even the popular-price chain stores were pulling out. Grant's announced plans in 1960 to close ten to twenty downtown stores per year, noting that 308 of 348 new branches it had opened in the past five years were in suburban shopping centers.

Reduced competition for shares of a shrinking retail pie failed to help those department stores that remained. They tried to economize by converting selling areas to warehousing or offices, but even this move was unable to stop profit margins from sinking even lower than they were during the Great Depression. Not only department stores but entire downtown areas were losing business. From 1948 to 1954 sales were booming for the nation at large, but the downtown share of retailing fell by one-fourth in thirteen of the largest metropolitan areas.

The loss of shopping, coming on top of the exodus of middle-class families and manufacturing firms, hit downtown hard. Scholars pondered the trends and questioned whether downtown had outlived its usefulness. Big-city mayors and civic leaders saw the same trends and found them intolerable. The shells of their cities were getting to look like black-and-white newsreels of the Great Depression, and early federal efforts to help were making matters worse by spreading a wasteland cleared for urban renewal projects that nobody wanted to build. Downtown storekeepers closed early and locked up tight, leaving behind empty streets that discouraged fearful residents from venturing out at all. With downtown business districts crumbling, cities faced fiscal ruin. Forces beyond anyone's control were pushing them into an economic back alley where they could die quietly.

Mayors and downtown business leaders were weak and getting weaker, but they still had enough influence to protect themselves before it was too late. Their campaign to reverse the trends turned out to have a staying power that no reasonable observer could have foreseen during the lean years for central cities.

The 1950s—prosperous Eisenhower years known for drift and complacency in public life—was a time of frantic activity to rebuild cities. Tight alliances of mayors, corporate executives, and civic leaders wielded money, power, and media access to get construction projects going. Reviving downtown had become a cause and a movement by 1957, when Connecticut General Life Insurance Company convened the leading thinkers and doers in city redevelopment for a national conference on the problems they faced. The fifty speakers and panelists were a *Who's Who* of the field, including government officials from Washington and the cities, real estate developers, professors, architects, industrialists, city planners, publishers, and bankers.

Their first problem was that most people who had a choice were opting to live in the suburbs. As experts committed to saving cities they could not bring themselves to respect the decisions average people were making, and rather than trying to understand popular taste they dismissed it as misguided. Lewis Mumford ridiculed Americans for arranging their lives to suit their cars, evidence to him that they had no life worth living. Dean John Burchard of MIT warned that those who liked the suburbs—"people who listen to the monotonous rhythms of rock-and-roll records while a carhop brings them chicken-in-the-rough and a chocolate malted"—were incapable of appreciating a better life.[1]

The experts, however, did not deny the faults of central cities. To the contrary, most believed that the older cities could not survive without drastic changes. The operative term for city housing, street layouts, and land use was *obsolete*. The typical street grid was outmoded, concluded architect Victor Gruen, and would have to be replaced. Downtown was not only a crisscross of inefficient streets but it was also cluttered. Conference members were eager to get rid of the clutter and to make plenty of space—for highways, parking garages, cultural institutions, and space for its own sake. The new downtown would have "a great deal of grass and flowers; there would be birds and fountains and fine buildings generously spaced." They envisioned "a complete reshuffling of land uses." Manufacturing, warehousing, and freight-handling operations would be gone. Offices, banks, financial firms, government agencies, hotels, restaurants, department stores, and specialty shops would be in. Downtown was also to be a center for the arts, education, and recreation; for theaters, concert halls, libraries, museums, schools, and sports stadiums. There would be close-in apartments for people who valued the cultural and educational opportunities of downtown.

To replace the obsolete city with this new vision would mean tearing down much of what was there. There was little talk of preserving historic buildings or keeping the traditional character of the city center. In order to save downtown, it was going to be necessary to destroy it. Since streets could not be replaced without knocking down the buildings that lined them, speakers argued that a complete remedy would be possible only through the redevelopment of the entire area. Clearing the downtown would not be enough; neighborhoods surrounding the business district were also obsolete. "The task," according to these authorities, was "renovating entire neighborhoods to provide a completely new land-use pattern." As an example of what was needed, conference members pointed with approval to the leveling of several hundred acres of southwest Washington, D.C., and the uprooting of no fewer than 24,000 people to make possible a "fresh start."

A reader searches the conference report in vain for some recognition that whatever else the city is, it is also a place where ordinary people live, work, and play. But these experts made no serious attempt to look at the city through the eyes of average people who needed homes, jobs, and recreation. They spoke more as guardians of the cultural values that cities represented, now threatened by suburban growth.

The same downtown boosters recognized, however grudgingly, that the suburbs they despised did have certain merits: more living space, room for cars, and relief from the grimness of overbuilding. They wanted to bring some of these qualities to the cities, but like the later generation of urbanists who decided to bring the suburban shopping mall downtown, they wanted to do it on their own terms.

Rejecting the unchecked commercialism of "a nation of doughnut stands" in suburbs that were growing too fast and with too little planning, they meant to exercise proper control over the rebuilding of cities. They believed cities should work from rational plans drawn up by "strong business leadership and a top professional staff"—in short, by people very much like themselves. Citizen committees would have a secondary role: "to crystallize public thinking and underwrite the success of community plans." Professionally planned projects, in contrast to the unrestrained decisions of suburban developers, would modernize the cities in a civilized way.

The downtown specialists' plans for rebuilding cities carried the imprint of elitism. With so little understanding of popular taste and even less interest in it, how would they ever figure out what would bring people to visit or live in the new buildings? And how could they rebuild the inner city so thoroughly without pushing out the very people and businesses that had not yet left for the suburbs?

Alliances: The Pittsburgh Model

To city officials the loss of downtown retail trade and the departure of businesses from prime commercial and industrial properties warned of a massive drain on the public treasury. American fiscal traditions left the cities responsible for raising their own revenues, with little help from states or the federal government. Local governments in 1957 raised more than two-thirds of their own revenues, with property taxes alone accounting for half the total. And the largest taxpayer in most cities was the central business district, which typically supplied a fourth or more of local revenue.

When businesses and shoppers deserted downtown, most of them moved far enough from the city to escape the municipal tax collector. Although mayors needed to make up the shortfall, they were reluctant to raise taxes or cut services and unable to persuade state legislatures to help. A more appealing strategy was to find ways to compete with the suburbs in order to stop the outflow. Almost all the major cities and many minor ones rushed to draw plans for rebuilding downtown. It was an unprecedented time for downtown planning, with some 700 central business district studies and plans published by 1959.

While the mayors commissioned plans, downtown revitalization as a practical matter was virtually invented by the business community.

In one city after another corporate executives took the lead in forming organizations and making proposals for action. In Pittsburgh, where downtown troubles started early, financier Richard King Mellon and his associates established the Allegheny Conference in 1943 to work for the postwar economic development of Pittsburgh, particularly of its downtown. Most conference members were the heads of corporations and local institutions, and only the heads were allowed to attend executive meetings. They found an unlikely ally in state Democratic boss David Lawrence, who ran for mayor in 1945 on a platform stressing leadership. He promised to work with the Allegheny Conference, overwhelmingly Republican, and he kept that promise during his fourteen years in office. The combination of Lawrence's political muscle with the economic resources and private sector influence of conference members was a formidable underpinning for what came to be known as the Pittsburgh Renaissance.

Other cities followed Pittsburgh's lead in linking the political clout of city hall with the economic strength that still remained in downtown boardrooms. Philadelphia had its counterpart in the Greater Philadelphia Movement, organized in 1948, and Baltimore launched its Greater Baltimore Committee in 1955. Sometimes a mayor took the lead in making the match; New Haven's Richard Lee put together the Citizens Action Commission in 1954. Sometimes the private sector organization that worked with the mayor came exclusively from the central business district, as in the case of the Minneapolis Downtown Council. And in some cities business leaders were active in downtown renewal without forming a special organization. In Boston, for example, the chamber of commerce contributed funds for a planning study that led to the redevelopment of the waterfront and the Faneuil Hall markets. But whether or not there was a formal organization, almost every city gave high priority to the interests of those executives who had not yet left downtown.

These downtown alliances rested on the shoulders of prominent citizens who preferred not to join the stampede to suburbia. Many corporate executives wanted to stay close enough to their financial advisers, lawyers, and advertising agencies for face-to-face dealings on important matters, and these specialists were already clustered in town. Legal restrictions kept bankers and utility executives from moving out, and heavy investments in downtown buildings restrained the heads of other large organizations. Newspaper publishers had a commitment to their downtown identity, as well as an interest in keeping economic activity alive in the heart of their circulation area.

Their attachment to downtown was more than economic. Many also valued their association with downtown clubs, art museums, and symphony orchestras, and they wanted to stay close to theaters, galleries, concert halls, and fine restaurants. In addition many intellectuals, artists, writers, and architects looked on downtown as a focal point of communication and culture. Taken together downtown-oriented executives, professionals, and intellectuals were a strong, articulate group with ready access to the mass media. They supported efforts to revive downtown, but they thought of it as a haven for the elite rather than a gathering place for average people.

Finding common ground with the mayors was not hard. Power plays were unnecessary to get a mayor's attention because elected officials were worried about downtown. Public and private interests seemed to converge; both sides wanted to keep businesses in the city, and both wanted redevelopment to offer opportunities for profitable —and taxable—investment. Although they might differ on questions of who should pay how much, their joint interest in scoring a few successes encouraged a spirit of compromise.

For mayors, promoting the downtown economy was just the latest expression of civic boosterism. Further, development plans for downtown fit into the time-honored tradition of using construction to generate political support, familiar from the distant past and still fresh in the memory from New Deal public works of the 1930s.

In these public-private coalitions, neither side imposed a narrow agenda on the other. With much give-and-take they drew up plans for projects that met both the economic needs of business executives and the political needs of the mayors. When it came to proposing specific projects, business leaders often operated with a very broad definition of their self-interest. The first three projects to come out of the Allegheny Conference in Pittsburgh, for example, were for smoke control, flood control, and the creation of a downtown park around historic Fort Pitt. While all three promised to improve the climate for business investment in the center of the city, critics would have had a hard time arguing that they were not also in the public interest. Corporate executives discovered that mayors shared their concern about the future of the business district, while politicians learned that business people were willing to support projects that would appeal to the voters. Both groups stood to gain if they could carry out some of the schemes they had in mind.

Highway Detours

Backed by a civic elite and an increasingly sympathetic press, the mayors and their business allies moved quickly to broaden their power base and find money to carry out their plans. Operating at a time when the federal government was just beginning to increase its domestic spending, they gave their support to highway and urban renewal programs not originally intended for downtown redevelopment and managed to turn both programs to their own purposes.

Their first success of this kind was with the federal aid highway program. The interstate highway system as first proposed would have had some 34,000 miles of freeways flowing across the country but skirting the major cities. Its only urban roads would have been a series of short connectors linking city centers to the bypass highways, with no consideration to relieving traffic bottlenecks in town or helping local commuters.

In 1954 the Eisenhower administration drafted legislation to fund the proposed interstate system, and groups interested in highways began to mobilize support for a big program. New roads were popular, and the highway lobby was influential, but Congress was not going to give automatic approval to whatever plan the administration put before it. In 1955 the Senate and the House rejected major highway bills by wide margins because of disagreements over financing, and then another measure with different funding provisions died in the House. Anxious members of the highway lobby began to look for additional political support.

One place to look for supporters was among big-city mayors, several of whom had already tried to persuade House and Senate committees that the worst traffic jams, and therefore the most pressing highway needs, were in the cities. Not only that, but Baltimore's Mayor Thomas D'Alesandro had identified traffic strangulation within cities as "the major problem facing the country." Further both mayors and representatives of downtown business associations had already made Congress aware that the urban interstate routes were essential for revitalizing central business districts.

The high cost of buying city land for highways and the complex engineering problems of fitting wide roads into built-up areas made urban freeways far less attractive to the highway lobby than mileage in suburban or rural areas. But Alf Johnson, president and chief Washington strategist of the American Association of State Highway

Officials, wanted a broad coalition in order to get a national highway program through Congress. To pick up more big-city support he began persuading state and federal highway engineers to add more urban routes to the interstate network. With little opposition, federal highway administrators proceeded to invite state agencies to propose an additional 2,200 miles of urban highways.

Late in 1955 the U.S. Bureau of Public Roads made these additions official when it issued a report showing interstate highway designations for one hundred urban areas, looking much like the road maps out of a 1980s atlas of American cities. For large metropolitan areas, a typical plan showed an inner belt road around downtown, an outer belt highway circling the suburbs, and one or more radial highways connecting the suburbs to the city center. Smaller metropolitan areas had plans for loop roads or spurs connecting downtown to the nearest interstate highway. City officials also won another concession. During 1955 and 1956 congressional hearings, city representatives argued that urban interstate routes should be built not only as connectors to the interstates but also to help the cities cope with their own traffic problems. They got what they wanted with a provision in the 1956 law giving local needs equal consideration with interstate commerce in laying out these routes.

By the time Congress considered new highway bills in 1956, the official designation of urban routes had made the commitment to cities much more explicit than before, and the book with maps of one hundred urban areas was available to every member of Congress. A bill offering 90 percent federal financing to build the interstate highway system passed the House, 388–19, and the Senate, 89–1. How important the promises to cities were in getting the program enacted is hard to know, but President Eisenhower commented later that the book showing routes in one hundred cities had sold the program to Congress.

The cities' share in the new program was substantial. The Federal-Aid Highway Act of 1956 provided for 41,000 miles of interstate highways, of which 6,100 miles were in urban areas. Although the urban routes were less than 15 percent of the total mileage, they were expected to cost more than the rest of the system combined. Later amendments enlarged the total system to 42,500 miles and increased the urban share to 8,600 miles, more than one-fifth of the total mileage. Before 1956 the twenty-five largest cities had only 480 miles of freeways completed or under construction, and more than half the total was in just three cities: New York, Los Angeles, and Chicago. By 1976 some 7,400 miles of urban interstate highways were open to traffic, accounting for most of the urban freeways in the nation. If new highways could help downtown by funneling people in and out more easily, the cities had accomplished a major part of their rescue mission by shaping the interstate program their way.

The mayors and their downtown allies were no weaklings when it came to spotting openings and snatching public funds. The program they remade to suit city purposes was nothing less than the largest public works program in history. Their takeover was all the more remarkable because it was contrary to the intentions of President Eisenhower and his adviser on the subject, General Lucius Clay. When Eisenhower discovered three years later that the interstate system was running freeways through congested major cities, he fumed that this was entirely against his original concept. Reluctantly he conceded that the book of urban maps had made firm promises to Congress, and the federal government could not unilaterally change routes established by federal-state agreements. Clay, who headed a presidential committee that proposed the 1956 legislation, also disowned the urban routes as perversions of what his committee had in mind. (By 1972 even Alf Johnson considered the urban interstates a legislative error.) That the big-city mayors and their allies prevailed against such powerful opponents was testimony both to their own skill and to the emerging opportunities to get federal resources for rebuilding downtown.

The Urban Renewal Takeover

Another program up for grabs was urban renewal. Like the highway program, its purposes were pliable enough to invite cities to define them according to their own needs. Enacted well before most downtown coalitions were up and running, it was in operation too early for them to reach for the money while Congress worked on the legislation. But there is more than one way to skin a federal program, and this time a gradual taking was the strategy of choice.

Urban renewal was a hybrid in its origins, born out of the overlapping purposes of two conflicting groups. Real estate interests had argued for a federal program that would help private enterprise convert run-down areas of cities into profitable developments. Housing advocates wanted federal help to get better housing for low-income slum dwellers. The two lobbies came together just long enough to give critical support to a slum-clearance program as part of the Housing Act of 1949.

The housing lobby put its stamp all over the legislative history of the program. Thus the "primary purpose of Federal aid in this field," according to the Senate committee report, "is to help remove the impact of the slums on human lives rather than simply to assist in the redevelopment or rebuilding of cities."[2] No matter what the Senate leaders may have intended, the law had loopholes. One was that it offered federal help to cities for demolishing slum housing, no matter what they built in its place, on the assumption that tearing down slums was a community benefit in itself. This provision invited cities to use federal money for clearing run-down houses on the edge of the business district and to replace them with offices, stores, or anything else.

When legal requirements stood in the way of important projects, they turned out to have little practical effect. One of the basic provisions was that urban renewal funds were only for "a slum area or a blighted, deteriorated, or deteriorating area . . . which the [federal] Administrator approves as appropriate for an urban renewal project."[3] What constituted a blighted area was open to argument, however, and city officials had good reasons to stretch the meaning of blight. Federal regulations that emphasized clearing the most unlivable areas conflicted with other rules requiring local renewal agencies to sell their cleared sites to private developers for rebuilding. Few developers were willing to build in the heart of the slums. Cities such as Newark tried in the early years of the program to plan middle-income housing in some of the worst parts of the city, only to discover that no developers were interested.

Soon city renewal directors were searching for "the blight that's right"—places just bad enough to clear but good enough to attract developers. Robert Moses showed the way in the early 1950s when he planned a renewal project around Columbus Circle in Manhattan in order to build the New York Coliseum. To make the area "predominantly residential" Moses gerrymandered the project boundaries around some nearby tenement houses. But in addition to making it residential, Moses had to make it blighted. According to testimony from the former chief architect of the city housing authority, only 10 percent of the tenements were substandard and only 2 percent of the entire area could be considered a slum. It became a slum when the city planning commission declared it blighted, and federal renewal officials accepted this declaration. Project opponents took the city to court because they had evidence that the area was neither residential nor blighted. The New York Court of Appeals ruled in favor of the city, arguing that local authorities had duly declared the area to be substandard and residential and, barring corruption or fraud, "there is nothing for the courts to do about it."

With both federal reviewers and the courts unwilling to investigate municipal findings, blight was in the eye of the beholder, and the slum clearance requirement of the law was no safeguard at all. It meant only that cities would have to start commercial or industrial projects by clearing houses. But since the houses in question did not have to be substandard, the effect of this restriction was perverse. If cities wanted federal money for downtown redevelopment, the law prevented them from clearing old factory or commercial areas. Instead they had to find houses—any houses—to demolish. It was tempting to clear whatever houses happened to be on the edge of downtown, and city officials gave in to temptation. Local renewal agencies themselves reported that almost 20 percent of the housing they demolished for renewal projects through 1961 had been in sound condition. The real figure was undoubtedly higher since these agencies tended to classify marginal houses as substandard in order to make a case for clearance.

The cities not only found ways around inconvenient requirements but also swung enough weight in Washington to do away with them. They took their case against the "predominantly residential" requirement to Congress and managed to legalize a series of exceptions. The Housing Act of 1954 allowed 10 percent of federal grants to be used for nonresidential projects as long as there were "a substantial number" of substandard houses in the area. In later sessions Congress removed the "substantial number" requirement and raised the nonresidential exceptions to 20 percent of total grants in 1959, 30 percent in 1961, and 35 percent in 1965.

The downtown business coalitions took a direct hand in changing the law. During hearings on the proposed amendments city officials ran into opposition from economy-minded members of Congress who worried that lifting the residential restrictions would lead to extravagant city demands for federal funds. City lobbyists won them over by bringing in conservative business leaders who normally opposed federal spending but now wanted help with rebuilding commercial areas. Leading these supporters were department store owners and mortgage lenders whose downtown investments were threatened by suburban shopping centers. Redevelopment, they maintained, was both a business necessity and a source of tax dollars for the city. The mayoral-business alliances scored again.

Tracking the Money

With administrative and legal reviews rubber-stamping city choices of renewal areas and with Congress waiving residential requirements, the urban renewal program was truly prime for taking. The downtown coalitions grabbed it. So complete was their takeover that by the mid-1960s it became more than anything else a way to pay for rebuilding downtown. Although Washington officials never conceded the dominance of downtown in urban renewal, the facts were clear to several experts who studied the program in the late 1950s and early 1960s. Robert Weaver, then federal housing administrator and soon to become the first secretary of housing and urban development, spotted the trend and some reasons for it: renewal chiefs were pushing hard for downtown projects because these were less controversial than housing, more dramatic, better taxpayers, and above all more attractive to the business establishment. When President Johnson's National Commission on Urban Problems studied the program in 1967–1968, its staff found that of 439 new projects approved from 1966 through 1968, no less than 65 percent were in or adjacent to central business districts. Later an analysis of nine cities over the entire twenty-five-year life of the program confirmed how dramatic the takeover had been: 52 percent of all urban renewal funds went for projects within a mile of the city center and 82 percent for projects within two miles of it.

Capturing the highway and renewal programs put massive resources in the hands of the downtown coalitions. The interstate highway system cost $105.3 billion to build (through early 1987), of which $57 billion, or 54 percent, went for urban routes. Downtown groups did not get all the urban funds, to be sure. Some "urban" highways were in small cities outside the country's metropolitan areas, and within metropolitan areas the federal aid program paid for suburban beltways, as well as routes into downtown. But the bulk of the urban highway dollars went into metropolitan areas, and within those areas even the beltways helped commuters go from residential suburbs to downtown connectors. The city center was the focal point of almost every urban highway network in the country. As for urban renewal, federal grants totaled $13.5 billion, of which a conservative estimate is that some two-thirds, or $9 billion, went for projects in or near downtown. For both highways and renewal, most of the outlays were in preinflation dollars, which would have to be about three times greater in order to approximate their value in the late 1980s.

In managing these multibillion dollar takeovers, the downtown coalitions demonstrated three basic strategies that would contribute to the success of later projects. First was the unexpected power of a mayoral-business alliance. Second was a free-wheeling operating style that moved back and forth from the cities to Washington, combining astuteness and ingenuity with a willingness to bend whatever rules got in the way. The successful skimming of highway and renewal funds established a third enduring principle for rebuilding downtown: financing projects without asking for local tax dollars. Since most cities were trying to rebuild downtown because their revenue base was shrinking, current tax receipts left little to spare. Few mayors could even think about raising local tax rates for something as unconventional and untested as a plan to rebuild the center of the city.

The highway program suited city financial needs to perfection. Its funding was 90 percent federal, 10 percent state, and nothing at all local. Urban renewal made a modest demand for the cities to cover one-third of project costs while the federal government would pay for two-thirds. But to make urban renewal easier for the cities, federal rules allowed them to pay their share by building public works to serve a project area. Under this option the federal government would, first, share two-thirds of the cost of such items as new schools or street improvements for a renewal project and, second, accept these public works at full cost as part of a city's required matching share.

With shrewd planning, a renewal agency could use public works to pay for its entire share of a project and could even bank and transfer leftover credits to use for other renewal projects. If normal spending for public works was great enough, a city could finance urban renewal without asking anything extra of its taxpayers. When Mayor John Collins and redevelopment director Edward Logue presented Boston's famous "90 Million Dollar Development Plan" in 1960, they proposed to use $30 million in city capital funds to get $60 million in federal renewal grants. Their plan was to pay for the city's share of the total by building neighborhood improvements such as new schools. By keeping their capital budget under control, they could build public works and carry out a huge renewal program without raising tax rates—certainly an offer too good to refuse.

Other cities were also fast learners. By 1968 the federal government was collecting only twelve cents of every local matching dollar in cash; the rest was all public works and similar credits. Like federal aid highways, urban renewal seldom had to appear on the budget that went to the city council. That way it bypassed controversies over new spending proposals and did not have to compete against other claims on scarce tax dollars. In troubled cities with reluctant taxpayers, off-budget financing was good politics, and it was here to stay.

Demolition by the Acre

Backed by influential coalitions, reinforced by expert judgment that downtown was obsolete, given the power of government to take private property and the budgets of two federal programs to pay for it, ambitious renewal chiefs were soon pulling down buildings by the hundreds in the hearts of cities. Where developers normally had to negotiate for years to fit together building sites out of the dozens of small parcels that made up every city block, renewal agencies could clear huge tracts in one stroke. Where developers bargained for land by the square foot, government took it by the acre.

The site cleared for Rockefeller Center in the 1930s, one of the largest private holdings in Manhattan at the time and considered a remarkable opportunity for an integrated development, consisted of just 12 acres. Downtown renewal projects were often three, four, even five times larger. Charles Center in Baltimore was 33 acres, Government Center in Boston 44 acres, Capitol Mall in Sacramento 59 acres, Gateway Center in Minneapolis 72 acres. In neighborhoods just outside the central business district, the projects were larger still: Wooster Square in New Haven was 235 acres, the Southwest project in Washington, D.C., 560 acres. These holdings were of a size not seen in American cities since the early land developers first laid out lot lines on the open countryside.

Then there were the 6,100 miles of federal aid highways approved for urban areas in 1956, to which another 2,500 miles were added over the years. The new highways, designed to rural standards, were big

space eaters in crowded cities. Three lanes in each direction, generous median strips to separate traffic flows, broad shoulders for breakdown lanes, and landscaped margins added up to a right-of-way 200
feet or wider cutting through built-up neighborhoods. Every few
miles a cloverleaf interchange demanded still larger land takings for
the sweeping curves of high-speed entrance and exit ramps.

By the late 1950s urban renewal and interstate highways were con-
verging on neighborhoods near the center of cities, uprooting families
by the thousands. Moving was a burden for those who lived in the
way of renewal and highway projects. Most were black or Hispanic,
and most were poor. Of all the families displaced by urban renewal
from 1949 through 1963, 63 percent of those whose race was known
were nonwhite, and of these families, 56 percent of nonwhites and 38
percent of whites had incomes low enough to qualify for public housing, which, however, was seldom available to them.

The highway program did not report much information about the
people it evicted, but casual observation showed that the urban interstate routes cut disproportionately through poor and minority neighborhoods. Highway planners preferred routes that would take run-
down housing, acting on the belief that eliminating slums would
benefit the community at large. Sometimes cost was a factor, since
rights of way were usually cheaper to buy in poor neighborhoods
than in wealthy ones. Sometimes local politics was a factor, since
people in well-off neighborhoods had better connections to mayors
and governors who could call off the road builders. In Nashville, for
example, engineering consultants originally recommended an interstate route that ran mostly through railroad property except for one
controversial section that would have eliminated several white-
owned businesses. State and local officials objected and asked for an
alternate route through the center of a black community, through the
campus of a black college, and through sixteen blocks of commercial
property filled with black-owned businesses.

Racism was also a factor. During the political jockeying that led to
the 1956 highway act, officials from several cities told highway lobby-
ist Alf Johnson that the urban interstates would give them a good
opportunity to get rid of the local "niggertown." This was not idle
talk, nor was the practice limited to the South. Very few blacks lived
in Minnesota, but the road builders found them. Miles Lord, later a
federal district judge, reminisced about his service as attorney general
of Minnesota overseeing interstate highway land takings in the

1950s. "We went through the black section between Minneapolis and St. Paul," he recalled, "about four blocks wide and we took out the home of every black man in that city. And woman and child. In both those cities practically. It ain't there anymore, is it? Nice little neat black neighborhood, you know, with their churches and all and we gave them about $6,000 a house and turned them loose onto society."[4]

Whatever the motivation, the poor and the minorities were the leading victims of the highway and renewal programs. And the victims were numerous. Through 1967 urban renewal dispossessed more than 400,000 families and federal aid urban highways some 330,000. The more ambitious a city was in its efforts to rebuild, the more concentrated was the damage. Los Angeles, for example, made an early start on its famous freeway network with state highway funds and then drew down federal aid to step up construction. With their unerring instinct for spotting strategic neighborhoods whose people were poor, minority, and without political influence, the highway planners found the city's main Mexican-American community, Boyle Heights, irresistible. They pushed no fewer than five freeways through this one neighborhood a few miles east of downtown. Baltimore, another ambitious city renowned in the 1980s for the sparkle of its new buildings, also took a heavy toll out of its residents during the early stages. From 1951 through 1964 public programs including highways and urban renewal tore down the homes of about 10,000 Baltimore families, of whom 90 percent were black. By the time the dust settled, low-income blacks had lost the equivalent of one of every five houses they lived in.

Low-income and minority families who lost their homes faced hard times. Low-rent public housing projects usually had long waiting lists, and suburban homes were out of the question. Middle-income people who were moving to suburbia at the time left some vacant houses behind in the cities but most of them at rents the poor could not afford. For black families the situation was close to desperate. While wrecking crews were pulling down their houses, a near-record number of blacks just up from the rural South were crowding into the cheapest apartments still standing in the same neighborhoods: 1.5 million blacks left the South in the 1950s, on the heels of the 1.6 million who moved to the cities of the North and West during the 1940s.

The highway and renewal refugees were under pressure to leave

established black neighborhoods, but they ran up against strong resistance when they searched for homes in white areas. Not only were
the residents often hostile, but many brokers and rental agents would
not do business with them. Financial institutions commonly refused
home loans to middle-income blacks who wanted to buy in racially
mixed neighborhoods. Most were in no position to buy in any case,
but they had to pay a rent premium because so few apartments were
open to them. Long before the civil rights movement had any impact
on housing discrimination, black families were trapped between the
racism of highway and renewal clearance and the racism of city
neighborhoods and real estate institutions.

Renewal and highway projects were systematically pounding low-
cost housing in the inner city to rubble, with the most active cities
demolishing the homes of the poor about as fast as vacant houses
were coming on the market. In Baltimore the total number of vacancies in sound condition at all price levels grew by only 5,700 between
1950 and 1960, at a time when renewal and highway projects were
pushing out 10,000 families. There was not enough housing to go
around. The best that relocation workers could do was to solve the
housing problem the way the czars allegedly solved Russia's economic problems: "The shortage will be divided among the peasants."

The Cover-up

A sense of fairness might have led the government agencies that were
responsible to offer the evicted reasonable help. That sense of fairness
was hard to find. Highway agencies had an obligation to pay property owners for their land and buildings, but the 1956 act made no
provision to compensate tenants, to help people find housing, or to
cover any moving expenses. For the first six years of the interstate
program, its administrators were under no federal pressure to help
with relocation, and only eight states acted on their own to make
small relocation payments.

When President Kennedy in 1962 recommended more generous
federal help with relocation, congressional opponents objected that
shifting money from construction to replacement housing would hold
up completion of the interstate system. As a result the Federal Aid
Highway Act of 1962 required no more than advisory services for
displaced families and offered to reimburse state highway departments for moving expenses up to a ceiling of $200 per family and

$3,000 per business firm. By the end of 1964 only twelve states authorized even these small payments. Most highway departments offered evicted tenants nothing more than advice on where to look for a place to live.

As for urban renewal, the law had several safeguards for relocation. It required local renewal agencies to submit a feasible relocation plan, backed by evidence that decent housing was available, as part of every application for federal aid. Beginning in 1954 the administrator of the federal Housing and Home Finance Agency had to certify personally that each city had an effective relocation plan. In addition Congress authorized federal cost sharing of certain relocation expenses starting in 1949 and then raised the amount and broadened the coverage in later amendments.

Renewal laws and regulations required cities to handle relocation as a serious responsibility within the program. Yet if the cities had too little public housing for the purpose and too few vacancies at the right price level in private buildings, how could they meet the requirement? Washington officials operated on the assumption that if city agencies could not find enough housing for relocation, they would report that fact to federal administrators, who would then tell them to postpone or cancel their renewal projects. But cities facing this problem had an alternative: they could lie about the availability of relocation housing. And if federal reviewers checked city statements on relocation as superficially as they checked their findings of blight, they in turn would lie to Congress and the public about the urban renewal program.

Before Watergate and later scandals responsible critics were slow to accuse government officials of lying, but as the Urban Renewal Administration compiled rosy relocation figures from local agency forms and released the grand totals as official truth, knowledgeable people became skeptical. Housing expert Charles Abrams, one of the first to voice his suspicions publicly, wrote that federal data showing almost every evicted family living in good housing were contrary to the known facts of slum life in American cities. He pointed a finger at city renewal agencies that were concealing their failure to meet relocation requirements by resorting to "misstatements of fact rare in the annals of official reporting."[5]

Independent researchers began to uncover deceptive city reports. According to the Boston Redevelopment Authority less than 2 percent of the families relocated from its West End project went into substandard housing. When a research team from Massachusetts General Hospital conducted a survey, they found 23 percent of relocated families living in substandard housing. Another study of these families discovered that the redevelopment authority used more exacting standards to rate the quality of the houses it tore down than it did to rate the houses where people moved. On this basis the authority could report that a family moved from a substandard house to a good one, when in fact the opposite was just as likely.

Soon federal investigators were also finding self-serving flaws in urban renewal records. In St. Louis, which had reported relocating everybody from two renewal projects into houses of standard quality, a random field check revealed twenty-three out of twenty-four from the first project living in substandard housing and twenty-five out of thirty-five from the second. Federal staff also caught renewal officials in the District of Columbia approving 68 percent of their relocation housing without looking at it and officials in Kansas and Missouri neither counting nor helping as many as half the people living in project areas.

A team of independent attorneys who examined documents used within the bureaucracy to certify relocation procedures and results concluded that an average of five to seven federal officials reviewing each project signed statements knowing they could not be true. They called their report *The Legal Lawbreakers*. Another attorney found the reason for weak federal enforcement in a sense of pressure to produce long-overdue results. With processing times of ten years or more for renewal projects before people had to be relocated, senior federal officials regarded anything that might cause further delay as rocking the boat. Further, decisions at that stage followed literally thousands of earlier administrative steps adding up to a process of massive proportions. A typical urban renewal application as submitted to Washington stood two-and-a-half-feet high and weighed fifty-three pounds. A relocation staff member would have to be either heroic or dense to try upsetting a project with so much paper behind it. Under pressure to avoid further delay, reviewers signed the form rather than disrupt the process.

The pressure to finish projects had a similar impact at the local level. City renewal chiefs, who were most responsible for the cover-up of relocation failures, were not opposed to providing good relocation housing or help with moving costs. When Robert Moses testified at highway hearings, he urged Congress to include federal funds for relocation expenses. He even argued for generous relocation assistance, over and above what was simply just and fair, as a way to prevent opposition to the badly needed urban highways. Moses and his counterparts in other cities tried to build relocation housing, but they could not get enough of it, largely because there was no political constituency pressing for it the way the downtown business groups pressed for what they wanted. Without the housing, good relocation was impossible. Unable to do the job the federal regulations called for, they were willing to tell whatever lies were necessary to get the projects built. As one of Robert Moses's admirers conceded: "He thought about people. But if it came to a project or people, he'd take the project."[6]

Casualty Count

What really happened to relocated families is hard to know because the official information is so unreliable. Even by government accounts, however, relocation assistance payments in the urban renewal program fell far short of the modest level authorized. Of all the families, individuals, and businesses evicted from 1949 through 1963, only about half received any relocation payments at all. Those who were paid got an average of $69 per family, $45 per individual, and $1,405 per business firm. While renewal officials reassured Congress and the public of the high priority they assigned to relocation, the money they spent told a different story: of all public outlays for urban renewal projects through 1968, just one-half of 1 percent went for relocation.

Studies of relocation by people outside government show that while renewal and highway projects were clearing away marginal, low-cost houses, they were pushing people into places that were better but more expensive, with rents typically higher by 20 percent or more. But the higher prices did not always bring better housing. Surveys found from one-fourth to one-half the families moving to homes that were substandard despite the cost increase. Researchers also identified social and psychological losses, which were more damaging. Highway and renewal planners had a knack for picking low-income neighborhoods where residents had deep attachments to friends, relatives, neighbors, churches, schools, and local businesses. For immigrants and other city dwellers who needed the security of a supportive neighborhood—"urban villagers" was Herbert Gans's term for them—eviction on short notice created nothing less than a life crisis.

The West End of Boston, cleared in 1958–1959, became a national symbol of the effects of urban renewal on people. Psychologists who studied the consequences found some 40 percent of the victims had severe, long-term grief reactions, including symptoms of depression, distress, and a sense of helplessness. They told interviewers: "I felt like taking the gaspipe"; "I lost all the friends I had." The story was similar when urban renewal cleared the Southwest area of Washington. Researchers there found people bearing a deeply felt sense of loss for years afterward, with one-fourth reporting they had not made a single friend since leaving the old Southwest.

A close look at relocation uncovered other abuses, worse than even the critics dared to imagine. While individual relocation workers may have tried to be helpful, some public agencies resorted to threats and harassment in order to get people out in a hurry. In San Francisco a federal court issued a restraining order to protect occupants who were being hounded out of residential hotels. In Camden, New Jersey, city authorities started demolition before all the residents were out, subjecting the ones who remained to vandalism, fires, streets blocked by rubble, and invasions of rats. People in the path of the Cross-Bronx Expressway in New York told a similar story: "As soon as the top floor of a building was empty, they'd start tearing off the roof and the top stories, even. While people were still living in it, they were tearing it down around their heads!" "Then started the muggings." "The rats were running like dogs and cats in the street." "I got old that winter."[7]

The research findings on relocation come mainly out of the urban renewal program, where the law made an explicit commitment to relocation assistance and federal funds were available. The highway program had no such commitment until later, and little is known about what happened to people who lived along the urban interstate routes. But if even renewal officials had to cover their tracks on relocation, the highway record was almost certainly worse. For anyone who wanted to avoid being victimized by civic improvement, the best advice was surely never to get in the way of plans for community progress.

Other notable victims of city rebuilding were the owners and employees of small businesses. Through late 1963 local renewal agencies reported evicting some 39,000 business firms; no figures are available on highway evictions of businesses. According to a federal survey of fifty local renewal programs, more than one-third of dispossessed firms went out of business—a rate significantly above normal business failures. Other studies indicate that small companies and retail and service businesses tied to neighborhood customers were especially vulnerable.

Now communities are concerned about keeping jobs and attracting business; it is strange to recall that the downtown coalitions began their campaign to improve cities by destroying thousands of small businesses. Neither renewal nor highway officials offered enough relocation help to keep small firms whole. Although they paid compensation for the loss of tangible property and for some moving expenses, neither program paid for the loss of goodwill—the reputation a firm had built up over the years and its network of customers—that could seldom survive a move to another area. Except for an allowance of $1,500 per firm for small businesses, urban renewal rules did not allow federal funds to pay for the value of a business beyond the worth of its physical property.

A study of 350 firms displaced by renewal or highway projects in Providence, Rhode Island, between 1954 and 1959 offers a look at what relocation meant for businesses. About one-third of the firms went out of business. Most of those that survived were doubly disadvantaged: they paid higher rents while their sales declined. Among small businesses, six of ten reported a drop in income after they moved, while only one in ten reported an increase. One of five owners who lost their businesses became unemployed, and one of five took retirement. The rest found other work, but nine of ten who went out of business earned lower incomes afterward.

The owners were devastated. For most, having to move on short notice destroyed the work of a lifetime. Many were immigrants who had struggled to set up businesses and had lived by the rules of hard work, thrift, and self-reliance. Now they could not understand what was happening to them: "The loss was more than just a building— my work is gone forever too. All of my customers have moved away. . . . [It] shook my confidence in my city and country—I never thought they would do such a thing." "They made me one offer—take it or leave it—and it wasn't enough. We didn't have a lawyer to fight them, so they beat us."[8]

Rebuilding cities through wholesale clearance had the same impact on long-established small businesses that it did on deeply rooted

residents of the old neighborhoods. While it may not have been possible to calculate fair compensation for pain and psychological loss, it
was possible to pay compensation for some costs: the time and expense of finding new quarters, expenses and income losses while
finding new jobs, full replacement cost for property, full moving
expenses, rent increases in new locations, and losses resulting from
demolition and clearance operations. Failure to compensate the dispossessed for these and other losses meant that government was
paying far less than the true cost of rebuilding cities. Instead city
programs had a Robin-Hood-in-reverse quality, with poor residents
and small business firms subsidizing the rest of the community. As of
1968 economist Anthony Downs estimated that evicted families
alone—not counting businesses—were paying uncompensated costs
of between $157 million and $230 million per year for highways and
renewal projects.

As far as business evictions were concerned, when renewal programs expanded in and around downtown during the 1960s, the
extent of the damage increased. The number of business evictions
jumped from 39,000 in 1963 to more than 100,000 by 1971. Federal
data also show continuing high rates of failure for dispossessed businesses—typically between 25 and 40 percent in big cities—for the
entire life of the renewal program.

Even with more generous compensation and fairer procedures, relocation would not have been easy. But the rebuilding strategies of
the 1950s and 1960s made it especially hard: the commitment to large-
scale clearance (replacing the "obsolete" features of cities), the staging of both renewal and highway programs at the same time, the use
of highway routes to clear low-income neighborhoods, and the determination of mayors and their allies not to stop projects over relocation
issues.

Eventually these strategies threatened enough people to force city
officials to look for more appealing projects such as the shopping
malls of the 1970s. But in the early 1960s an effective cover-up con-
cealed the facts from the public at large. Only a few experts and the
obscure victims knew that the self-satisfied government reports on
relocation—"the relocation staff did wonders through sympathetic,
patient and helpful attitudes" [Chicago]; "a noteworthy achievement
for which credit is due" [New York]—were dishonest. The press at
that time was generally supportive of city efforts and one-sided in its
coverage. When New York city planning commissioner Lawrence

Orton, together with sympathetic members of the Women's City Club, went to the press with solid evidence that Robert Moses's official reports were undercounting displaced people and misrepresenting the harsh treatment given to them, all but the *Post* refused to print it.

The national press was equally uncritical. *Time* ran a five-page cover story on the rebuilding of cities in 1962 without a word about relocation problems. The article projected optimism and claimed "the big cities are riding the crest of a renaissance." Noting that the cities were clearing thousands of badly blighted acres, the author reported on only one relocated family, who moved into a brand-new Chicago housing project. "It's like a dream," Mrs. Willie Adams said, "only better. Everything is new and clean—and no cockroaches."[9]

Adding color and action to downtown: New Year's Eve at Horton Plaza, San Diego. *The Hahn Co.*

Bringing back people: St. Patrick's Day parade passing under the skyways of St. Paul. *City of St. Paul PED.*

Clean, comfortable settings for family outings: Faneuil Hall Marketplace, Boston. *Boston Redevelopment Authority.*

City stagecraft: annual Winter Carnival in downtown St. Paul. *City of St. Paul PED.*

(*above and opposite*) Street entertainment in San Diego. *City of San Diego.*

The traditional city as a place for civic ceremonies: Boston's Quincy Market, 1876.
The Bostonian Society/Old State House.

Downtown in its prime: retail row on Boston's Washington Street, late nineteenth century. *U.S. Bureau of Public Roads, National Archives (from Boston Landmarks Commission).*

(*opposite*) The grandeur of early department stores: Chicago's Marshall Field & Co., 1907. *Lloyd Wendt,* Give the Lady What She Wants (*Chicago: Rand McNally, 1952*).

(*below*) The legacy of commercialism and a prototype of the shopping arcade: Milan Galleria, late nineteenth century. *Rotch Library Visual Collection, MIT.*

Downtown in the new cities of the west: San Diego, early twentieth century. *City of San Diego.*

Still vibrant in the 1950s: Chestnut Street, Philadelphia. *Rotch Visual Collection, MIT.*

Another face of the 1950s: Boston's Scollay Square before clearance. *Greater Boston Chamber of Commerce.*

If the new projects built on the ruins of old neighborhoods had been great popular successes, they might have erased the memory of injustices committed to clear the land. But when the private, elitist vision of the downtown coalitions took shape on the ground, it did not inspire popular admiration or enjoyment. Cities were building projects for narrow groups of users more than for the public at large, and most of them were big, isolated, self-contained complexes.

Since most of the rebuilding was within a mile or two of the center of the city, the new projects were planned for people and activities that city and business leaders considered appropriate for downtown locations. In most big cities about one-third of the land rebuilt under the urban renewal program through the late 1960s went for housing, typically apartment towers for the well-to-do.

The high price of new houses was not just a result of developers searching for profit. It was consistent with the goal of mayors and business executives—"a tax-paying, culture-loving, free-spending middle class," as political scientist James Q. Wilson described their motives. If the aim was to attract big spenders to live downtown, an essential part of the marketing strategy had to be to keep the public at large away from their doors. Those who could afford in-town housing objected to both the people and the environment of downtown. A 1959 survey in Baltimore, for example, discovered that high-rent payers in other parts of the city cited the "class of people" as one of the main reasons that they would not move downtown. Architects designing projects for protection against the unruly city had to avoid any features, such as benches, that might prove attractive to casual visitors.

The few renewal projects that made a feature of preserving existing houses were also intended for upper-income residents, who would demand protection from unacceptable people, traffic, and noise. In Philadelphia the realtor who chaired Mayor Richardson Dilworth's city planning commission thought renovated Georgian houses on Society Hill might be prestigious enough to bring affluent people back to downtown. An essential part of his strategy was to establish a large enough area—he had 1,000 acres in mind—as exclusive turf for the wealthy.

Dilworth was enthusiastic about the idea and took political risks to support it. In a city with a large black population, the racial implications of pricing housing in renewal areas for the wealthy were disturbing, but he faced them openly: "We've got to get the white [leadership] back. . . . We have to give the whites confidence that they can live in town without being flooded." The only flood on Society Hill was a torrent of high-income whites who made it their preserve. Between 1960 and 1970 the area went from 20 percent black down to 6 percent black, and median family income increased almost 400 percent.

Office buildings were another prominent feature of the first cycle of rebuilding. They too were intended for private use by an elite group of business firms and professionals who wanted the latest and best in office space and who could pay for it. Pittsburgh's renowned Gateway Center started with a real estate survey that identified a market for larger and more prestigious offices to be used by the city's big businesses. In the office towers that went up in the 1950s, most of the space was committed in advance to large Pittsburgh corporations. U.S. Steel, the Mellon Bank, and Alcoa put up new headquarters, and with a gift from the Mellon Foundations the city built an underground garage topped with a landscaped public plaza named Mellon Square.

Office complexes such as the ones in Pittsburgh were not as private in character as new luxury apartment projects. They did, after all, bring in thousands of white-collar workers. But except for a single hotel, there was little in these buildings to attract the public at large; they were no more than workplaces. Even the public plazas were mainly for office employees to use on their lunch hour. Pittsburgh and other cities were building office districts that were busy from nine to five but deserted at night and on weekends.

Office complexes did not have to be private. In the early 1930s Rockefeller Center had demonstrated that office buildings could work well in a public setting crowded with visitors. Rockefeller Center contained mainly office buildings, but it also had a world-famous theater in Radio City Music Hall, shopping arcades, an ice rink in a sunken plaza with an adjoining restaurant and outdoor sculpture, a pedestrian mall to Fifth Avenue, famous murals in the main lobby, a nightclub and an observation deck, a gigantic Christmas tree, and broadcasting studios open to public tours. In contrast to this variety of activities and features, most office complexes in renewal projects focused narrowly on serving the immediate needs of their corporate tenants.

Cities also cleared land for public buildings: civic centers, municipal offices, hospitals, schools, museums, concert halls. But even these projects, intended for broad groups of users, usually had an isolated look. Planners and architects were following principles for downtown development that kept the public away.

Designed for Isolation

Typical redevelopment projects had three features that cut them off from the rest of the city: they were very large, built to serve just a single function, and laid out in ways that emphasized their separation from the surrounding area.

The exceptional size of downtown projects was in keeping with expert opinion that only a thorough and spacious rebuilding could rejuvenate cities. Professional notions about blight also encouraged a clean sweep of older areas. Slum reformers believed that blight was bound to spread from one building to another. The best solution was a total one: radical surgery to remove all blighted properties at once.

Large projects could have been an advantage for the cities. With unparalleled opportunities to level vast building sites rather than shoehorn projects into tiny parcels, renewal directors might have done much more for the public than the best of the private developers of earlier times. Judged by what was built during the 1950s and 1960s, they did much less.

With so much space at hand project planners made a deliberate break with the conventional city layout, which they considered obsolete. Instead of siting the new buildings along established streets, they set them far apart from one another in open, parklike settings. Tall towers placed in a garden—the vision advanced by Le Corbusier and other leading architects—was the underlying concept for Gateway Center in Pittsburgh and dozens like it across the country. These projects usually cut off existing streets to create superblocks of open space, in contrast to the uninterrupted flow of Manhattan streets through Rockefeller Center. The wide spaces between buildings were seldom inviting to pedestrians, however. Roads, ramps, and parking areas split them up and made them hard to cross on foot. The towers were isolated, and the pseudo-parks around them had no intimacy, variety, or highlights.

The new projects followed city planning orthodoxy of the time by sorting out the clutter of old cities and segregating allegedly incompatible activities that might interfere with one another. Typical projects served single-purpose, specialized functions. An office development was equipped to service offices and the people who worked there: nothing more. A housing complex was for its residents: nothing more. New York even built a specialized project for the performing arts, Lincoln Center, rather than mix concert halls and theaters among offices, stores, and restaurants. Shopping, if it went beyond a few convenience stores, was generally considered an undesirable, incompatible land use in places designed for other purposes. Combining offices, shopping, restaurants, and hotels in a single mixed-use project, the most fashionable real estate idea by the late 1970s, was taboo. As a result large areas of the city were given over to single-purpose projects that were distinctly uninviting to the public at large—sometimes intentionally, as with housing complexes, and sometimes inadvertently.

This downtown renewal formula was a blueprint for isolation. Its repetition from city to city gave the projects a deadly uniformity that did not speak well for the underlying strategy of merging public and private interests in development. Meanwhile the clearance of familiar landmarks and the separation of new complexes from their older surroundings went a long way toward obliterating any local color or sense of place. The few exceptions stood out prominently. In Baltimore's Charles Center, built in the 1960s, new buildings joined older ones saved from the bulldozer, and a theater, hotels, and apartments added points of interest among the office towers. Most large projects blended poorly with surrounding streets, and with their superblocks and open spaces they seemed to fit the suburbs better than the centers of cities. Although they usually found takers for their rental space, they added little to the attractiveness of downtown and won no popularity contests on their own merits.

Nobody Knows the Rubble I've Seen

Having uninspiring projects rise from the ground was not the worst outcome for a city. Many cities saw nothing at all rise from the ground.

Federal rules for urban renewal directed a sharp separation between city renewal agencies and developers. The city was responsible for planning a project and carrying it forward until the land was cleared and ready for new construction. Just before it was ready city officials were to invite proposals from developers and then select a winner to complete the work according to plan. Developers had no role at all during the advance planning. In principle, city officials were to make up their minds about the sort of project they wanted and only later find a developer.

The last step usually turned out to be the hardest. In Detroit planning for the Gratiot residential project started in 1947, two years before enactment of the federal renewal program. By 1952 city officials had converted it to a federal aid project, drawn up a plan for rebuilding the area, and announced an auction to select a developer. Nobody bid for it. To make the project more inviting, the city changed its plan to allow more construction. Another auction a year later produced only two bids. Six months later the high bidder revealed his own plan, which was so poor that city officials refused to approve it. By late 1954 city officials turned for help to a committee of business people who knew something about marketing land. After another year they found a developer who bought the site. Following more delays, the first houses opened in late 1958. Until then the city had nothing to show for its highly publicized effort except fields of rubble known locally as ragweed acres.

In Newark a similar story was unfolding. Local renewal officials announced slum clearance in the North Ward in 1952, and by 1956 they were ready to market the land. When their promotional campaign failed to generate any developer interest, they knew they were in trouble. After beating the bushes for another year, director Louis Danzig finally roused several firms to make bids and auctioned off the land. The high bidder, however, was unable to come to terms with federal officials on mortgage insurance he needed to start building. Danzig needed one more year to find a developer qualified to take the project, and to sweeten the deal he had to promise to override the city's competitive bidding procedure on the final plan.

Newark officials, bruised by the experience, decided to let future developers tell them in advance where they wanted to build. After coming to terms with a home builder interested in their next project, however, they discovered that Washington officials would not approve this violation of federal policy, but the federal regional office in Philadelphia had faced the rubble problem so often that its staff winked at Newark's tactics.

Although Robert Moses in New York selected developers before he planned projects, almost everyone else followed the federal rules. To involve developers early would have risked trouble not only with Washington but also with the courts. If a city agency negotiated with a developer long before it was ready to sell the land, it would be vulnerable to lawsuits challenging its procedures for making competitive awards. Besides, allowing the developer to help draw up the project plans could have raised legal questions about whether the city was taking land for a private purpose rather than a public one.

So city officials had to make plans based on their own feasibility studies and their best judgment, but when the time came they were often unable to find developers to take the site off their hands. St. Louis had its "Hiroshima Flats" and St. Paul its "Superhole." Vacant lots littered with junked cars, piles of garbage, and rat nests were the most visible results of thirteen years of work on the ambitious Ellicott project in Buffalo. "Trees that were saplings when the land was cleared have grown tall," wrote the *New York Times*. A dozen years after the federal program ended, some cities were still trying to sell their shopworn projects. In May 1986 the *Times* published an aerial view of thirty beachfront blocks in the Arverne section of New York City, cleared for renewal in the mid-1960s and still lying abandoned twenty years later while the city waited for a Prince Charming to bring them back to life.

The rubble problem was not just anecdotal, and it was not limited to the early years of the program. Although Washington officials kept claiming steady progress in the sale of land to developers, the record was poor to the end. As late as 1971 more than half the projects begun between 1960 and 1964 still had land unsold, and only the very earliest projects—those begun between 1950 and 1959—had completed two-thirds or more of their land sales. Excluding developers from project planning led to results that could only make a skeptical public even more skeptical about the way cities were rebuilding downtown.

The Freeway Revolt

The downtown coalitions had been carried away by a vision of radical change for downtown, but their efforts to force this change were not working. Highway building was the first element of downtown renewal to run up against tough, project-threatening opposition. Local controversies began to surface almost as fast as state highway engineers were able to put the 1956 highway act into operation. The road builders had every reason to think they could deal with local opposition as they always had, by brushing it aside or making minor concessions. When residents of Boyle Heights in Los Angeles protested the Pomona and Golden State freeways in 1957 and 1958, the highway engineers who had already routed three freeways through this neighborhood paused just long enough to make a slight change of alignment before they went on pouring concrete.

The time-honored tradition of minimal concessions or none at all failed to work in San Francisco in 1959. There citizens who were upset when a double-deck elevated highway cut off their view of the much-loved Ferry Terminal persuaded the city's Board of Supervisors to stop the freeway system just where it was, before it did any further damage. The supervisors vetoed two planned extensions and left the Embarcadero Freeway with its stub end hanging in midair. Even while most other cities were pleading for federal aid, San Francisco was turning down $60 million in highway funds. Federal and state highway officials were amazed at this turn of events.

If the San Francisco action was an eye-opener for the engineers, it was a source of encouragement for highway opponents in dozens of other cities. In the early 1960s highway protests too strong to ignore spread to all parts of the country: Baltimore, Memphis, Milwaukee, Seattle, and San Antonio among others. In the mid-1960s the press discovered these controversies as a national movement and gave it coverage as well as a name: the freeway revolt. The protesters were managing to stall urban highways and by the late 1960s even to stop them altogether. "A bare fifteen years after the Interstate program commenced," wrote Daniel P. Moynihan in 1970, "it is just about impossible to get a major highway program approved in most large American cities."[1] Highways were stopped in cites as different from one another as Philadelphia and Phoenix, Miami and Minneapolis, and New Orleans and Chicago. And increasingly the highways that generated controversy were the ones planned for downtown.

The driving force behind the antihighway movement was indignation, and people had good reason to be indignant. The highways that generated controversy were most often the ones that threatened to destroy low-income neighborhoods. Highways under attack in Baltimore, Boston, Kansas City, Los Angeles, and St. Louis would have run through low-income black communities. While highway engineers continued to believe that eliminating poor neighborhoods was a blessing for the city, those who lived and worked in the path of the highway were angry enough to fight back.

Aside from threats to residential areas, the other reasons for indignation were environmental or aesthetic. Plans to demolish historic houses in Baltimore, rows of sycamore trees in Cambridge, and part of a city arboretum in Seattle led to protests. A fourteen-lane bridge planned over Baltimore's Inner Harbor prompted the same outrage as the defunct freeways that would have damaged prized areas in San Francisco. The highway controversies in central cities were over issues that had little to do with transportation.

Insensitivity to nontransportation values reached deep into the highway bureaucracy. Consider this statement from the federal Bureau of Public Roads describing with pride the road network its engineers wanted to build: "The pavement area of the system, assembled in one huge parking lot, would be 20 miles square and would accommodate two-thirds of all motor vehicles in the United States. New right-of-way needed amounts to 1½ million acres. Total excavation will move enough material to bury Connecticut knee deep in dirt. Sand, gravel and crushed stone for construction would build a wall 50 feet wide and 9 feet high completely around the world. The concrete used would build six sidewalks to the moon. . . . Lumber and timber requirements would take all of the trees from a 400 square mile forest."[2]

The highway revolt countered this engineering dream with an appeal to another strongly held American value, the defense of one's home. Although each protest group operated in its own style, saving neighborhoods from the bulldozer was the theme. A Cambridge protester with a gift for satire put the theme to music, in a parody of Lerner and Loewe's "The Street Where You Live" from *My Fair Lady*:

Oh I used to walk down this street before
But they've kicked out all the folks I used to meet before
And the neighborhood
Now is gone for good
There's no street on the street where I lived.

When the interstate highway program got under way in the 1950s, it had exceptional public support. For the sake of highways conservatives set aside their normal objections to federal intrusion in local affairs, and liberals stretched their priorities for public spending by calling for "better schools, better hospitals, better roads." Newspaper editorials were warmly supportive, and even journals of critical comment on public affairs found the need for new highways so compelling that they raised no serious questions.

To get a sympathetic hearing, the opponents had their work cut out for them. They usually formed a protest organization, recruited as many members as they could, and held large public meetings to demonstrate support. Media coverage was essential for recognition. Protesters learned to make news by sending their best speakers to public hearings, creating visible confrontations whenever they could, and staging demonstrations in front of government buildings. Some who managed to build city-wide coalitions were able to turn out huge numbers of people for mass rallies in the most prominent locations at the most critical times. Although big-city newspapers were usually boosters of development projects for downtown, their reporters could not ignore the drama of ordinary citizens confronting the establishment with charges of community injustice.

Other protest tactics worked too. Sympathetic engineers and planners could attack the technical adequacy of government transportation plans, and occasionally protesters went to court to challenge highway departments on procedural grounds. The strategies were as varied as the protests themselves, and in the end the political system responded to causes that could turn out large numbers of supporters over a long period of time. The high visibility of freeways planned for the center of the city, combined with the practiced political skills of civic leaders in the big cities, made these roads more vulnerable to attack than suburban highways.

One of the surprises was the failure of the highway lobby to squelch this opposition. The powerful interest groups that backed federal highway aid in Washington—the automobile, oil, and trucking industries—did not rally around their program at the local level, perhaps because eliminating a few city freeways did not pose much of a threat to the overall system. State highway departments and public works commissioners were left to defend the urban roads, and their claims to technical objectivity were beginning to sound hollow.

Growing disenchantment with urban highways in intellectual circles gave an extra measure of legitimacy to the protests. Starting with
the belief that average people did not observe proper limits for their
use of private cars, a growing body of critics argued that new highways would not relieve congestion but would simply encourage more
driving. If the net result of highway construction was to bring more
cars into the city, according to this indictment, transit systems would
lose passengers, congestion would increase, and there would be fresh
demands for another cycle of road building. Lewis Mumford in 1958
predicted that new highways and parking garages would eventually strangle the city centers with traffic, driving out remaining
businesses.

As the interstate system was put in place in the 1960s and 1970s,
professionals and journalists joined in the attack. Most pronounced
the urban interstates guilty on all counts in the indictment as soon as
they were open. Their book titles outdid one another in hostility: *Dead
End, Road to Ruin, The Great American Motion Sickness, Autokind vs.
Mankind, Superhighway-Superhoax.* This attack, one-sided and over-
drawn, marked a changing climate of opinion that made mayors and
business leaders listen more carefully to angry citizens.

Measured in highway miles, the freeway revolt had a smaller impact than its national scale and media attention would suggest. By
1976, 86 percent of the planned urban interstate routes—7,413 miles
of a planned 8,600—were open to traffic, so the protests came too late
to block construction of the bulk of the system laid out for cities. But
highway miles do not tell the whole story. The routes that were not
built include many sections that would have devastated in-town
neighborhoods. Measured by the number of people displaced, interstate highway construction became less destructive after 1969, with
monthly displacement figures falling by 79 percent from 1969 to 1976.
Further, the protests had a chilling effect on plans for future urban
highways. As the opposition spread, highway officials shelved plans
for new urban expressways, and federal spending for city transportation turned to upgrading existing roads and public transit.

As far as the rebuilding of downtown was concerned, the highway
protests cut off one of the two main sources of money, the federal aid
highway program. Much of what the mayors and their allies wanted
was already accomplished, however, and federal funds would still be

available for public transit to cope with future needs for downtown access. More important, the freeway revolt was an early warning of rising public resistance to any projects designed to tear apart neighborhoods, including urban renewal.

Losing Urban Renewal

Urban renewal was even more important to the downtown coalitions than the federal aid highways. It gave them a way to assemble and clear land in and around downtown, to use that land for what they wanted, and to do it almost all at federal expense. To the mayors and their business allies it was a lifeline of support for cities struggling to stay afloat.

The same reactions that generated the highway revolt threatened to cut that lifeline for downtown. If people living in the 200-foot-wide strip planned for a freeway could protest and win, it stood to reason that the much larger communities threatened by urban renewal could do the same. Although the first wave of people to be evicted for renewal projects did not organize much resistance, other neighborhoods learned a few lessons from their experience—lessons about the nature of civic progress and the value of relocation promises. When the renewal agencies drew up plans for more projects, they ran into more determined and skillful opponents.

New York was the bellwether of opposition to urban renewal. As in the case of the San Francisco freeway revolt, the first success story did not come from a protest of the poor but from the political know-how of the middle class. After a series of urban renewal scandals, Robert Moses left his post as head of New York's slum clearance operations, and Mayor Robert Wagner set up a new agency with a mandate to rebuild the city in less authoritarian ways. Searching for a place to build middle-income housing, the agency settled on a desirable location at the edge of Greenwich Village for its first renewal project. The neighborhood was desirable enough to have attracted a group of middle-class professionals, some of whom had already managed to stop a road through Washington Square park. One of the leading activists was Jane Jacobs, an accomplished critic of urban renewal whose incisive book on the rebuilding of cities was almost completed at that point. This agency, set up to rescue the city's urban renewal program, had picked the wrong place to start.

Jane Jacobs and her neighbors knew enough about urban renewal to realize that once the city managed to take the first few steps toward a project, it would be hard to stop them, so they organized an uncompromising attack from the beginning. In early 1961 the agency took the seemingly harmless step of asking city government approval to apply for federal funds for a preliminary study of the area. Recognizing this move as the first commitment to a renewal project and suspecting that the city already had plans to destroy their neighborhood, opponents orchestrated a sophisticated campaign. They spoke up at public hearings and council meetings, visited city officials, and filed a lawsuit challenging the designation of the area as blighted.

Mayor Wagner was facing a tough battle for reelection in the 1961 Democratic primary. The day before the vote, he came out against the West Village project. After his reelection the City Planning Commission formally removed the designation of blight, and by January 1962 the project was dead before it started. To reinforce the bellwether effect, West Village activists gave advice to people in two other project areas on how to fight the city, and their neighborhood organization took part in the successful campaign against the proposed Lower Manhattan Expressway.

Renewal projects were vulnerable to neighborhood attacks even when the opposition was not as formidable as the West Village group. After the early clearance projects earned a bad name for the program, many cities switched to projects that cleared only the worst buildings and renovated those that could be saved. To make this new approach work, renewal officials had to come up with neighborhood plans that would persuade residents to fix up their homes. As a practical matter they had to listen to local people if they wanted them to improve their property. Although these renovation projects were not as destructive as wholesale clearance, they still threatened to push out owners who could not afford to upgrade their homes, tenants who could not pay rent increases, and everyone who lived in buildings slated for demolition. Skeptics called this new strategy for neighborhood improvement the "financial bulldozer."

The neighborhood rehabilitation projects generated their own controversies, usually centering on how much of the area would be cleared, how much help people would have with renovation, and how much relocation housing would be built. Renewal agencies had to come to terms with residents if they wanted even minimal cooperation. By the mid-1960s almost every big city had a political brawl over urban renewal, and some had more than one.

Downtown interests had a stake in these controversies because neighborhood groups could make urban renewal much less useful for rebuilding the city center by holding clearance to a minimum. New political stirrings at the time made it easier for low-income people to influence programs like urban renewal. With the rediscovery of poverty as a national issue in the early 1960s, Presidents Kennedy and Johnson made the War on Poverty a central feature of domestic policy. Under the Economic Opportunity Act of 1964 federal grants for local antipoverty agencies usually bypassed city hall and went directly to private organizations that had representatives of poor people on their boards. These community action agencies soon created an independent organizational base for local activists, giving them budgets, offices, staff, and status that they could use to fight city hall. Federal support reinforced a growing belief that residents of low-income neighborhoods had a right to share control over government programs in their areas, with urban renewal a prime case in point.

The civil rights movement and growing black militancy made city officials especially cautious about imposing projects on reluctant minority neighborhoods. By 1964 protests over living conditions were common in the black neighborhoods of northern cities, and racial violence had come to Chicago, Cleveland, New York, and Philadelphia. In the summer of 1965 the Watts area of Los Angeles had the worst rioting the country had seen since Detroit in 1943. The police called in help from the National Guard, and after several days of fighting thirty-four people were dead, hundreds were injured, and 4,000 were under arrest. The violence in black neighborhoods continued in 1966 and 1967, with the most serious outbursts leaving widespread destruction and three dead in Chicago, twenty-three in Newark, and forty-three in Detroit.

President Johnson's Advisory Commission on Civil Disorders investigated the riots and concluded they were the result of legitimate grievances of black people. When the commission analyzed the sources of unrest, it found urban renewal evictions among them. Inadequate housing was one of the top three complaints and urban renewal a significant complaint in many cities—specifically that there was too little community participation in decision making and that the programs were "Negro removal."

Looking further into what government had done about the conditions that gave rise to grievances, the commission learned why urban renewal was a problem. Staff members investigated three cities that were well known for the high quality of their urban development programs: Detroit, New Haven, and Newark. All three were champions at getting federal funds for housing and urban renewal, and all three had serious riots. A count of low-income houses built and low-income houses destroyed in these cities went a long way toward explaining why renewal was a sore point with the black community. Detroit had built 758 low-income houses with federal programs since 1956, while demolishing 8,000 low-income houses for urban renewal. Since 1952 New Haven had built 951 federally subsidized houses while clearing 6,500 low-income homes. Newark had a large low-income housing program that had built 3,760 dwellings since 1959, but the city had evicted 12,000 families for urban renewal, public housing, and highway construction during the same period.

Big-city mayors wanted to keep the peace even more than they wanted to succeed with urban renewal. Earlier, black neighborhoods had been the targets of choice for both renewal and highway projects, but now the rioting sent a message: "Don't tread on me." There might be a way for mayors to have their renewal projects and still keep the peace, but that would mean treating black neighborhoods as something more than a land reserve for downtown expansion.

With citizen participation taking hold as a form of politics and with rioting understood as a form of protest, renewal planners had to give up any ideas of large-scale clearance. If cities could no longer level in-town neighborhoods, if they could no longer push minority groups out of their homes, if clearance projects were vulnerable to political protests and legal maneuvers, what good was urban renewal for re-building downtown? It was still a way to clear factories and ware-houses on the edge of downtown, since there were few residents to complain and up to 35 percent of federal renewal funds could go into projects that involved no housing. Also, some neighborhoods, and even whole cities, had not yet learned how to stop clearance projects. Even where housing renovation was the only feasible treatment for a neighborhood, renewal was still a way to make interesting old houses in convenient locations attractive to a new class of well-to-do home buyers—the sort of people who could work downtown and enjoy its cultural advantages. Urban renewal, even diminished, remained an important resource for downtown planners.

The political climate of the 1960s continued to reshape the uses of renewal, however, and the downtown coalitions had only a few years left to exploit its remaining possibilities. When people talked about the urban problem, they no longer meant the decline of downtown. Now they meant the plight of poor and minority groups in slum neighborhoods. A new awareness of poverty not only pushed downtown out of the spotlight but encouraged Congress to tighten the reins on urban renewal. A series of amendments starting in 1966 gave top funding priority to projects that built houses for low- and moderate-income people and required all residential projects to consist mainly of this type of housing.

After Richard Nixon's election in 1968, Housing and Urban Development secretary George Romney pushed urban renewal ahead with so much energy that 1972 became the peak year for project starts in the history of the program. But he also kept the pressure on cities to meet the new housing priorities, and for the first time top federal officials acknowledged relocation abuses openly. Romney's assistant secretary in charge of renewal told a conference of local officials: "It has often been said by our critics that we have been unresponsive to the relocation needs of project residents. It has been said, for example, that urban renewal is nothing more than Negro removal. . . . We have been accused of violating the law and of contravening our own administrative regulations. And today we are being called 'legal lawbreakers.' . . . It is time to be honest with each other and to admit that there is some validity to these allegations."[3]

Whether the cities could have found a way to use renewal for rebuilding downtown while still meeting their housing and relocation obligations is an open question. By the early 1970s, even while Romney was working hard to strengthen urban renewal, President Nixon had decided to disentangle the federal government from the seemingly endless local controversies that surrounded this and other grant-in-aid programs. His New Federalism strategy of switching control over federal grants from Washington to states and cities included merging urban renewal together with other programs into a single source of funding that the cities could use flexibly for almost any type of development project. The new community development block grants, enacted in 1974, were awarded according to a formula instead of responding to proposals for specific projects, and federal regulations were cut to a minimum. After twenty-five years the urban renewal program was over. Cities were still free—freer than ever—to use federal community development funds for downtown projects. But the downtown coalitions could no longer get those funds designated in advance for the projects they wanted. With their main source of off-budget financing gone, they would now have to compete against other city and neighborhood claims for a share of each year's community development grant.

The political pressures of the 1960s made an impact on the downtown coalitions as well as on federal urban programs. Even coalitions as powerful as the one in Pittsburgh recognized that it was time to change the agenda in order to keep the peace. Starting in the mid-1960s corporate leaders worked on projects to send black students to college, hire and train the unemployed, lend money to minority business people, and improve a low-income neighborhood once marked for clearance. In 1968 the Allegheny Conference hired a new director, conceded that it had "failed to recognize the urban crisis" in the past, and announced its commitment to a "social Renaissance."

Mayor Lee's New Haven coalition also had to slow down, listen to critics, and put some projects on hold. Community activists mobilized opposition to a highway proposal and several urban renewal projects and together with a city-wide coalition demanded more construction and less clearance. Lee responded by setting up eight neighborhood corporations to share power over antipoverty programs, giving neighborhood organizations an advisory role in urban renewal, and bringing the Hill renewal project to a halt for several years. Business leaders did the same things as their colleagues in other cities: they hired minority workers, helped neighborhood organizations, and financed low-income housing. Meanwhile they put the rebuilding of downtown on the back burner.

Persuasive Protests

Political pressure sent downtown coalitions a clear warning. Most big-city mayors and their business allies understood that they could no longer evict large numbers of people for the sake of revitalizing downtown. No other conclusion made practical sense, and even with hindsight it is hard to understand why the urban experts and city officials failed to anticipate the political reaction and to act on it earlier. Perhaps the most plausible explanation is the one Lewis Mumford suggested in connection with the highway program: "When the American people, through their Congress, voted . . . for a twenty-six-billion-dollar highway program the most charitable thing to assume about this action is that they hadn't the faintest notion of what they were doing."[4]

The same could be said of the many urban experts—Mumford included—who recommended wholesale clearance and rebuilding as the only solution to the problems of the central cities. No doubt most assumed that the clearance and relocation would be humane, compassionate, and generous. But this assumption in turn seemed to rest on nothing more solid than political ideology.

To a generation of liberals who had lived through the New Deal and World War II, government was a benevolent force in society that could be trusted to do good. And during the 1950s it was an article of liberal faith that government was needed to redress imbalances created by the private sector. John Kenneth Galbraith's *The Affluent Society*, a book with wide influence at the time, argued that the private economy was flooding the country with frivolous consumer products while more legitimate needs were going unmet because government was not doing enough: "To create the demand for new cars we must contrive elaborate and functionless changes each year and then subject the consumer to ruthless psychological pressures to persuade him of their importance. . . . In the meantime there are large ready-made needs for schools, hospitals, slum clearance and urban redevelopment, sanitation, parks, playgrounds, police, and a thousand other things. Of these needs almost no one must be persuaded. They are unavailable only because . . . the money to provide them is unavailable."[5]

Anyone who argued for public programs as meritorious as slum clearance was in good company in the 1950s. Not only was the purpose a worthy one, but a halo left over from the patriotism of World War II made government—particularly the federal government, which would be supervising both urban renewal and highway construction—seem fair and trustworthy. Not only liberal intellectuals put their confidence in government at the time; most other people did the same. According to opinion polls, 80 percent of the people had great trust in government in the late 1950s, a figure that dropped sharply after the mid-1960s.

Political liberals were not the only source of support for the clearance strategy. In most cities the business community, more inclined toward conservatism, still supplied the civic leadership for urban renewal. Recently one of the country's leading business organizations in the field of public policy, the Committee for Economic Development, sponsored research to identify the contributions of local coalitions of business executives and public officials to city development since the 1950s and came up with glowing findings: "Public-private partnerships are a source of energy and vitality for America's urban communities. Successful experience with such partnerships spans the decades and the country. It is up to the leaders in government, business, labor, nonprofit organizations, educational institutions, and civic associations to carry this experience forward."[6]

Nobody can deny the central role of business executives in the rebuilding of downtown areas or their right to celebrate the handsome projects of the 1980s that result from their efforts of twenty or more years ago. But where were these business leaders when Baltimore bulldozed the houses of 10,000 families, 90 percent of them black? Or when New York tore the top stories off still-occupied buildings to get the last tenants out? Or when Los Angeles pushed five freeways through its main Mexican-American neighborhood? Or when Providence evicted hundreds of small firms with inadequate compensation, driving one-third of them out of business? Or when San Francisco had to be restrained by court order from hounding tenants out of residential hotels? The answer must be that they were deeply implicated in these events. One of the federal officials who dealt with San Francisco's renewal program said of its director, Justin Herman: "Herman could move rapidly on renewal—demolition or construction—because he was absolutely confident that he was doing what the power structure wanted insofar as the poor and the minorities were concerned."[7]

Public officials and business leaders had been indifferent to the damage their programs did to people in the way. Urban experts who had recommended large-scale clearance either did not take the trouble to find out the effects on the victims or else shrugged them off as a reasonable price to pay for progress, especially since somebody else was paying it. But by the early 1970s business and civic leaders alike recognized that the days of big clearance projects were over.

Progress But No Applause

The pause in downtown renewal in the late 1960s was a good time for stocktaking. After a twenty-year campaign the protest over clearance was not the only problem, but there was progress to report as well. New office and apartment buildings had an importance out of proportion to their number. They were concentrated in and around downtown, in the spotlight of the news media and in view of the daily flow of commuters. Many cities that were early starters had their first major projects either completed or well under way, and their downtown coalitions could point to symbols of revival in brick and mortar or, more likely, in concrete and glass. Beyond the symbols there were also improvements in highway access; most of the urban freeway routes planned under the interstate system were open to traffic by the early 1970s.

The movement to rebuild downtown led to an impressive increase in office construction in the 1960s. During the 1950s new office buildings added 58 million square feet of office space to the downtown districts of the thirty largest metropolitan areas, with New York accounting for almost half the total. (Among the other leading office producers of the 1950s were several cities with active downtown renewal programs: Pittsburgh, Chicago, Philadelphia, and Denver.) By the 1960s new construction added more than twice as much office space—132 million square feet—to the central business districts of these metropolitan areas. New York's share fell to one-third as other cities accelerated the expansion of their office districts. Once more, cities with major downtown renewal programs ranked high in office construction, among them San Francisco, Atlanta, Boston, and Baltimore.

The pickup in office construction was an important indicator of economic strength for the cities. Despite strong competition from the suburbs they were managing to hold onto a major share of the country's growth in office and service activities. The downtown business centers of the thirty largest metropolitan areas captured some 20 percent of all office construction in the nation during the 1960s.

These new offices brought welcome job opportunities, but office buildings alone were still not producing the kind of downtown that city residents found attractive. Pittsburgh had its Gateway Center with jobs for 22,000 people where only 4,000 had worked before, new downtown highways, some sixty new buildings, and air pollution control that made the city cleaner and more livable. Yet even friendly observers were disappointed. Jeanne R. Lowe, who wrote sympathetically about the rebuilding of cities in the 1960s, questioned whether the Pittsburgh Renaissance was a success: "Pittsburgh residents do not dawdle downtown, or come back down there after work and on weekends. Despite the golden Hilton Hotel at Gateway Center and the civic arena's telescoping roof, there is little to attract or hold people there."[8] Pittsburgh historian Roy Lubove, less committed to urban renewal, called the new downtown "an enormous filing cabinet, which operates between the hours of 9–5," and condemned its "expressionless stainless-steel facades."[9] Jane Jacobs, a severe critic of urban renewal, wrote angrily of what the cities were producing with their billions of dollars in federal funds: "Cultural centers that are unable to support a good bookstore. Civil centers that are avoided by everyone but bums, who have fewer choices of loitering places than others. Promenades that go from no place to nowhere and have no promenaders. Expressways that eviscerate great cities. This is not the rebuilding of cities. This is the sacking of cities."[10]

These were telling criticisms, not because of the points they scored against uninspired architecture, but because they emphasized that the downtown projects had little appeal for anyone. They suggested that whatever clientele the downtown coalitions had in mind for their projects had little to do with typical city residents or visitors.

Since the plans themselves often included sketches of new projects, three irreverent city planners got the idea of investigating the intended public for downtown by studying the sorts of people who appeared in these sketches. Using planning reports published between 1958 and 1964, they found the people drawn as young, well dressed, and white—at a time when cities were becoming noticeably older, poorer, and blacker. The recurrent character types who wandered through the new plazas and office complexes or lived in the new apartment towers included The Gentleman with the Briefcase, The Fashionable Lady, The Boulevardier, The Viewer, and The Young Lovers.[11] This exercise uncovered an attempt by the downtown coalitions and their design staff to appeal to a sophisticated and affluent public. The bias against average people was clear; these downtown plans aimed at improving public taste rather than satisfying it. In contrast to suburban developers who reached for the middle of a mass market, downtown planners were searching for people who were hard to find. Perhaps the elite types who appeared in their drawings could be sold on downtown, but at best their numbers would be small.

The problems of marketing downtown apartment projects were also symptomatic of this search for people with highbrow tastes. Sociologist William Michelson studied survey data on the living choices and preferences of a sample of city and suburban residents in order to see how many of them really wanted the kind of housing that downtown planners were promoting. He found that about 85 percent of the people preferred to live in single-family homes, and most wanted to live on lots of one-third to one-half acre. Eight people of ten went to work by car and fewer than one in ten by public transit. And even if the time and cost were equal, nine of ten who drove to work wanted to keep driving.

Michelson then searched his sample to see how many people in it matched the full profile of suburbanites that the planners hoped to attract to downtown living, that is, people who owned single-family homes but wanted to move to apartments, who wanted to move from a large lot to a smaller one, who wanted to move from their present neighborhood to one closer to the center of the city, and who would choose to go to work by transit rather than car if the time and cost were the same. Of 748 people in the sample, not one fit this profile. His conclusion had to be that downtown plans were a misfit, or as he titled his article, "Most People Don't Want What Architects Want."

The new downtown was profoundly out of touch with popular taste and with developers who normally built for a mass market. The key decisions on downtown projects were not made by developers, since urban renewal procedures excluded them from advance planning, but by a professional staff who hoped to attract a trendsetting elite. In time some of the trendsetters did find their way to the new projects, but the response from the public at large ranged from indifference to disappointment.

When the renewal era came to an end, the downtown coalitions were at a turning point. They had built strong alliances, captured federal funding, and sharpened their skills in local politics. Their crusade for downtown was by no means a failure. In fact they had laid the groundwork for successes that would come later in response to new opportunities and new strategies. But their vision of radical change, their abuse of low-income and minority residents, and the elitism of their plans brought their own campaign to a standstill.

One troublesome question remained unanswered. Suppose their vision had been less grandiose and their program gentler. Would they have succeeded during the renewal era? Probably not, because timing worked against them in the 1950s and 1960s. Developer interest was too limited and fragile to make use of cleared sites. Would earlier contact between city officials and developers have made a difference? Probably so. It would have discouraged cities from starting projects when the demand for sites was weak. Gearing renewal to realistic prospects for selling the land would have led to more cautious clearance, parcel by parcel, beginning with the most desirable locations. There would have been less demolition, fewer protests, and smaller projects closer to the existing grain of downtown. Letting developer interest set the pace for rebuilding might have made for less drama but also less hardship. As important, developers would have brought another point of view to bear on the rebuilding of downtown, one oriented toward marketing projects for the broad middle class. That point of view could have improved the prospects for commercial success as well as popular acceptance.

After the binge of clearance was over, city officials were more willing to listen to developers, and they looked with growing interest at successes in the suburbs.

Would the Shopping Mall Play Downtown?

If real estate developers ever thought they might take their place among the experts who were drawing plans for downtown, they were in for a rude awakening. When the International Council of Shopping Centers asked about opportunities for retail developers in the urban renewal program, a top Washington official let them know where they stood: "You are buying the land at a discount. One of the reasons is that you have agreed to improve it according to this plan. You can't draw on your imagination and decide for yourself what would be better for you or the site. It has to follow this plan. For that reason, it is sold at a discount."[1]

Even if developers were kingpins in the new suburbs, their job in urban renewal was to take over projects conceived by the experts and to get them built no matter how botched the plans were. The federal manual wrote a script in which city officials were on stage by themselves during Act 1, they shared the stage with the developer during a very brief second act, and the developer's team transformed a rubble field into a successful project during Act 3. If the developer made his entrance according to the script, he had to follow plans drawn up in Act 1 by city staff who knew too little about real estate or popular taste. The project unveiling that was to be the grand finale of Act 3 usually put the audience to sleep and got a scathing review the next day.

By making developers into accessories after the fact, the renewal coalitions threw away a chance to learn how to build for the crowds rather than for the elite. Most developers of the time, unlike the downtown experts, were not critical of the suburbs nor were they trying to educate people to higher standards of taste. Pragmatic business people eyeing the bottom line, they saw the suburbs as a frontier and did their best to respond to the culture of people who bought tract homes and loved their cars. Departing from the traditions of prewar custom builders who put up a small number of homes under contract to individual clients, a new breed of merchant builders learned how to build hundreds of thousands of new homes a year for sale on the open market. They organized enterprises capable of buying and subdividing raw land, putting in streets and utilities, designing projects for middle-class tastes and pocketbooks, financing the entire operation on favorable terms, and marketing what they built.

By the 1960s developers had mastered these techniques not only for tract houses but for industrial parks and shopping centers. And the shopping centers were a sharp contrast to downtown renewal projects: designed to be as inviting as possible to a broad group of users and kept open days, evenings, and weekends.

The regional shopping center looks in retrospect like the inevitable outcome of mass automobile ownership and suburban growth, but its emergence in the 1950s was a dramatic event. Newspapers wrote glowingly about the advantages of "markets in the meadows": places totally planned for the consumer that made more sense than the helter-skelter competition of the average Main Street, offering free parking for thousands of cars and one-stop shopping convenience in spacious weathertight surroundings. This was strong rhetoric, but the reality was that shoppers could avoid wearisome, traffic-clogged travel to downtown and noisy and crowded streets and shop at their leisure.

The developers and retailers responsible for these centers had created something strikingly different from their closest forerunners, the few shopping districts with built-in parking that graced certain prewar suburbs. Those districts were meant to embellish residential communities for the well-to-do. Kansas City's Country Club Plaza, for instance, opened in the 1920s with small clusters of specialty stores set among landscaped parking areas on blocks studded with Grecian urns, Italian marble statues, bronze fountains, and Spanish filigree gates. Suburban branches of city department stores in the 1930s similarly were small operations featuring high-fashion, top-price lines rather than the full selection of a downtown store. The postwar retail developers, however, went for the mass market, not the carriage trade. By bringing department stores together with seventy or more midline shops, they tried to create a retail destination with the pull and character of New York's Thirty-fourth Street rather than Fifth Avenue. By duplicating the drawing power of downtown, they gambled that the new regional centers would dominate suburban retail markets.

In going for high volume in the suburbs, developers broke away from established retailing principles. Commonly accepted marketing theory held that suburban locations were appropriate only for convenience goods, those daily necessities purchased frequently, while downtown was the place for more prestigious shopping goods—the general merchandise, apparel, furniture, and household items that people bought after comparing variety and value from a wide selection. Not bound by retailing dogma, the early regional center developers thought differently.

Just as the past showed the limits of aristocratic retailing, demographic projections for the future profiled a suburban market well suited to developers' ideas. As statistics from the 1950 Census rolled off the presses, they revealed a big and rapidly expanding middle class. For retailers this was a much better market than the luxury class of the 1920s because the number of households was much larger and the demand for quality merchandise was reportedly tied to group buying habits. In addition its family orientation and preference for informal, outdoor leisure activities created enormous demands for new products, products not supplied effectively in the downtown stores.

To build the big regional shopping centers, developers needed department stores to draw customers to the center, to attract the apparel shops, shoe stores, and other small retailers who would lease space, and to get financing from the major insurance companies that backed these risky ventures. The big retailers were reluctant players, however. "Department store owners wouldn't even consider locating their stores in the middle of a field, away from traffic," recalled David Bohannon, the developer of Hillsdale Shopping Center in San Mateo, California, one of the earliest centers. They believed sidewalk frontage was critical for drawing customers into the store, and putting parking in its place seemed reckless. With huge investments downtown, department stores also were fearful of cutting into their own sales volumes and abandoning their semimonopoly location. In 1947 Gimbel's of New York boasted of being "all trunk and no branches."

If department stores were slow to see that suburbanization would change consumer buying habits, competition eventually helped developers persuade them to move. Caught in a squeeze of low productivity, rising costs, and competitive pressures from rapidly growing chains such as Sears and Wards, department stores were pushed into making changes. And making the necessary changes downtown was too hard. The cost to remodel unwieldy flagship stores was high; more important, executives had little control over the surrounding environment that was steadily weakening their competitive position. They could build branch stores long before cities could solve traffic problems or halt the deterioration of middle-class neighborhoods. Although branches might cut into parent store volumes, in the dog-eat-dog competition for suburban trade, department stores were bound to lose business to somebody, and many executives decided "better it should be lost to themselves than to strangers."

Retail giants such as Macy's and Allied Stores were among the first to reverse corporate policy and locate their new stores in planned shopping centers. Moving into a planned center was not only a way to solve parking problems but a way to limit competition through the developer's control over the makeup and management of the entire project. Further, department stores extracted low-cost leases and other concessions from developers who needed them as anchor tenants. The benefits were compelling, and by the early 1960s developers and department stores had banded together to build regional shopping centers.

To make this alliance work, developers laid out buildings and parking for a complicated mix of stores, arranged financing, found suitable tenants, negotiated leases, and managed an ongoing operation. They needed to know as much about merchandising as about real estate to be successful. They had to find ways to draw people to the center, persuade them to stay for long visits, and get them to shop not just in department stores but in as many of the other stores as possible. Design, management, and negotiation—everything had to be geared to selling consumer goods.

There were few precedents for a planned and controlled shopping environment, no standards for the right amount of parking, and many questions about the best combination and layout of stores. Leading mall developers were candid about how the industry blundered along to a workable model by "a process of discovery," the "halt leading the blind," and "success by accident." During the 1950s a handful of entrepreneurs and department store executives experimented with the first regional centers. Within a few years the early mall builders were able to define a marketing strategy, an economic structure, and a physical form that worked well enough to serve as the prototype for an expanding industry.

The first regional shopping center, an open air mall called Northgate that opened outside Seattle in 1950, set the pattern by lining up stores in the middle of the site, surrounding them with parking, and turning them inward to form a pedestrian corridor for easy walking and comparison shopping. Northland near Detroit, a pioneering project that opened in 1954, demonstrated the advantages of going beyond commerical needs by furnishing lavish public spaces with flower beds, sculptures, fountains, benches, music, and imaginative lighting. Although both retailers and mortgage lenders were uneasy with this approach, early success at Northland confirmed the argument of architect Victor Gruen that an enjoyable total environment would bring people in and get them to stay. "More people," he reasoned, "—for more hours—means cash registers ringing more often and for longer periods."[2] By 1956 the opening of the first enclosed, climate-controlled mall, at Southdale in the Minneapolis suburb of Edina, made shopping still more comfortable year round and completed the basic model. It was a model that avoided the elitism of early renewal projects and demonstrated enough popular appeal to make downtown planners sit up and take notice.

Sanctuaries for Shopping

At first glance some people took regional shopping centers for clones of downtown with parking and pedestrian malls added, but this was a nearsighted view. A closer look showed that developers had lifted the most productive types of stores from downtown—those selling brand-name clothing, jewelry, shoes, cards and gifts, candy, and specialty food items, as well as those offering toys, sporting goods, books, cameras, cutlery, luggage, records and musical instruments, and even pets. They passed over the furniture stores, five-and-dime variety stores, key shops, liquor shops, used-book stores, bargain basements, second-hand stores, pawnshops, trinket places, "going-out-of-business" stores, and, of course, the discounters. Malls offered services but of a certain kind: beauty and barber shops, cinemas, community rooms, home finance companies, banks, medical offices; perhaps a post office, shoe repair shop, stamp redemption center, cleaner, photographer, or travel agent; but rarely a coin laundry, tailor, or appliance repair shop. The regional shopping center was for the most efficient merchants, not the start-up businesses or unprofitable, failing, or marginal enterprises.

Just as the selective retailing strategy led to a standardized group of tenants, it presented an idealized version of downtown. Developers believed that suburbanites had little nostalgia for downtown's hit-or-miss retailing, pushy crowds, dirty streets, or dress-up shopping rite. Seeing the projections for rising incomes and standards of affluence, they assumed suburbanites wanted something better, though more casual and informal, and they built a shopping environment to match.

In ambience and retail mix the suburban model of success turned its back on the market-driven chaos of downtown and left little to chance. As landlord of the entire shopping complex, the developer applied a measure of control unparalleled in downtown, and he wanted a hassle-free environment for shopping comfort. Merchandise was delivered, garbage compacted and picked up, and the mall cleaned daily—all behind the scenes with the sights, sounds, and smells kept away from shoppers. Mall personnel oversaw security operations, ridding shoppers of the sidewalk peddlers, Bible-pushing preachers, winos, prostitutes, panhandlers, or drug hustlers they might encounter downtown. The manager of an amusement arcade, kicked out after twenty-two years in Southdale, understood why his operation had fallen from favor: "I suppose the reason would probably be that the kids cause problems, that they sit and loiter. They swear, and the adults don't like it. They once-in-a-while will mooch money: Can I have 50 cents for the bus?"[3]

Developers had a big stake in making shoppers comfortable because their profits depended on heavy foot traffic and impulse buying at the small shops lining their malls. They earned no profit from the bare-bones leases and sweetheart deals they had to give the anchor department stores. To cover costs and earn a profit, they counted on the mall shops, especially those producing the highest sales volumes.

When developers refer to mall economics, they generally mean the distinctive revenue streams behind their money machines. Tenants pay a minimum rent, which typically covers insurance, real estate taxes, management, debt service on the mortgage loan, and an acceptable return on investment. (Since the inflationary 1970s new leases generally allow developers to pass along any increases in real estate taxes to the tenants.) Tenants pay their own utility expenses. On top of that, they pay common-area-maintenance charges—that is, a share of the expenses for cleaning and maintaining everything outside the space they occupy, including the pedestrian mall, parking area, delivery service facilities, and public restrooms. They also hand over money for a share of mall promotional expenses. With these revenues, a developer counts on breaking even financially. The developer's extra profit comes from an additional rent based on a tenant's sales. A tenant's minimum rent is pegged to a specific level of gross sales at which the store becomes profitable. If sales surpass this breakpoint, the developer collects some percentage of a tenants' gross sales, known as overage.

With business profits tied so closely to operating performance, developers had strong incentives to keep tight control over the shopping environment. They wrote long, elaborate leases governing opening hours, signs, window displays, lighting, merchandise lines, and promotional activities. By maintaining uniform, high standards of appearance and a strategic tenant mix, they hoped to attract crowds to the mall for long visits and multiple purchases.

The idea behind the mall was to create a sanctuary for shopping. In searching for a workable form, developers and their architects subscribed to much of the same city planning orthodoxy that inspired downtown renewal projects. They built single-purpose centers on large sites that segregated shopping from other activities. These principles worked better for them than they did for the downtown planners. In the hands of the mall builders city planning ideas were turned to the tastes of the average person. What they built was segregated but inviting. All that parking surrounding the retail core made for easy access and also protected the mall from nearby development. Removing the commotion of other activities encouraged visitors to concentrate on shopping.

The goal was commercial, but developers found that the way to achieve it was to provide an overlay of entertainment, relaxation, art and sculpture, civic goodwill, and space for community meetings and public events. A few thought of themselves as city builders or believed that shopping malls should serve as community centers to fill a void in suburbia. Others simply followed the pattern of successful regional centers. In time intense competition from discounters and other mall developers drove some to search for alternatives to the prototype. Faced with rising costs for building and operating malls, a few cut back the amenities and pared down their centers, but the biggest mall developers reasoned that it was better to compete by creating a place where people would mix leisure with shopping. So they built bigger malls with more recreational activities—movie houses, amusement arcades, ice skating rinks. Some provided space for churches, auditoriums, employment agencies, and personal counseling. Still others built satellite centers with office buildings and set aside land for apartments or hotels. By the early 1970s the mall had become a new community center.

By providing safe, comfortable spaces open long hours, developers made their retail centers inviting to a broad cross-section of the population. For teenagers the mall was a safe place to hang out, an updated scene for romantic rituals, and a significant source of part-time jobs. For the elderly it was a safe place to meet friends, an antidote for loneliness, and even a track for walking exercise. With few community-wide alternatives or popular street corners in suburbia, malls filled the social gap. Besides, no one had to spend any money to take advantage of the mall.

Increasingly the newer malls featured monumental central courts ornamented with sculpture, dramatic interior displays of light, and eye-catching graphics and floor designs that went far beyond commercial standards. In an intensely competitive environment the central court became an integral part of the developer's thrust to establish his mall as the premier community meeting place. It was more than a place to relax and meet friends; it was also the stage for promotional events that would draw more shoppers. And as developers built larger and more elaborate superregional malls in a drive to increase sales volume and block competitors, their central courts became bigger and more lavish.

The high priority given to public spaces was feasible in part because of low land costs. It was an unusual strategy, however. In a business that measures success in sales performance per square foot, the mall builders dedicated many square feet to social gathering. At first they tried to keep their common space close to 10 percent of total leasable area. As they built two-level malls, the figure grew to more than 16 percent in order to accommodate the setback design, ramps and escalators, and construction support necessary for a second level of retail shops. In malls with huge central courts the common area took up as much as 20 percent of the floor area rented to retail shops.

Defining the promotional thrust this way posed greater risk than increasing the annual advertising budget because brick-and-mortar investment was a long-term financial commitment. Yet the public space was a good investment. When energy costs and inflation accelerated in the early 1970s, developers cut back their spacious central courts but did not eliminate them.

The track record for mall builders in the suburbs was an unqualified success. In the 1950s and 1960s, while city officials coped with the dashed hopes of urban renewal, developers increased their output of malls tenfold and with few failures. By 1974 15,000 shopping centers were capturing more than 44 percent of the nation's retail sales (excluding automotive products and building materials, which are rarely sold in malls), and 800 big regional malls accounted for nearly a third of this total. By all the industry benchmarks—dollar value of construction contracts, retail sales volume, amount of gross leasable space—the regional mall was an economic powerhouse. And it had become a national common denominator, an experience few could not relate to. In following their commerical instincts, developers had produced something with more than commercial value.

The success of the suburban mall made it a logical model for mayors and their business allies to consider as they grappled with the problem of reviving downtown throughout the 1960s and 1970s. How much of that success came from popular attachment to cars, from the appeal of enclosed shopping sanctums, or from the unmet need for social centers in the suburbs was uncertain. But nobody doubted that the suburban mall had struck pay dirt; successful ones were already drawing more than a million people a month. For downtown planners who wanted to keep retailing alive, the question was whether a transplant could take hold in the city. The suburban mall gobbled up acreage, but sites downtown were smaller and more expensive. Also building would take longer and developers would have to deal with politicians and bureaucrats whose reputation for delivering on their promises was less than compelling. Since the odds were against an initiative by mall developers, what were cities prepared to do to bring them downtown?

Competing with Easy Street

The race to build regional malls did much to shape developers' notions of the elements that made a project feasible. The key to capturing a market was a prime site in the path of growth. For Edward J. DeBartolo, the nation's largest shopping center developer, cities were barely visible on a map contoured by swirls of suburban activity linked together by highways. Any one cluster of 15,000 to 20,000 people was too small a market for a regional mall, but put a mall right in the center of several with a toll-free interstate weaving through, and it was sure to be a winner. Checking one such location from his company plane, DeBartolo took a long look and said: "We got 'em! We can write our own ticket down there."[4]

Being able to move fast was a high priority. Once developers convinced department store executives to go to the suburbs, these retailers lost little time gearing up for expansion. Life insurance companies wanted to write mortgages for what they considered the Cadillac of investments, secured not just by real estate but by long-term leases from national retail chains. Local regulators and citizens were in step with growth, and zoning conflicts were rare. In that environment, most malls went up fast—within one and a half to two years. Time was money, and competition was intense. "Every good developer had a backlog of 15 projects," said Ernest W. Hahn, one of the nation's top five mall developers. "The problem was to get them built . . . to get there before somebody else did." And having a pipeline of projects kept large firms going, even when some malls ran into snags. With numerous deals on hand, they had flexibility to put new projects into production while they resolved such problems as the pullout of an anchor store.

With all the complexities of mall development, however, moving fast and maintaining an inventory of deals demanded a skilled organization. DeBartolo built what he termed "a beautiful machine— the most complete set of in-house services in the business": a specialized staff of 300 with lawyers, accountants, sales forecasters, traffic analysts, purchasing agents, architects, designers, and engineers. These machines were big producers. Between 1971 and 1976 the country's leading mall developers—Edward DeBartolo, Melvin Simon, Ernest Hahn, Alfred Taubman, and James Rouse—turned out more than ninety malls.

The 1960s and early 1970s were the go-go years of shopping center growth, when there were so many good sites that one veteran in the business claimed "you could almost throw a dart and develop." With ideal conditions in the suburbs, few mall developers bothered to look anywhere else. Downtown did not appear as a viable alternative. Despite the new office buildings reshaping big-city skylines, people were not moving back to town in numbers large enough to count. Further, expensive land, tight building spaces, and complex building controls persuaded the typical developer that building a mall downtown would amount to "betting the company."

In the race to build, the big mall developers acquired the strength to act as pioneers. They created organizations with a productive capacity that matched the efficiency of their selling machines, and as competitors snapped up remaining sites, these well-staffed organizations would need something else to do—go downtown, perhaps. After coming to terms with the exacting dictates of department store magnates and national chain store retailers, they were masters of drawn-out negotiations that one developer compared to the "exasperating red tape of a non-profit governmental agency." Most important, as large, well-capitalized firms, they had staying power. When the going got tough, as it would downtown, they had the financial strength to see a deal through the sometimes glacial pace of development.

A Tonic for Tired Cities?

To move as fast as they did, developers grabbed onto the current model of a workable mall, retreading it until competition drove them to something new. In the 1960s that prototype was the enclosed form pioneered at Southdale. Developers tinkered with details, adding a third and a fourth department store and more specialized shops. Architects came up with new configurations—L, H, T, X, cross, or pinwheel shapes—as they jockeyed space to give all the anchors equal billing or worked around difficult sites. These distinctions were relevant for the specialists. As long as developers could find seventy-plus acres in the cornfields, with no adjacent structures or existing streets to set building limits, the mall conformed to a predictable prototype: a low-lying island of stores surrounded by acres of open parking lots.

This prototype had possibilities for downtown. The retail core of the mall seemed well suited to an urban setting, with its high-density, high-value commerical space linked to public areas and built to standards consistent with long-term investment objectives. Making the core compact was a way to keep walking distances comfortably short when developers built in the suburbs, but it also matched the demands of high-cost land downtown because it packed in a huge amount of activity. For example, Woodfield outside Chicago in Schaumburg, the world's largest enclosed mall when it opened in 1972—2 million square feet of space for 215 shops and 4 record-sized department stores—fit its structures into an area smaller than three city blocks.

Whether the mall had value as a solution for downtown was something experts debated. On the inside, the prototype had several elements that appealed to critics of urban renewal: a mix of activities, a setting for pedestrians, large public spaces, and dense crowds to create excitement and provide the security that comes from eyes on the street. The single-ownership feature of the mall also fit with business thinking on how to make downtown shopping more competitive. Unified management would enable decisions to be made on behalf of a whole shopping area easily and quickly, without having to negotiate common business hours or display standards with each of a hundred independent-minded merchants. By "owning the whole town," a mall developer could try out marketing concepts on a scale that was impossible in the traditional city center.

Yet many people who worried about downtown were uncomfortable with commercialism. On a singular occasion in 1963, academic experts, developers, architects, and urban designers gathered at Harvard University to discuss the potential of the shopping center as a nucleus of inner-city activity. When James Rouse, the keynote speaker, explained how his firm integrated a church and an arts program into one of its malls in order to fill a community vacuum, Harvard professor Serge Chermayeff "got up and absolutely denounced everything I had said and what we were doing," Rouse recalled. To Chermayeff, mixing the arts with commerce was "prostituting legitimate uses," and having a church or arts in a mall was an "outrage."

One of the few critics who saw lessons for downtown in suburban shopping centers was Grady Clay, real estate editor of the *Louisville Courier-Journal*. Clay found much to admire in the best centers: new standards of quality, a compact retailing core ready-made for pedestrians, and public spaces well suited to civic ceremonies. In contrast to the "vast symmetrical open spaces" planned for urban renewal projects, Clay believed that shopping centers such as Northland with their "humor, inventiveness, and ingenuity to enliven display and entertainment" held "promise of the future" for downtown.[5]

Most design critics harped on the standardization of shopping malls, citing the repetition of chain stores, the imitative fixtures, and the absence of diverse street activity. Few credited the mall with producing an important public environment, and even fewer saw any potential in it for following the tradition of other notable architectural forms linked to commerce: the downtown movie palaces and great railroad stations. Intellectuals who wrote about cities had strong biases. They overlooked the community function of shopping malls because they failed to understand suburbia and the people who liked living there.

Yet even while the urban experts were praising downtown as a cultural bastion for the elite, the suburbs were overtaking central cities as the places where most people lived. Critics whose profession was to put current events into a big-picture perspective missed the meaning of long-term population trends. By the late 1960s when city officials began thinking about bringing the mall downtown, the suburbs were so clearly the preferred life-style for most Americans that no downtown retail center could rely solely on city dwellers as a retail market. Downtown malls would also have to attract middle-class people from the suburbs.

Meanwhile the mall itself was changing shape. The prototype of the 1960s continued to service the industry, but as competition intensified, a few developers experimented with innovative concepts more relevant to downtown. Rouse tried to make the routine mall more exciting by packing in more activity. At Echelon in New Jersey and at his new community of Columbia, Maryland, he planned the mall as a suburban equivalent of downtown by building on large sites and joining shopping to apartments, offices, and hotels, as well as to places for entertainment and cultural events.

More activities, yes. But following conventional wisdom, the offices, hotels, and theaters were housed in separate buildings nearby, not in the enclosed mall. Texas developer Gerald Hines took a more decisive step when he opened his Galleria in 1970 in City Post Oak, a rapidly growing suburb of Houston. In building the Galleria, Hines said he was trying to define a new prototype, "a whole new urban form that the American public doesn't know exists." He mixed several different activities: boutique shopping, first-class lodging, prime-quality office space, and recreation in the form of a private athletic and social club on the roof and a hockey-sized ice rink dominating the skylit, center space of the mall. Hines broke almost all the rules of mall building: retail shops were stacked on three levels, and high-rise hotel lobbies and office buildings fed directly into the mall. Everything was compressed onto a 33-acre site (less than half the area typical for a suburban mall), with more than half the parking space loaded into underground garages.

The Galleria was iconoclastic in another way: it had only one department store, Dallas-based Neiman Marcus, known for its elegant and unusual luxury goods. The mall's small shops were equally prestigious, including New York speciality stores such as Mark Cross, W. & J. Sloan, Tiffany, and a Park-Bernet art gallery. Geared to up-scale shoppers, the Galleria led the way for a special type of mall retailing. "Sears wouldn't have a chance in this shopping spa. Here, it's Neiman-Marcus: 188,000 square feet of compelling opulence," commented a writer for *Architectural Forum*. The huge ice skating rink was another draw (especially in hot, humid Houston), offering shoppers and rink-side cafe customers entertainment with shopping in a suburban version of New York's Rockefeller Center: "Refreshment kiosks. French cuisine. It's not everywhere you can munch petit fours while watching Peggy Fleming skate for charity."[6]

The Galleria spawned no suburban imitators, but it was a direct forerunner of Water Tower Place, a mixed-use complex that opened in Chicago with one of the first big-city malls in 1976. According to vice-president Norman Elkin at Urban Investment Development Company, the firm that developed Water Tower Place, "The Houston Galleria established the mixed-use development with urban pos-sibilities. It was a pace setter watched closely by others in the indus-try; it had a great impact. Although it was not downtown, it suggested the possibility of a new type of downtown mall."

All along developers had been trying to distinguish their malls from the competition by creating a thematic attraction. Through the choice of interior materials, colors and textures, art work, lighting, landscaping, and other finishing touches, malls were dressed to fit many moods: American regionalism, country village life, Euro-pean culture. Some such as the Galleria consciously offered urbanity —glitter, gloss, and entertainment—in spirit, rather than place, as an attraction.

When Ghirardelli Square opened its hillside plaza overlooking San Francisco Bay to a crush of visitors in 1964, this unique conversion of red brick factory buildings to a retail center demonstrated that a col-lection of shops selling unusual goods could draw shoppers to an offbeat but striking in-town location even without anchor department stores. A similar conversion, the Cannery, opened nearby soon after-ward, and together they gave form to a new expression of shopping as entertainment. The magnets—a collection of specialty shops, res-taurants, and unusual public spaces—were new and different, but the specialty malls in renovated buildings fit with the differentiation going on in the suburbs.

Ghirardelli Square and the Cannery represented the next architectural progression by putting a mall into old buildings and using downtown itself as a theme for the mall product. The small, local entrepreneurs who pioneered these projects were not professional retail developers, but they were processing downtown in a framework that was already working in the suburbs. Only a few took note, however. These developers were not part of the big league, and their projects deviated so far from the mainstream of mall retailing that this connection was lost until ten years later when critics began to discover why Boston's Faneuil Hall was such a popular success, able to draw the suburban middle-class back downtown.

Roadblocks

Even if new concepts were beginning to stimulate interest in downtown, transplanting the mall still posed hard problems. First, access was a major issue. When developers searched for suburban sites, they looked at locations close to major highway interchanges. As more and more interstate highway links opened in the 1970s, nearly all large cities had at least one major road leading into downtown. Several cities, New Haven and Sacramento, for example, even rerouted interchanges to get them close to planned retail projects. But good highways were not enough to get shoppers downtown; they also had to get through downtown streets and out of their cars without sacrificing convenience. That was not an easy task, even in the suburbs, where developers ran into traffic congestion caused by a location too close to the interchange. As a result, they learned that off-site access roads, deceleration ramps, and turning lanes were nearly as important as a prime location to bring drivers to the center.

Parking problems downtown were even more formidable than access. Parking had to be plentiful and close to the stores. Developers followed the industry's standards that were based on a battery of technical specifications detailing the amount, layout, pattern, and size of parking spaces. Behind the requirements, however, was a simple yardstick: make the parking lot big enough to accommodate all visitors during the peak shopping period—the last Saturday before Christmas. Applying these suburban standards meant searching out large sites. If the industry was calling for 5.5 spaces for every 1,000 square feet of selling space, a typical regional center with 600,000 square feet of stores would consume more than 30 acres just for parking areas.

These requirements jammed tight against a set of forces downtown that demanded a different solution. Relative to costs for suburban land, downtown blocks were prohibitively expensive for the large amounts of surface parking that surrounded the retail core. Also, city officials, having absorbed the lessons of the highway revolt and urban renewal protests, were under great political pressure to keep sites small. The unavoidable conclusion was that parking would have to go underground or into multilevel structures next door.

As radical as it seemed, breaking the conventional ground-level connection between the parking lot and the mall was not out of the question. Technical solutions were available. For almost any site, architects and traffic engineers could design connections between the mall and the parking lot to make the trip from one to the other easy and direct. Several suburban malls such as Houston's Galleria already had vertical parking arrangements. Rising suburban land costs were pushing some developers in this direction, while strong retail demand stimulated others to add more stores to their malls by building over parking lots and adding new garages.

The real issue was downtown. Garage structures were expensive, and overlaid on high-cost land (that would have to be cleared of buildings) they jacked up the cost of providing free parking for shoppers. Developers also worried about whether the department stores would accept this solution. Concerns about safety raised another red flag. Even with appropriate lighting and patrols, developers questioned how consumers already worried about street crime would feel about walking through garages.

When developers and their architects planned suburban malls for the convenience of shoppers, they did their best to avoid psychological obstacles such as traffic-crowded streets, subway-type corridors, long stairways, and winding garage ramps because it was important for shoppers to think they were close to the mall. Architects had kept mall buildings compact to make sure shoppers would cover the distance from one anchor store to another. Three to four city blocks was the maximum straight-line distance many designers believed a shopper could walk comfortably.

If the mall had to be compressed further to fit downtown, there was an obvious technical solution: go vertical. In shifting to tall buildings, however, developers faced extra costs for passenger and freight elevators, escalators, and structural components necessary to support and service more than one level. Two-story construction had already added a 20 percent building premium; if malls rose above this level, costs would jump higher. Like the parking rearrangement, this solution was linked to consumer acceptance. Developers were wary. "Once we get to three or four levels, and the customer can't find his car anymore, we might be in trouble," said an East Coast developer. "The logistics, particularly parking, are the most important thing— not the number of stores."

All of these issues—access, parking, and scale— were familiar to city officials and downtown executives figuring out ways to improve retailing. For years they lobbied for federal highways and city parking structures close to shopping districts. In a short burst of activity between 1957 and 1962, some fifty cities tried to keep the retail core compact and competitive by closing off selected downtown streets to traffic and landscaping them in suburban style to create low-cost malls. More cities closed shopping streets through the early 1970s, but as an attempt to revitalize downtown shopping, the pedestrian mall flopped. Most lacked the ample parking, coordinated shop hours, and careful maintenance shoppers found at suburban malls; worse, the trees, benches, and fountains attracted vagrants and boisterous kids. Pedestrians stayed away, merchants left, and stores remained vacant. After these well-publicized street closings turned into wastelands, many cities such as Boston, Toledo, and Seattle moved to reopen the streets, take away the furnishings, and relandscape the sidewalks.

Everything that was easy to do in the suburbs was harder downtown. Moving the mall threatened to throw a wrench into developers' production machinery because the solution that worked so well for them in the suburbs would not fit downtown. The prototype was adaptable, but developers could not make all the necessary changes themselves. First, they needed city government to assemble enough undersized parcels for a center, sell the land at a reduced price, share the costs of traffic improvements and parking comparable to suburban standards, and shepherd projects through the political and bureaucratic maze. Second, mall building had to move in step with another dynamic, a private business politics full of its own conflicts and compromises. To build a mall, developers had to bargain with department stores and lenders over location, size, makeup, and design. As for locating downtown, department stores had hardly looked back ever since developers convinced them to leave for greener pastures.

The Gatekeepers

Shopping center entrepreneurs built giant corporate enterprises from tentative ideas, borrowed money, and intense personal drive. Working their way up from small strip shopping centers to large regional malls, they owed their allegiance and their fortunes to the suburbs. Several started with a toehold in construction, marketing, or finance, but they had no historic ties to downtown and little, if any, investment there.

The department stores that worked with developers once had strong ties downtown. During the early 1960s department store executives made limited, selective investments in their flagship stores downtown, but this was window gloss while corporate planners shifted their focus to the suburbs. California's Broadway-Hale Stores led the way by giving up numerous downtown locations in order to concentrate on branches in regional centers. Other department store chains such as Allied Stores, Federated Department Stores, and the May Company first made a bow to their downtown interests but then changed direction once they discovered the benefits of aggressive branching with stores in regional centers. The payoff from expansion was fast. The May Company reported that after opening fifteen suburban stores within five years, its branches accounted for 55 percent of total company sales volume in 1964, up from 43 percent in 1959.

If the new retail strategy did not immediately eliminate the downtown store, it was only a matter of time. Allied's *1963 Annual Report* stated: "With completion of these two units, the Company will have three major stores in Houston, all well located relative to the medium to better income areas of the city. . . . There will be no downtown location once the present home furnishing unit is closed. However, a Joske store will be within fifteen minutes driving time of every Houston home, via the express roads which ring this dramatically growing city."[7] If corporate strategists set out to ring the city with suburban branches, why would they invest in downtown?

Anyone who wanted to build a downtown mall had to face the fact that department stores were leaving the cities. By the early 1970s their corporate profits were tied to sales in suburban shopping centers. For Broadway-Hale, Allied Stores, May Company, Federated Department Stores, and Montgomery Ward—the nation's largest department stores—shopping center sales represented no less than 60 percent and sometimes as much as 80 percent of total corporate sales volume. For Sears, Dayton-Hudson, Allied, and Macy's, which entered the competition as mall developers themselves, the stakes were compounded.

Tapping new markets was not the only reason to go to the suburbs. They went to keep discounters and other rivals away from their doors. Beginning in the 1950s, discount stores such as Zayre, Caldor, K-Mart, and Woolco had emerged as tough competitors, seizing a large share of the retail market. Between 1960 and 1970 as their sales volume soared from $2 billion to $24.4 billion, the discounters replaced full-price department stores as the number-one general merchandiser. (Department stores, in comparison, registered sales of $16 billion in 1970.) Department stores were not likely to gain market share by investing downtown because the competitive threat from the discounters was centered in the suburbs.

Developers understood the consequences of this competition for their business because many were building malls to the dictates of department stores that picked out their own sites years in advance of demand. When the time was right, the department store would bring in a developer to build, own, and operate the mall space connecting anchor stores. By the early 1970s at least three of the nation's biggest mall builders—DeBartolo, Rouse, and Hahn—were developing most of their projects under such joint arrangements. Operating in this way, developers relied on the department store to do the market analysis for new mall locations. Hahn, for one, felt that the function of his firm was to supply sites and centers for department stores. As for whether department stores chose sites wisely, another leading developer once told Hahn executive John Gilchrist, "If you have two good anchors located in hell, you can still rent 300,000 square feet between them."

The power behind the anchors' position derived as much from financial criteria as it did from their power to pull in customers. Developers got their financing from the large insurance companies that supplied mortgages mainly on the basis of tenant leases signed in advance. As a precondition to granting a loan, these lenders required long-term commitments from retailers who could show a minimum net worth of $1 million, known to the industry as "triple-A" or "credit" tenants. With revenues from enough leases backed by the credit status of such tenants, they had confidence that the mall would at least break even and cover the debt service owed to them. To meet their terms, developers usually had to rent 70 percent of the center's retail space to triple-A tenants. Since few speciality stores or local retailers had this rating and would take large enough areas, department stores were essential for financing a regional center.

The economic alliance linking department stores, lenders, and developers was powerful. In the rough-and-tumble business climate when shopping centers were sprouting all over suburbia, industry leaders pointed to this three-party consensus as a useful set of checks and balances against projects too weak to survive. As a merger of complementary resources the alliance was productive, but it set up developers for a tricky balancing act.

Developers' dependency put them in a vulnerable position, squeezed between domineering department stores and inflexible lenders. They ran the risk of losing the development opportunity if they failed to sign the necessary anchor tenants or of undermining the economic structure of the project by giving in to too many demands of the anchors. These giant retailers swung so much weight in shopping centers that the Federal Trade Commission eventually tried to curb their power plays. Between 1972 and 1976 the commission filed complaints against most large department store chains, arguing that the terms they extracted from developers amounted to unfair methods of competition based on their economic power. Specifically the commission objected to their demands for approval rights over other tenants and for the exclusion of discount stores from the malls. Without contesting these charges, one department store after another signed consent decrees promising to cease and desist from such tactics.

No matter what the out-of-court settlements said, department stores still had more than enough leverage to keep getting what they wanted. And if one developer did not want to cooperate, another would. What department stores wanted was determined increasingly by corporate managers as family-run, independent stores either closed or sold out to giant national holding companies during the 1960s and 1970s. Meanwhile mass merchandisers such as Sears and J.C. Penney tightened their hold on the retail market with hundreds of new stores. As a result of growing concentration in the retail industry, central management controlled the funds that went into new stores. Geared for mass distribution, department store managers made decisions by the book on the basis of financial return targets. And the big, inflexible organizations were headed in only one direction, seemingly unable or unwilling to risk new ideas like returning to downtown. To store executives enjoying their power and control over suburban malls, cities must have seemed disorderly and threatening.

Department store conservatism stymied several early downtown efforts. In the mid- to late 60s, for example, Rouse tried to build a mall in the center of Norfolk, Virignia, "one of the greatest retail vacuums in America," he recalled. "We spent eight years, we spent over a million dollars and never could get a department store to come. At that time there was no alternative [to the department store as anchor], at least in anybody's mind." In the early 1970s department stores in Los Angeles and Salt Lake City took the unusual step of building new flagship stores as part of downtown malls, but these privately initiated ventures were special cases backed more by corporate prestige than retail logic. To those in the industry the real change would come when cities attracted major retailers and major developers. At the time the odds that retailers would change their negative attitudes toward downtown seemed small. At the margin, however, one thing was quietly working for downtown: the ripe development climate that had made suburbia an easy place to build new malls was changing at an accelerating pace.

Searching for New Locations

As developers finished a record number of superregional malls in the early 1970s, their pipeline seemed to be running dry. Although the driving force of department store expansion had not yet run its course, a network of shopping centers was already well established in the suburbs of major cities. In some areas mall construction had already gone well ahead of population growth and if, as expected, that growth slowed, additional malls could oversaturate the market. Projected cutbacks in highway construction were another signal that the future held fewer opportunities. After an intense boom period, the supply of virgin territory was shrinking, and competition among the biggest mall builders was making it all the harder to buy a good site in a promising market.

The search for sites was compounded by a rapid buildup of suburban growth regulations during the early 1970s. Prompted in part by the environmental movement and in part by opposition to further growth, suburbs across the country were putting in place demanding review and permit requirements for proposed developments of all kinds. These had the effect of stretching out development times and

raising costs, while also giving opponents of shopping centers repeated chances to block them. Further, the mood of local citizens and
their representatives was turning increasingly hostile to development, particularly in places hit by high growth in the recent past.

The antidevelopment climate cast a psychological pall over the industry, and many developers felt conditions would only get worse. In
the keynote address at the 1972 conference of the International Council of Shopping Centers (ICSC), president Ernest Hahn projected an
unsettling period ahead as the industry confronted antitrust actions
against department stores, proposed federal tax code changes eroding real estate benefits, continuing decay of downtown areas, litiga-
tion by tenant stores against developers, and mounting state and
local regulation. "Many ecologists, planners, assessors and elected
officials," he said, "think of shopping centers only in terms of cars,
seas of asphalt, traffic congestion and an abundant source of tax
revenue. As a result, property taxes, restrictive zoning and unrealistic
architectural demands are either stopping center development entirely or putting it on the borderline of being uneconomical."[8]

The list of problems continued to multiply. Construction costs
mounted and energy prices skyrocketed. The infrastructure necessary for regional shopping centers—water mains, sewer connectors,
and road improvemens—was another new element in the cost equation. In the past suburban governments had been willing to pay for
some of these facilities or to use local bond issues to finance them, but
by the early 1970s the suburbs were increasingly pushing developers
to pay the bills. On top of local regulatory snags, the newly created
federal Environmental Protection Agency (EPA) posed an even more
direct threat to suburban mall development. In an effort to prevent
automobile emissions from lowering air quality in places that already
met pollution standards, the agency drew up regulations in 1973 to
restrict the construction of major new parking facilities in the outer
suburbs.

Developers felt besieged on all sides, on the defensive against envi-
ronmentalists, ecologists, and citizens. "If government doesn't make
it impossible to do business," said Albert Sussman, executive vice-
president of ICSC and a key spokesman for the industry, "it will
surely end up making it more costly, more frustrating and less
profitable to stay in business. If it took you two or three years to
develop your last center, you can expect it to take four or six years for
your next center."[9]

Developers groped for new strategies to adapt to the dwindling number of suburban sites and keep their big organizations active. Many built smaller malls in secondary retail markets that had been passed over before. A few looked to overseas markets. Others made profitable improvements to older, existing malls by enclosing open air centers, adding new department stores, and renovating the common areas. A handful began to think about urban sites.

Reappraising city locations, according to Taubman, resulted from "economic reality." Building new supportive systems like roads, sewers, water, and other utilities was "less economical than searching out developed lands in urban areas where such systems already exist." As the nation grew increasingly concerned about energy conservation, rising gasoline prices, and double-digit inflation, such downtown staples as central location, mass transit systems, and higher-density living emerged from a cloud of negativism and appeared more rational and efficient than before. When asked at a 1974 conference why developers were turning downtown, Hahn cited three reasons: energy problems, mass transit, and the EPA. Although building downtown would not be easy, at least developers found a welcome mat. "Cities were doing positive things to bring developers in, like helping with finance," said Sussman. "They were not antagonistic."

Although most department stores continued to map out aggressive five-year expansion plans, by 1973 a few were voicing tentative interest in the possibilities of a downtown store. Young, affluent couples beginning to settle in selected neighborhoods close to downtown offices made the near-downtown location look as though it was on an upward trend, remarked Norman Elkin of Urban Investment Development Company. Additionally the problems of building downtown had a flip side. The way Elkin looked at it, a store in one of these locations would be safe from competition longer than outlying centers because it would take years for anyone else to build another mall.

Yet developers and department stores remained cautious and selective in identifying downtown possibilities. If the development climate downtown seemed more hospitable than in the suburbs, that was not enough to make a shopping mall succeed. Developers wanted sites that would meet retail standards for an economic proposition. "It is painfully apparent," Hahn remarked at the 1972 ICSC conference, "that we in the shopping center industry cannot bootstrap blighted downtown areas into viable well-balanced city cores solely by the development of retail facilities. The social and economic problems of blighted areas are much too large for our limited industry to solve by itself. Of what value are shiny new stores filled to the ceiling with merchandise if they exist in a vacuum of poverty, unemployment, and social despair?"[10]

Developers who turned to downtown in search of new markets were mavericks. Most developers looked at downtown and still saw a quagmire. In addition to bringing along the department stores and the lenders, they would have to deal with city government every step of the way on land assembly, street changes, traffic plans, and building codes. "We have no expertise in that area . . in [downtown] financing, leasing, and all that," said Herbert Simon, president of Indianapolis-based Melvin Simon & Associates. "But the biggest thing we don't have is the patience to wait five or six years and then have the whole project go out to bid. We've been fortunate enough—or unfortunate enough—to be kept busy in conventional shopping centers."[11]

By the time developers were beginning to sift the possibilities for downtown malls, city officials and urban professionals were reaching a new consensus about what was appropriate for downtown, and the shopping mall was an important part of their vision. Downtown planners and business coalitions had never abandoned their hopes for reviving retailing, and the intervening decade had produced a number of models for them. Downtown renewal projects such as Charles Center in Baltimore and Prudential Center in Boston incorporated shopping areas. In 1964 the first downtown mall in the country, Midtown Plaza, opened in Rochester, and others followed in the early 1970s in New Haven, New Rochelle, Bridgeport, Buffalo, Sacramento, Worcester, Salt Lake City, and San Bernardino.

These large-scale construction projects were not the only models for cities. Ghirardelli Square and the Cannery showed that contemporary shops could blend with a historic setting to form a downtown showpiece. Trolley Square in Salt Lake City and Larimer Square in Denver later expanded on the concept by creating larger pedestrian districts for specialty shopping organized around historic buildings and period furnishings. In the late 1960s Minneapolis improved on earlier street closings by redeveloping Nicollet Avenue as a permanent pedestrian mall with enclosed walkways at the second-story level that later connected to the IDS tower with its dramatic atrium.

The 1960s was a time of experimentation downtown. The record showed that downtown malls were feasible, but it also showed that they were tough projects. Planners in New Haven and Sacramento ran into one obstacle after another trying to assemble land, attract a developer, get commitments from department stores, and line up support from downtown retailers who feared the mall would take away business. With delay compounding delay, these projects took ten years or more to complete. Some never got off the drawing boards.

Architects and developers ran into delays working with rigid building codes. Land costs were another obstacle; even with urban renewal writedowns, some developers saw no way to compete with the suburbs on rent. Further along in the process, developers had to counter retailers' worries about crime, nighttime safety, and shoplifting, even though these problems were not unknown in the suburbs. Leasing was slow, and they usually had to make rent concessions.

With so many trouble spots, cities had to work hard to interest developers. In San Bernardino the city built the two-level air-conditioned pedestrian mall and parking facilities in order to bring in a potential developer to provide the stores. Although this initiative was probably necessary, building the core of the mall in advance added extra costs and management problems for the mall shops and public spaces.

Early experience produced no clear-cut results on performance. Some centers did reasonably well, but their retail sales still fell short of industry-wide benchmarks. Others went through difficult times because their merchandise was dull, their stores were not matched to the needs of local shoppers, or the purchasing power of the downtown market fell short of expectations. Some such as Baystate West in Springfield and Worcester Center held on in spite of a weak start, but others such as Constitution Plaza in Hartford converted the retail space to other uses. Considering the overall track record, many developers agreed with this 1976 assessment by *Fortune* magazine's Gurney Breckenfeld: the "fizzles, failures, and abandoned downtown projects far outnumber the successes."[12]

If the case for downtown retail development had to be made strictly on the merits, city boosters would have been hard pressed to find the right language. Downtown prospects had not improved much by the end of the 1960s, but suburban options were deteriorating enough to make some developers take a more wide-eyed look at the cities.

An early attempt to make a pedestrian mall by closing off traffic: Fresno, California, 1964. *Portland Cement Association.*

Transplanting the suburban mall: Glendale (California) Galleria, opened 1976.

Making the suburban layout urban: Water Tower Place, Chicago, opened 1976.
Urban Investment and Development Co.

Combining activities in a new mixed-use prototype: Water Tower Place. *Urban Investment and Development Co.*

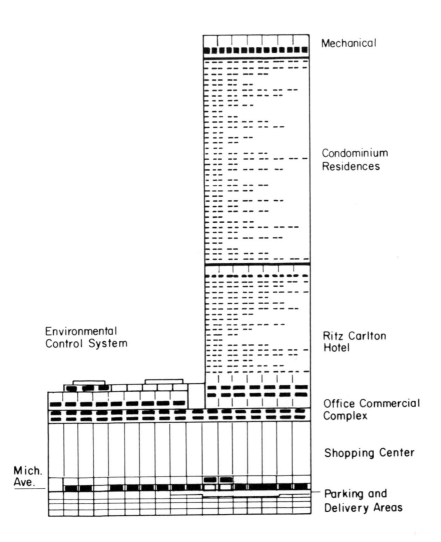

Mechanical

Condominium
Residences

Environmental
Control System

Ritz Carlton
Hotel

Office Commercial
Complex

Shopping Center

Mich.
Ave.

Parking and
Delivery Areas

WATER TOWER PLACE

Blending history and leisure with specialty stores in an off-beat location: Ghirardelli Square, San Francisco, opened 1964. *Saskia Ltd.*

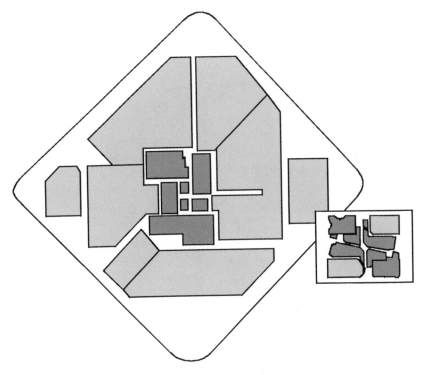

The standard suburban layout—a retail island surrounded by a sea of parking—would have to be compressed to fit downtown: Southdale shopping center, suburban Minneapolis; Santa Monica Place, downtown Santa Monica, California, with parking in garage structures.

The problem in Pasadena: Plaza Pasadena threatened to cut off the civic auditorium from the rest of downtown. *City of Pasadena Community Development Commission.*

GARFIELD AXIS

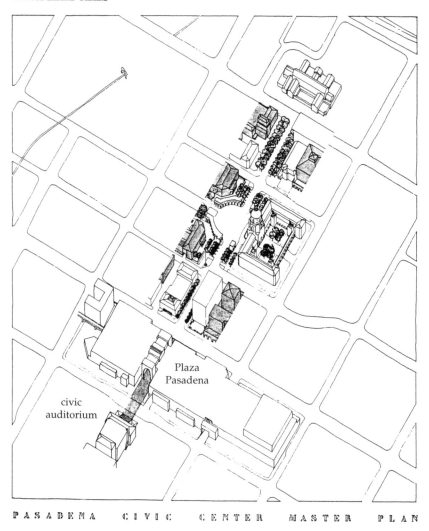

Plaza
Pasadena

civic
auditorium

P A S A D E N A   C I V I C   C E N T E R   M A S T E R   P L A N

The solution: a glass-enclosed archway through the retail mall. Plaza Pasadena.

Building pedestrian links: St. Paul skyway leading into Town Square/Saint Paul Center. *City of St. Paul PED.*

Mall exteriors that deaden downtowns: street frontage along Town Square/Saint Paul Center.

Trying for livelier streets: an early Horton Plaza plan. *The Jerde Partnership, Inc.*

Making a clear connection to downtown: Horton Plaza entrance with obelisk marking stairway to performing arts theaters. *Centre City Development Corporation.*

Pasadena: No Bed of Roses

A few pioneering mayors and mall developers got together for reasons of their own in the early 1970s, but the word on the street was that nobody could manage to turn an honest dollar out of rebuilding downtown. The problems were beyond help, at least for the foreseeable future. Mayors might promise improvements, but urban experts saw city government squeezed between rising costs and a depressed tax base and warned of a coming fiscal crisis. Racial conflict was worrisome and threatened to get worse. President Johnson's commission investigating civil disorder had predicted that the country was heading for a garrison state with two societies: "one, largely Negro and poor, located in the central cities; the other, predominantly white and affluent, located in the suburbs."[1]

University scholars were also hanging crepe for a funeral. Political scientist Douglas Yates studied the cross-pressures facing big-city mayors and described their near-paralysis in his book *The Ungovernable City*. Economist Kenneth Boulding concluded that the modern world had destroyed the capacity of cities to make decisions affecting their own future. The city was a leftover from another age—"something that nobody loves, and what nobody loves will die."[2] The public at large seemed to agree. In a 1974 Gallup opinion poll, interest in city living sank to a new low, with almost nine people of ten wanting to live in a suburb or small town. Among people who lived in big cities, more than half said they were afraid to go out at night. Cities, in short, were heading for a fiscal crisis, turning into a garrison state, ungovernable, out of control, unloved, unlivable, and frightening. Worse, this was not just street wisdom but the considered judgment of informed, thoughtful people with no axe to grind. The outlook for rebuilding cities had hit rock bottom.

Where, then, was a good place to try building a downtown mall?

Surely not in the biggest, most dangerous, riot-torn, deficit-ridden cities, but perhaps in a small city where the problems were still manageable. A city like Pasadena, where 115,000 people lived in single-family neighborhoods, racial tensions had never reached the boiling point, taxes and services were reasonable, and the community managed to stage a nationally televised Tournament of Roses parade every New Year's Day. Pasadena had downtown problems, to be sure, but the city at large was far from hopeless.

When the redevelopment agency began negotiating with Ernest Hahn in 1971, retail developers across the country followed events in Pasadena with great interest. As far as they were concerned, the downtown experiments in the 1960s were little more than curiosities far from the mainstream of mall development. To bring downtown into the mainstream, a nationally known developer would have to score a clear success. Within a few years Faneuil Hall Marketplace would provide that success, but in 1971 it was still bogged down for lack of a capable developer.

Hahn's interest in Pasadena seemed to be the first test of whether an accomplished mall builder could adapt standard shopping center principles to an in-town situation. Pasadena could show whether there were solutions to the problems of site layout, parking, department store demands, financing terms, and local politics. Above all mall building was always a race against time and competition. Now the question was whether a seasoned suburban developer could run his usual race in the heart of downtown or would have to run it wearing leg irons. Whether, in addition, a downtown mall could flourish in spite of crime, fear, racial tension, and fiscal strain was a different issue to be tested in another time and place.

Retail conditions in the center of Pasadena resembled those of big-city downtowns in the late 1960s. Block after block of Colorado Boulevard, once a flourishing commercial thoroughfare, had become a source of wounded pride and sagging revenue. Retail sales had been on the decline since the mid-1950s, rents were low, vacancies high, and the 1920s buildings were too small and shabby to attract a high level of trade. As retailers shut their doors, dead stretches of street frontage made shopping even less appealing. And as downtown retail sales declined in real dollars—more than 10 percent alone between 1966 and 1969—property and sales tax collections sank, eroding the city's revenue base. If city government did not take some initiative, further decline seemed inevitable.

City officials wanted a shopping center to reverse the loss of business and tax dollars, but they also wanted it as a symbol to show that Pasadena was making a comeback. With population on the decrease and court-ordered school busing stirring racial fears, civic and business leaders wanted to prevent white flight. A more attractive downtown, they reasoned, would help to keep the middle class happy with Pasadena, and a shopping center would be an important catalyst to revive downtown. It promised to bring people back to Colorado Boulevard, where fancy shops and handsome civic buildings used to set a tone of distinction for the entire community.

Despite its declining sales, Pasadena was a market that fit Ernest Hahn's description of a suitable downtown opportunity: a place with enough purchasing power to support a regional mall. Per capita income was higher in Pasadena than in most other cities in Los Angeles County. Downtown still had one popular department store, the Broadway, and more exclusive shopping just beyond Colorado Boulevard that attracted visitors as well as residents. Several industrial firms had located in Pasadena to be near the California Institute of Technology and its associated Jet Propulsion Laboratory. A few companies had set up their headquarters downtown, and a new freeway to Los Angeles was nearing completion.

When city officials approached Hahn in 1971, company executives saw that downtown Pasadena could tap something like a typical suburban market. With this goal in mind they intended to follow the industry prototype by building an enclosed, two-story, air-conditioned mall, anchored at each end by a well-known department store. John Gilchrist, later president of the Hahn Company, believed Pasadena had a community feeling more like that of New England and the Midwest than of suburban Los Angeles. People who lived there would want to shop there if they could. No novel environment was necessary. All the company had to do was to build an ordinary mall acceptable to department stores and mortgage lenders. What Hahn executives considered satisfactory for shoppers, however, did not fit downtown.

Inventing a Transplant

Unlike the outer suburbs where whole farms turn over to commercial use, a downtown site large enough for a mall is a patchwork of small parcels, covered with buildings, extending across a few city blocks and the streets between them. Developers have to carve out their building pads without disturbing landmarks or disrupting important civic places. When Hahn overlaid his plans on the three-block site city officials had chosen, the prototype layout split the heart of downtown and walled off a main axis on Garfield Avenue linking public buildings on either side of Colorado Boulevard. That was unacceptable to the Pasadena Redevelopment Agency (PRA). The issue was the ability of the public to see and get to the Pasadena Civic Auditorium from the steps of the library, or vice versa. Hahn had to find a way to adjust the prototype because a three-block mall would have killed the deal. "Over the Garfield axis, we would have walked away," recalled former redevelopment chairman Cornelius Pings. "We had to have the view, or no project."

City officials also were concerned about dead space where the mall structure faced Colorado Boulevard, the route of the Tournament of Roses Parade; they insisted that Hahn line this side of the boulevard with small stores. Street-facing stores also fit with city officials' desire for a symbol of civic progress. They wanted "something different from the great bland fortress," said architect Paul Curran, project director for Charles Kober Associates.

Making these adjustments proved troublesome. Hahn had never developed a mall with streetfront stores, and at first they did not seem feasible. To begin with, the automobile-oriented logic of the suburban prototype worked against it. Parking would be underground or in garages behind the mall, so most people coming to Plaza Pasadena would not enter the mall from Colorado Boulevard but from elevators and walkways coming out of the parking areas. Streetfront stores would be out of the flow of shopper traffic, and their rental value would be low.

The stores in question added up to little more than 3 percent of the total retail space, but they cut into the space of interior stores and service corridors, jeopardizing what mall developers believed was the right layout for mass merchandising. Security was another problem. If the streetfront stores also had doorways inside the building, a thief who broke in at night could gain entry to the entire mall. Hahn executives stood firm against the PRA for some time. But they heard the same argument from the architects, looked back on the walled-in structure they had built in an earlier redevelopment project, and concluded the PRA was right.

Community groups wanted to keep Garfield Avenue open as a pedestrian street running through the project. Hahn objected because this plan was at odds with the basic idea of a shopping center. The J. C. Penney store at one end of the mall would have been cut off from the rest of the center. "It wouldn't work," Penney's management told Curran. "We might as well be in Cucamonga!" Hahn and the anchors wanted an uninterrupted flow from one department store past the mall shops to the other, a conventional shopping center that could be enclosed and air-conditioned to compete on equal footing with others nearby.

Slicing through the mall to preserve a view threatened to upset more than the design plans. PRA officials wanted control over a wide interior corridor in order to keep it clear of obstructions and open to the public even when the mall was closed. This unconventional zone, the Garfield Pedestrian Mall, was hard to reconcile with the normal operation of a private shopping center. To Hahn's mortgage lender, turning part of the structure into a semipublic section meant a loss of financial security. Executives of both anchor stores worried that the corridor would become a public easement beyond the control of mall management, and J. C. Penney people were especially concerned that city staff might interfere with design and display decisions just outside their main entrance.

After years of debate, public forums, and plan revisions, Hahn's architects found a solution to the design problem that suited the merchandising dictates of the mall prototype. They pierced the facade with monumental triple arches and a glass-enclosed opening that runs through the retail center over Garfield Pedestrian Mall. "The glass arches frame the Civic Auditorium," said Curran, "making it more of a visual monument." Plaza Pasadena was a double break-away from the prototype, with its streetfront stores and framed view corridor; it was distinctive enough to win an award from *Progressive Architecture*. As with Quincy Market, the pressure to solve problems generated innovative solutions that improved the project.

As Curran and his architectural team worked through design after design trying to find a solution acceptable to the PRA, the public review groups, and the developer, they scaled their plans to an 11-acre rectangular site. But even with the PRA empowered to take the land it needed, downtown sites could never be packaged as neatly as the cornfields of suburbia. As with most other redevelopment projects, even limited clearance provoked conflict. When the PRA revealed that the Pasadena Athletic Club building was slated for demolition, several citizen groups protested that it was an architectural landmark worth saving. The Athletic Club occupied a prime merchandising spot at the southeast corner of the site, and Hahn had promised it to the Broadway, then the only committed anchor tenant and codeveloper of the retail center.

In response to citizen concerns, the PRA asked Curran to cut a notch out of his site for the Athletic Club building. Curran came up with new proposals, but they would either have forced changes in the department store's cost-efficient prototype or moved it farther away from the underground parking. All of Curran's alternatives would have pushed part of the Broadway behind the six-story Athletic Club, making the store less prominent from the street. As far as Broadway executives were concerned, no plan would do except demolition. These alternative plans did not work for Hahn either because they cut back the size and depth of the mall shops, leaving less prime retail space to rent.

Supporters of preservation were fighting from a weak position. Confronted with the anchor's intransigence, the PRA board was reluctant to keep up the pressure because Broadway's negotiators threatened to walk away from the project if the Athletic Club stayed. As Pings saw the issue, "If it had been a first-class building, we would have built a larger project, but the Athletic Club was really a pretty crappy building; attractive on the outside, rotted on the inside." Opponents filed petitions, organized a postcard campaign, and tried without success to get the building listed on the National Register of Historic Places. Taking aim at management's sensitivity over customer loyalty, they persuaded many residents who were Broadway shoppers to cut their credit cards in half and send the pieces to corporate headquarters.

The owner of the Athletic Club finally antagonized the preservationists himself by starting several legal actions as bargaining chips to get the best possible price for his property. Vulnerable on one side to delay from lawsuits and on the other to withdrawal by the anchor, the PRA negotiated a price with the owner of the Athletic Club to move ahead with demolition. By April 1976, more than four years after starting negotiations with Hahn, the city was ready to begin clearing the site.

Sweetheart Deals

What made a shopping mall into a fragile, time-consuming venture was a series of necessary agreements that were hard to pull off under the best of circumstances; they were overwhelming downtown. A developer had to fit together commitments from department stores and lenders; city review and approvals of environmental impacts, design, and public finance; and city agreements on parking, scheduling, terms of assistance, and the division of development responsibilities. Each step needed long negotiating sessions, and the agreements reached in one set of negotiations had consequences for the others, so that the entire process of collecting commitments and support was like clearing multiple hurdles set out side by side.

The first hurdle was securing a commitment from the Broadway. Because it was a popular midpriced retailer with proven ability to draw shoppers into its existing downtown store across the street from the proposed mall, Hahn believed it was the essential anchor and key to the entire project. If Broadway agreed to relocate, Hahn believed he could then persuade J. C. Penney, which also had an older store downtown, to move into the mall. But neither Hahn nor the city would go very far on a speculative basis. The PRA would not make a major financial commitment before signing an agreement that would tie Hahn firmly to the project, and Hahn would not come to the table to negotiate a deal before he had a firm commitment from the Broadway.

Broadway's executives were prepared to listen. They wanted a new store to replace the old one, but they also had strong economic reasons not to budge at all. Despite the age of their store and its declining sales, they could run it for years more at a profit because its operating costs were low and would get even lower when their current lease expired. Also, they were opening new stores in competing malls in nearby Arcadia and Glendale. "They wanted to cover their downside—take no risk at all—by paying what they were then paying and getting a new building in the process," said John Gilchrist. Timing was working for them, too. "No other anchor was interested at all in being the first. They wanted a sweetheart deal to go in."

Pushing against this inertia was hard. For years developers had been persuading downtown stores to move to the suburbs, and now they had to make a new case. The traditional conservatism of department stores made them unlikely candidates to go against the tide, and their demands—for preferential lease terms, generous parking standards, and prototype store designs to match those of suburbia— were nonnegotiable. In a typical suburban situation a developer had some flexibility in making department store deals; he could take some losses as long as the project was good overall. Downtown, however, economic pressures on all sides ruled out this type of maneuvering. Costs were higher, leasing would take longer, and operating risks were greater. Also, lenders typically charged a premium for financing a downtown project. The fact that parking would be in underground garages with the mall built on air rights over the city-owned facility added legal complications. All these extras restricted the trade-offs Hahn could make to balance the demands of department stores.

At a minimum, just to get Broadway's attention, he had to provide a subsidy that would bring operating costs for a new store in the mall down near the current level for the old Pasadena store. In a typical suburban deal the first anchor would be given a pad of land free or at cost to build its store, plus its share of parking at no cost. But this was only a partial solution here because building a new 150,000-square-foot store would push Broadway's expenses beyond its current baseline figure even before other operating costs such as property taxes were added. Broadway's managers wanted a deeper subsidy.

Funding that subsidy was the city's job. Even before the city had formally selected Hahn as developer, the PRA had hired consultants to figure out how to relocate Broadway. On the basis of this analysis, the price tag for buying out Broadway's interest in its present location ran to about $3 million. To assist the project in this way, however, the PRA had to extend its redevelopment boundaries to include the Broadway block so that the PRA could use eminent domain powers to acquire the site.

To nail down Broadway's commitment, Hahn offered its owners a big piece of the project—50 percent of the ownership in the mall— sweetening the move across the street by turning it into a lucrative financial opportunity. Making Carter Hawley Hale a co-owner suited the PRA's interests because with a stake in the project, the retailer was less likely to renege on its commitment. The deal combined public money and private profits passed through a private conduit. First, the PRA compensated Broadway for its existing lease interest with a severance payment the anchor turned over to the developer. With this $2.5 million lump sum payment, Hahn agreed to provide a building shell for the department store at a below-cost rental. Counting in profits Broadway would receive as a mall partner, its annual rental plus property taxes and insurance would be in line with its current costs. With little or no cash outlay, Broadway got a new store and a 50 percent share in the mall profits for no more than its existing operating expense. When Broadway's management wanted to get out of the equity deal two years later, Hahn came up with new terms just as favorable to the department store.

Personal relations also counted heavily in making this deal possible. For many years Hahn had had close professional and social contacts with Philip Hawley, president of Carter Hawley Hale Stores and at any one time might be negotiating with him on a number of projects. Jerome Lipp, president of the Carter Hawley Hale real estate arm, was an experienced advocate of redevelopment, who knew how to bargain from either side of the table. As executive director of Sacramento's redevelopment agency in the 1950s, he had managed the clearance and renewal of the skid row area adjoining the state capitol. Years later, then working on the private side for Carter Hawley Hale, Lipp initiated Broadway's involvement in redevelopment projects in Glendale, Culver City, and Hawthorne.

In negotiating with J. C. Penney as the second anchor for Plaza Pasadena, Hahn and the PRA once again paid for a drawing card. These negotiations too were drawn out; Penney management, which had a reputation for hard bargaining and attention to detail, demanded favorable terms before making any commitment. Meeting their demands took time and money consistent with the one-sided bargaining power that is the norm in the mall business. To get department stores for their suburban centers, developers had to subsidize them; when development shifted to downtown, the ante went up, and city government helped pay the bill.

Pledging Future Taxes

The economics of building a mall downtown meant that the public subsidy had to be big. Meeting the demands of the anchors was one reason. Providing free parking in expensive underground and multilevel parking structures was another. Working within smaller sites, building to higher fire code standards, and financing a longer construction period also added extra costs. Operating expenses, maintenance, and security were higher too, and they put pressure on Hahn to ask high rents of potential tenants.

Strictly as a private venture with no outside help, high costs made projects such as Plaza Pasadena infeasible because the economic value of a downtown mall typically fell below its total development cost. The greater risk of building downtown was another discouraging factor. Because downtown was not a growth market, retail sales and profits were much less secure than for a suburban mall. With repeated delays, a downtown project was especially vulnerable to increases in carrying costs and other up-front expenses that could cripple it before it got started. Minimizing up-front costs is a normal way for developers to do business, but under the marginal conditions of downtown, this became a critical objective, and Hahn fully expected the city to share the risks.

None of this came as news to the PRA. From the early planning studies, city officials knew they would have to pour money into the project to attract a developer. By the time they opened early discussions with Hahn, they were planning to buy all the land, relocate businesses and residents, demolish the buildings, improve the surrounding streets, and sell the parcel to Hahn at a price well below their cost. To make a downtown mall competitive, the city planned to take responsibility for building, financing, and maintaining enough parking garages to meet suburban retail standards.

As the PRA moved from preliminary planning to spelling out what it wanted in the mall and getting realistic figures, estimates of the cost of the subsidy almost tripled, rising from $14 million or $16 million in 1972 to $41 million in 1976. Yet the price Hahn could afford to pay for the parcel, based on the size of the project and the income he could earn from it, remained relatively constant—between $4.4 million and $4.9 million. As a result, the public subsidy grew larger. Although the city's commitment to assemble land and improve the area was far-reaching, it was not unusual. To stimulate office development downtown, the PRA had given the same kinds of help to several other projects in its 340-acre downtown redevelopment district. The cost for Plaza Pasadena was another matter though. The PRA had shelled out subsidies ranging from $1 million to $3 million for other projects, but Plaza Pasadena was on a scale of its own.

The high cost of downtown land hit Plaza Pasadena harder than the office projects. As a shopping center, Plaza Pasadena had a horizontal, two-story suburban layout with much less income-producing space than office towers on equivalent sites. This low-density use of the land made it less valuable for development, requiring the PRA to write off $16.6 million, or 40 percent of what it spent to buy and clear the site. By far the biggest item was $21.8 million for parking, the result of trying to match suburban standards in a crowded downtown setting.

The city was determined to get the project built and to do it without federal funds. The earlier Pepper Project, the first—and last—federal urban renewal project in Pasadena, had been a political disaster. Massive clearance had uprooted hundreds of low-income black families and displaced neighborhood businesses, delays had been interminable, and getting developers to complete the work had been a continuing agony. Eventually the federal Department of Housing and Urban Development took over ownership and proved to be an inept landlord. With the Pepper Project experience behind him, Pings decided to do it without federal money or not at all. To find the money Pasadena, like other California cities, turned to tax-increment financing.

Tax-increment financing, a system for redeveloping blighted areas, dates back to 1952 in California; by the mid-1970s seventeen states had authorized this form of financing. It allows city redevelopment agencies to pay their expenses for a project by keeping the increase in property tax collections that normally results from new construction and rising assessments in a project area. Using this revenue stream as collateral, redevelopment agencies issue tax-exempt bonds and operate with much greater fiscal autonomy than the federal urban renewal program ever allowed. To start the process, a redevelopment agency draws boundaries for a special tax-increment district, holds public hearings to establish that the area is in blighted condition appropriate for redevelopment, and presents a project plan to the city council for approval. When the council approves the plan, the existing assessed value of property in the district, called the tax base, is frozen for the benefit of local governments that have been collecting taxes from it. Afterward any tax revenues that result from increases in the tax base flow from the county collection office to the coffers of the redevelopment agency.

Politically tax-increment financing is a redevelopment director's dream. Once committed, the money rolls in with a minimum of effort, exempt from the annual appropriation struggle over scarce tax dollars. Since the bond issues based on this income are not direct obligations of the city, they do not have to go on the ballot for voter approval once the city council endorses them. In California the administrative machinery necessary to move this process is relatively simple, legal standards for establishing blight and drawing boundaries are liberal, and discretionary powers over the uses of tax increments for redevelopment purposes are broad. As an instrument of public policy, tax-increment financing is controversial, but as a revenue raiser there is no question that it provides cities with a treasure chest for redevelopment.

Even with all the advantages of tax-increment financing, the high cost of building a downtown mall was a problem. Underwriters and investors, rather than federal renewal officials, would determine whether a project was feasible; the bonds would have to meet their standards. In terms of scale, redevelopment financing represented big business. When the PRA issued its bonds for land acquisition in 1976, the $32 million offering (the first part of a two-stage borrowing) set a record as the largest issue of tax allocation bonds in California. But for these bonds to be salable, the projected tax increments had to be large enough to cover the interest charges and repay the principal. By the standards of the bond market, Plaza Pasadena could not support the heavy subsidy because, as a low-density user of land, the mall by itself could not generate enough tax increments to service the necessary debt.

The PRA's way around this problem was to phase downtown redevelopment, starting with office projects that would generate surplus tax-increment revenues. Executive director Gerald Trimble estimated that office buildings, with a large amount of taxable space on a small amount of land, would yield a return of about fifteen-to-one on public redevelopment outlays. The stores and restaurants that he wanted for downtown would produce only a one-to-one return on public investments, however. By putting office buildings first, Trimble bought six years of lead time to organize Plaza Pasadena while piling up public capital.

The PRA planned from the start to capture as much in downtown property taxes as possible by drawing the boundaries of the redevelopment district around privately sponsored buildings just nearing completion. When the downtown redevelopment plan was approved in 1970, the assessed value of the district was nearly $21 million; with two new office headquarters and a major hotel by the end of 1973, the tax base jumped to $27.5 million, producing an increment of more than $815,000 for that fiscal year. The income from such costless projects provided the agency front money to pay early bills for the mall project.

By drawing tax-increment district boundaries strategically and staging office development early, the city took care of the huge subsidy for Plaza Pasadena without stirring up taxpayer protests. In a community as sophisticated and organized as Pasadena, Trimble and PRA board members knew the project would need all the political protection they could give it. "We expected political trouble—abuse, delay, lawsuits," said Pings, "and we had strategies to deal with opposition." Trimble, newly appointed as redevelopment director, set out to build a record of achievement while keeping a low profile. He moved quickly and quietly, holding environmental impact hearings early and getting the key agreements and approvals signed before opponents could create problems. But although Trimble and the PRA board managed their business with an aggressive tack, they were still vulnerable to opposition.

Protective Maneuvers

Public help was essential to close some part of the cost gap between city and suburban shopping malls. Tax-increment financing made the politics manageable by shifting the payment to future years and leaving revenues from the existing tax base untouched. Still there was no denying that it would eventually cost the community money by tagging future collections to pay off project expenses. The need for subsidy made political approval harder in the cities than in the suburbs, where government left mall building to the developers.

Government spending had to follow procedures that opened the way for opponents to make their objections count. Even with tax-increment financing, redevelopment agencies did not have the autonomy of public authorities that build bridges, tunnels, and toll roads without voter or council approval. The PRA had to take its plans and bond proposals to the seven-member board of directors, Pasadena's city council. Opponents could bring pressure on these elected officials to turn down PRA projects or their financing. Further, citizens had standing to bring lawsuits to stop projects on both technical and procedural grounds. At every turn Pings and Trimble had to consider the politics as well as the economics of their project. When the two considerations came into conflict, they had to choose between holding down public costs and protecting their political base. Downtown projects pushed city governments to operate with a blend of political and developmental skills that had no parallel in the suburbs.

The lawsuits Pings had expected turned up on schedule. Genevieve Graydon, a retired U.S. Internal Revenue Service employee and long-time Pasadena resident, lodged a complaint with the IRS trying to prevent the city's use of tax-exempt bonds for a private project. Shortly after Hahn and the city signed their agreement in 1975, she sued the PRA, arguing that the project area was not blighted. These actions were the work of a single individual, but they put a legal cloud over Plaza Pasadena that would keep investors and lenders away until they were resolved. Although the IRS complaint and the lawsuit were delay factors, the issues they raised did not lead to wider opposition.

In trying to keep the lid on interest costs for an already expensive project, however, the PRA made a decision that opened the door to serious political problems. Trimble had a choice of ways to finance the $41 million project. Redevelopment agencies could sell either tax allocation bonds or lease revenue bonds; the immediate advantage of using one over the other was cost. With tax allocation bonds the future tax increment is pledged as security against the public debt, and the city has no further obligation to repay the bonds if the additional tax yield from the project area is not large enough. With lease revenue bonds the city, as lessor, undertakes a direct obligation to make the necessary payments. City involvement gets the bonds a higher rating, makes them more marketable, and lowers the interest rate the redevelopment agency has to pay. Acting on advice from bond counsel, the PRA chose the less expensive approach. On a bond issue the size the PRA planned to sell, an interest rate differential of even a quarter of a percentage point would produce a large saving in the total interest cost.

By going after this economic benefit, the PRA took a big political risk. The agreement between the city and the PRA was in the form of an ordinance subject to approval by the city board of directors; if enough voters signed petitions, it would be subject to a referendum. The entire project, in effect, could be on the ballot for a city-wide vote. So when the city board authorized the PRA to issue more than $20 million in lease revenue bonds to finance land acquisition, mall opponents seized their chance to try to block it. To Trimble's surprise they succeeded on the first round by filing petitions with more than 5,700 certified signatures, enough to get the question on the ballot.

The leader of the referendum campaign was Christopher Sutton, a twenty-two-year-old who worked on a small Pasadena newspaper while attending UCLA. Spurred on by an accumulation of grievances, Sutton organized Pasadenans for Responsible Planning, a group consisting mainly of well-educated people with political affiliations that cut across party lines. Minority groups were conspicuously missing from the opposition, perhaps because the PRA had made a special effort to persuade the black community of the benefits of redevelopment. To get minority support, the PRA had made commitments on job training, minority contracting, and access to construction jobs.

Picking up on discontent with the city's annual operating loss on its recently completed convention center, plus opposition to public subsidy for private business, Pasadenans for Responsible Planning emphasized four reasons for blocking the mall project. First, property taxes were at stake and would increase as a result of the project. Second, the retail center was a major risk for the city treasury. Third, its design was unimaginative and left no room for alternatives. And fourth, the public had not been given a chance to discuss the issues because the PRA had been secretive. Moreover, opponents argued that with lease revenue bonds, the city had sidestepped a vote on a long-term public commitment and had ignored creative proposals and constructive criticisms.

Critics were bothered by the fact that while the review procedures for Plaza Pasadena were technically correct, Trimble's swiftness had undercut the process. In a staff report to the planning commission that never saw the light of day, one city planner complained that twenty-two public hearings required by law had sidestepped the important issues by restricting discussion to the most limited questions. The significant hearings, he claimed, "took place behind closed doors in the offices of the *Star News*, the Chamber of Commerce and the Redevelopment Agency."

Some public officials also felt shut out of the conversation. Robert Oliver, an economics professor at the California Institute of Technology long active in public affairs, told the board of directors, "Four years ago, as a member of the Planning Commission, I asked repeatedly for meetings dedicated to a discussion of the Livingston-Blayney report [which recommended the retail center] and long range plans for Pasadena. But I was told to wait until the Redevelopment Agency had a specific proposal. It was too early. Then, when a tentative proposal was presented we were told that agreements with the developer had already been signed. There was no turning back. Suddenly it was too late."

Confronted with a legal threat to the retail center, the PRA made quick work of the referendum drive. Although Pings and Trimble doubted whether their opponents had the votes to win, they were not taking any chances. Working around the clock, Trimble and the PRA's bond consultants converted the financing to tax allocation bonds that were not subject to a referendum, and the PRA won quick approval from the city board of directors for their new plan.

The PRA's tactics stirred up more controversy. Trimble was blunt in his assessment: "Well, they [the city directors] had a choice, it was not going ahead or changing the method of financing." In making the switch, however, PRA board members did not read the referendum petition as a message that most citizens opposed the mall. Their own soundings still showed general support, but they worried that a well-organized campaign could do them in. Pings considered the whole affair typical of Pasadena, a town with a history of voter initiatives. "You can get people to sign almost anything," he said. "With paid staff or volunteers, you can get signatures."

Opponents circulated more petitions and filed another lawsuit, but Trimble outmaneuvered them once more by bringing the first bond issue to market before they could get to court. PRA members worried enough about political fallout to hire a public relations firm for a few months to repair the damage, while Trimble did his best to rebut the charge that the mall would raise property taxes. Pings and Trimble believed they had a mandate to get the mall built, and for that purpose they were prepared to cut some corners. "Critics would call it crass political expediency; and it was," said Pings. "But it was legitimate, viable, and we were open about it. We had political support in the council. We were insufferable, but we were right."

Dealing with strong opposition was one of the potential complications of building malls downtown. In the suburbs opponents of development concentrated their fire on the zoning and regulatory approvals necessary to get a project started, but once the approval battle was over, the developer was usually home free. Downtown, where the city had to lend a hand throughout the development process, its exposure to political conflict lasted longer. Besides, the complexity of public-private deals made it hard for city officials to debate alternatives in public forums that would satisfy citizen activists. If they shut the door too tightly on citizen involvement, however, they might pay a high price to get their project built. After Plaza Pasadena was already open, PRA critics kept up their fight by organizing a referendum to put the city board of directors in charge of future redevelopment. Before the matter could come to a vote, the directors gave in and clipped the PRA's wings by converting it from an independent authority to a city department.

Sharing Troubles

Hahn and the PRA learned public-private development together. When they began there was no tested game plan for sharing decisions or responsibilities. California's redevelopment legislation gave cities a flexible source of money without holding them to special operating procedures. Local officials used their freedom to make early contact with a developer, and from then on they improvised. Pings and the PRA board acted on a clear mandate to build a retail center, but they considered themselves amateurs in development. Trimble put together a strong staff, but they were learning too. Hahn was an expert in developing malls, and he was involved in other redevelopment projects, but they were still in their early stages. The saving grace was that they started with a mutual recognition of inexperience all around. "I drove down to [Hahn's headquarters at] Hawthorne," said Pings, "and talked with Ernie. After 10 minutes, we both shook hands, agreed we didn't know what we were doing. Each of us went back to our offices and told our staffs to make it work."

Operating outside the urban renewal program, the PRA and Hahn quickly established a working relationship very different from the arm's-length, command-and-control stance set forth in federal rulebooks. From the start they decided on a project that was feasible for both, and they shared an interest in getting it done. Their relationship was based on mutual dependence: each side needed the skills and resources of the other for the retail center to jell. The PRA needed Hahn to line up the anchors, get the private financing, find the tenants, design and construct the building, and manage it after opening day. Hahn needed the city to assemble land, relocate people and businesses, deliver financial assistance, smooth the way with regulatory reviews, and handle the politics. Yet the troubles of building a mall downtown tested the ability and perseverance of both sides.

By staying involved from start to finish, the PRA was on hand to untangle problems. As costs escalated, Trimble found new ways to help the project. When lawsuits and opposition jeopardized the bond sale, he reworked it to bypass the trouble. When California voters in

1978 approved an initiative known as Proposition 13 that clamped a tight lid on local property taxes, the PRA renegotiated its deal with Hahn to offset this unexpected threat to its tax-increment financing. In sharing the risks of building a mall, the city also provided much-needed protection.

For Hahn working as a partner with the city was an advantage and a stumbling block at the same time. On major decisions such as design, he was not free to act alone as he could when he built suburban malls. City ownership of the garage helped make the cost competitive with suburban projects, yet it also prevented Hahn from controlling the parking as tightly as a mall developer normally does and complicated his deals with the anchors by introducing city negotiators as a third party. Hahn had to turn over information on expenses and income that he considered confidential. And because each side wanted to be sure that the other was sharing risks at all times, they tied their spending to explicit schedules. With a tight agreement, Hahn had assurances that the PRA would put in money before he spent heavily on construction, but the same agreement took away his freedom to time his moves to suit changing business conditions.

When Plaza Pasadena opened in September 1980, the ribbon-cutting fanfare celebrated a decade of public activity as much as the opening of a business. After all the problems over design, anchor demands, opposition lawsuits, delays, cost escalations, and Proposition 13, just getting to opening day was an achievement. It had taken nearly ten years of planning, negotiations, and crisis management, but compared to the city's still-unfinished Pepper Project, the record was good.

The frictions were, in the end, productive. Design features that were controversial at first later turned into accomplishments. The streetfront stores and the public space passing through the mall distinguished Plaza Pasadena from suburban shopping malls in ways that helped integrate it with downtown. And city officials were able to shape the project according to their conception of public needs without forcing the developer into an untenable position.

On the big issues that led Pasadena to want a mall in the first place, the city got what it wanted: an attraction that brought people back downtown, a symbol of success and competence, and a competitive shopping center that kept Pasadena sales at home. Once Plaza Pasadena opened, the long-term decline in downtown retail sales quickly reversed itself, with sales in the major retail categories doubling in real dollars between 1978 and 1982. This downtown turn-around helped stem the outward flow of sales and sales taxes to regional malls in neighboring towns.

The mall's completion also sent a signal to other developers. Even before Plaza Pasadena was completed, the PRA's campaign to attract major corporate headquarters to downtown Pasadena had produced an impressive roster of firms including Parsons Engineering, Bank-americard, Pacific Bell, and Kaiser Permanente. Plaza Pasadena was a prime element strengthening downtown, but its contribution is hard to sort out from other, complementary changes that took place. As a location for office employment, Pasadena's opportunity came with the completion of the Foothill Freeway in the early 1970s that con-nected the city to the skilled labor pool in the rest of the region. At the same time the retail center figured in the decision calculus of specific office projects, according to Trimble. "We committed to those com-panies and developers that Plaza Pasadena would be built. They were relying on it. Avery Label Company and Parsons certainly felt it was important."

Plaza Pasadena also helped make the climate right for new shops to move into the 1920s and 1930s two-story buildings along Colorado Boulevard where rental space had gone begging for many years. To the west of the mall, in the historic district of Old Pasadena, one development group is investing $60 million in rehabilitating small buildings for offices, restaurants, and specialty shops. To the east, on the old Broadway department store site, the $200 million Plaza Las Fuentes project of office space, a hotel, stores, and entertainment is under construction. According to development director William Rey-nolds, the city's ability to attract developers who bring good design to downtown comes from the success of Plaza Pasadena.

What counted most for Pasadena was that it got the project built, and it lived up to expectations. For other cities watching, Pasadena demonstrated that downtown malls could be built, but they were fragile, vulnerable ventures. Fitting them in among existing streets and buildings was hard, anchor stores held out for unconscionable deals, small groups of opponents had the power to slow them, and larger protests could cripple their public financing. On top of every-thing else, totally unpredictable events could be life threatening. City officials had anticipated the high cost of Plaza Pasadena, but the enactment of tax-cutting Proposition 13 changed the rules in the mid-dle of the game by making a drastic reduction in tax-increment revenue. The public financing equation unraveled, and consultants warned of shortfalls that would prevent the PRA from repaying its debt on schedule. A surge of taxable construction in the rest of the downtown redevelopment district later bailed out the PRA, but the scare was vivid enough to remember.

With a thin margin between success and failure, downtown malls demanded greater skill and ingenuity than suburban ones. Developers did have to run their race in leg irons, but with enough help from the city they could make it to opening day. Pasadena anticipated a national trend: as more and more cities took the initiative to bring the shopping mall downtown, a new type of public entrepreneurship came into its own.

6

Entrepreneurial Cities and Maverick Developers

While Pasadena struggled for ten years to complete its mall, more than fifty other cities decided to start their own retail ventures. Although Padadena showed that massive subsidies would be needed to wrench these projects loose from a retail industry still attached to the suburbs, downtown coalitions ranked shopping malls high on their agenda. Every city had its own reasons, as public officials and civic leaders kept groping to figure out what made sense for downtown and what the public would accept. But no matter whether a city's immediate problem was to save a historic building, remove an eyesore, or demonstrate the mayor's competence, the favorite solution of the 1970s was to build a mall.

A Landmark in Boston

Boston's decision to build Faneuil Hall Marketplace was exactly in tune with the mood of the times, yet it was more the result of close calls and lucky breaks than of a calculated choice in city hall. The city came close to pulling down the historic buildings in the 1950s and later nearly took the project away from the architect and developer who came up with the idea of turning them into a shopping arcade.

The once-elegant market structures began to outlive their usefulness by the early 1900s when delivery trucks jammed the narrow, congested streets and merchants began to leave. By the 1950s the market was dingy, deteriorating, and partly deserted. In 1956 the City Planning Board marked it for clearance to make way for office buildings.

Three years later the Cambridge consulting firm of Adams, Howard, and Greeley drew up the first plan that advised the city to keep the three buildings as a marketplace. Kevin Lynch, an MIT professor and urban design specialist responsible for much of this plan, soon learned what some of the city's political leaders thought of historic preservation. After he finished briefing a State House committee on the new recommendations, one of the legislators took him aside to check whether he had heard his name correctly and, if so, whether he was Irish. When Lynch assured him that both points were correct, the representative whispered to him, "Tell me, why do you want to save these old Yankee buildings?"

Saving the decayed buildings did not become established as city policy until the 1960s, when redevelopment director Edward Logue consulted with architectural historians and decided they were worth saving. He set the process in motion by persuading the chamber of commerce to undertake a renewal study of the waterfront area and then used the study to secure federal funds for a more detailed plan. Both the chamber's study and Logue's plan were explicit in proposing to renovate the market buildings, and city council approval of the downtown waterfront renewal plan made it official in 1964.

The renewal plan justified saving the market area as "one of the finest urban spaces in America" but was less than clear about what to do with it. Shopping was only one of several possibilities. The plan recommended keeping the few restaurants and retail food outlets that were there and improving the market by adding offices, other businesses, and apartments.

While the redevelopment authority was busy moving the food wholesalers to other quarters, Ben Thompson turned up one Sunday to photograph the interesting old buildings and began to think of how he might renovate them. Intrigued by the prospect, he pored over early photos and drawings of the Faneuil Hall markets and found in them a sense of action and excitement that he wanted to bring back to modern Boston. For ideas he thought about Tivoli in Copenhagen, Ghirardelli Square in San Francisco, and the Farmers' Market in Los Angeles. He also started talking to Logue.

Thompson was a businessman as well as an architect. He had learned about merchandising as the founder and head of Design Research, a retail chain specializing in contemporary home furnishings. As owner of a successful restaurant in Harvard Square, he also knew the food business firsthand. Thompson saw a way to bring the traditional market back to life as part of a merchandising strategy with food as the theme.

By the time the redevelopment authority was ready to invite com-

petitive proposals from developers, Thompson had found a Philadelphia sponsor who wanted to build the sort of retail center he had in
mind. In late 1970 the firm of Van Arkel and Moss, with Thompson as
architect, submitted a proposal emphasizing retailing. They planned
to use the central Quincy Market building as a food arcade and to
renovate the two adjoining buildings for retail stores on the ground
floor with offices and either a hotel or apartments above. Two other
developers who made proposals intended to have fewer stores and
more offices, one even featuring a corporate headquarters in remod-
eled space behind the old facade.

The redevelopment authority awarded the project to Van Arkel and
Moss and set up a series of tight deadlines to get the project financed,
leased, and into construction. When Van Arkel and Moss was unable
to meet any of these deadlines, the authority took back the project.
Thompson promptly started a national search for a more capable
developer but found little interest among the people he knew. The
redevelopment authority, meanwhile, decided to protect the buildings by starting exterior restoration under a federal grant for historic
preservation.

With more time to find a new client, Thompson wrote to James
Rouse at the suggestion of a mutual friend. This time he had gone to
the right address: Rouse not only wanted to do a downtown retail
center but had a special interest in food markets. He had been experimenting with food courts in several of his suburban malls and was
pleased with the results at Sherway Gardens near Toronto and
Paramus Park in New Jersey. Rouse took one look at the Faneuil Hall
site and said, "Damn, if this kind of thing can succeed in Toronto and
Paramus, here right in the heart of downtown Boston it ought to be
possible to produce a very special kind of place."

Rouse and Thompson agreed at once to work together and told
Mayor Kevin White and redevelopment director Robert Kenney in
the spring of 1972 that they wanted to develop the market complex.
White and Kenney were more than encouraging. "It was like we were
the knight on a white horse; we were just embraced that we were
coming in to save this project," according to Rouse. While he and
Thompson went about refining Thompson's earlier plans, they
started negotiating the terms of an agreement with the city.

Meanwhile one of the previous competitors for the project, Roger
Webb, submitted a second proposal to Kenney. His plan was to renovate only the two warehouse buildings on either side of Quincy Mar-

ket, leaving the city to improve and manage the central building. Webb and his partners were Bostonians prominent in architectual preservation, and he had recently renovated the old city hall. Their proposal was not for a retail center but for equal amounts of office space and stores in the north and south buildings.

In December Kenney took Rouse and Thompson totally by surprise when he told them he would recommend giving the project to Roger Webb at the meeting of the redevelopment authority two days later. Rouse called his friends in Boston at once to ask them to talk to the mayor and anyone else who could help. When the authority members put off their decision, supporters of the Rouse-Thompson plan gained precious time to campaign for it. Several influential Boston bankers and property owners, convinced that Rouse and Thompson were more likely to build something of value for downtown, put pressure on Mayor White to intervene. A group of downtown executives who favored Rouse and Thompson organized themselves as Neighbors of Government Center and urged White to conduct a careful review of the two proposals.

While White pondered his decision, the redevelopment agency, Municipal Research Bureau, and Neighbors of Government Center studied the competing proposals. It was clear that selecting Rouse as developer would offer the best prospect for creating a large retail magnet in the market buildings; choosing Webb would mean saving the historic buildings without a retail focus and without the pageant of food and people that Rouse and Thompson envisioned. But the reviews focused less on what each developer would build and more on what they would do to repay the city's investment. Rouse was willing to guarantee a return of at least $600,000 a year to the city, to be paid before debt service and operating expenses, while Webb proposed to take a limited profit and turn the rest of his rental income over to the city without making any guarantees.

When the city council held hearings on the two proposals, Boston developer Norman Leventhal, speaking for Neighbors of Government Center, told them he did not think the Webb group had the marketing expertise to handle this project. As Leventhal described the situation, Webb would have an unsupervised contract with no accountability and no obligation to provide a return for the city. The council committee on urban renewal recommended giving the project to Rouse and Thompson by a unanimous vote.

By that time Rouse got to see the mayor. At White's suggestion, they took a walk through the run-down market buildings and stopped for a cup of coffee at a little restaurant still in business. Rouse recalls White saying, "I understand that you bulldoze your way through anything you see that you can't get done; you just bulldoze your way through." "No, we don't do that," Rouse replied, "but I'll tell you this: we'll fight hard for what we believe in and we will try to overcome every single roadblock there is." "How do I know you're going to do what's best for Boston?" White asked. "I don't want one of these damned buildings that really isn't right for Boston." Rouse offered to work closely with the mayor: "I'll meet with you once a week to report on everything we're doing, step by step. You can watch it all the way." As a former student of architecture at Williams College, White wanted to be involved in the design enough "to be sure they didn't muck it up with neon signs on the roof or something like that." Rouse offered him that opportunity but left town without knowing where he stood. Two days later, in late March 1973, the redevelopment authority named the Rouse Company as developer.

The Boston decision to have a downtown shopping mall was far from straightforward. It started with a decision to save the market buildings because of their architectural merit, and for most people in city government that was always the main consideration. A fire that destroyed the historic Clinton poultry market across the street in 1971 reinforced their fears that if the Faneuil Hall markets were not soon renovated and reoccupied, they too might be lost. For the redevelopment agency the market complex was becoming a white elephant demanding much care and expense and providing little return. They were eager to find a developer—almost any developer—who could figure out a way to make use of it without destroying its historic character.

Nor did the redevelopment staff have any notion that retail stores in market buildings might be designed to attract large crowds of visitors to the city. "Our idea," according to research director Alex Ganz, "was to serve the growing residential market near downtown, plus office workers, and maybe increase Boston's share of retail trade just a little." But their search for a developer led to Rouse and Thompson, who did have a strategy to bring in large numbers of people for shopping and entertainment. The eventual choice of Rouse and Thompson did not mean that city officials shared their high expectations—in fact, they did not—but that key business leaders and Kevin White were impressed by Rouse's commerical success and Thompson's imaginative plans. Their proposal promised reasonable financial returns for the city while replacing the ruin outside the mayor's window.

The Boston story of chance events and happy accidents is not very different from the way other cities got started. Luck was usually as important as rational calculation. The slow pace of urban renewal in the 1950s saved Quincy Market from the bulldozer, and the readiness of the business establishment to pressure Kevin White in the 1970s gave Rouse and Thompson a chance to build their symbol of downtown revival.

James Rouse: Mixing Pleasure with Business

The development team of Rouse and Thompson brought to the project special abilities that would not only help to get it built but would make it succeed even beyond the expectations of city officials. Thompson's plans were a striking achievement in themselves, fresh and ingenious in the way they adapted old buildings to new uses. Rouse added an equally essential ingredient: he knew how to turn the visions of an inspired designer into a project that could meet the commercial demands of investors, mortgage lenders, and merchants. "Profit," according to Rouse, "is the thing that hauls dreams into focus"; and he would shape these dreams into high-volume sales and high-rent space. He would go for a broader market than the restricted clientele of Thompson's avant-garde furniture stores and upscale restaurant. Unlike the earlier urbanists who wanted to rebuild cities for the elite, Rouse's approach was to entertain middle-class shoppers and make them feel comfortable.

By the standards of the shopping center industry, whatever Rouse and Thompson did was bound to be unconventional. They were trying to fit a modern retail operation inside the walls of 150-year-old warehouses on a crowded site in the heart of the city. Only a developer with nerve and skill could do the job, and Rouse had those qualifications. A self-made man who started out as a mortgage banker, he switched to shopping center development at the age of forty when regional malls were a new idea. He helped refine the concept by building one of the first enclosed, air-conditioned malls in the country in 1958. By the time he was fifty he embarked on another pioneering venture, building a new city of 60,000 from scratch at Columbia, Maryland. Intending Columbia as a model for future suburban growth, he took the unusual step of convening a group of social scientists and other academic advisers for ideas on planning and servicing the new community.

By the time Rouse met Thompson, he had been trying for ten years to build a shopping center downtown, first in Fort Lauderdale and then in Norfolk, Virginia, before throwing in the towel. Each abortive effort made him try harder, and when the Boston opportunity came his way in 1972, he was fifty-eight years old and eager to try again.

Rouse's innovations usually had some underlying social concept. In his suburban malls he tried to create community centers. At Columbia he tried to demonstrate the advantages of a comprehensive plan for neighborhoods, parks, schools, shopping, jobs, and a town center. Further, while racial conflict was tearing other cities apart, he made a special effort to build racially integrated neighborhoods in Columbia.

He also had a special reason for wanting to build downtown shopping malls. Retailing, he believed, was one of the most important activities for regenerating cities—"a critical triggering ingredient"—because its appeal was potentially so broad. "Everything else in the center of the city serves a particular market," he said. "Offices are for office workers, the theater is for people who go to plays, the art museum is for people who go to see art. But everybody is involved in the marketplace, and as it is lively, appealing, and attractive it draws people to the center of the city." Even Boston officials who wanted nothing more than to save the historic structures would also welcome a project that drew crowds back to the city, and Rouse was prepared to use his opportunity for that purpose.

Rouse had the resources to be an innovator at the Faneuil Hall markets. By the early 1970s his network of successful regional malls had given him the credentials, skills, and business contacts he would need to handle a project as risky as this one. Rouse had also organized a company capable of putting visionary ideas into operation. The complexity of shopping center development demanded the talents of many experts and the leadership of more than one executive. When we speak of Rouse's work on Faneuil Hall Marketplace, we are describing the work of a managerial team headed by James Rouse as chairman and Mathias DeVito as president of the Rouse Company in the 1970s.

Rouse had an operating style well suited to working in new and unstructured situations. Unknown obstacles did not discourage him;

he was an optimist who believed that close calls are normal in real estate and that "the development business primarily consists of finding a way to overcome crises." His colleagues did not always share this view, and Rouse sometimes had to calm anxious members of his own board. While he was working on Columbia, one board member called to ask whether the company was in trouble. Rouse said, "Of course we're in trouble; we're always in trouble." His director told him that Wall Street was upset because of a report that Rouse was unable to raise any more money for the sewer system in Columbia. Rouse acknowledged that the report was correct. Asked what he intended to do about it, he replied, "I haven't the foggiest notion what we're going to do about it, but we'll find an answer."

With his high tolerance for risks and complexity, he was able to persuade his board to go along with projects such as Faneuil Hall but sometimes only by the skin of his teeth. When Faneuil Hall was in its early stages and he was still juggling all the risks while trying to handle increasingly complicated negotiations with the city, he made the mistake of having his project chief describe the full situation to the board. They were horrified, he recounted: "My God, there were demons at every step." The board wanted to withdraw at once, but Rouse convinced them to allocate another $500,000 to move ahead, and from then on he was able to keep up the momentum.

Aside from a cheerful acceptance of crises, Rouse brought with him a conviction that the major obstacle to overcome was a negative frame of mind about downtown and its future. When he agreed to do the Gallery at Market East in Philadelphia at the same time as Faneuil Hall, he faced the doubts of the public, department store executives, and prospective tenants that a retail center could draw customers to that "unsafe, dirty, inconvenient" part of town. But he had resources beyond personal persuasion to win over the skeptics. His impressive track record in the suburbs helped convince investors and merchants to give his latest ideas a chance, and he had influence with business people who wanted places in his suburban malls. "We had one hell of a time leasing the Gallery," he reported, but he was expanding his Cherry Hill Mall near Camden, New Jersey, and was prepared to make package deals: "We were finally very up front with the fact that any merchant who wanted to come into Cherry Hill also had to come into the Gallery."

Rouse was truly exceptional among developers in his willingness to take on the political battles that sometimes came with downtown territory. To get the Faneuil Hall project, he acknowledged "pulling every legitimate pressure we could find—which was *everything* we could find—from anybody who knew the city, knew the mayor. We did marshal a hell of a lot of support." Later, in order to build Harborplace in Baltimore, Rouse had to get voter approval in a special referendum. To win the election, he threw himself into the campaign like a professional: "Our goal was that every political club in Baltimore on election day would have to be handing out sample ballots that were for us and against the opposition, and every political club in Baltimore did. The black churches distributed 50,000 handbills in favor of Harborplace." To win support in a mostly black city, he met with fifty leading black ministers and promised minority jobs and business opportunities in the project. He was an effective campaigner, blending business purposes with his sense of social mission. "We just made our case," he explained, "and our case was honest and valid and should have been supported." Any developer would have been ready to state a case, but few would have been willing to mobilize political clubs and churches, and still fewer could have masterminded an election campaign.

A Public Market in Seattle

In many cities the decision to build a downtown mall was part of a search for something warmer and more inviting than bulldozer-style redevelopment. When Seattle officials made plans to level a retail district for an uninspiring renewal project, the city's residents took matters into their own hands by voting down the project and directing city government to renovate it instead.

The shopping area they saved was the Pike Place Market, a seedy yet colorful and popular produce market on the edge of downtown where local farmers had been selling fruit and vegetables to the public since 1907. During World War II close to half the farmers in the market were among the Japanese-Americans taken away to prison camps; many lost their land and their businesses forever. The number of farmers selling in the market dropped from more than 500 in 1939 to about 50 in 1949. By the 1950s the market was devastated, and the arcade buildings that housed it were in danger of collapse. Spurred on by downtown business leaders, the city planned to replace it with offices, apartment towers, and hotels.

By the time the city was ready to present a plan for federal approval, public opposition to urban renewal was on the rise across the country. Led by Victor Steinbrueck, a charismatic architecture professor at the University of Washington, opponents collected more than 50,000 signatures for a voter initiative to save the market. Rather than accept the initiative, a city council committed to the project decided to put the measure on the ballot in November 1971. To the surprise of most political insiders, it carried by a vote of 60 percent.

At one stroke the initiative killed the renewal project and set up a 7-acre historic district around the core of the market together with a historical commission dominated by market supporters to oversee its restoration. City officials found a decision thrust upon them, but unless they acted quickly, time and neglect would destroy the market without a need for bulldozers.

Mayor Wes Uhlman, his agency heads, and most of the city council read the vote as a new statement of what the public wanted for downtown. It was an abrupt repudiation of the business coalition's goal of a thoroughly modern city center dedicated to economic development. From their perspective the shabby Pike Place Market was a symbol of doom: a "decadent, somnolent fire-trap," according to former mayor Dorm Braman, and "a scab on the backside of downtown" according to others.

Victor Steinbrueck and his allies were operating from a different set of beliefs. They wanted to preserve places that gave Seattle a special flavor—places that evoked its history, even if they were undistinguished, unprofitable, and unsavory. One Seattle architect called the market "an honest place in a phony time." Steinbrueck's objection to sanitizing the city was a clear challenge to the notion of civic progress that inspired most urban renewal projects. Steinbrueck and his supporters managed to change the debate over downtown from a narrow concern with economic development to one that considered issues of design, livability, and historic value.

Mayor Uhlman gave high priority to renovating the Pike Place Market, partly out of understandable respect for a cause that had just demonstrated its strength at the polls and partly because the views of the market supporters fitted his own sense of what was right for the city. In the late 1960s Uhlman had been active in the campaign to preserve Pioneer Square, another historic area on the edge of downtown. He explained the controversy over Pioneer Square as also a clash of values between progress and preservation. "The old establishment," he said, "wanted to tear it down to build two glass office towers. They expected to make a lot of money. I wanted to save it because it was human scale. Buildings put up around 1910 were all scaled for people, not like the black towers you see now."

Uhlman's commitment to bring the Pike Place Market back to life fit well with other stands he had taken to bring more attractions downtown, including an aquarium, apartments ("downtown should have a 24-hour population," he said), and retail arcades within new office buildings: "We wanted street activity and interest—a people city."

The decision to renovate a downtown market in Seattle came from a shift in public opinion away from tear-it-down renewal and toward the care of popular landmarks. The landmark in question was no architectural treasure, but it was an unusual retail market that people looked at with affection—a once-bustling, colorful farmers' market offering fresh food of exceptional quality. When cities chose to build retail centers in the 1970s, they had different notions of retailing in mind. What the voter initiative called for was not a shopping mall in the contemporary suburban sense of that term but an old-fashioned produce market that used to be popular and might work again in Seattle.

John Clise: The Coalition Builder

Pike Place Market restored according to the terms of the citizen initiative could not operate as a profit-making venture. The initiative provided no money for the renovation, and the Historical Commission it created was a watchdog agency with no developmental responsibilities. Huge public subsidies would be necessary to rebuild the battered market, yet the farm-stand proprietors could not afford to pay even the going rent for commercial space.

Nor would a developer have the freedom to mix higher rent payers among the farmers. The Historical Commission had a veto over tenant selection, and its members were determined to shape the market their way—with untried local businesses and no national chains. Flushed with victory in the election, they approached their new responsibilities with a combination of ideological fervor and religious devotion. "A lot of them were endowed as having come by the Holy Grail," reported a city staff member who tried working with them. And they kept an iron grip on market tenants. When a food stand called the Manila BarBQ began to sell a new Philippine-style sauce, the commission ordered it removed because the original approval was for southern-style barbecue sauce only. No commercial developer could tolerate these restrictions and stay in business. As a result city government created the Preservation and Development Authority to renovate and manage the market on a nonprofit basis.

The leading entrepreneur for this project was a public official, John Clise, who served first as property manager of the authority and then as executive director from 1979 to 1983. Clise earned his real estate credentials in a family business and his political credentials as a member of the movement to save the market. He had managed old Seattle buildings before, but few commercial buildings anywhere had the accumulation of problems he found in these structures: "pipes drip, valves fail, circuits blow, roofs leak, drains plug, and floors crumble," he wrote in an early report. While tenants screamed, Clise had to placate them long enough to get a patch on each fresh breakdown. The best solution he found was to run repair and maintenance operations directly out of his own office in the market basement.

The political demands of Clise's job were extreme even for a public sector developer. He had to deal with fiercely independent shopkeepers determined to fight any increase in their heavily subsidized rents, raucous street characters who used the market as their hangout, citizen activists who hated government and regarded any compromise as a sellout, historic purists who wanted to preserve every crumbling inch of the old buildings, hard-eyed mortgage lenders who read only the bottom line of each transaction, and city council members who wanted Clise to shield them from controversy while running a clean operation in the black.

A warm, friendly bear of a man, he dealt amiably and openly with all these groups. He worked patiently to find tenants the Historical Commission would approve and then regulated their business operations strictly enough for ideological preservationists but realistically enough for a merchant to make a living. To keep the vital subsidies flowing, he had to hold this squabbling coalition together in support of a long series of separate projects. He cultivated the necessary political support through endless negotiation to accommodate even such marginal groups as the street musicians who played in the market. After years of bargaining with them over where and when they could perform, he reflected on the outcome: "Our grey hairs are getting more numerous but there does seem to be relatively good harmony."

Clise was comfortable with the turmoil that was part of the charm of Pike Place Market. As he made his daily rounds through the stalls and passageways, he separated brawling drunks and lent a hand to stumbling ones. Working at his rolltop desk, he looked casual and relaxed, surrounded by a clutter of antique signs, old office equipment, and gadgets from the past. One almost expected to see him wearing a green eyeshade. Picking old reports out of overflowing pigeonholes and searching his pockets for scraps of paper on current projects, he seemed only a step away from administrative chaos.

Yet when it came to raising money, he showed the same entrepreneurial flair and rule-bending skill as other development managers. When he needed a key market building certified as historic in order to be eligible for tax write-offs, he faced a real problem. Most of the structure had been rebuilt after a fire in the 1940s, and the city's preservation officer declared it "a building of little redeeming architectural value that is 98 percent new." With help from market supporters and the Historical Commission, he mounted a campaign that eventually drew in Washington's Senator Warren Magnuson to get the necessary certification.

Proving St. Paul's Competence

While some cities were building markets in order to preserve cherished landmarks, others were building them in order to cover over some disaster. If any single factor was responsible for St. Paul's decision to build a downtown mall, it was civic embarrassment at the failure of earlier efforts, at looking bad in comparison with its twin city of Minneapolis, and above all at the vacant site known as "superhole" in what used to be the retail heart of downtown.

Beginning in the early 1960s the combined leadership of business, labor, and city government worked to rebuild downtown St. Paul. The cornerstone of their efforts was a twelve-block, 43-acre urban renewal project in the center of town. In typical renewal style, the city assembled land early and then went out to look for developers. Although the agency in charge had a history of clearing more land than it could sell, the project area had ten new office buildings by 1974, and the city had built two and one-half miles of enclosed skyways connecting new and old buildings at the second-story level.

Meanwhile suburban competition was killing retailing in downtown St. Paul. Between 1954 and 1963 more than fifty shopping centers of all types with close to 8 million square feet opened in the suburbs of the Twin Cities. Renewal officials completed the devastation by demolishing some 350 stores between 1963 and 1975, while the newly built skyways took pedestrian traffic away from remaining street-level shops. According to the local press, the number of stores in downtown St. Paul dropped from more than 400 in 1963 to 160 in 1975.

The renewal agency picked a site for a retail center in the main commercial district along Seventh Street. Between 1967 and 1971 three developers showed interest in it, but in the end all walked away. Meanwhile the agency cleared more land and pushed out more stores; two blocks on Seventh Street stood empty, and seven blocks in the old retail core now had no stores on the street.

By the early 1970s the business community and city renewal staff agreed that the most pressing downtown problem was the disappearance of shopping. A chamber of commerce study in 1973 concluded that the central district needed a people-oriented attraction and with an eye toward neighboring Minneapolis reported that the skyways built so far "were not people places like Nicollet Mall." This report also proposed a major retail development that would cross Seventh Street at the superhole site and would connect Dayton's and Donaldsons, the two large department stores remaining downtown.

To move the plan along, the chamber of commerce set up a committee of business leaders with Robert Van Hoef, a banking executive experienced in downtown planning, as director. Van Hoef promptly hired the consultants who had worked on Nicollet Mall to do a plan for a Seventh Street mall. Renewal agency staff meanwhile made plans for a retail project to link the two department stores. They envisioned an enclosed center patterned on suburban malls, plus a hotel and office tower above the stores.

These ideas were promising, but without a developer in hand they were just one more set of drawings in a cabinet already bulging with forgotten plans. Van Hoef commissioned a display model and a six-screen slide show and began a national search. During 1974 he turned up only two developers willing to shell out even the small cost of preliminary studies without a city guarantee to reimburse them if the project fell through: Carlson Companies, a Minneapolis-based hotel chain, and Oxford Properties, a Canadian firm specializing in mixed office and retail projects. Their initial proposals for the Town Square complex were in line with Van Hoef's ideas and the plans of the city renewal agency, but they were slow to make commitments. By the spring of 1976 Carlson Companies had cut the size of its planned hotel, and Oxford had decided to build only a first phase of its project; neither had found financing, and Oxford had no prospective tenants willing to sign leases.

George Latimer: The Mayor's Glue

When George Latimer took office as the new mayor in June 1976, the time was at hand for a city decision on whether to proceed. Major public financing was crucial to the project since both developers expected the city to pay for more land, a parking garage, an enclosed mall along Seventh Street, and skyways connecting the new project to nearby buildings. Yet the city was in poor financial shape with a high level of debt, pressing needs for capital investment, and rising operating costs. Latimer was a labor lawyer who had run as a Democratic-Farmer-Labor candidate with strong ties to trade unions and almost none to the business community. He had made no promises to the downtown business establishment and had never even met its leaders. As he put it, "We didn't drink in the same bars."

Soon after the election Latimer had to decide on his priorities. The problems of downtown were all too visible, with empty holes from urban renewal "competing for historic designation." In deciding where to focus his energy he wanted to find projects that needed his personal involvement and would produce demonstrable results. Town Square looked right from both points of view, and many elements were already in place, but the situation called for a special resource that he could bring to it: "the glue that the mayor has to bring people together." He sensed that big egos would be involved in this development and that the key figures would want to deal with the mayor on important decisions. He also sensed that the downtown business community had done a great deal of work so far and was not getting an adequate response from city hall. By working with them he could broaden his base of support while establishing himself as an effective leader. Latimer became the chief public sector entrepreneur for Town Square.

Fiscal considerations were not important in deciding to move ahead, according to Latimer, because even a successful downtown project would make only a small difference to the taxpayer. He wanted Town Square for other reasons. Most important was "to make it a better city, to bring people in." In addition to attracting shoppers, he thought Town Square would encourage people to live in the city and therefore make downtown more than a nine-to-five office district.

Latimer wanted the shopping mall in order to promote the city's economic development too. Looking back, he contended that other investors would never have come to St. Paul without Town Square and the Science Museum, another project built around the same time. From the outset he believed the new retail center would have an important psychological effect by overcoming negative images of city government left over from the unfinished renewal projects. He believed it gave people a sense of accomplishment and a feeling that the city could act positively: "When I speak of cleaning up the riverfront or building an outstanding park, people now take it seriously."

Some city officials who shared responsibility for Town Square thought its overriding purpose was economic development. According to Eugene Kraut of the St. Paul Port Authority, "The infrastructure for economic development is more than streets and sewers. If you bring a businessman to town to persuade him to invest in the community, you have to be able to take him to a good hotel and good restaurants and stores." In addition Kraut thought the retail and hotel jobs generated by Town Square were important: "Many people need these low-skill jobs; they would be on welfare without them."

Gary Stout, who headed Latimer's Department of Planning and Economic Development, also thought of downtown retailing as part of the infrastructure for economic development. "Developers are not impressed by Chamber of Commerce brochures or market analyses," he said. "They are impressed by other people's projects." Stout credits Town Square for persuading several other companies to build in St. Paul.

Developing a downtown shopping mall served different purposes for different people. Van Hoef minimized economic reasons and stressed the contribution of Town Square to the character of downtown: "We realized we were building a downtown that was not a people city. We had aluminum, glass, steel, but nothing to attract people. We didn't want that kind of city. Do you know of a good city that doesn't have retail activity?" One reason for the popularity of shopping malls among the downtown projects of the 1970s may have been that they promised to combine the virtues of a more attractive downtown with the virtues of economic development, while most other projects promised either one but not both. And in the case of St. Paul, building a retail complex was a way of removing a civic sore spot and replacing it with a symbol of accomplishment.

A Porno District in San Diego

Every decision to build a downtown shopping mall seemed to begin with some local quirk. In San Diego the problem was public rest rooms under Horton Plaza park. Once the terminus for Wells Fargo stagecoaches, then the core of a thriving downtown and the transfer point for city bus lines, this small park was the traditional place for band concerts, political rallies, and public celebrations. But San Diego's growth explosion after World War II—it went from twenty-fifth to eighth largest city in the nation between 1950 and 1980—sent the city sprawling outward and took away the clientele of the downtown stores, theaters, and hotels. The old center soon turned into the local skid row and adult entertainment district. Once-pleasant hotels became run-down single-room-occupancy buildings, theaters and movie houses featured X-rated films, and retail shops gave way to sleazy bookstores and bars for visiting sailors.

As the Horton Plaza park became an oasis for vagrants, alcoholics, and street people, other citizens complained increasingly about the safety of the park and the poor condition of its underground toilets. Preparing for the city's two hundredth anniversary in 1969, the city council voted $90,000 to improve the park and rest rooms, but the chief supporters of this appropriation argued convincingly that the money would be wasted unless the city improved the surrounding area. The city planning department then began to study renewal possibilities for a three-block area near the park. Advocates for the study—led by San Diegans, Inc., the downtown business organization—argued for revitalizing the much larger run-down district in that part of town.

Under the pressure of their logic, the study area grew from three blocks to five, then nine, and then fifteen. The planners proposed a combination of commercial and federal office buildings, a hotel, and housing. A consulting firm studied the prospects for selling cleared land to developers and concluded that the most likely demand would be for office and hotel space, with apartments as a secondary possibility.

A big plan was in the making for downtown but with no attention to a shopping center. The city made commitments to rebuild this depressed area without deciding what to do with it. With the election of Pete Wilson as mayor in 1971, the downtown plan had an influential friend in city hall. Wilson ran on a platform calling for stricter control of growth to prevent the "Los Angelizing" of San Diego. Impressed by the political constituency working for downtown development, he quickly saw that revitalizing the city center could produce a tangible success as part of his strategy for limiting suburban growth. With Wilson's support the city council approved a redevelopment plan for the fifteen-block Horton Plaza area in July 1972. San Diego had already gone some distance to protect the integrity of its cleaned-up rest rooms.

Further studies continued to identify office space as the most marketable use of project land, with hotels second, but they also emphasized the importance of street-level retailing to complement the offices and hotels. An economic consultant argued that retail space would diversify the downtown economy and stimulate further development in the future, and city design specialists argued that stores were important to bring people into downtown streets and break the monotony of rows of offices.

To move the project closer to reality, the city organized a national competition that gave developers great freedom in proposing what to put on the site. Only three entries were persuasive enough to consider seriously, and all three proposed significant retail activity. Two of the competitors were Ernest Hahn and James Rouse; the third was San Franciscan Lyman Jee.

Hahn proposed to build from 500,000 to 750,000 square feet of retail space, the equivalent of a regional shopping mall. To make this amount of retailing feasible, however, he maintained that the city or other developers would have to build several thousand houses or apartments downtown, as well as nearby hotels and a convention center. Rouse made no demands for development outside the project area and proposed to build 1.75 million square feet of office and retail space, a 1,000-room hotel, and a pedestrian walkway to a marina five blocks away. Jee proposed a development of 1 million square feet in a mixed office and retail center, plus some low- and moderate-income housing.

Choosing either Hahn or Rouse to do the project would have meant building a major retail center, on the scale of a large suburban mall, in the heart of downtown. Before the selection committee had made a decision, Rouse withdrew his proposal in order to cut back his new ventures during a building slump. This left the choice between Hahn and Jee, or between a retail center and a mixed-use development as the focus of the project.

The city staff was divided on whether downtown should have a shopping center. One group, led by community development director William Gerhardt, thought there was little chance of getting retail development and favored office buildings. Several other staff members wanted to emphasize shopping because it would add life and color to downtown. "Most people thought shopping wasn't feasible," recalled downtown planner Angeles Leira, "but Hahn was a maverick and he thought it could be done. When he proposed a retail center, we were jumping for joy!"

The competition between Hahn and Jee was one-sided in any case. Hahn's track record was overwhelming, and if anyone had the qualifications to build a major retail center in the depressed heart of San Diego, it was surely Ernest Hahn. The selection committee worried that Jee might be unable to come up with financing for his project. In May 1974 the city selected Hahn as developer, citing his experience with retail development, his local ties to San Diego (where he had already built a successful regional mall and was negotiating to build another), his special capability in redevelopment projects, and his commitment to the revitalization of downtown San Diego.

In San Diego the decision to have a downtown mall was more straightforward than in the other three cities. Historic preservation was not a consideration at this point (although it would be later), and there was no superhole crying to be filled. Nor was there a sense of protest against earlier bulldozer-style renewal since San Diego had not been active in urban renewal.

Embarrassment was a key element in the decision once more, in this case over a porno district and skid row. There was no Seattle-style preservation movement that wanted to save it as an honest record of the city's seamier side, and there was every reason to expect public enthusiasm for a plan to get rid of it. If a credible developer had proposed building offices and hotels, city officials might well have agreed. Downtown retailing was deader in the highly suburbanized cities of California than in most of the rest of the country, and the few city staffers who favored a retail center had a hard time persuading anyone to listen to them.

San Diego was a discouraging place for a downtown mall. In comparison with Boston, Seattle, and St. Paul, the city hardly had a recognizable center. Its small office district and run-down stores were a poor starting point for development, and there was no tradition of in-town living. The problem in San Diego was to create a downtown rather than to bring one back to life. In this setting the city's proce-dure was to find a qualified developer interested in downtown and then to follow his judgment.

Ernest Hahn: Endurance and Flexibility

Risk taking is second nature to real estate developers, but those who were willing to build retail centers in places like San Diego's porno district in the early 1970s had an extra measure of optimism. They were the counterparts of public sector managers in that they too were operating in uncharted territory where they would have to find new solutions as fast as they learned what needed to be done. The leading pioneers—Ernest Hahn in the West and James Rouse in the East—brought with them a special operating style that helped city officials work out new forms of public-private action.

Hahn had started as a general contractor and then had organized a company that became the largest developer of shopping centers in California and one of the largest in the nation. By 1975 his firm owned eleven regional shopping malls and had thirty more under way. Start-ing in the late 1960s Hahn began to build malls in redevelopment projects in several small California cities, including Culver City, Hawthorne, and Fairfield. By the time he entered the larger cities of Pasadena, Long Beach, and San Diego, he and his staff had already learned how to work with city governments. Together with his pro-tégé and future company president John Gilchrist, he headed a team with a proven capacity to operate in the complicated world of rede-velopment. Hahn had achieved a prominence in the shopping center industry that made other developers watch his downtown ventures with interest to see whether they might set a trend. And like Rouse he had reached a point in his career where he could afford to take risks in order to build a pinnacle project.

Hahn was willing to start projects without resolving every issue in advance. He would get a project going on the basis of general agree-ments and then deal with the details one at a time. An adept and persistent negotiator, he went into most situations with great con-fidence that he could find the right trade-offs to make a deal work and persuade others to go along with his solutions. His readiness to live with open-ended and uncertain situations made it possible for cities to start projects without having all the answers in hand. Once a project was under way, Hahn's confidence worked like a self-fulfilling prophecy. As city officials and his company invested more and more energy and resources, both became increasingly committed to completing the project. When the stakes were large enough, both were eager to strike workable bargains.

In a field marked by an urgent sense that time is money, Hahn's endurance record is unusual. Horton Plaza was eleven years in the making from the time he was named developer to opening day. At about the same time he worked for a dozen years to build a mall in suburban Marin County north of San Francisco. Neither Hahn nor his executives can recall abandoning a regional shopping center in midstream, although they can recall many temptations to do so.

Flexibility was another feature of the Hahn style. It was as though he started with only a vague notion of what each finished center would be like but with a commitment to craft a unique project to fit the time and place of its development. John Gilchrist considered the slow process of doing downtown retail centers an advantage in disguise: "it gives us time to improve the project, to get better tenants."

Time worked for the Hahn Company when staff members paid attention to community objections in order to learn what the public wanted and then came up with new plans to give it to them. University Town Centre, a regional shopping mall near the University of California San Diego campus, was almost a casualty of local controversies in the early 1970s. When the first plan generated strong opposition, Hahn scrapped it and hired another architect whose designs were closer to what nearby residents seemed to want. Working with an organized forum of community groups, executives Ronald Hahn and William Doyle agreed to expand the retail center to include 300 houses and apartments joined by pedestrian and bicycle paths, with a 7-acre canyon kept open for public use.

In a further departure from industry practice, they agreed to build 150,000 square feet of space for low-rent activities for community groups and to work with local people in selecting appropriate tenants. Political pressure resulted in an ice rink, day care center, health facility, folk art museum, repertory theater, amusement arcade, food market, professional offices, art gallery, disco-restaurant, and rooms for adult education classes and club meetings in the mall. Ronald Hahn estimated that these nonprofit or low-profit activities cost the developer almost $7 million.

But after the mall was open, nobody at the Hahn Company complained. Hahn executives considered the extra cost an inadvertent investment that paid off handsomely. Sales and rent receipts were far above expectations, making the center one of the company's best performers. Staff members credited these results to the community services that attracted people and persuaded them to stay longer than visitors to other shopping malls. Center manager Gordon Jackson agreed that "in the long run, participation has produced a better product." The Hahn Company repeated such features as the ice rink/ food court combination, meeting rooms, and extension classrooms in its newer projects. Further, a staff member with responsibility for analyzing community life-styles served on the team that planned future retail centers.

This demonstrated interest in adjusting plans to local tastes sent a message to other cities that some developers would custom-build projects for them. Hahn knew how to build malls that people regarded as community symbols. In Pasadena he went along with plans for the very expensive arched passageway in deference to local wishes. He then hired muralist Terry Schoonoven—"a local Michelangelo"—to decorate the walls and ceilings with local vistas while school classes came to see the artist working from his scaffold. Hahn reported with pride that people thought of Plaza Pasadena as "our mall" rather than "Hahn's mall."

Company executives pointed out that the special problems of working with city governments proved to be manageable. One of these problems was sharing decisions, recognizing, as John Gilchrist put it, that "the city which invests so heavily in a project is entitled to a say in its design and timing." Working mostly in California, where local growth regulations are among the toughest in the country, Hahn negotiators grew accustomed to difficult suburban politics. State law prevented direct contact between developers and elected officials, and the development team was often uncertain of local government approval until the last minute. Public-private conflict was normal.

With the antigrowth politics of California suburbs as his benchmark, Hahn found real benefits in having the city as a partner and being able to negotiate, a process that brought more advantages than disadvantages. In part, this was because Ernest Hahn is a superlative negotiator with a low-key, unassuming manner that disarms local officials. When his unpretentious presentation surprised a city council that had braced itself for high-pressure salesmanship, a visiting consultant reported: "By the time Ernie got through they would have given him anything he wanted. Fortunately he didn't want anything illegal, because they would have given him that, too."

Working in downtown projects, Hahn and his company also had to deal with the fishbowl problem: learning how to share confidential information on project costs and returns with public officials. "If you were asking them for financial help," said Gilchrist, "you had to show why you needed it. You had to share your figures." Hahn's staff usually sent sensitive documents to consultants working for the city, who used them as background for public reports without direct quotations and without turning them over to city staff. Neither Hahn nor the city negotiators wanted to open their working documents to project opponents who might be preparing legal briefs.

The most important contribution of developers like Hahn to the new entrepreneurial style of city governments was their confidence that direct negotiation is a way to resolve problems. Gilchrist claimed that negotiating with city officials over downtown projects was not much different from bargaining with anchor department stores. "They have to get certain things to make a deal work," he said, "and we have to get certain things." If interests were too far apart, no project would move ahead. "The best evidence that negotiations are fairly smooth," according to Gilchrist, "is that projects are being built."

Gerald Trimble: The Public Sector Developer

San Diego took a double dose of entrepreneurship by signing on Ernest Hahn as project developer and then hiring Gerald Trimble away from Pasadena to manage Horton Plaza for the city. Trimble brought many of the skills that flourish in the private sector: a technical grasp of complex developments, a tenacity in pushing projects through to completion, and an ability to invent workable solutions to unexpected problems. But his background was entirely in the public sector, and his entrepreneurship put the city in a strong position for the decade of deal making that went into Horton Plaza. Trimble's base of operations was the newly created Centre City Development Corporation (CCDC), a nonprofit corporation empowered to represent the city in negotiating with Hahn and to take responsibility for planning and managing the Horton Plaza project. Trimble believed the agency was set up to deal with developers in a businesslike way, with business people on the board. It was needed also, according to

Trimble, because the city council and planning staff did not understand real estate, were suspicious of many necessary transactions, and were uninformed about costs.

But Trimble was no uncritical supporter of either the project or its developer. He considered the early plans for Horton Plaza very poor and pressed Hahn to make changes in its fortress-like design. He kept bargaining for a city share of the revenues from Horton Plaza until Hahn agreed. And he insisted on deals that would be defensible politically, even when they imposed questionable costs on the Hahn Company.

Once he made his deals, however, he was a forceful advocate for them and for the project. There was almost no organized opposition to Horton Plaza, so he had no need for the tactics he had used in Pasadena. But he spent hours meeting individually with city council members who were opposed or uncertain, trying to nail down their support before decisions came to a vote. He described his approach as educating council members on such matters as why the city should sell downtown land at a lower price than it paid for it. He marshaled facts and arguments and cited comparable prices for other California retail centers.

Trimble's technical command and persuasive skills, however, were not enough to overcome disagreement based on values or ideologies. Some city council members voted consistently against the project because they were flatly opposed to spending public money for redevelopment no matter what the economic justifications might be. With two members unshakable in their disapproval, the project came within a hair of losing the two-thirds vote it needed for a renegotiated agreement in 1979. Even with strong mayoral support and no organized opposition, the thin margin between success and failure kept Trimble and his board pushing aggressively to protect Horton Plaza.

In both Pasadena and San Diego Trimble's operating style became an issue in itself. Some critics complained of inadequate opportunities for the public to consider or debate the plans he promoted so energetically. Others objected to the rule bending that was typical of bureaucratic entrepreneurs. One of Trimble's staff members in Pasadena had this to say: "In my opinion, he has little regard for what is right or wrong as far as regulations are concerned. He will stretch them right to the limit of what he can get away with."

Trimble and other public entrepreneurs found ways to accomplish results in the field without repeating the brutality of the urban renewal and highway building programs. The question that remained was whether they were justified in cutting corners on public accountability for the sake of finishing projects. The answer depended on the priorities of the time. For those who valued citizen participation and open public debate more than completed projects, Trimble's style was hard to take. But for those who had been through years of participation and debate and now valued results—as long as the deal makers followed proper legal procedures—Trimble's style was made to order. In any event Trimble was doing what his board members wanted. Dean Dunphy, chair of CCDC, summed it up from his point of view: "If you're going to avoid the ruffling of feathers, you're not going to get things done. Aggression is, in fact, a required characteristic of his job. The role that he is performing is one of real estate developer, and that is an occupation not normally found in city government. He's playing the private sector guy with all the public power."

The old downtown in Pasadena: once flourishing, then a source of wounded pride and sagging revenues. *The Hahn Co.*

A new image, ten years later: Plaza Pasadena.

What the city wanted: street-facing stores. Plaza Pasadena.

The developer's strategy: a regional mall downtown. Plaza Pasadena.

Getting rid of an embarrassment—Superhole, one of the rubble fields left by urban renewal in the heart of St. Paul. *City of St. Paul PED.*

A symbol of city competence: office towers seen from the city's enclosed park. Town Square/Saint Paul Center. *City of St. Paul PED.*

A green oasis in cold weather: Town Square Park. Town Square/Saint Paul Center. *City of St. Paul PED.*

Interior pathways designed and paid for by the city. Town Square/Saint Paul Center. *City of St. Paul PED.*

The Pike Place Market in its heyday, 1915. *Museum of History and Industry, Seattle.*

(*opposite, top*) Sketch of Pike Place Market by Victor Steinbrueck, leader of the campaign to save the market, published to mobilize public support. *Victor Steinbrueck, Market Sketchbook (Seattle and London: University of Washington Press, 1968).*

(*opposite, bottom*) After millions of dollars in renovation, the structures were sound, but the market looked the same. Pike Place Market.

(*top and bottom*) The theme of Pike Place Market: produce from nearby farms and fish from nearby waters.

A slice of history preserved in Pike Place Market: the last hat blocker in Seattle.

(*top and bottom*) Below-market rents make unconventional stores possible: a pawn shop, and a herbal pharmacy.

7

Deal Making

Not long ago a city administrator who kept cutting and patching deals with a developer while sinking millions of public dollars into a private project could reasonably have expected to be out of a job and facing a grand jury. Yet as soon as city officials freed themselves from the straitjacket of urban renewal, they began to negotiate special deals to suit each project and to spend public money even before a deal was done. In comparison to the cramped style of the renewal era, public negotiators were operating more like developers and less like rule-bound bureaucrats.

Testing the Waters

Cities continued to make the opening moves, spotting potential projects and places to build them, but they made them differently. After the freeway revolt and the renewal protests most downtown coalitions had learned to avoid projects that would destroy neighborhoods or tear apart whole business districts. Instead they worked at compact projects on small sites, trying to create centers of intense activity rather than showpieces of spacious planning. Their new style dealt at once with the design critiques of earlier projects and the political resistance to wholesale clearance.

If microsurgery was going to replace the bulldozer, downtown shopping centers were the right size. The central Pike Place Market designated for restoration fits within a 7-acre site, and Fanueil Hall Marketplace fits within 6½ acres. In both cases officials were renovating existing buildings rather than clearing. Town Square sits on just over 4 acres of land that were easy to assemble. Part of the site was left over from urban renewal clearance years earlier, and the rest became ripe for taking with the closing of a W. T. Grant store that occupied most of it. Once these cities had a compact project in hand, most resisted the temptation to make it more ambitious by leveling the surrounding blocks.

Of the four cities we studied in detail, only San Diego drew up plans that called for a moderate amount of clearance: 6½ blocks, or 11½ acres, for the retail center. But this was not the sort of clearance that would lead to citizen protests. Instead of threatening a neighborhood of homes, the major threat it posed was to a porno district and skid row. Pornography has a wide following but no advocates, and most voters were likely to consider the city better off without it. San Diego had not done enough urban renewal to sharpen local sensitivities against the bulldozer, and the total number of evictions was not large. The project moved out 230 long-term residents from the hotels plus 58 business firms.

In other cities the search was also on for key sites that were small, prominent, good for retailing, and close to the downtown core if not in it. Baltimore made room for the Harborplace mall by adding just 3.2 acres of prime waterfront land to its 33-acre Charles Center–Inner Harbor project. Similarly Cincinnati found a place for its Fountain Square Plaza, an office-hotel-retail complex, by adding less than 2 acres to an earlier renewal project. Of seventy-one malls, nearly half took up fewer than 5 acres; the median size was 5.7 acres.

Some cities economized on land clearance by planning retail malls next to established department stores. This strategy not only minimized property takings but also made projects more attractive to developers. Instead of having to sell land to department stores at little or no profit, they could develop high-profit space for mall shops between the anchor stores. Town Square in St. Paul connects to an adjacent Dayton's department store, with only a single anchor store built as part of the project. The Gallery at Market East in Philadelphia is a mall with a new Gimbel's at one end and a venerable Strawbridge & Clothier at the other; and the Grand Avenue in Milwaukee consists of one new and one renovated arcade linking two established department stores. By building alongside an established store, a city could fit its project into the heart of downtown with only minimal disruption. Otherwise the search for a site usually led to some convenient location just outside the traditional retail core, such as Faneuil Hall Marketplace a few blocks from Boston's Washington Street shopping area.

After scrapping the urban renewal manual, city officials started talking to potential developers early to discover whether anyone wanted to build what they had in mind. Instead of working in isolation and learning later that their plans were unmarketable, they were able to decide on the size and makeup of projects with a realistic sense of private sector response. This reality testing was a major reason for the improved track record for downtown projects.

In San Diego early contact with developers resolved the doubts of city officials about what was feasible at Horton Plaza. Ernest Hahn's proposal to build a retail center led the city in that direction when the prevailing opinion among city staff was that developers would have little interest in downtown retailing. In San Diego as in other cities, reality testing continued through years of discussions with the developer as both sides sent up trial balloons to discover what would work.

When San Diego selected Hahn as the developer of Horton Plaza in May 1974, the city council gave him exclusive negotiating rights to prepare a detailed development agreement within ninety days. For the next three and one-half years the council kept voting extensions while Hahn talked with department store executives to find out what it would take to bring their stores downtown. City officials meanwhile came to the realization that their development ambitions were outrunning their managerial capacity. While Hahn chased department stores, they took the time to establish CCDC as a new nonprofit corporation to manage the project for the city and brought in Trimble as its executive director.

St. Paul went through a similar process. The two developers of Town Square, Carlson Companies and Oxford Development Group, made their first proposals to the city in early 1975. While the city voted extension after extension, both companies checked out the feasibility of their early plans. Carlson scaled back the size of his hotel when he was unable to get financing for it, and Oxford decided to build its office towers in two stages when executives had trouble leasing space in advance. Mayor Latimer reorganized the city's development agencies to shore up public control of the big project that was coming, and he put pressure on the Port Authority to help out by taking responsibility for an underground parking garage. By late 1977, nearly three years after the original proposals, the developers were able to come to terms among themselves, the Port Authority, and the city to make a firm start on the project.

This commitment of time to test project feasibility transformed advance planning from a city hall operation into a mutual exploration of opportunities and problems. The result was a more informed sense on all sides of what was realistic and where the obstacles were.

In addition, talking back and forth put an end to the elitism of earlier downtown planning. Developers and retail executives were almost always trying to figure out how a project could attract the masses. Except for a handful of upscale ventures, they had their sights on the broad middle of the market rather than the thin ranks of highbrows with money. Since developers took the lead in discovering what was feasible, they had plenty of scope to promote their own ideas about how to make projects popular. It was a full turnabout from the time when a federal renewal official had told shopping center developers not to use their imagination but to build according to the city's dictates.

Deals to Match Projects

Most cities approached their new retail projects with a standard opening offer: they would supply the developer with a site ready for building, sell it below cost, and take responsibility for building a parking structure. But there was no ready formula for pricing this setup or for working out specific terms of an agreement. City negotiators were usually willing to cut a special deal on price and to tailor design terms for each project. The deal, however, would have to meet the needs of both city officials and the developer. For the city the basic need was to make the project politically defensible; for the developer the bottom line was economics.

The basic agreement on Faneuil Hall Marketplace had terms that worked for both the city and the developer. After the redevelopment authority bought the property, relocated the remaining merchants, took down a poorly placed highway ramp, and put in new utility lines, normal renewal practice would have called for selling the site to the developer at a reduced price. Instead staff members came up with an unconventional proposal. They believed they would be better able to protect the historic buildings, the main purpose of the project, by keeping them in public ownership instead of selling them to the developer. Selling the market buildings might have looked too much like selling the Boston Common. This arrangement had advantages for the Rouse Company as well because it minimized start-up costs. The company faced extraordinary early expenses to renovate the interiors of the old structures, but by paying an annual rent for the expensive downtown site instead of a lump sum to buy it outright, it could hold down the need to borrow money.

In setting the rent Rouse would pay, the redevelopment authority again departed from convention in a way that gave advantages to both the city and the developer. The city's primary goal was a guaranteed income from the property. In addition, officials no longer thought of themselves as donors making a grant for a public purpose. They considered themselves coinvestors in a potentially profitable venture, and they wanted a share of the returns as compensation for their risks. At the same time they recognized Rouse's interest in keeping his annual payments in line with the actual performance of the project, which was hard to predict.

They negotiated an agreement for Rouse's rent to take the form of payments in lieu of taxes, and they phased in these payments over a three-year period corresponding to successive completion of the three market buildings. Rouse agreed to pay $200,000 in the first year of operations, $400,000 in the second year, and $600,000, or 20 percent of gross rental income from retail tenants, whichever was larger, from the third year onward. This deal gave the city two political benefits: a guaranteed income from the property plus a chance to share upside gains. At the same time it limited Rouse's payments to the guaranteed minimum unless the project was a big success. Boston was one of many cities that began to negotiate for a form of profit sharing in the 1970s. Baltimore, Milwaukee, Philadelphia, and others followed suit, as did San Diego, which tried to tie Hahn's payments to the performance record of Horton Plaza.

By the 1970s city officials expanded their aid inventory for downtown projects, adding to their bargaining chips for striking deals. On top of land assembly, cost write-down, and parking provision, they began to build more of the supporting facilities for shopping malls: new streets, skywalks, parks, and plazas. In a few cases, such as Philadelphia, they even built the mall structure itself. They became more imaginative brokers of financial support to sweeten a deal, using their contacts and proposal-writing skills to raise money from business organizations, historic preservation societies, private foundations, and federal agencies that still had programs for cities. Drawing on a wider variety of financing techniques—leasing land and buildings to developers and floating tax-exempt lease-revenue bonds—some put together complex transactions that broke new ground for public finance.

City negotiators used more elaborate aid packages to cope with the serious obstacles they faced. These were no simple giveaways; the complexity of the projects, plus continuing frictions and conflicts, led to hard bargaining on all sides. When the St. Paul Port Authority took responsibility for building a garage under Town Square, for example, its staff had to negotiate air rights agreements with two developers, determine what supports to build for structures above the garage and where to build them, establish a formula for sharing the cost of these supports with the developers, and work out logistics when all the contractors were swarming on the site at once. At one point negotiations went on for thirty-two days straight, with eleven lawyers.

Operating with new forms of aid, city negotiators improvised deals to get projects built. San Diego, for example, tailored its support to help Hahn line up the essential department stores. When Hahn began courting anchor tenants, he discovered that one glimpse of conditions around Horton Plaza was enough to frighten them away. To minimize their exposure to the street scene, he used to take them to the roof of a nearby office building for a bird's-eye view. When the president of one retail chain insisted on a closer look, Hahn reluctantly took him past the Pussycat Theater, the Saigon Bar, and the $10-a-night hotels. While walking, they came upon a skid row denizen who was urinating into his own shoe. Hahn said nothing, hoping the incident would go unnoticed. But his visitor tugged at his sleeve and said, "Ernie, did you see what that man is doing?" Ever the enterprising salesman, Hahn replied, "He is going to need new shoes, and if you had a store here you could sell them to him."

After the first series of rebuffs, Hahn realized he could not get a department store downtown unless he could promise that conditions were going to improve. His next move was what he called "an old developer's ploy." First, he got the city to say it would do certain things if the stores were there. Then he approached the businesses and assured them of city support if they came into the project. Finally he signed them to letters of agreement subject to the city making good on its promises.

Hahn and the department store presidents wanted a commitment from the city to clean up some of the shabbier parts of town by building several thousand houses and a convention center. In his first proposal Hahn had asked the city to develop housing in the run-down and partly empty industrial areas between Horton Plaza and the shoreline. By 1976 the presidents of Robinson's and Mervyn's announced publicly that they would join the project if the city met their conditions, including the development of a marina, housing, and a convention center nearby. With backing from Mayor Wilson and lobbying by the downtown business organization of San Diegans, Inc., the city council approved plans in 1976 for 4,000 houses, a marina, and a convention center in two newly created redevelopment projects south and west of the retail site. These undertakings were an exception to the tendency of cities to limit themselves to small, strategic projects. They made up for San Diego's underdeveloped downtown and set the stage for two anchor store commitments and for a firm deal between the city and Hahn the following year.

St. Paul also came up with unusual forms of aid to suit the special problems it faced with Town Square. Downtown St. Paul was in such desperate shape that no developer would risk building a retail complex there without a generous measure of help. For Mayor Latimer the political imperative was to do whatever was necessary to avoid any more abortive projects. City officials plunged in with far-reaching assistance and carved out a public role that ran through all stages of the project, from start-up to management.

First, St. Paul handled typical city functions: feasibility studies, land assembly and write-down, parking construction, street and sidewalk improvements. Then the city broke through conventional public-private boundaries by deciding to act as developer for critical parts of the complex. In the original plan the city proposed to build a three-story glass-roofed galleria that would pass through the office-hotel-retail complex and form its main shopping axis and to build skyways connecting Town Square to neighboring buildings. When a reduction in the size of the hotel necessitated a new design, city architects eliminated the galleria and substituted three levels of public space, a pathway to the stores, skyway connections, and a 30,000-square-foot public park enclosed on the rooftop. For all these public elements of the project, the city took responsibility for financing, design, construction, ownership, and operation.

The deal in St. Paul was an agreement for joint public-private development, which suited both the city and the two developers. It suited the developers because it relieved them of the considerable expense they would normally bear for public spaces to bring people to their doors. By knocking at least $13 million off the development cost for Town Square, St. Paul materially reduced the risk of opening a shopping mall in a weak downtown location. But giving help in the form of a generous amount of public space, with city officials deciding on its design and management, also suited Latimer's purpose of creating a civic showpiece. In addition, spending city money for a park and walkways was easier to justify politically than turning over a check to the developer, since the new public areas would be an amenity for the community as well as an asset for a private project.

Development by Consensus

The elaborate aid packages that cities put together drew them more deeply into the supervision of retail centers. As they shared more of the risks, they asked for greater control. When they took charge of developing parts of the project, shared control was the most practical way to proceed. The details of building a shopping mall are almost infinite. While it was possible to settle some of the big issues in advance, as the St. Paul Port Authority tried to do in its marathon negotiations, there was no way to anticipate all the details far in advance of the actual work. Further, the demands of mutually dependent construction procedures overlapping in time and space ruled out the hands-off control style of urban renewal. For St. Paul to cut a straightforward deal, prepare and transfer the property, and then watchdog the developer's performance until the project was done according to plan was out of the question.

The deal in St. Paul and in the other cities was an implied agreement to share both design and management decisions throughout the development period and to cope with problems by renegotiating earlier understandings if necessary. Frequent trips back to the bargaining table were a way to get projects over unexpected obstacles. They were also a way for the cities to work on details that would otherwise be left to developers, and sometimes these details were as important as the character of the public park on top of Town Square.

To simplify construction management, St. Paul agreed to hire the same architects who were designing Oxford's office and retail complex. Oxford had a long-term relationship with Skidmore, Owings, and Merrill, a firm well known for the clean, modern look of its glass-box office towers. Skidmore's design for the park showed a mostly open area that could be used flexibly for many purposes but that had little within it to attract anyone. Its hard surfaces and open plan looked more like a sleek office building lobby than the green oasis that city staff had in mind. Gary Stout, Latimer's development director, called the design "disastrous."

Stout took a St. Paul delegation to visit Oxford's Toronto Dominion Square project in Calgary, which served as a model for Town Square. It too had a rooftop park, one that made fuller use of water and landscaping to create gardens that Stout liked. He tracked down the landscape architect responsible for the Calgary park, brought him to St. Paul, and prevailed on him to do a schematic design for Town Square Park. With this scheme as a starting point, Stout persuaded Skidmore to draw a new plan featuring water, plants, and a different layout with distinct spaces for recreation, exhibits, and public events. Even with the new plan, he worried that Skidmore's fondness for clean surfaces might produce a barren look. To be sure he could fill the park with greenery, he doubled the architect's order for plants.

Most of the deals struck gave developers and their designers plenty of latitude to be inventive, but they also gave city officials a chance to step in when the plans fell short of expectations. Even the most inventive developers had lapses, and the two-way check on project plans proved useful in one city after another. Boston, for instance, had a greater voice in development decisions at the Faneuil Hall markets than it would have had in a more customary arm's-length relationship with a developer. During an early stage of planning, Rouse wanted to build a partial roof connecting the three market buildings in order to protect shoppers against New England weather. Although Thompson was strongly opposed to covering any part of the celebrated buildings, Rouse might well have insisted, but he had made a last-minute promise to consult with Mayor White step by step while the project was under way, and White settled the matter quickly by ruling out an enclosure.

Once cities expected to share major decisions, they no longer pressed for deals that spelled out everything in advance. For developers it was not unusual to launch a venture before straightening out the details, but for normally cautious public officials this freewheeling style was something new. In St. Paul Latimer got Town Square into construction before he confronted the question of how much the city would contribute toward the cost of heating, cooling, cleaning, and maintaining all the public spaces within the retail complex. After Oxford's president forced the issue, it took five years of on-and-off negotiations to produce an acceptable cost-sharing formula.

San Diego ran even greater risks by cutting a deal on Horton Plaza that had huge holes in it. The first development agreement committed the city to finance and build a 2,000-car parking garage but left wide open the terms on which Hahn would lease it. Worse still, city negotiators had found Hahn's first project plan unsatisfactory but put off decisions on the makeup and design of the center. Meanwhile the city was ready to start buying land and relocating people on the basis of an unfinished agreement. Hahn too was taking risks since he had no way of knowing when the city would build the housing and convention center it had promised. But the agreement gave him the right to drop the project if the city failed to carry out its commitments, if the anchor stores withdrew, or if he could not arrange financing. The city had no such protection once it began assembling land because its holdings would be of questionable value without Hahn to convert them into a commercial operation.

San Diego and St. Paul took extra risks by leaving issues open because their alternative was even less attractive. Waiting to work out the operating cost agreement in St. Paul and the parking lease and project design in San Diego could easily have added several years to the already snail-paced start in both places. Besides, the agreement that counted most was not about project specifics but about sharing major decisions. As long as the mayors were sure of their seat at the negotiating table, they could live with gaps in the deal. With both the cities and the developers pouring increasing resources into a project, both would have big stakes in finishing it, and there was always tomorrow to work out the issues that remained.

Development by consensus was a key to city success in mall building. It meant that the cities were no longer big brothers in advance planning, and developers were no longer the master builders who took over once the plans were done. Cities and developers that depended on each other had to find deals both could accept. And with development handled through ongoing negotiations, each separate deal was less than conclusive; most were incomplete and temporary, subject to revision by mutual consent.

City Hall Deal Makers

Before city governments could handle development negotiations successfully, they had to change. Until the 1970s the technical staff that managed redevelopment was seldom knowledgeable enough about real estate to do a critical analysis of a developer's figures, let alone calculate a reasonable public subsidy for a project. But as real estate development became more professionalized, a growing number of people acquired the knowledge for this work. The Boston Redevelopment Authority brought in Stewart Forbes, a Harvard Business School graduate and member of a leading Boston development firm, as a real estate consultant and then as deputy director for development. Forbes's analyses revealed several flaws in Rouse's arguments during negotiations over his annual payments. Mayor Latimer recruited an experienced deal maker, Gary Stout, who had learned about real estate development while directing downtown revitalization for Portland, Oregon. Other cities relied on specialized consulting firms knowledgeable about project economics and the development industry. San Diego worked closely with the San Francisco firm of Keyser Marston Associates from the earliest stages of planning Horton Plaza. When Trimble took over as chief negotiator, he continued to use Keyser Marston's advice on such questions as how much to charge Hahn for the land and how much of the project the city could afford to finance.

Aside from acquiring new technical skills, the cities moved their retail projects along by making changes in their own administrative systems. The agencies that dealt with developers were regulators, not promoters, and by the 1970s their regulation had come to include a maze of reviews, hearings, studies, and approval requirements known collectively as the "permit explosion." In suburbia developers were often tied up for years in pinball tactics that bounced them from one agency to another and sometimes back again for a second round. City officials who wanted to promote development tried to offer a more direct approval process, and those who worked on retail malls usually used informal pressure to keep paper shuffling and foot dragging to a minimum.

Several cities took the extra measure of establishing a new organization to manage downtown development and the deal making that went with it. In St. Paul Latimer reorganized city government soon after his election to consolidate planning and development functions in a single agency under his control. Seattle set up the Preservation and Development Authority to renovate the historic core of the Pike Place Market rather than ask existing city agencies to do the job. And San Diego established CCDC with its independent board of directors drawn from the business community.

Creating new staff positions and new agencies was a way of promoting downtown development without making massive changes in the bureaucracy. It added a small group of people in leadership positions and gave them high status, high salaries, and unusual freedom to wheel and deal on behalf of the city. Once they made their deals, they usually worked as advocates and expediters for the projects they had negotiated. Trimble served as the main point of contact between Hahn's project manager for Horton Plaza and city government agencies. Trimble, for example, set up and attended meetings with the building department to go over fire safety features of the project and checked back later to make sure all problems were resolved. In St. Paul the new development agency set up a fast-track review system that allowed construction to proceed stage by stage at Town Square while the architects were working on plans for the next phase.

Deal makers in city government did not throw out paper pushers. Instead they found ways to work alongside them. While most city staff in regulatory and development offices kept doing their jobs in the usual way, certain agency heads and senior officials kept pressing them to cut through red tape on projects in which the city was an investor.

The mayors backed up their deal-making aides by getting personally involved as troubleshooters from time to time. While St. Paul, for example, was wooing Dayton's and Donaldsons to anchor Town Square, the suburban town of Woodbury approached these same stores with a proposal for a competing mall. But Woodbury needed a special ramp from an interstate highway to make its mall possible, and Latimer lobbied the metropolitan planning agency to disapprove the highway connection. At the same time he lobbied the department stores to stay in downtown. Mayoral troubleshooting was an extension of the new relationships between city government and downtown developers. It meant that once a city cut a deal for a project, the developer could count on behind-the-scenes help from city hall.

Coping with Crisis

Between the closing of the deal and the opening of the mall, the typical downtown project lurched from crisis to crisis. While the developer, city officials, department store executives, and mortgage lenders tried to work out their many conflicts, business slumps, tax changes, lawsuits, company takeovers, and rising interest rates produced calamities that rained down on these projects like biblical plagues. And emergencies came without much letup. While San Diego negotiators were working with Ernest Hahn on Horton Plaza, for example, there were three mayoral elections, three economic recessions, bouts of double-digit inflation that sent interest rates soaring, two lawsuits challenging the project, a change in ownership of the Hahn Company, and enactment of the tax-limiting Proposition 13 that paralyzed public financing of redevelopment in California.

Coping with unpredictable events was a crucial test of the new decision sharing. For developers, going back to the drawing board was not unusual, although having to consult with city representatives was a complication. City negotiators, in contrast, had to learn how to take apart a development deal and put it together differently. In Horton Plaza all the buffeting from outside events led the inside decision makers to come up with nine different design plans, four changes in anchor tenants, and three major overhauls of the original deal in addition to dozens of minor ones.

City negotiators and developers were ready to strike new bargains to handle surprises; in effect, their deals were never final. After Boston selected the Rouse Company to develop the Faneuil Hall markets, both sides sorted out misunderstandings and spelled out terms in ways that changed the original deal. Under the new agreement city officials calculated Rouse's lease payments as a percentage of his rent roll, but they first made a deduction to recognize his exceptional operating costs in this downtown location. Rouse in turn agreed to make additional lease payments on any income over $3 million a year, up to a preset ceiling.

Soon after the negotiators came to terms, restoration workers found the buildings in worse shape than anyone had realized. Because water leakage over the years had rotted many of the old beams, the cost of restoration was going to be more than the city could afford under its federal grant. Rouse estimated that he would end up spending an extra million dollars because of the water damage—exactly the sort of unforeseen problem that made downtown mall development risky. He had not yet signed the lease and wanted the city to reduce his payments by a million dollars during the first three years.

The redevelopment authority agreed to reopen negotiations. Although Rouse's staff wanted to be compensated in full for the higher construction costs, city negotiators argued that downtown rents had already increased enough to offset part of these costs. They were ready to acknowledge Rouse's point, but they also wanted to avoid the difficult problem of verifying the cost of extra repairs. After discussions that ran more than a year, they gave Rouse most of what he wanted in exchange for a still greater share of future revenues over $3 million, up to a cap of 25 percent of income after the adjustment for operating expenses. City negotiators were willing to make concessions because they considered the project risky and wanted Rouse to have financial incentives to get it done as soon as possible.

Public-private deals were open to more sweeping revisions, with cities and developers swapping responsibilities. Horton Plaza faced a life-threatening financial crisis in the late 1970s, five years after Hahn started work on the project. The original deal committed San Diego to assemble the land, rebuild streets and utilities, expand Horton Plaza Park, and build a 2,000-car parking garage. Enactment of Proposition 13 in a statewide taxpayer revolt in 1978 cut the city's property tax rate and crippled its ability to finance the project out of tax increments collected in the district around Horton Plaza. To keep the project alive, Hahn offered to make annual payments in lieu of taxes equal to what he would have paid before Proposition 13, to make an interest-free advance toward the purchase price he would later pay for the land, and to build more of the parking himself instead of holding the city to its obligation. Trimble gave up a half-block site he had planned to lease to Hahn in exchange for a share of retail rents from the mall stores.

As construction costs and interest rates kept escalating during the following two years, even this revised deal financially strapped the city. In 1981 Trimble and Hahn went back to the table once more, and this time Hahn agreed to build all the parking, including more than 3,000 spaces for Horton Plaza and 450 to honor a promise the city had made to the developer of an adjacent office building. By taking full responsibility for the garages, Hahn had saved San Diego millions of dollars, and Trimble in turn was willing to cut the price the city would charge for the land. Hahn argued that because of the many concessions he had made he should pay nothing at all for the site. But each revised deal still had to meet political tests. Although there was some merit to Hahn's position, Trimble was sure that giving him the land would endanger city council support. With a municipal election approaching, he already had his hands full explaining why Hahn was going to pay only $1 million for a site that had cost the city $18 million. Three special provisions helped Trimble sell the deal politically: Hahn's earlier profit-sharing agreement on rental income from mall tenants, a new agreement for Hahn to pay the city a percentage of parking revenues, and a commitment to share the net cash flow from office space planned for a second phase of construction. Further, Trimble was able to point to interest savings on $5 million in loans and advances from the Hahn Company as another form of compensation.

The complexity of these deals provided plenty of bargaining chips for the negotiators, but what was at stake was more than role swapping. Escalating construction costs and municipal bond rates were pricing the project out of the city's reach. Even while Trimble and Hahn kept striking deals, the public cost climbed relentlessly from $29 million in 1977 to $49 million in 1979 and up to $54 million in a mid-1980 plan. In late 1981 Trimble and Hahn agreed on a deal that cut the public investment back to $33 million while the developer's cost more than tripled since 1977. Although city concessions fell far short of offsetting Hahn's new costs, the deal was tolerable for Hahn, salable for Trimble, and consistent with the tax limits mandated by Proposition 13.

Negotiable Designs

Problem solving also led developers and city officials to change the physical design of projects. More often than not, their design revisions made the downtown malls more distinctive and better able to compete with suburban shopping centers.

The story of Horton Plaza is one of steady change in the character of the project, from an early plan dismissed as "a suburban shopping center set on four levels of parking" to one of the most unconventional retail centers in the country—a blend of theme park, theaters, and department stores in a compact, multilevel, open-air plan that left very few industry standards unbroken. All this happened even though participating department stores were opposed to changing the rules. Most of it happened because there were problems that everyone wanted to resolve, and the solution to each of these problems moved the project, one step at a time, further and further away from the tried and true suburban mall.

Parking is a revealing example. One of the basic attractions of suburban malls has always been plenty of free parking and when developers built malls in the cornfields they were able to surround them with enough parking space to handle even the Christmas rush with room to spare. But downtown land is much too expensive to be used for parking lots, and garages are costly. Further, large parking structures around the malls cut them off from the rest of downtown, defeating the underlying goal of bringing people into the business district. Nor is it necessary to build so much parking as part of the project since some shoppers come by public transportation and others from the downtown itself—nearby offices, hotels, and convention centers. After Plaza Pasadena opened in 1980, Hahn and Trimble had direct experience with the misapplication of suburban parking standards to downtown. With two levels of underground parking built an enormous expense, the lower level was empty most of the year, and a survey showed that 18 percent of the shoppers were coming by bus or on foot.

Yet department store executives had suburban parking standards in mind for any new shopping center, and when Hahn made his first detailed proposal to San Diego in 1974 he insisted that the project would have to conform to the customary ratio of at least five parking spaces per 1,000 square feet of retail floor area. At the time of the first formal deal between Hahn and the city in 1977, two department stores had expressed no more than conditional interest in the project, and the parking standard remained unchanged. By 1979 the project had become more attractive to department stores. Hahn had four lined up by then, and the three that were first to enter wanted larger stores than in the original plan. In the revised deal at that time Hahn agreed to build more of the parking himself, but he and Trimble together were no longer willing to give the department stores as much parking as in the earlier agreement. From his position of greater bargaining strength, Hahn was able to eliminate 300 spaces by shaving the ratio without losing any anchor stores.

Department stores were in a squeeze once more when the financing pressures of Proposition 13 forced Trimble to make the site smaller and Hahn to make corresponding cuts in the dimensions of their building pads. This move violated another taboo by forcing the stores to build three levels of shopping instead of their usual two. Despite these affronts to the usual expectations of department store executives, interest was growing, and Hahn was able to bring in two higher-line stores, Broadway and Nordstrom, the latter in exchange for the promise of a place in Hahn's suburban University Town Centre.

By 1981 the new agreement that transferred total responsibility for parking to Hahn took out 270 spaces promised in 1979 while adding more than 100,000 square feet of retail space. Already convinced that conventional standards were excessive for downtown, neither Hahn nor Trimble worried about this cut. The city planning staff in San Diego favored less parking as a way to encourage more people to use public transportation. Hahn persuaded department store executives to go along by promising that when extra spaces were needed during peak evening and weekend periods, their customers could use nearby office parking space that he controlled. For the Christmas rush he worked out a shuttle bus arrangement between other downtown garages and Horton Plaza. When still further cost cutting was necessary, a new agreement in October 1982 eliminated 100 more spaces without serious protests from the anchor stores.

In short Hahn and Trimble were able to plan an unconventional retail center on a compact site by starting with a traditional proposal acceptable to conservative anchor tenants and then changing it in stages as the project progressed. Normally the anchor stores would have been able to resist any changes they disliked by using their great bargaining power with the developer, and normally they would have had great influence over the entire project. But Hahn was able to limit their influence during the planning period. As the list of interested department stores grew, he had the leverage to change his plans without breaking up his strong collection of anchors.

While reducing the space for parking made the center more compact and opened better connections from adjoining streets, Trimble and Hahn also found other solutions that made the mall less like its suburban counterparts. In the first flurry of activity after Proposition 13, Trimble started negotiations with one developer who wanted to put up a twenty-story office tower in the project area and with another who wanted to build a hotel. Both would improve Horton Plaza's balance sheet by paying for their sites and by generating future tax increments. They would bring in more people and create greater diversity, coupling a hotel and office building to restaurants, department stores, specialty shops, and performing arts theaters. The result would have the intense activity of a mixed-use complex combining attractions for day and night.

A few years later Hahn followed the same strategy for improving his own balance sheet. After agreeing to build all the parking and to swallow other large-cost items, he had to find ways to economize.

One way was to pack more usable space onto the site. Hahn's retail center grew from 563,000 square feet in the original deal to 650,000 in 1979 and 780,000 in 1981. When he and his architect, John Jerde, restudied the plans to find a way to fit two large parking garages into the scheme, they decided to do away with a proposed ice skating rink. To save money on both construction and operating costs, they defied industry standards once more by scrapping plans to enclose and air-condition the mall. While losing the ice rink may have been unfortunate, an open mall was well suited to the exceptionally agreeable climate of San Diego, where sun and sea breezes would even reinforce the Mediterranean quality that Jerde wanted to achieve. Taking away the enclosure also helped integrate the project more successfully with surrounding streets and buildings.

As far as city negotiators were concerned, Hahn could have his redesign in exchange for taking over increasing financial responsibility for the project. This was the essence of the deal during the last few years of negotiation. The changes Hahn wanted—a more compact development, on more levels, without an air-conditioned enclosure—met his needs without upsetting Trimble or city officials. There was little reason for anyone to believe the project would suffer as a result, and its unusual character could be a strong selling point in competition with the conventional malls that were ringing up sales in suburban San Diego.

The Relationship Is the Deal

The provisional deals that cities made with developers were well suited to these downtown projects. Their looseness allowed both sides to move ahead without having to resolve every issue in advance and left plenty of freedom for creative problem solving. Deals meant to be revised, however, are not easy to enforce or to explain to the public.

When Hahn took over responsibility for the parking garages, he sited one on the edge of the project facing the Gaslamp Quarter, a historic area where property owners were renovating turn-of-the-century buildings and replacing remaining porno shops with more respectable enterprises. The Gaslamp merchants and city officials were anxious to have a lively street at this edge of Horton Plaza, and Hahn agreed to build 20,000 square feet of retail shops at ground level rather than line this side of the street with garage walls. During the late stages of design, however, the Hahn company found that they could get enough parking spaces without extending their garage all the way to the street. There would be a leftover parcel 50 feet wide and 350 feet long bordering the street, with enough room for another commercial building.

Hahn Company president John Gilchrist checked with Trimble, and both agreed it would make no sense to have a row of stores as part of a garage fifty feet back from the sidewalk, even though that is what their formal disposition and development agreement (DDA) specified. Without taking time to amend their agreement, they decided to omit the retail space for the time being and to figure out a more appropriate way to complete their side of the street by using the leftover site for a new building.

When Horton Plaza opened for business, its street frontage facing the Gaslamp Quarter was a mess. Construction barricades were still in place, and an unpaved strip fifty feet wide led to the cagelike rear of a concrete parking structure six levels high. Gaslamp retailers were furious. City councilman Uvaldo Martinez called this back end of Horton Plaza "a disgrace . . . and an absolute affront to the Gaslamp Quarter." The Hahn Company proposed temporary improvements until a stronger real estate market would justify a new office-retail building. Trimble wanted to move faster toward a long-range solution. He proposed buying back the unused site and turning it over to a developer who would build six stories of loft-style apartments with retail stores at street level. His plan was consistent with the city's goal of encouraging more people to live downtown, and it met the needs of the Gaslamp merchants across the way. But local reporters began to raise troublesome questions about the nature of the development agreement in which Hahn had promised to take care of the problem without additional compensation.

Trimble understood that the city would have to pay Hahn something for the 50-foot site, for seventy-five parking spaces that would be taken out of retail use and set aside for apartment residents, and for a new ventilation system after the six-story building sealed off the open end of the garage. He estimated a total payment of about $1.3 million to cover these items. The press simplified this transaction as payment of $1.3 million for a small strip of land, and they compared it to the $1 million Hahn had paid for the entire 11.5 acres in Horton Plaza. Hahn's payment in reality was not for the land but for a business opportunity hedged about with restrictions on what to build and handicapped by his agreement to pay for all the parking, share profits with the city, and make a series of interest-free loans and advances. But in the shorthand of the press, it was what he paid for the land.

The job was to explain to a suspicious press and council that the transaction was not a giveaway. Explaining that neither payment represented a price for the land was one thing. There was also the matter of the formal disposition and development agreement, widely understood as a solemn contract and not a temporary deal. As critics put it, "The city would pay the Hahn Co. to let Hahn out of an agreement that Hahn has been unwilling or unable to meet." When reporters went to San Diego's legal department to find out why the city would not simply sue Hahn to get him to build stores along the street, they began to discover that deals could have loose ends. A city attorney described the DDA as "a legally enforceable document" but explained that "some items are listed in more or less general terms. We could go to court on any DDA, but I can't recall that we have in the recent past." More important, he described the DDA as "more or less a working partnership between the developer and the city, with CCDC as the middleman." John Gilchrist spoke similarly: "The DDA is a general partnership agreement. It has to allow some flexibility."

City council members, Gaslamp Council activists, and most civic leaders soon rallied around Trimble's proposal. They were anxious to resolve a troublesome problem and understood the nuances of development deals well enough to feel no outrage. But the flexibility that developers and city officials both want is at odds with the general belief that a deal is a deal. In recent development practice a deal is only a milestone marking the status of negotiations at some point in time. The basic deal is a commitment to keep going back to the bargaining table as long as there are problems to settle.

The deals that cities cut with developers had the ring of a highly entrepreneurial style. City officials took on the functions of originating projects, advancing the money and staff to launch them, testing the waters for private sector interest, and finding a developer. After getting over these early hurdles, they continued to take heavy risks by operating on the basis of incomplete deals and pouring public funds into land assembly while developers still had escape hatches available. As coinvestors in private projects, cities were also subject to the normal business risks of recessions, inflation, anchor store withdrawals, and company takeovers. Their deals provided for returns as well as risks, sometimes including profit sharing, but future income was exposed to the further risk that shoppers might not like the unconventional malls.

Downtown projects depended on adroit deal making; they also depended on a climate of opinion that gave city negotiators the freedom to wheel and deal. By the 1970s voters and elected officials had reasons to accept wheeling and dealing on behalf of the city and to understand it as deal making in the public interest. Hard times with inflation and recession had generated widespread support for economic development and for projects to revive downtown business. The sorry state of downtown intensified public impatience for results and encouraged elected officials to take the risks of bold action. Moreover, the removal of most federal rules after urban renewal folded in 1974 invited cities to improvise their own ways of managing development.

The nature of the projects also gave city officials wide leeway to operate on their own. These were complicated ventures involving cities with developers, retailers, and financiers. Hammering out agreements that might run to 150 pages of fine print demanded not only time but flexibility. To have any chance of succeeding, the negotiators had to meet behind closed doors. When cities managed to find negotiators with real estate competence who could hold up their end of the bargaining, the most practical way to proceed was to let them act as deal makers authorized to represent the city. If they gave away too much, elected officials could always vote the project down. And the negotiators were careful to cultivate public support by making sure their deals met political as well as economic standards. Finally, they kept the public trust by negotiating financing plans with special care. When it came to sharing project costs with the developer and figuring out how to pay the bills, city negotiators understood that no matter how badly they needed the money, they would have to keep their fingers out of the pockets of local taxpayers.

8

Getting and Spending

After city officials got up from the negotiating table, they had to figure out how to pay for their promises. With Washington on the retreat and municipal budgets under strain, cities' traditional financial arteries were tightening steadily. Juggling their budgets just to keep up municipal services, most mayors were in no position to ask voters for special funds for downtown retail projects.

In cutting deals, city officials tried to avoid making outright cash grants to developers. They assisted projects in other ways, such as by offering tax abatements, leasing city-owned land or buildings, and making loans to be repaid at below-market rates or on deferred schedules. They kept public spending under control by choosing small sites and negotiating the best cost-sharing formulas they could get. But one way or another they had to come up with subsidies to cover the premium for in-town land and parking, offset the carrying charges for slow-moving projects, and overcome the reluctance of retailers to venture downtown. These facts dictated the size of the bill cities agreed to pay in order to compete with the suburbs.

That bill varied widely from city to city. In thirty-nine projects completed between 1971 and 1985 the public contribution ranged from as little as 3 percent up to 83 percent of the development cost. In half the projects the public share fell between 20 and 50 percent, with a median of 32 percent. For the full Pike Place Market projects, the public share came to 34 percent; for Town Square, 21 percent; for Faneuil Hall Marketplace, 28 percent; and for Horton Plaza, 25 percent.

Paying without Pain

This level of cost sharing added up to more public money in the deal than most local officials ever acknowledged. When we asked mayors and top city administrators how much they had put into their new retail centers, typical answers were "not a penny" or "very little." Further questioning revealed that most did not consider federal aid to be money the cities spent, nor did they count off-budget outlays as actual spending, and when project appropriations were spread over several years, they lost track of what was spent in the past. To calculate what cities actually spent, we counted all their expenses for studies, plans, administration, land, relocation, and construction, regardless of whether the money came from higher levels of government, bond issues, or local appropriations. Even federal grants were a form of city outlay since the cities could have applied to use them for other purposes.

In comparison with past practices, the cost-sharing arrangements for downtown malls put most cities on the line financially. Although urban renewal projects often required cities to come up with contributions that were equally large, most took advantage of federal regulations that allowed them to pay with public works instead of cash. Cities that did their retail projects under urban renewal, such as Seattle and Boston, were therefore able to put in almost no money of their own. But most downtown malls came too late for renewal funding, and cities had to pay hard cash for bills that ran to more than $20 million in St. Paul and more than $39 million in San Diego.

City officials coped with the big subsidies by searching for painless ways to pay them. The first obvious strategy was still to go to Washington. As federal funds became scarce, city deal makers tapped into financial techniques that called on local resources or future project income: revenue bonds, tax-increment bonds, hotel or other special use taxes, loans from city agencies, and cash advances from developers. Some of these procedures were standbys of public finance, others were creative applications of methods commonly used to finance private developments, and one—tax-increment financing—was a legislative solution tailored for the problem at hand. The logic of using one or another of these techniques varied, but the political imperative was consistent: to avoid going after current tax appropriations.

Some of the costs did not show up on the city budget because they were the responsibility of an independent redevelopment authority. Other public costs were shifted to nonlocal taxpayers because the subsidy came from federal tax advantages. Still other subsidies were hidden because they diverted only future revenues from the municipal treasury, or they drew on city funds only if the project ran into financial trouble. And still other parts of the bill would not show up in a conventional accounting because cities paid them by letting the developer increase the value of the project through building more rentable space. Whether these devices amounted to hoodwinking the voters or stretching public resources creatively is an issue we discuss later. In the 1970s, however, few observers raised questions because these were pragmatic solutions to build sought-after projects, and their applications were too novel (or unknown) to generate widespread criticism.

The Federal Pipeline: Good to the Last Drop

For over two decades Washington served as the vault from which city officials could draw funds to rebuild downtown. After the urban renewal cutoff in 1974, they could still tap community development grants and special-purpose awards for housing, mass transit, historic preservation, and economic development. Some of this money came with strings attached, but city officials found ways to make the dollars work for them.

The Pike Place Market demonstrated what skillful fund raisers could still do with the federal aid catalog of the early 1970s. To renovate the crumbling market while keeping rents low enough for farmers demanded giant subsidies. Since the voter initiative made no provision for paying the bill, Mayor Uhlman and his staff had to figure out how to do it. They created the Preservation and Development Authority (PDA) to take responsibility for the historic core, funded it with $100,000, and channeled service contracts its way to get the agency off the ground financially. But for the big money Uhlman turned to Washington. An urban renewal project had already been approved for a 22-acre area, including the 7-acre core of the Pike Place Market slated for preservation. Even with drastic changes from clearance to renovation, the same renewal plan could still serve as Seattle's ticket to federal funding.

Seattle officials had no financing plan to cover all the restoration and development they wanted for the market. Their strategy was to divide the market into a series of twenty projects, look for federal grants for each one, and stage the work as they found money. Uhlman gave high priority to Pike Place and did much of the fund raising himself, following this tactic to the point where his critics accused him of spending more time in Washington than in Seattle. He had strong support from influential members of the Seattle congressional delegation, led by veteran senator Warren Magnuson. "We got far more than our share," Uhlman confided with a look of satisfaction. "When I became mayor in 1969, the federal flow was $39 million. Within a year it was almost $300 million."

As federal programs changed, Seattle's fund raisers were quick to shift from one source to another. By the time the Pike Place project was under way, the federal government was dismantling urban renewal. To help cities finish projects in midstream, the Department of Housing and Urban Development offered special "urgent needs" grants. Seattle got what it could from urban renewal and then went after urgent needs funding. After urban renewal was merged into the community development block grant program in 1974, it tapped that source as well. When the shutdown of the Boeing Aircraft assembly lines pushed Seattle's unemployment rate close to 20 percent, the city became eligible for special federal aid priority and exploited its advantage to the hilt. Seattle scored with the Carter administration's Urban Development Action Grant (UDAG) program too. The city even landed a grant from the Urban Mass Transportation Administration to build a cog railway down the steep hillside from the market to the waterfront. With a shift of plans, it used the money to build a stairway instead.

Because of superlative grantsmanship combined with a large federal aid budget left over from earlier appropriations, Seattle was able to finance almost all of the Pike Place project with $40 million in federal money. The only costs to the city were minor property tax losses resulting from the transfer of private market buildings to the tax-exempt PDA and occasional staff time not charged to federally funded projects. Seattle satisfied urban renewal cost-sharing requirements by building public works near the market and in other project areas.

To stretch the federal grants as far as possible, PDA director John Clise and his staff combined them with private mortgage loans. By approaching Seattle bankers with some $10 million in federal commitments for the historic core and by showing them conservative mortgage requests for properties that were sure to attract tenants, the PDA managed to raise about as much from private lenders as from Washington.

The aggressive raids on the federal treasury and leveraging of grants notwithstanding, money was always in short supply. When the authority needed additional cash for one of its projects, Clise found a way to sell a market building to private investors who could use the federal tax benefits allowable for rehabilitating a historic structure; the PDA protected itself by negotiating a long-term management contract to keep effective control of the property. Selling income tax benefits constituted one more form of federal subsidy for the Pike Place Market, and the technique was so novel for a public authority that Clise kept the transaction in low profile. Before these tax incentives were sharply cut back under the Tax Reform Act of 1986, the PDA repeated its maneuver for most of the other market buildings in order to cope with chronic budget problems.

For Seattle the timing was highly favorable for heavy federal funding. Later, even if the take was not as large, other cities kept finding their way to the federal till. The new UDAG program had a small pool of funds in comparison with earlier levels of support, but as the main federal program intended for redevelopment, it still brought money downtown. UDAG funds helped pay for half the projects we surveyed that were built after 1978.

Dwindling federal aid did not stop city officials from starting projects. Many were willing to live with uncertainty and improvise. Even more than their counterparts in Seattle, city officials in St. Paul took risks by starting Town Square without knowing how they would pay for it. Seattle could simply have stopped if the money ran out midway, since the different sections could operate independently of each other. But in St. Paul the project was a single unified complex for which the city had agreed to build public spaces and skyways to adjoining buildings. Although Town Square had its origin in a leftover urban renewal site, the project was built too late to use renewal funds for anything besides the superhole block.

The mayor and other city officials went far out on a limb by signing agreements with the developers and even starting construction before they had a firm plan for financing the public part. The city council voted to use federal community development block grants to buy extra land around the superhole site and then authorized a $5.9 million public galleria without providing either a funding source or a plan for covering operating costs. Apparently council members expected to use tax-increment financing, unaware that the tax-increment district they had set up for a 1974 bond issue had actually lost value since then and the prospects for early increments were poor. Gary Stout, Latimer's director of planning and economic development, learned from his Washington contacts that the Department of Housing and Urban Development was getting ready to make the first UDAG awards. The stated purpose of the program, to fill financing gaps in public-private economic development projects, was right for Town Square, and Stout lost no time filing an application. After negotiation and energetic lobbying, St. Paul plucked one of the first plums from the new money tree.

By drawing on urban renewal for superhole, a community development grant for the additional block, and a UDAG award for the public space, St. Paul managed to cover close to 60 percent of its $20 million share out of federal funds. For the rest of the money, the city used a strategy of layering one source on top of another. Latimer persuaded the port authority to issue bonds for the parking garage, later sold to Oxford at cost. By remapping the tax-increment district and floating new bonds in 1978, the city raised another $5.3 million. Then it negotiated a recovery of $3 million from Oxford for structural elements built at public expense that would also serve commercial parts of the complex, such as support columns for the retail floors and space for an underground food court. The sale of land and development rights from the newly cleared block added another $700,000, and the city managed to find private contributions to make up the rest. St. Paul put together a package of many parts, but the main source aside from federal aid was its own tax-exempt bond issues. These were tax-increment bonds, but in the event that the tax district failed to generate enough increments, the city pledged to make up the difference out of general revenue.

This turn to the city's own taxing power was a signal of what many other communities did as federal aid became harder to find. In part the switch was from one form of federal aid to another. Their bond issues were exempt from federal taxes and consequently sold at much lower rates of interest than taxable bonds. St. Paul's bond issues in 1978, for example, were marketed at rates of between 5.4 and 5.6 percent, fully three percentage points lower than prevailing rates for long-term, taxable government bonds. Instead of using federal grant appropriations, cities were using income tax subsidies to raise money from private investors. Either way, federal taxpayers as well as local ones were contributing to their projects. For the cities tax-exempt bond subsidies were preferable in some ways. As long as their bonds

were salable, they could avoid the delays of federal application procedures, the whims of Washington officials, and the uncertainties of
program funding.

Digging into Local Resources

Layered finance was only one strategy cities used for their downtown
retail projects. San Diego, like other California cities, had an active
preference to avoid using federal renewal funds in order to maintain
local control, and planned Horton Plaza from the outset as a nonfed-
eral project. Because of the high cost of land assembly and site preparation, San Diego had to come up with $39 million, considerably more
than the public outlay for Town Square.

San Diego taxpayers put up most of the public share but in indirect
ways that were less noticeable and less painful than through city
council appropriations. Nearly $15 million came from tax-increment
bonds. This off-budget financing meant that any increase in property
taxes collected from the area around Horton Plaza was reserved to
pay for redevelopment expenses. By 1977, years before the project
went into construction, the funds were flowing. Assessed values in
the redevelopment district had grown 265 percent, and the city was
capturing close to 80 percent of the district's tax revenues with annual
increments at nearly $1 million, or more than four times what it could
have expected in the absence of the special districting. These new tax
dollars would otherwise have gone to pay for city, county, and school
district expenses now supported instead by city and county taxpayers
at large. Until the bond payments were met, additional tax revenues
from the district were unavailable for other public outlays or for cutting local tax rates. To that extent they represented a cost to San Diego
city and county taxpayers.

San Diego officials were able to raise an exceptionally large amount
of money through tax-increment financing by capitalizing on some
special assets. They saw a bonanza coming from office and hotel
development, staked their claim early, and poured the new tax dollars into the coffers of the Horton Plaza project. First, their timing was
just about perfect. When they defined a tax-increment district in 1974,
downtown property values were still depressed. Second, they drew
the boundary to include blocks where they knew buildings would
soon be sprouting and where they thought they could steer more
investors. Third, they made sure the new developments paid taxes.
One of the projects in the works was a federal court and office build-

ing that covered three of the fifteen blocks in the district. As a federally owned building, it would have been tax exempt and therefore would have reduced the tax base of the area instead of adding to it. But they persuaded federal officials to lease it from a private owner, who would pay full taxes on it.

Another special asset was Ernest Hahn's personal commitment to fund the project. Between 1979 and 1982 the Hahn Company supplied $4 million in interest-free loans and advances to the CCDC to help with cash-flow problems. After the Trizec Corporation bought out Hahn in 1982, the company asked for repayment of the $4 million in order to improve its rate of return from Horton Plaza. Trimble and his staff scrambled to find a way to repay the loans without jeopardizing the project, but funds were tight and interest rates high. No proposed solution seemed to work until Ernest Hahn suggested that if the city issued more tax-increment bonds, he would personally bid for them at a low rate of interest.

San Diego taxpayers funded close to 30 percent of the city's contribution in another form. CCDC turned to city government for as much help as it could get and managed to arrange a loan of $9.5 million from the city's capital improvement funds and other municipal sources. The effect was to divert city funds and to postpone other projects for the sake of keeping Horton Plaza alive and solvent.

The rest of the money came from the project itself. Land sales to Hahn and other developers in the project area raised 10 percent of what the city needed. The remainder—about 17 percent—came from such project revenues as temporary leasing of land and interest earned on cash set aside for later expenses.

San Diego officials proved as adept as those in other cities at turning up diversified sources of funding, although in San Diego all the sources were local. On the other hand, they had more than the usual amount of cooperation from the developer. Still, San Diego demonstrated that under the right circumstances, it was possible to finance an ambitious downtown redevelopment program with no direct federal aid at all—and this at a time when most mayors considered it heresy even to think about rebuilding their cities without generous federal funding.

Safe Money for Risky Projects

If financing the public portion called for search-and-create strategies, financing the private portion of downtown malls called for marketing strategies. Developers had to work at selling lenders on downtown. A mall downtown put the spotlight on a factor that shopping center lenders usually took for granted: location. Financing suburban malls was synonymous with investing in population growth and retail volume, but not so downtown. Judging by conventional criteria, lenders saw all the trends going the wrong way: population was declining or stagnant at best; per capita purchasing power had not kept pace with the nation at large; and total employment was still declining despite the surge in office jobs throughout the 1970s. As fiduciaries responsible for other people's savings, how could lenders pledge insurance premiums, pension contributions, and passbook deposits for these risky retail investments when the economics looked so grim?

Downtown had a big image problem. Nowhere was this more evident than in St. Louis, a city falling into ruin so quickly that its main export was reportedly used brick. After several years of planning and false starts, the deal for the $175 million mixed-use project of St. Louis Centre was finally ready to go in 1981. The city had negotiated a $35.5 million public financing package, and the developer, Melvin Simon & Associates, submitted a loan application to Teachers Insurance and Annuity Association (TIAA). On the day the investment committee was to decide on the loan, the *New York Times* ran a front-page story about the death throes of St. Louis. TIAA's loan officer immediately pulled the application off the day's agenda. "The person who wrote that story didn't know what was going on," remarked Simon's executive vice-president, Randy Foxworthy. "We brought a Teachers executive out to St. Louis, showed him evidence of a recovery, and convinced him the *Times* article was wrong. Then we resubmitted the loan and got it approved."

For both the city and developer a key strategy for bringing shoppers downtown was to offer a different shopping experience, but to most lenders unconventional projects in highly visible locations were an invitation to professional disgrace. When Rouse started working on Faneuil Hall Marketplace, he had approximately twenty suburban centers to his credit and a national reputation as a successful innovator whose career spanned thirty-five years. That was enough to persuade TIAA to promise a long-term loan once the market was open for business. But even with TIAA's commitment in place, getting a construction loan was close to impossible.

The Chase Manhattan Bank of New York was willing to provide half of the $21 million Rouse needed if Boston banks would take care of the rest. Rouse found Boston bankers too cautious to take the idea seriously. Loan officers saw red ink flowing from the lack of an anchor department store, a location far away from suburban purchasing power, and the high costs and unknown problems of renovating a decaying produce terminal with a watery basement.

They disapproved as well of the local, independent, creative merchants Rouse had signed up. "We looked at the tenants," recalled Ephron Catlin, vice-president of the First National Bank of Boston, "and none of them had a credit rating. They were a bunch of nobodies." Catlin, one of the few supporters Rouse had among Boston bankers, tried to organize a consortium to put up the construction money. The handful of bankers willing to consider participating insisted that Rouse prelease a third or more of the retail space to creditworthy chain stores. Rouse met their requirement by signing the Magic Pan, a national restaurant chain, to take 32,000 square feet on the second floor of the Quincy Market building.

Bringing in one established tenant to offset the nobodies was not enough to put the consortium together, however. Mayor Kevin White finally got on the phone to the same local banks that had pressured him to select Rouse as developer. He used friendly persuasion, asking them to finance the restoration of an important landmark, and he also went further. Several loan officers who later joined the consortium spoke of taking "a lot of pressure from the mayor" and of "public" and "community" influence as factors in their decisions. Whether arm-twisting or appeals to civic responsibility did the trick, White was instrumental in solving the financing problem.

The story repeated itself in other cities—Philadelphia and Lexington, Kentucky, in particular. In both places developers ran into similar roadblocks, and they needed city hall and the downtown coalitions to loosen the conservative tendencies of local lenders. In Milwaukee, Dayton, and Detroit, downtown business coalitions themselves came up with equity funds to back up their political support.

Despite the problems, large commercial lenders stepped into downtown mall projects, though gingerly. Prudential, Equitable, Connecticut General, Metropolitan, and Travelers were each the sole long-term lenders for one to three projects, and Aetna financed five. Without TIAA, however, fourteenth in rank among the nation's largest life insurance companies, there would not have been much new retail investment downtown. As a group, the big life insurance companies financed more than a third of the seventy-five projects we studied, but no other lender backed the trend the way TIAA did. In the early 1970s when investors still considered downtown a retail disaster area, TIAA was making mortgage commitments for Worcester Center and Faneuil Hall in Massachusetts, Rainier Square in Seattle, Plaza Pasadena and three more California projects; and then commitments for the Galleria at White Plains, Harborplace, Louisville Galleria, City Center Minneapolis, Stamford Town Center, St. Louis Center, Horton Plaza, and St. Louis Union Station.

As one of the nation's largest private pension funds, entrusted with the staff retirement savings for nearly all private universities and colleges, as well as other nonprofit educational institutions, TIAA seemed an unlikely backer of risky ventures. Its loan officers made their decisions on the same limited facts available to others, but they read them differently. What others saw as a problem, they saw as an opportunity: projects with enough risk to justify a premium return.

The premium they were looking for was a return of one-quarter to one-half percentage point above the interest rates they charged for a conventional suburban mall. From the developer's perspective, this was a small consideration. "Our relationship with TIAA is long-standing and it is good," explained Hahn president John Gilchrist. "We could get flexibility and understanding from Teachers. It didn't make sense to look around for other lenders to save one-half percent." Teachers had financed close to 90 percent of Hahn's shopping centers, and while National Life and Accident had backed some Hahn centers, according to Gilchrist "they wouldn't touch downtown."

In looking for extra risk and extra returns, TIAA was no novice. As a specialized lender for shopping centers, it had been a maverick before, working a special niche (along with Equitable and Connecticut General) by making the earliest shopping center loans in the 1950s for DeBartolo, Taubman, and others who had been turned down elsewhere. By the mid-1970s the suburban field was crowded, and TIAA started searching for other investments where it could still earn a premium. After more than twenty years of retail experience, TIAA had a skilled staff and a president and chairman, William Greenough, who directed staff to put aside the usual parameters when they evaluated unconventional projects.

"For loans like Faneuil Hall," TIAA vice-president Carol Nichols recalled, "there was a lot of hesitancy on the part of local lenders. When we looked at Faneuil Hall, however, we were putting our confidence in the strength of Boston." Faneuil Hall deviated from every one of TIAA's mall standards, particularly for parking, anchor stores, and national tenants. The risk of this unconventional project was acceptable, in part, because TIAA wanted to finance each of the three buildings separately as completed, and this matched Rouse's plans as well. Rouse's track record and long association with TIAA also counted heavily.

TIAA did not go along with the Rouse Company on every project; it decided against funding the Gallery in downtown Philadelphia. Nor did it loosen its customary grip on the terms and conditions of tenant leases or the structure of its own deals with developers. "It had to be the same," remarked Nichols, "since everything else was new, more expensive, more risky, and involved more approvals." As for the special provisions that came out of the developer's deal with the city, these were no more troublesome than the problems of thrashing out agreements with department stores in the suburbs. "In downtown," according to Nichols, "we were just trading the city for the anchors."

Downtown projects also fit with TIAA's conception of social investment. While Greenough maintained that it was not the function of TIAA to subsidize good causes with faculty savings, the organization preferred investments with broad social purposes as long as they also met high standards for financial returns at acceptable levels of risk. Projects to revitalize cities played to this sense of social purpose. Such unconventional projects were only a small part of TIAA's total investment portfolio, however. The first Faneuil Hall disbursement of $15.1 million in 1978 was one of 199 transactions that year totaling $630.3 million. And TIAA's calculated risk taking paid off well by conventional measures. Since the 1960s Teachers consistently outranked its peer group of life insurance companies in investment performance.

While TIAA's investment strategy and long-time relationships with shopping center developers led it to finance downtown malls, its presence on the scene was a stroke of good fortune for the cities. Downtown developers who searched for financing in the 1970s were up against a shortage of money for long-term, large-scale projects. Inflation was soaring, and life insurance companies had to stand on the sidelines with their funds in short-term, liquid investments while policy holders took out record loans against their life policies at low interest rates stipulated in standard contracts.

TIAA was in a special position. As a pension fund, it collected savings on a regular and predictable basis and offered no loans against member contributions. To the contrary, TIAA's own restrictions kept pension money locked in so that it could contract to make large-scale loans many years in advance. This was exactly the type of commitment developers needed for their downtown retail projects. TIAA had the luxury of continuing its business policies on an unchanged course while other major shopping center lenders were shifting gears. Simon vice-president Randy Foxworthy exaggerated only slightly when he recalled Teachers as "the only lender with any money to lend and they had a never-ending supply."

TIAA's success with downtown malls did not bring along a rush of other lenders even after the general investment climate warmed. While the big institutional players placed the regional mall high on their preferred lists, downtown malls were another story. A field of few lenders, tight deals, and premium rates continued to make city malls hard to finance. Developers found alternatives by getting lenders to form consortiums or taking them in as partners. From TIAA's perspective enough lenders were in the field in the 1980s to wipe away their first-in-the-door interest premium. On the other hand the shakiness of the financing pressed developers to put in more equity than in suburban malls. "The ground rules are changing," remarked A. Jerry Keyser, a leading consultant on redevelopment finance. "The early deals went through old networks and drew on established relationships. Today the deals are tougher. The old business of putting in no equity is disappearing."

Dovetailing Dollars into Joint Ventures

Putting public money into private projects was nothing new. From the network of private canals in the nineteenth century to industrial plants and waste treatment facilities in the 1960s and 1970s, states and cities had used their borrowing power to promote business ventures that promised to improve local economies. But there were few workable precedents for mixing public and private funds in projects like the downtown shopping malls. When cities financed land purchases, site improvements, parking garages, and other components of the retail centers, they were developers as well as lenders. Leery of tying up funds in projects that might never see the light of day, they tried to gear their spending to the developer's progress.

If city officials worried that developers might not finish on time, developers worried that city governments might not come up with all the promised money. The problems that both sides had with financing fed these fears. Each would have favored a spending schedule based on the principle of "you first." Since cities took responsibility for the early activities, they had to go first. Yet they could not sell redevelopment bonds without evidence of genuine developer commitment to a project.

California attorney Joseph Coomes hammered out an agreement with the city of Hawthorne that soon became the model for that state's downtown retail malls. It solved the problem of up-front money by having the developer advance the purchase price for the land to the redevelopment agency. This early payment represented a sufficient developer commitment to allow the city to sell its bonds. The property that the agency assembled then served as collateral for the developer's advance. Hawthorne officials were also unwilling to start building the garage before the developer started building the mall, but part of the garage was under the mall. To find a solution, both parties negotiated a construction contract allowing the developer to construct both the garage and the mall, drawing down funds from the agency and the private lender in line with a specific formula.

In effect, if not in precise legal form, cities became partners in complex business transactions. They adopted businesslike practices to make sure projects were completed. The stakes were too high and the risks too great for either city officials or developers to try to get over the hurdles by improvising on their own.

City officials also began to act more like business investors by bargaining for financial returns over and above normal tax collections. Boston's agreement with the Rouse Company called for annual lease payments based on a percentage of rental income in lieu of property taxes. This early example of profit sharing has been in force long enough to demonstrate results. By the mid-1980s Boston was collecting some $2.5 million per year from Faneuil Hall Marketplace. Because the city invested no cash of its own to match federal contributions, these payments represented the sort of bounty that mayors used to dream of getting from urban renewal. Even after allowing for property taxes lost from the two market buildings that used to be in private ownership, by 1987 Boston was ahead by more than $15.5 million.

The true return on public investment is less spectacular although still impressive. A fuller accounting should consider all public outlays as though they had come out of the city budget since Boston might have put the federal and state dollars to other uses. The city began to shell out money for planning and engineering studies in 1962, and it paid for the north and south market buildings plus business relocation expenses and exterior renovation between 1965 and 1975. These heavy outlays were all before the galloping inflation of the late 1970s. The Rouse Company made its first full lease payments in 1979, seventeen years after government spending began and in postinflation, devalued dollars.

With appropriate discounting to reflect the actual timing of expenses and the long-delayed payback, the yield on the public investment through the end of 1987 was less than 1 percent. If annual payments continue to increase at the 1982–1987 rate through 2002, the tax deal will generate a return of 8.5 percent for the forty-year period. Adjusted for past inflation and for future inflation at recent rates, this return would be 2.5 percent in constant dollars. Adding in the residual earning power of the structures at the end of 40 years increases the real return to 4.5 percent.

Coming at a time when inflation was wiping out returns from any investment with fixed earnings, the city's tax deal produced a good payback, in addition to other benefits to the city from the marketplace. If Boston had taken the dollars it invested in the marketplace and put them instead into long-term U.S. Treasury bonds, the return over forty years, after inflation, would have been less than half what the city can expect from Faneuil Hall Marketplace.

Inflation cut down the return from the marketplace too. So did the long-deferred payback and the concessions the city made in renegotiating the deal with the developer. But the biggest single factor limiting returns is that no one had any idea how much income the project would generate. As revenues skyrocketed past the Rouse Company's projections, the profit-sharing arrangement failed to bring in as much money as the lease formula might have allowed because the city had set too low a cap on total payments.

Profit sharing nevertheless produced extra benefits. So far Boston has taken in 40 percent more than it would have collected through conventional property tax channels. Automatically indexed to how well the marketplace does each year, payments are not dependent on a bureaucracy to reassess property values or a city council to approve higher tax rates. As a source of revenue for municipal operations, the intake is only a small item in a big-city budget. But the results of profit sharing are helpful politically for city officials who take financial risks to pursue public objectives.

Only cities with the most favorable circumstances could stage a repeat of Boston's gain from Faneuil Hall. But whether or not the downtown malls turned into gold mines, city negotiators tried increasingly to go into business with developers. Since they were sharing heavy risks, many wanted to share the rewards of successful projects.

San Diego expected to earn future income beyond tax increments from Horton Plaza. Although Hahn repeatedly resisted Trimble's proposals to share parking and rental revenues with the city as part of the initial deal, he eventually went along with this idea in exchange for city concessions during later bargaining. In the end the Hahn Company agreed to pay San Diego 10 percent of gross rental income in excess of base rents from shopping mall tenants, 10 percent of net cash flow from office space planned for a second phase of construction, and 31 percent of gross parking revenues beyond the amount needed to amortize Hahn's cost of building the parking facilities.

Over time a growing proportion of cities succeeded in trading their mall outlays for future returns. When cities changed their financial assistance from grants to loans, they stipulated a return in the form of a loan payback. Of twenty-five projects that opened from 1971 to 1980, none required loan paybacks; the number with loan paybacks increased to nine out of thirty-one projects that opened from 1981 to 1985. Specific profit-sharing agreements also became more numerous. Between 1971 and 1980 three projects out of seventeen for which we have information involved profit sharing. From 1981 to 1985 thirteen additional projects out of twenty-four had profit-sharing agreements. As of 1988 most of the sixteen projects with profit sharing were performing up to expectations in terms of retail sales or actual cash returns to the city, and only four were doing too poorly to generate profit-sharing income in the near future.

In the process of bargaining for financial reciprocity, cities made more productive use of public dollars than when they acted only as financial donors to downtown projects. Financial returns, however, were never the main purpose that city officials had in mind. Those that bargained for loan paybacks and profit sharing were careful not to threaten the viability of a project, and when the malls opened, the public looked for other kinds of success.

9   Open for Business

While Faneuil Hall Marketplace, Pike Place Market, Town Square, and Horton Plaza were under way, the once-lonesome frontier of downtown retailing was getting crowded. A small band of pioneers opened the territory in the 1960s, but by the mid-1970s developers, city officials, and retail executives were busy staking out choice in-town sites all over the country.

More than one hundred new downtown retail centers opened for business between 1970 and 1988. In the early 1970s, the best known were Crown Center in Kansas City and ARCO Plaza and Broadway Plaza in Los Angeles. Between 1976 and 1979 the list grew to include Water Tower Place in Chicago, Faneuil Hall Marketplace, Pike Place Market, the Gallery at Market East in Philadelphia, Omni Center in Atlanta, Renaissance Center in Detroit, St. Anthony Main in Minneapolis, the Market at Citicorp in New York, the Shops at Station Square in Pittsburgh, and the Glendale Galleria and Hawthorne Plaza in the Los Angeles area. The 1980s brought openings at a faster pace, with Plaza Pasadena, Santa Monica Place, Harborplace in Baltimore, and Town Square in 1980; Georgetown Park in Washington, Fountain Square South in Cincinnati, and Long Beach Plaza in 1981; Embarcadero Center in San Francisco, the Louisville Galleria, and the Grand Avenue in Milwaukee in 1982; Canal Place in New Orleans, South Street Seaport in New York, Gallery II in Philadelphia, and Charleston Center in West Virginia in 1983; National Place in Washington, City Center in Minneapolis, Copley Place in Boston, and Tabor Center in Denver in 1984; Horton Plaza, Tivoli in Denver, St. Louis Union Station, and St. Louis Centre in 1985; Riverwalk in New Orleans and Charleston Place in South Carolina in 1986; Bayside Marketplace in Miami and the Conservatory on Nicollet in Minneapolis in 1987; and

River Center in San Antonio, Union Station in Washington, and 900 Michigan Avenue in Chicago in 1988.

Downtown retail centers swept the country at a rate that demonstrated what cities could accomplish. Developers built where cities greased the way. Cities were coinvestors in three of every four projects from 1970 through 1985, with the median public share amounting to nearly one-third of total development cost. Private money bankrolled half of the few downtown malls that opened in the early 1970s, but from then on city governments became key financiers of an accelerating trend. By the 1980s they were sharing development costs for more than four of every five new projects.

Although cities turned to a development industry notorious for copying past successes, the downtown projects were not suburban transplants. They had to be unorthodox in order to work. The downtown malls were also different from each other. Three kinds of projects predominated. One was the regional shopping mall, anchored by one or more department stores and offering a wide variety of shopping goods aimed at the middle of the market. This type came closest to a copy of the tried and true suburban model, but Plaza Pasadena illustrated how even the familiar regional mall became something else in the process of moving downtown.

The festival or specialty mall was a step further removed from suburban shopping centers. Faneuil Hall Marketplace was the prototype, offering an unusual collection of small local shops without the proved draw of anchor department stores. Most festival malls emphasized food and entertainment, plus offbeat wares. An important part of the strategy was to make the mall special by highlighting its historic associations, opening it to waterfront vistas, and enlivening the public spaces with street entertainers and festive decorations.

The third variety of downtown mall was the mixed-use project, combining retailing with two or more other activities such as offices, hotels, a convention center, or housing. The idea was to bring together activities that would be mutually reinforcing, such as stores that would appeal to hotel guests or business visitors and that in turn would help attract people to the hotels and offices. Water Tower Place, completed in 1976, was the pacesetter for downtown mixed-use projects. It combined eight levels of upscale shops, the big-name department stores of Marshall Field and Lord & Taylor, a Ritz-Carlton Hotel, an office complex, luxury condominiums, four movie houses, and a performing arts theater.

Although festival and specialty malls received overwhelming attention as symbols of downtown revitalization, they accounted for fewer
than three of every ten retail centers built in the cities between 1970
and 1985. More than four of ten were mixed-use projects, and the
remaining three were regional malls.

This three-way classification, however, brushes over local differences. The downtown prototypes served as points of departure for
developers and architects who tried to come up with a solution
geared to each city. Most struck some variation on a theme, and a few
drew their inspiration from more than a single source. Horton Plaza
in particular combined the retail selection of a suburban regional mall
with the entertainment of a festival market plus the diversity of a
mixed-use development.

But the downtown projects still had much in common. Almost all
followed the suburban strategy of aiming at the middle of the market.
They excluded such low-end establishments as discount stores and
factory outlets, and only a handful featured collections of luxury
shops. Further, each prototype seemed to find its own decor clichés
and its favored national chains. If mall owners eventually copy each
other's styles, future travelers may have a hard time telling one festival market or mixed-use project from another. So far, however,
cities have avoided the monotony of suburban malls, and the projects
we have studied in detail stand out sharply from each other.

Most downtown centers share another characteristic that cities
wanted: although small in land area, they are big businesses, with
more than seventy-five stores and typically 200,000 or more square
feet of retail space. Their size alone makes them prominent drawing
cards with a capacity to fill the streets with visitors and the public
coffers with tax dollars.

The frictions and the crises, the deal cutting and the renegotiation,
all had their impact as the malls took shape. Their tangled history of
conflicts and compromises might have led to projects as misshapen as
the proverbial camel—an animal thought to have been designed by a
committee. Yet a look at the results shows well-organized centers
calculated to bring people to the city and profit to the developer.

Faneuil Hall: Marketing the Unusual

For professionals who work at planning and building cities, Faneuil
Hall Marketplace is the outstanding city development project of an

era. To Edward Logue, who spent the 1950s renewing New Haven, the 1960s renewing Boston, and the 1970s running building programs for New York State, this marketplace was done so brilliantly that "if it had opened a few years earlier it might have saved the urban renewal program." When he learned that we were going to interview James Rouse, his main suggestion was: "Ask why he didn't do it sooner."

To appreciate why the experts are so taken with Faneuil Hall Marketplace, it helps to know about the long years of disappointment with organized efforts to rebuild American cities. Public housing, a New Deal slum clearance plan to build attractive homes in well-planned neighborhoods, led instead to the notorious projects that became lodgings of last resort. Urban renewal was the postwar hope for reviving worn-out cities, but its best-known products were red tape, half-vacant sites, and pompous developments that nobody could like except their architects.

Lyndon Johnson tried a fresh start in 1965 with the model cities program, which proposed to focus the full range of federal aid programs in a sweeping plan to make the poorest neighborhoods livable and to build "cities of spacious beauty and lively promise." The results were another letdown: overregulation and underfunding in Washington and only marginal improvements to housing and public services in the cities. One more hopeful experiment from the Johnson administration was called "new towns in-town," an imaginative scheme to build entire new communities with good housing for the poor on surplus federal land in seven cities. Local opposition either killed every proposal outright or stalled it indefinitely.

By the mid-1970s urban specialists had been working nearly forty years without producing a truly popular, nationally recognized achievement. Urban renewal, model cities, and new towns in-town were all dead, and public housing was barely alive. Disillusioned voters were turning their attention away from the urban crisis to the energy and environmental crusades that sparked the interest of a new generation of activists.

City experts and the urban press were aching for at least one big success, and Faneuil Hall Marketplace finally gave it to them. It hit a series of themes just right for the time. For a mass public that had just discovered gourmet food, the central arcade served it up in volume and with flair. For a public with a fresh interest in history, the market presented authentic 150-year-old buildings and cobbled paths rich with historic associations. For a generation that had discovered sidewalk cafes and bustling piazzas in Europe, the market brought these pleasures home.

Although both the desperation of the experts and the fads of the moment contributed to the instant acclaim for Faneuil Hall Marketplace, the project was an impressive accomplishment in its own right. Thompson and Rouse converted the old structures and the spaces between them into a unique shopping mall, opening it to nearby streets and making it inviting to passers-by. The background is history, but the foreground is late twentieth-century retailing. Each of the three market buildings uses three levels, starting with the basement, for store space totaling 220,000 square feet. Rouse and Thompson found room for 160 stores and 30 to 40 bull market pushcarts by using every corner. The storekeepers made the most of their small spaces, moving incredible volumes of food and merchandise across the counters from tiny work areas behind.

The market has a clear layout. To find food stores, you go to the central Quincy Market building, where forty of them are concentrated together with ten cafes and informal restaurants. To find larger restaurants with more elaborate menus, you go to the North Market building, which has nine of them, counting four operated by enterprising Ben and Jane Thompson. The rest of the North and South Market stores sell a medley of clothing, art, toys, jewelry, handicrafts, home furnishings, and assorted souvenirs. Among those shops are several national or regional chains such as Ann Taylor, Crabtree and Evelyn, and Crate and Barrel.

Merchandising methods evolved after the market opened. Rouse and Thompson's plans for the food arcade called for some stores to sell items to take home and others to sell food to eat across the counter. The original provision merchants who had never moved out were given a chance to stay in the market at low rents, but their leases restricted them to selling take-home food as they had before. One day a produce dealer who had too many ripe pineapples on hand decided to sell them by the slice and found he did much better that way. Soon he went from pineapple slices to assorted fruits on skewers ("fruit kabobs"). Butchers who could not do enough business selling prime cuts soon put in steam tables for selling meat sandwiches, barbecued chicken and ribs, and hot sausages. Within the first few years fast food took over most of the central arcade.

The market's popularity exceeded everyone's expectations. Door estimates climbed from 10 million people the first year to 12 million in

1978, when the entire center was open. By the mid-1980s it drew 16 million visitors a year, as many as Britain and three times as many as Mexico or Hawaii. Sales figures of $233 per square foot astounded Boston financiers in 1976. By 1987 the figure was close to $500. In comparison with typical shopping center performance, these results were off the scale.

Contrary to the widespread belief that festival malls attract a free-spending crowd, the high sales figures resulted more from the volume of customers than from what they bought. A shopper survey undertaken by the Rouse Company in 1977 found that 16 percent of the visitors spent nothing at all, and the median expense was only five dollars. Fewer than 15 percent of the visitors spent more than twenty dollars.

The marketplace had a special appeal for young adults: half the visitors were between the ages of eighteen and thirty-four. This concentration of the postwar generation at the market gives some support to the general impression that it is a haven for young urban professionals, or yuppies. But the customers are not especially affluent; the median household income of visitors in 1977 was $19,500, close to the median family income of metropolitan Boston.

One of the great surprises was the pulling power of the marketplace beyond the city of Boston. Thompson never intended it as a tourist attraction, and redevelopment authority analysts expected it to attract mainly local residents and downtown office workers. The Rouse Company's own projections in 1972 figured that tourists would be important customers of the market but underestimated how important they would be. Only one in four visitors in 1977 lived in the city of Boston, while close to 40 percent came from the suburbs. Ten percent came from the rest of Massachusetts and more than one-fourth from other parts of the country. In all, 37 percent of the shoppers described themselves as "visiting Boston as a tourist" in comparison with the 28 percent tourist share forecast in 1972. Within a few years, the tourist share climbed to nearly half of all visitors.

In short Faneuil Hall Marketplace was more than a local institution, and its appeal outside the city helped to raise sales far above the figure that Boston bankers considered unattainable. But depending on tourism can be troublesome because tourist fads come and go. Project manager James McLean in the 1980s hoped to attract a steadier clientele from the nearby office district by adding businesses to meet their needs, such as a store specializing in clothes for working women.

Because sales have been so strong, tenant turnover has been low: only 15 percent in the first eight years, and this despite the unusually short three-year leases the Rouse Company wrote in order to be able to fine-tune the tenant mix after opening day. Since the market turned out to be a money machine for sales, the city prospered from its formula tying the Rouse Company's annual payments to rental income from retail tenants. Yet the market has not been a spectacular success for its developer. According to James Rouse, it does not rank among the company's top projects. Several older suburban malls are "far more profitable," Rouse reported, but he was confident that in time Faneuil Hall Marketplace will be equally productive.

One of the problems has been the high operating cost. As part of the deal with the city the Rouse Company agreed to take full responsibility for security, maintenance, trash collection, and snow removal. Rouse gave high priority to these operations and asked his staff to spare no expense to keep the market safe and well maintained. As an admirer of the Disney organization, he sent McLean to Disneyworld to learn how to clean and maintain an attraction that draws a million people a month. Disneyworld is known not only for the technical proficiency of its maintenance but also for its almost compulsive standards of neatness and repair.

The Rouse Company, like other shopping center developers, covers the cost of city taxes, maintenance, and service operations by passing them along to the tenants as special assessments on top of the rent. By 1983 these charges totaled $27 per square foot of retail space, plus $13 more per square foot for over-the-counter food merchants, who generate an extra load of trash. These costs were far out of line with normal retail center charges that rarely exceeded $5 per square foot. At Faneuil Hall Marketplace fast food vendors in the mid-1980s were paying about $40 per square foot for base rent, plus a percentage of sales, and the Rouse Company assessed them another $40 in tax and service costs.

The steady escalation of these pass-through costs led to something approaching a tenant revolt in 1983 when the tenants' association filed a class action lawsuit alleging that the Rouse Company exaggerated its costs and charged more than a proportional share of tax and upkeep costs to the tenants. While the case was in court, some tenants charged that they were under unfair pressure from the Rouse

Company to sign waivers promising not to take part in the lawsuit. In 1986 the merchants negotiated a $3 million out-of-court settlement with Rouse.

Why are maintenance costs so high? Part of the answer is that collecting and hauling away 25,000 pounds of garbage from the market every day and steam-cleaning the cobblestone pavement several times a week demands a large maintenance crew. Of McLean's 110 employees in 1983, 55 were on the janitorial staff. Because of the nature of the market's business, much of their work was unavoidable, although keeping Disneyworld standards without charging Disneyworld admission fees is a problem in itself. Another large outlay went for a security force of twelve permanent members with one deputized police officer on duty at all times. This cost was high because of the downtown location, as developers had anticipated when they first thought of moving in from the suburbs. McLean, who previously managed a Rouse center in the suburbs, reported more vandalism and shoplifting at Faneuil Hall Marketplace than at a typical suburban center, and because he had a large security force and a relatively small area to patrol (no parking lots or garages), he reported more arrests than at suburban centers. Most of his security problems were minor thefts and vandalism to outdoor benches and trees, with no break-ins or major damage so far.

James Rouse was satisfied with the degree of security at Faneuil Hall and his other busy in-town projects. According to Rouse, the crowds are the best source of safety: "Security is never a problem with enough people; crowds drive away crime." About fifty visitors (out of 16 million) reported having their wallets lifted in 1985, and twelve pickpockets were arrested. McLean credited the arrests for deterring other criminals. On a late night visit to Faneuil Hall Marketplace, we were struck with the effectiveness of the security force. When two young men who had apparently stolen something ran down a food aisle at top speed, three guards appeared out of nowhere, quickly nabbed one of the runners, and hustled him out of sight.

The Faneuil Hall project is certainly not trouble free, but on balance it is a reasonable success for the developer, a major attraction for the city, and a clear asset for the tax collector. It has brought people downtown, both from the Boston area and from other parts of the country, in numbers that are evidence of its popularity. It has remained a national and international symbol of city revitalization.

Pike Place: Preserving the Past

Rouse and Thompson spoke of "jumble" and "chaos" as important elements of a festival market. Pike Place Market has jumble and chaos to spare. The odd sizes and shapes of its old buildings and the maze of corridors winding up and down the different levels set the stage. The stores themselves make up a collection like no other. Because of below-market rents and the curious selection standards of the Historical Commission, Pike Place Market features stores that would never be found in an organized shopping center and some that would hardly be found in the downtown of any contemporary American city: a Bible shop, a tattoo parlor, a stand selling rubber stamps, another selling wood fiber roses, a denture repair service, a knife sharpener, a Filipino take-out stand, a Bolivian restaurant, a day-old bread store, a calligraphic card store, a bingo hall, four used clothing stores, a pawnshop, a used book store, a used comic book store, the last hat blocker in Seattle, Tenzing Momo's oriental herbs and teas, Afghan crafts, and Malay, Turkish, and Yugoslav delicatessens. These exotic stores give the Pike Place Market the atmosphere of a museum of retailing, combining living displays of endangered species from American cities with a sprinkling of small businesses from distant corners of the world.

Like Faneuil Hall Marketplace it is a specialty center focused on food, with no anchor department stores, housed in historic market buildings, and located at the edge of downtown overlooking the waterfront. Its layout is about as far as one can get from the ordered harmony, unified design, and tasteful landscaping of a suburban mall or even the classical symmetry of Quincy Market and its two parallel structures. In the historic core twenty buildings of assorted sizes and shapes stand on both sides of an L-shaped street where delivery trucks park and unload. To go from one building to another shoppers usually have to walk out to the street, where they dodge trucks and handcarts. With no enclosure covering the sidewalks or roadway, they are at the mercy of the notorious Seattle climate ("a fine city if you don't mind living inside a car wash"). In addition to breaking the suburban rules about keeping loading operations out of sight and sheltering the customers against the weather, the Pike Place Market also falls far short of retail parking standards: a nearby city garage and several open lots together provide only a few hundred spaces.

The part of it closest to a shopping mall is a two-block arcade running through the Main Market building along the western side of Pike Place. Here people push their way through the crowded space between produce, fish, and crafts stands on either side. This main arcade is the focal point of the market, much like the central corridor where Quincy Market merchants sell across-the-counter snacks. The theme of Pike Place Market, however, is not fast food but a harvest of vegetables and fruit from nearby farms, plus schools of fish from nearby waters looking almost alive on open beds of ice. Displays change with the season: strawberries, asparagus, and mushrooms in the spring; raspberries, blueberries, cherries, peppers, and tomatoes in the summer; peaches, pears, and apples in the fall; and clams, oysters, crabs, mussels, salmon, sole, and perch most of the year.

Two more features set Pike Place Market apart from suburban malls: all the merchants are independents, and the buildings are old enough to be considered historic for the Pacific Northwest, since most were built between 1907 and 1917. The restoration emphasized structural repairs and improvements to wiring and plumbing, with no contemporary stylistic changes to disturb the period-piece atmosphere. The buildings are simple, functional, and unobtrusive. One expects to see antique brick and carefully highlighted architectural details, but in fact the walls are wood and plaster, the floors are simple planks or common paving materials, and the handrails are iron pipes. Architect George Bartholick, who was in charge of the renovation, defined success as having "the market community . . . barely aware of any changes when the job has been completed."

Store designs are equally unobtrusive. Since the merchants had to pay for their own fixtures, as in typical shopping centers, most tried to hold down the budget by using simple, traditional counters and window displays. Although the Historical Commission sometimes reviewed their plans with painstaking zeal, it did not lay on the customary rules calling for uniform signs and shopfronts, nor did it prevent the merchants from using low-budget materials. The result is an informal atmosphere within the stores, with merchandise set out according to the owner's inclination and with virtually none of the sophisticated, imaginative displays that are part of high-powered suburban merchandising. Most of the farm stands are no more than simple wooden bins holding fruits and vegetables.

Housekeeping standards are casual. This is no sanitized Disneyworld. It is a busy, littered market, kept tolerably clean but showing all the signs of hard use. The daily operations that suburban malls carefully conceal from the shoppers—delivering and unpacking merchandise, hosing down fish and vegetable stands, taking away the leftovers—are not only out in the open but usually underfoot. Disorder is part of the attraction and the spectacle of a traditional marketplace; it also reminds shoppers that the food is fresh, not preserved and packaged for long shelf life.

A large market even by suburban standards, the entire 22-acre complex has some 820,000 square feet of retail and office space, with shopping mainly in the central 7-acre historic district and office space mainly in the outer sections. The historic core has 235 businesses operating in 379,000 square feet of retail space. Food stores account for about 40 percent of the total in the core, with another 40 percent selling mainly handicrafts, gifts, and used goods. About 15 percent offer professional or neighborhood services such as health care, legal services, dry cleaning, and haircuts. The remaining few are the hard-to-classify places like the bingo and tattoo operations. Only about 75 merchants at any one time are farmers, but they create the image that draws the crowds.

Visitors to the market are a broader cross-section of people than shopping malls attract or tolerate. According to John Turnbull, former staff director for the Historical Commission, the market has been scruffy by intent: "We want graffiti. We want winos and vagrants." Turnbull conceded that the commission does not want graffiti everywhere, nor does it want crude and tasteless scrawls, but it has set aside certain walls, under the watchful eyes of a committee of local artists, where graffiti are welcome. The artists decide which to keep, and they do keep many. As for the winos, "Vagrants and street people are part of the scene; they have a right to be here," Turnbull says. "Seattle police in general tend not to disturb winos who swig from their bottles in public places as long as they do not annoy others." (In every other shopping mall we know, security guards are trained to deal with drunks by offering polite assistance in getting them home, by taxi if necessary, but in any case to edge them firmly off the premises.) Turnbull maintained that the market's tolerance of vagrants, street people, and graffiti makes good business sense. Tourists are attracted, he said, "precisely because it is un-touristy." These practices give the market a raucous character that is authentic and even refreshing in comparison with the orderly restraint and polite atmosphere of suburban malls.

The Pike Place Market is also unusual in renting only to independent business people and in having the owners on the scene. In more than nine of ten market establishments the owner is involved in daily management, and almost all have at least one member of the owner's family working there. Part of the Historic Commission's intent has been to help start-up businesses, and more than half the establishments in the market are the owner's first venture. The commission works with people who face special problems getting started: a third of the businesses are owned by women and almost a fourth by minority merchants, nearly twice the ownership rates for women and minorities in Seattle at large.

This strong presence of local, start-up merchants has personalized the shopping experience at Pike Place Market, but it has not led to the burst of entrepreneurial vigor one might expect. Market director John Clise observed that "many owners are not good managers. They run their businesses as hobbies. They are content to take out their salaries and don't think about profits." This personal style contributes directly to the low-key atmosphere of much of the market. It also means that despite the low rent and good location, many businesses do not succeed.

In only a few cases has the market been a business incubator: a spice and coffee shop started at Pike Place and became a chain, and an Italian grocery set up other branches. More often the market has been an incubator only in the limited sense of helping someone set up a new business that was able to survive under the protection of the Pike Place complex.

One of the more successful entrepreneurs in this sense is Shirley Collins, owner of a busy kitchenware store, Sur la Table. When she started out, she was able to afford only a small space in a run-down market building at a rent of $45 a month. As the business began to prosper, she joined with two other merchants to renovate a small art deco building within the historic district, with the help of a loan from the Small Business Administration and a mortgage from a local bank. An early activist in the campaign to save the market, Collins wanted to serve a broader community of customers than the suburban hostesses who took up advanced cooking in the 1970s. "I don't like the 'gourmet' label for my store," she said. To diversify, one of her strategies was to stock commercial-grade supplies such as durable Elephant chinaware to sell to small restaurants. In addition, she and her husband, Alf Collins, a food writer and restaurant reviewer for the *Seattle*

Times, scouted street stands near European markets for inexpensive kitchen gadgets to import.

Market managers have taken steps to bring in poor people, including sponsoring some 300 subsidized apartments that create a low-income clientele on the site. In addition, they leased space to many economy retailers, such as the used clothing stores, the pawnshop, and an army-navy surplus store. They paid for restaurant equipment to enable the Church Council to operate a low-cost cafe in one of the renovated market buildings. The result is that Pike Place Market has something for almost everyone. While suburban malls usually aim at the middle of the market, Pike Place tries to cover the low end as well.

Despite its chaotic appearance Pike Place Market is no less controlled than the carefully managed malls of suburbia; only the purposes of the control are different. While commercial mall owners select and regulate their tenants for the sake of maximizing total sales, the public agencies responsible for Pike Place Market use their control for the sake of helping merchants start businesses, preserving traditional retailing, and bringing in businesses to serve the poor.

The controlling agencies also have another important impact: to protect firms already there by restricting new competition. Although the commission has approved tenancies for many similar businesses, they select new tenants with a view to keeping competition within limits. Shirley Collins, formerly a member of the Historical Commission, observed that "the Commission wavers when new merchants propose to do what existing ones do." They do not stifle competition totally, she explained, noting that other stores in the market besides her own sell kitchen equipment. But when someone proposed to open a cooking supply store close to Sur la Table, the commission vetoed it. "They seemed to be protecting me," she said, "even though I didn't speak against it." The chaos of the Pike Place Market, in short, is a finely tuned sort of chaos.

The Pike Place Market is a popular success. It draws large numbers of people: from 20,000 on weekdays to 40,000 on Saturdays, more than doubling the number of visitors since the renovation began. These survey figures add to an annual total of more than 7 million, not far below the turnout for a typical regional mall in the suburbs.

We have little information on who the customers are, but large numbers of middle-income people and tourists stand out. Turnbull described the customers as mostly not the poor but the middle class and the upper middle class. The prices are not noticeably lower than in supermarkets, but the quality of food is better. Although management gave high priority to finding tenants who would serve low-income customers, John Clise also believed the market was attracting mostly middle-income people. He even noted signs of "gentrification in the food": as merchants discovered that customers were willing to pay more for higher quality, they switched to better and more expensive produce.

Tourists come in large numbers, but the merchants complain with some justification that they come more to look around than to buy. During the summer more than half the people in the market are tourists; yet in a survey of merchants, two-thirds reported that tourists supplied less than one-fourth of their business.

Annual retail sales, according to management estimates, were $20 million to $30 million by 1983. This volume was far below the comparable figure at Faneuil Hall Marketplace, with a similar number of businesses occupying only 60 percent as much retail space. In sales per square foot the Pike Place estimates were the equivalent of $53 to $79, compared with $350 in Faneuil Hall Marketplace at that time. Interviews with Pike Place merchants confirmed that most handled only a low volume of business. More than half reported fewer than 100 paying customers on a typical day; and two-fifths reported an average sale of less than $5, two-fifths an average sale between $5 and $20, and only one-fifth an average sale over $20.

The more commercialized approach of Faneuil Hall clearly generates greater dollar returns than the low-key, casual style of Pike Place. Since rents and maintenance costs are low, many Pike Place merchants can live with small sales volumes. But even with low rents, their profit margins are thin and their incomes modest. Turnbull noted that some stores take in only $100 a week but pay weekly rents of $30 to $60. Notable exceptions are the fish stands, which pay low rents on long-term leases while ringing up sales as high as $1,500 per square foot in 1983 and $4,000 by 1987.

Sales volume was not the prime purpose of renovating Pike Place Market, however. As far as the public and most city officials are concerned, it is a huge success. The old buildings are no longer in danger of collapse, and the renovated space is filled with small businesses. Vacancies are not much of a problem because a merchant who decides to give up a business usually sells the lease to someone else who is more than willing to accept the same terms in exchange for the low rent. Seattle voters wanted to preserve the old market, and it was preserved. Once back in operation, it was popular.

Activists across the political spectrum have considered Pike Place Market not so much a real estate project as a crusade. According to Harriet Sherburne, one of the leaders of that campaign and later the city's director of the Pike Place project, "anti-renewal groups on the right joined liberals and anti-Vietnam protesters who wanted to save the market." After the renovated market was open for business, it meant many things to many people: help for the poor, treats for the tables of the gourmets, entertainment for the family on a Saturday afternoon, and a boost for tourism.

In John Clise's view, the market is a "sacred cow." "Politicians hear good things about it from the public," he says, "and they have little disposition to interfere with it. Critics do not usually go public, because they would face a public committed to the market." Yet Clise discovered that there are sharp disagreements over how to judge the performance of the market and its managers. The Preservation and Development Authority (PDA) has become subject to conflicting demands: to act in a businesslike way but also to serve as an incubator for start-up firms; to cover its operating costs but also to deal gently with unbusinesslike tenants.

A city council report in 1981 brought many of these conflicting expectations to the surface. Among the criticisms it leveled at the PDA were these: the authority had run at a deficit in almost every year of operation, had insufficient liquid assets to meet current obligations, and needed steady financial support from the city government. Clise's letter of rebuttal pointed out that the PDA had a current surplus of more than $300,000 in 1981, that it had always met its obligations to creditors, and "our payment schedule is more rapid than the City's." He defended the reserve level by arguing that the PDA was created for public purposes, not to generate a large surplus of funds.

Although Clise made a good defense of the market's management, his exchange with the city council revealed underlying conflicts between the ideals of historic preservation and the notion that the market should operate on a sound financial basis. More profitable businesses could strengthen the market and help it pay its own way. Preservationists, however, object to businesses that cater to well-off customers on the ground that they would change the historic character of the market.

Yet some of the people who were most active in renovating Pike Place Market question whether its historic function was to serve low-income people or to make the most of economic opportunities. Harriet Sherburne argued that the market always reflected the changing tastes and interests of its times and always served a cross-section of Seattle society. To James Mason, the first Pike Place project director for the city, the historic functions of the market were "to create conditions for economic enterprise" and to "provide a place for immigrants to make a living." Mason argued for allowing market business to change rather than "spraying plastic" over whatever is there at a particular time. Seattle preservationists who made a social cause out of saving the market, however, have done their best to block it from turning into a fun house for yuppies. And the PDA, unlike a private developer, does not have the freedom to select strong tenants and negotiate favorable leases in order to improve its finances.

The preservationist outlook, which was so critical for saving the market, also led to conflicts over security problems. The market's location across the street from Seattle's sleaze district, together with the management's tolerance of deviant characters, made it easy for a certain number of criminals to join the crowd and operate at the market. Virginia Felton, public relations director for the authority, conceded that drugs are sold at the market and believed there is no way to stop it: "It's that type of place."

PDA managers have favored cleaning up some of the adult entertainment places nearby in order to reduce the security problem, but the same historic preservationists who watchdog the market object to eliminating porno shops. Still, the city did ignore their protests long enough to close a doughnut shop across the street that had served as a hangout for runaways and a notorious center of child prostitution. But further cleanups are unlikely, and the drug dealers will probably continue to work the rambling corridors and odd corners of the crowded market.

Despite these problems and disagreements, the Pike Place Market is a great success for the city. It is a crowd pleaser and an asset to downtown. Few people are aware of the massive public subsidies that made the renovation possible and even fewer of the financial tightrope that the market authority still walks. Clise was right to call it a sacred cow: even former critics came to recognize its value. The Downtown Seattle Association, sponsor of the infamous proposal to bulldoze most of the market, now counts itself among the "men of vision" of that earlier time and claims credit as "an active participant in planning for the Pike Place Market."[1]

The renovated market demonstrates once more that blending history with food is a winning combination. In fact, if the food is good enough, the buildings do not have to be very outstanding or historic. (As a Victorian music hall song described the pleasures of going from landmark to landmark in old London, "It's fun to study history—and the pubs along the way.") And a well-conceived attraction can assemble large crowds even without suburban parking lots and high-powered merchandising. Pike Place Market also shows that downtown retail centers can serve low-income customers without driving away the middle class. But it is not a likely model for other cities because the large federal subsidies that paid for it are no longer available. Further, it falls far short of the sales volume that either developers or tax-hungry cities expect, and it may turn out to be vulnerable to competition from newer centers with greater commercial sophistication. When Seattle decided to let the Rouse Company develop a retail center as part of its downtown Westlake Mall project, we asked PDA director Harris Hoffman how he felt about the forthcoming Rouse project. He answered with a single word: "worried."

Town Square: Making the Setting Special

Although cities started retail centers for different reasons, all faced a common problem: how to compete with established suburban malls. The need to compete led mall developers to build distinctive centers offering the public either a new environment or unusual shopping. Some, like Faneuil Hall Marketplace and the Pike Place Market, compete on both counts. Town Square, on the other hand, has conventional stores in an unconventional setting.

The retail makeup of Town Square is like that of a suburban mall compressed into a smaller space. Its anchors, Donaldsons and Dayton's, are the only full-line department stores in downtown St. Paul. The Donaldsons store is new, built as part of the Town Square complex; the Dayton's store was an existing one linked to the new center by a short skyway hookup. The mall shops occupy only 106,000 square feet, including a small retail area added to the Dayton's skyway passage three years after the opening. Oxford Properties divided the space to make room for just fifty-two stores plus an underground food court with fourteen snack counters.

Town Square has no special theme. It serves up a mix of general shopping goods with some emphasis on items for downtown employees and business visitors, such as stationery and office supplies, business equipment, and fashions for working women. To satisfy the out-of-towner's itch for a souvenir, it has a few handicraft shops and the Minnesota Store, which specializes in such local items as wild rice, booklets of Scandinavian humor, Paul Bunyan carvings, and recordings of the St. Paul–based radio program "Prairie Home Companion."

Town Square is a mixed-use development, the most frequent type of downtown retail center. Within a single structure covering two city blocks, shoppers can walk through three levels of stores to the enclosed rooftop city park. Flanking the retail core are a 250-room hotel on one side and office towers of twenty-five and twenty-seven stories on the other; underground is a 500-car garage. Without going outside, visitors can cross four skyway bridges to surrounding office buildings and Dayton's department store, as well as to the entire skyway network that winds through twenty-six downtown blocks.

The internal layout is tightly packed, with the office building lobbies pressing close to the retail shops on one side and the hotel lobby close on the other. The four skyways converge on the retail hub with its store-lined passageways. Escalators and an elevator carry people from one shopping level to another and to the park on top. Waterfalls, trees, and shrubs fill the space between the escalators, and the water splashes from the park down through two levels of mall stores and then into a collecting pool in the below-ground food court. The park has no fewer than 250 types of plants, thanks to Gary Stout's determination to avoid a cold, barren look. A huge glass roof lets in sunlight (when it is available), and trees and flowering shrubs alongside the moving water create the sense of a greenhouse even when the sky is gray. Besides greenery, the park has play areas, an open theater, and a place for exhibits.

With the skyways, office towers, and hotel bringing people into the retail area from different directions, while the park draws some of them upstairs and the food court lures others downstairs, it does not take much of a crowd to fill the center of Town Square with action. Even with people in motion, however, the atmosphere is not that of a bustling market. Town Square looks like an office building with wall surfaces of polished stone and storefronts of shiny contemporary design. The fountains and landscaping offer some relief from the hard, clean look, but the shopping area resembles a collection of stores one might find within an office building or a hotel.

The appeal of Town Square is that of an uncommon setting. Its combination of closely linked activities has no parallel in the suburban malls around St. Paul. It is similar to some of the downtown retailing in Minneapolis, and particularly to the City Center project built by Oxford Properties at about the same time. But the enclosed park is a unique feature within the Minneapolis–St. Paul area, and it has few parallels anywhere: the park makes Town Square a sight to see.

Another factor that helps it compete with suburban malls is its excellent access to the rest of downtown St. Paul. The downtown area is compact, with office buildings, banks, city hall, hospitals, apartment towers, theaters, and museums all in walking distance of Town Square. Distances are short, and the skyway system makes walking easy, with heating for the cold winters and air-conditioning for the hot summers. According to city officials St. Paul has the longest skyway system in the world. At a crossroad where four skyways meet, Town Square is a logical starting point for visitors who want to enjoy the warmth of glass-enclosed bridges while they look out on snowy downtown streets.

Although Town Square is well connected to downtown at the second-story skyway level, it is not at all inviting at street level. From the sidewalk it has the appearance of a gray-walled fortress. No storefronts enliven the street, and the most prominent openings are driveways to the hotel entrance and the underground garage. Only a few small doors lead from the sidewalk to the shopping area. Since the original plans called for Seventh Street to flow directly into a public galleria within Town Square, the barrier walls at street level are especially disappointing.

Mayor Latimer recognized early that this was a poor plan, but his design staff could not persuade Oxford's architects to make more than minor changes. Still dissatisfied with the design, Latimer asked Oxford executives to reconsider it. After some small concessions, Oxford president G. Donald Love insisted the plans were reasonable and argued that his stake in the design was as big as the city's. According to Latimer, Love had been so reliable and cooperative in working out earlier problems that he could not bring himself to make a major issue of the street-level design at that point; it would have been "out of proportion." Reluctantly city officials went along with Oxford's plans.

The shopping mall at Town Square got off to a slow start. On opening day in October 1980 only twenty-five stores were in place, most of them national chains. Two years later the mall was 90 percent leased, and by 1984 it was full. In 1986 after a few stores had closed and mall managers decided not to renew others, the vacancy rate was 7 percent.

The public turnout, however, was strong from the beginning. Locating a shopping mall on the skyway network with office towers on one side and a hotel on the other meant that thousands of people pass through it every day. Oxford executives in 1983 estimated the daily flow of passers-by as 40,000, more than enough to give storekeepers a fair chance to catch impulse buyers. Sales figures were reasonable: $171 per square foot in the mall shops by 1982, up to $185 in 1983 and $200 in 1985. Oxford's managers claimed this record was one-third higher than sales at competing suburban malls, but results for the two department stores were mixed. Dayton's general manager Reuel Nygaard was satisfied that his company's $10 million investment in remodeling at Town Square had paid off; Donaldsons director Wallace Holznagel reported in 1985 that Town Square "has not performed at the level of our other stores."

One problem with Town Square's shopping mall was its small size in comparison with suburban competitors. During the planning stage Oxford executives thought the mall could thrive by serving mainly downtown employees. They discovered in a 1982 survey, however, that less than 40 percent of the shoppers worked downtown, with most of the rest coming from outlying St. Paul and its suburbs. Within that broader trade area, most people who were interviewed said they preferred suburban malls because they were more convenient and because they offered a larger selection of items to buy.

Oxford executives and city officials found these survey results persuasive and searched for ways to develop a critical mass of stores nearby. The city promoted a World Trade Center with eighty shops next door and another downtown mall at Galtier Plaza a few blocks away. Meanwhile Oxford's management tried to bring in trendy establishments to strengthen Town Square. In early 1986 Oxford sold most of its U.S. properties to the rapidly expanding Bell Canada Enterprises, whose executives endorsed Oxford's strategy for Town Square. Later the new owners merged Town Square with the World Trade Center and renamed the entire complex Saint Paul Center.

Town Square so far has been a marginal performer for the developer but a big success for the city. In a downtown devastated by urban renewal, Town Square came to life as a civic showpiece with its unusual park and mixed-use complex on a hub of the skyway system. Although its retail record is less than sparkling, sales were strong enough to encourage other developers to build more shopping nearby. As of 1987 the new stores were not yet doing well either, but Mayor Latimer and his business allies had at least made a start at reviving downtown retailing, exactly what they had in mind when they decided to back Town Square.

Horton Plaza: Designing Fantasies

"This damn place should have as little resemblance to a typical shopping center as possible. I don't want to see a bench, a tree grate, a handrail or anything else that has ever been used before. I want it utterly unique!" These marching orders from Ernest Hahn to architect Jon Jerde made innovative design into a competitive strategy for Horton Plaza. With too few people in the center of San Diego to support a large retail center, Hahn counted heavily on suburban customers. But San Diego shoppers already had their pick of well-equipped suburban malls, including three of his own: Fashion Valley, Parkway Plaza, and University Town Centre. To pull suburbanities past the regional malls and into downtown, he needed something special.

Horton Plaza as a result traveled a long way from early conventional plans intended to make department store executives feel they never left the suburbs to a final design that follows no known prototype. It teems with action: four department stores, 150 specialty shops, a farmers' market, two performing arts theaters, four sit-down restaurants, a dozen fast food counters, a seven-screen movie house, mimes, musicians, carts, and vendors. This huge center jams 900,000 square feet of retail space into a tight, five-level structure. It zigzags around two landmarks saved from the wrecking ball: the Balboa Theater, a sixty-year-old Spanish Renaissance Revival movie house now being turned into a contemporary art museum, and the small Golden West Hotel designed by Frank Lloyd Wright's son, John. A 450-room hotel on one corner of the site opened in the fall of 1987, and plans for a second phase would add 300,000 square feet of terraced offices on top of the two seven-story parking garages. Horton Plaza is a new blend of regional shopping mall, festival marketplace, and mixed-use development.

One way to make it competitive was to have a novel design;

another was to put together an unusual combination of stores. The Hahn team worked both ways. By lining up four strong department stores and complementing them with mall shops selling clothing, shoes, jewelry, home furnishings, and gifts, they matched what the suburban centers had to offer. Then they more than matched the competition by adding full-service restaurants, a farmers' market, a repertory theater, a deck of six sporting goods stores, and a cluster of unusual specialty shops. By opening day in August 1985 no less than 40 percent of the tenants were new to the San Diego area, and Horton Plaza was the only place to find them. The newcomers included Boudin's Bakery, a San Francisco institution renowned for its sourdough bread; Stefanel, an Italian clothing chain whose only other California branch was in Los Angeles; and the Price of His Toys, a Beverly Hills toy store for adults featuring robots, high-tech games, and exercise equipment. Although Horton Plaza was not the exclusive location for most of its stores, the San Diego area had no comparable collection of national drawing cards—such as Abercrombie & Fitch, Banana Republic, and Laura Ashley—together with branches of two- or three-store chains known locally for unusual merchandise.

Hahn's decision to do without an enclosure and air-conditioning was a money saver that helped him pay for parking garages when the city could no longer afford them. It also tied in with the strategy of making Horton Plaza different because Jerde would have greater design freedom in an open-air setting. Hahn recalled waking up at two in the morning and thinking, "We're going to take the damn roof off of this thing, and we're going to make it look like part of the city, and we're going to make it exciting, . . . and it's got to have businesses that are different from those we find in the suburban area." He called Jerde in the middle of the night and said, "Take the damn roof off of it and see what you come up with." Jerde yelled with excitement, according to Hahn, because "he hated to be restricted to designing the toothpaste tube sort of air-conditioned environment prevalent in the normal suburban center, and suddenly his imagination and his talent took off."

As Jerde came up with new and unconventional plans, Hahn faced a tough job of persuading department store executives to go along with them. He understood why they would object: "A plan in which one couldn't see from one end to the other, that wasn't the traditional 32-feet wide at all places, that did not have all levels of the mall in a normal plane, defied all the criteria the department stores were used to in the regional shopping centers." Although the anchor stores were firmly committed to Horton Plaza by then, Hahn still had to mount a special campaign to loosen their attachment to the suburban prototype. He managed to bypass the usual store planners and made his pitch directly to the heads of divisions and chairmen of boards who had "the imagination of good merchants."

Hahn also pressed his mall tenants to be innovative. He made new use of the developer's control over store designs by demanding individualism in place of the usual conformity. The Hahn organization's design criteria told tenants explicitly: "Horton Plaza is an outdoor urban mall with a . . . design theme built around a vision of the mall as an extension of the city street system. Standard store designs that have been developed for suburban shopping center locations will not be appropriate." After directing merchants to change whatever storefront they used in suburban malls, the design guide urged them to create a "one-of-a-kind retail environment" through displays expressing unique qualities of their business. The result is a center of undeniable originality that wraps its merchandising function in layers of novely, fantasy, and visual delight. It is a monument to shopping as recreation and to selling by entertainment. With the exuberant colors of the Los Angeles Olympics (where Jerde served as design director), fun and make believe in the spirit of Disneyland, and architectural imitations on the scale of the ones at William Randolph Hearst's castle at San Simeon, it is also very Californian.

One of the qualities that makes Horton Plaza special is its layout. Instead of making it easy for shoppers to find their way around, Horton Plaza teases them with a maze full of surprises. On the outside the softly colored walls of its four department stores line up with the street grid. But once inside the visitor finds a series of curved, wandering pathways connecting buildings of odd sizes, positions, and shapes—including triangles, pie wedges, and terraced crescents. "People don't walk in straight lines," according to Jerde. "They like to curve and angle, dodge and weave. They like steps and ramps. People like to loiter, too, so there must be plenty to catch and hold the eye of the customer." Jerde pushed this idea to an extreme. His main path through the center struck architecture critic Donald Canty as "a meandering, multilevel pedestrian way that is a dizzying melange of architectural elements . . . repeatedly bridged, balconied, arcaded, and festooned."[2]

Jerde had worked closely with Deborah Sussman on the 1984 Olympic Games, and he brought her into Horton Plaza as a consultant on graphics and colors. Together they recreated the pastel shades and stagelike settings of the Olympics, emphasizing soft blues and blue-greens, mauve-violets, aquas, magentas, peach, coral, and rust. Each section has its own design themes, hues, and lighting, with special visual effects such as a nighttime gallery of neon signs in one district.

The architectural borrowings include a prominent triangular structure suggestive of the Cathedral of Siena, walkways in the style of Venetian arcades, four dancing topiary hippos looking fresh out of Disneyland, and plenty of Moorish, Mediterranean, Victorian, and contemporary architecture. Adding to the sense of a theme park are a district with the carved wood and brass fixtures of an old English town and another with the multipaned windows and roll-up doors of an industrial street. Individual stores also pretend to be in other times and places: the movie theaters are 1930s Art Moderne, the Heaven Pop Cuisine restaurant is a 1950s diner, and the America's Cup Bar & Grill has a modern yacht decor. Some of the features mix different styles in striking ways, such as artist Joan Brown's forty-foot Egyptian obelisk faced with colorful California tiles.

While Hahn and Jerde were determined to create something new and different, they also intended it to fit comfortably with the rest of downtown. Hahn wanted the center to look as though it grew parcel by parcel like most city neighborhoods: "We're going to do things downtown that would normally be there if it were built, not at one time, but over a period of time, with individual landlords and individual businesses vying for the attention of the public."

Horton Plaza's outpouring of unusual shapes, colors, and designs makes it into something more than a natural extension of downtown, but Jerde thought of it as a retail neighborhood that happened to have distinctive architecture. He called his design "a new kind of city zone—just as SoHo and Beacon Hill are zones."[3] To help connect it to the city he built a grand staircase entrance from Broadway and made sure all the department stores had windows and entrances on the street. With an eye to detail, he tied the surrounding sidewalks into his internal paths by using identical paving blocks throughout.

Horton Plaza also incorporates reminders of the old downtown. Nordstrom's tiled dome echoes the one on the nearby Balboa Theater, and facade castings from the seventy-year-old Knights of Pythias building decorate a mall structure that replaced it. When Jessop's

Jewelers moved its downtown store into Horton Plaza, Jerde found a central spot for the popular street clock that had been standing on its sidewalk since 1907. He maintained visual connections to nearby streets by locating large windows and arches where the views are interesting and by orienting the upper levels to make the most of sweeping outlooks over the city, its harbor, and the California coast.

Another important connection to the city is Horton Plaza park, once a focal point of downtown activity but an eyesore by the 1960s. The city renovated and landscaped this small park to make it a suitable gateway for the retail center. Because of pressure from preservationists, the restoration followed the original plans of San Diego architect Irving Gill, including his previously unrealized design for a colorful light show in the classical fountain. The result is a handsome green square where people can turn from Broadway to walk into the shopping complex.

During the renovation the city took out the notorious underground toilets whose condition had led to the entire renewal project. Horton Plaza now serves the important though unheralded function of providing public rest rooms for downtown. Hahn and Jerde used these facilities to make still another connection with the city by locating them well within the project where they bring people to the food court and the sports deck.

Horton Plaza attracted attention within retail trade circles and in the national press. Even before it opened, the *Wall Street Journal* identified it as the forerunner of "the next generation of shopping centers." The *New York Times*, which rarely writes about California shopping centers, took note of it as "architecturally stunning" four months before opening day. A week after the opening in August 1985, the *Times* ran a feature article calling it "more ambitious than most previous efforts to create a new environment in the city." Journalist Robert Lindsey went on to describe the center as "a kind of urban village set in the heart of the city, with . . . twisting streets and walks set in an extraordinary architectural framework."[4]

Design critics who do not normally review shopping centers spotted Horton Plaza as a new breed. Sam Hall Kaplan, urban design critic for the *Los Angeles Times*, found it "a refreshing departure from the usual hermetically sealed, climate-controlled, predictable, homogenized shopping malls" and "one of the more ambitious and distinctive shopping complexes to rise out of the dust of urban renewal over the last decade." Paul Goldberger, the *New York Times* architecture critic, recognized it as a sharp break from earlier down-town prototypes. "Horton Plaza," he wrote, "is surely the most im-portant shopping mall to be built in any American downtown section since the Rouse Company got the idea of putting together some boutiques and ethnic food vendors to create the Quincy Market in Boston."[5]

Hahn's and Jerde's intention to create a fun-filled setting for shop-ping made a strong impression, delighting some critics and overpow-ering others. Goldberger opened his review with this observation: "There is a bit of Disneyland inside every shopping mall, struggling to get out. In Horton Plaza in the center of downtown San Diego, the struggle is over: Disneyland has burst through with a vengeance." He found the results exciting but also observed that "its almost untamed spirit, which is so energizing on a first visit, may well pale over time." Donald Canty, writing in *Architecture*, thought there was so much exuberance that the design and colors were "positively assaultive." He sympathized with the intentions but thought the results went too far in this "strenuous, even desperate effort to make downtown com-petitive with suburbia and induce people to come to a part of the city they have shunned for a long time."[6]

One test of innovation is whether a project provokes controversy. Horton Plaza did that too. Speaking at a public hearing in San Diego in 1981, Michael Sullivan of San Diego's Save Our Heritage Organiza-tion had this to say: "I am appalled by the arrogance of the architec-ture planned for the center. It is disgusting." And San Francisco architect Herbert McLaughlin put it down as "one of the most dangerous projects in the U.S. because it will in all likelihood be immensely popular. The issues of attention to detail and permanence were glossed over or denied. It's very kitschy, very much a stage set, very L.A."[7]

Sam Hall Kaplan, in contrast, was positive in his response to this "dazzling display of urban design, architectural allegories, festive decorations, sprightly coloring and conspicuous commercialism." He doubted, however, whether it was possible to create an instant suc-cess: "You cannot throw various urban design elements together, say 'poof,' and expect a 'people place' to evolve overnight. That takes time and a maturation process particular to each city."

Kaplan's sense that it is too early to judge the results applies with equal force to retail sales. The center was a good draw during the first year, however. Shoppers came from throughout the suburbs, and most made repeat visits; they were a reasonable cross-section of income groups with a median above that of the area at large; and three of four went downtown specifically to go to Horton Plaza. It drew a younger crowd than other centers in the area, and one-third of the visitors were from out of town. Horton Plaza rang up first-year sales like no previous mall in the company's history: $240 per square foot, which placed it among the top five centers in the Hahn portfolio. The number of people who visited the center was equally impressive: nearly 14 million over the course of the year. Of the four department stores, Nordstrom reported sales above its projections; Mervyn's performed about as expected; and the Broadway and Robinson's fell short of management targets. By the end of the year, the Hahn Company had leased 95 percent of the mall space.

Although Horton Plaza got off to a strong start, first-year performance is not a reliable measure of how well a center will do once the novelty effect wears off, so judgments of retail success are still premature. Nevertheless, completing the project against heavy odds and building a new downtown prototype are noteworthy achievements in themselves. Beyond the architectural embellishments that attracted critical attention, Horton Plaza is one of the most serious attempts so far to integrate a new retail center with the rest of the city. Its prominent openings to the street and careful attention to connecting details mark a new level of sophistication, especially in contrast to the barrier walls and pasted-on shopfronts of earlier efforts. Hahn and his colleagues measure the results in terms of quality as well as net income. Opening in Hahn's sixty-sixth year, Horton Plaza is in many ways the jewel in the corporate crown.

Hahn Company executives are confident of the center's performance once they take it through the inevitable start-up troubles. "There's no doubt that in the long run it will be extremely successful," Hahn predicts. "We have deep pockets. The company is in a position to sit there four or five years and do it right."

Popular Success and
Critical Dismay

By 1979, after the last phase of Faneuil Hall Marketplace was open, *Newsweek* writers saw evidence of a general revival of cities. They opened a feature article on the subject with a glowing paragraph on Boston: "Boston Mayor Kevin White slumps comfortably in the front seat of his official car and smiles with satisfaction at the visible progress his city has made. Just 100 yards from city hall is bustling Quincy Market—formerly a deserted waterfront area and now a crowded festival of chic shops and restaurants. Farther on is the site of Copley Place, a planned $250 million office-apartment-shopping complex. . . . Middle-class families are refurbishing Boston's neighborhoods. As White's car makes its way through a light layer of snow, he talks about peace in the school system after years of unrest over integration, about a new air of optimism throughout the city. 'Boston,' he says, 'is incredibly healthy.' "[1]

For the hard-pressed mayors of the 1970s, this kind of recognition was golden. It worked well for Kevin White, who spent sixteen years as mayor of Boston before taking up a prestigious professorial appointment at Boston University. Although White's successful rebuilding of downtown led eventually to a public perception that he was not paying enough attention to the city's neighborhoods, downtown projects in other cities were still magic with the voters. St. Paul's George Latimer won a fifth two-year term in 1983 and a four-year term in 1985, against opponents who complained that his devotion to downtown came at the expense of the neighborhoods. Pete Wilson won reelection twice in San Diego, and after eleven years as mayor he ran successfully for the U.S. Senate. Neil Goldschmidt revitalized downtown as mayor of Portland, Oregon, and went from there to become federal secretary of transportation and then governor of Oregon. In Baltimore, scene of one of the most striking downtown development programs, Mayor William Donald Schaefer won a landslide 72 percent of the vote in 1983 against a challenger who charged he had not done enough for poor districts, and he went on to win the governorship in 1986. Schaefer came to national attention mainly for his support of Harborplace and other downtown projects, which earned him a special spread as part of *Time*'s cover story on James Rouse ("Cities Are Fun!") in 1984.

Most of the new projects more than lived up to their sponsors' expectations. Their popular success no doubt owed much to the deliberate strategy of creating controlled, secure environments at a time when people were still uneasy about walking the streets of downtown. "The hunger for a safe place in the city was widespread," said Ben Thompson, in explaining why the crowds came. Beyond that, however, a combination of good luck and good planning made the downtown malls into a near-perfect match for emerging public tastes in the 1970s—the time when the American public rediscovered food and history.

The craze for trying new foods was well under way in the 1960s and by the 1970s had turned into a national preoccupation. Chefs became television personalities, and their cookbooks climbed the best-seller lists. Julia Child, James Beard, and Craig Claiborne were media celebrities. When the food processor burst upon the scene, it encouraged even beginners to try gourmet cooking. Ethnic foods, rare seasonings, exotic cheeses, and newly discovered vegetables took up more and more space in the stores. When a public made anxious about air and water pollution began to worry about what carcinogens might be lurking in the frankfurters, health food and organic food started moving from obscure cult stores onto the supermarket shelves. Craig Claiborne in 1984 attributed twenty years of incredible growth in the demand for new foods to higher incomes, travel, a weakening of the Puritan tradition, and greater sophistication on the part of food writers. He saw the food movement and its results as something of a landmark in human history: "There has never been an age when the public—and I take into consideration kings and queens and princes and shahs and czars and the moneyed folk of this country and Europe—could dine on such elegant fodder, even in private homes."[2]

Even downtown retail centers that did not specialize in food had a few stylish restaurants, and almost all had stores specializing in the latest equipment for the aspiring cook. Calvin Trillin caught the spirit of contemporary downtown retailing when he checked out stores on the renovated waterfronts of old cities: "In my version of a melancholy walk on the waterfront, I find myself walking through a cold Atlantic mist along the docks of some East Coast city, wearing a turned-up trenchcoat, making the best approximation of the traditional clip-clop sounds on the cobblestones that can be expected from a man in crepe-soled shoes, and ducking into a passage that turns out to be the entrance to a gourmet kitchen-supply shop called something like The Wondrous Whisk—where I soberly inspect imported French cherry pitters and antique butter molds and Swedish meat slicers."[3]

While the public was enjoying the pleasures of food, it was also taking a new interest in history. The preservation of historic buildings, once the concern of antiquarian societies and ancestor-worshiping *Mayflower* descendants, began to change into a popular cause by the 1960s. The wholesale destruction of historic areas for urban renewal and highway construction in the 1950s went a long way toward raising concern over the older areas of cities. Boredom with modern architecture no doubt played a part as well. In the housing and design journals that featured fashionable styles of living, contemporary homes in the suburbs were giving way to renovated Victorian town houses. By 1966 Congress sensed enough political interest to enact the National Historic Preservation Act, which established a National Register of Historic Places and new federal reviews to protect historic structures. Boston city officials were determined to save the Faneuil Hall market buildings because of their historic significance; San Francisco citizens rallied to stop freeway construction that threatened the view of their historic Ferry Terminal; and in New Orleans a popular protest stopped a freeway that would have damaged the French Quarter.

The number of communities with official commissions to protect historic districts grew from about 100 in 1966 to 500 in 1976 and 1,000 in 1982. So too with the number of properties and districts listed in the National Register of Historic Places: from 1,200 in 1968 to 2,400 in 1970, 11,000 in 1975, and 37,000 by 1985. Preservation also became a political movement with the skill and strength to get favorable tax treatment in 1976 and again in 1981 for owners who renovated old buildings. When Congress eliminated most tax shelters in 1986, it made an exception for historic rehabilitation tax credits.

The nation's bicentennial celebrations in 1976 stimulated greater interest in the American past. Cities across the country staged special events in their historic areas, most notably the tall ships events in several East Coast cities where old sailing vessels called on the seaports. Victoriana enjoyed a remarkable revival in the museums, in the interior decoration trade, in home furnishing stores. Nostalgia was in, and it was marketable. A scrap dealer who handled salvage from the New York subway system mounted old subway handstraps on wooden bases and sold them through an advertising slogan, "Hang on to a piece of the past."

For the cities the marketability of nostalgia meant that some surviving wrecks had cash value. By the mid-1970s city officials were delighted when they discovered a downtown block they had neglected to bulldoze. Some of these places became backdrops for retail centers that allowed shoppers to look out on turn-of-the-century surroundings. Even the new cities of the West, such as Pasadena, were able to fit modern shopping malls among civic buildings that dated from the 1920s or earlier. Still more fortunate were cities that had venerable shells suitable for groups of stores: railroad terminals, granite warehouses, and even a few structures designed for stores in the first place.

Among the new downtown retail centers with recycled historic buildings were Ghirardelli Square in San Francisco, once a chocolate factory; Faneuil Hall Marketplace; the South Street Seaport in New York: Larimer Square in Denver; St. Anthony Main in Minneapolis; and the Old Post Office Building in Washington. Some incorporated older buildings alongside others that were new—projects like Charles Center in Baltimore, Horton Plaza, Grand Avenue in Milwaukee, and the Gallery at Market East in Philadelphia. One of five downtown retail projects included buildings old enough to lend a touch of history, at least by local standards. And even projects that were entirely new could still capitalize on history, such as Baltimore's Harborplace adjoining the restored U.S. frigate *Constellation*. In sum, city officials and developers were ingenious in exploiting the wave of nostalgia that swept the country.

The swerves of public taste in the 1970s came partly from a new generation of consumers. As the decade began, the leading edge of the postwar baby boom entered its mid-twenties. Between 1970 and 1980 the number of people between the ages of twenty-five and thirty-four grew by nearly 50 percent, adding 12 million young adults to the population. And the baby boomers created their own life-style. By marrying late, pooling two incomes, and having fewer children, they put together an income package large enough to indulge their zest for the good life of shopping and entertainment.

While the journalistic image of the city-loving, high-living yuppie is a caricature that does not fit most of this generation, cities did have a special appeal for many who were raised in suburbia. For single people and married couples without children, city living had much to offer, and the poor quality of urban schools was not the obstacle it had been to the families of the 1950s and 1960s. A home in the city offered working married couples quick access to downtown jobs, a good selection of take-out foods and ethnic restaurants, and no demanding lawns or gardens. Only a minority of the baby boomers chose to live in the city, but that was enough to create a market for downtown retailers. Further, this was the best-educated generation in the country's history. Whether its members lived in the city or the suburbs, many were looking for sophisticated entertainment and unusual products to buy—and so the success of city centers with performing arts theaters and novel shopping malls.

Shopper surveys at the new downtown malls confirmed a connection between their success and the maturing of the baby boomers. Half the shoppers at Faneuil Hall Marketplace in 1977 were between eighteen and thirty-four years old when little more than one-third of the area's adult population was in this age bracket. Similarly Town Square drew half its visitors from this age group, and Horton Plaza pulled in fully 60 percent of its customers from the same category.

In contrast to the many fumbles of the urban renewal period, cities managed to do several things right when they built their retail projects. They learned from suburban malls how to make secure, controlled environments; they changed the suburban prototype enough to create unusual projects suited to downtown; and they offered themes that matched emerging public tastes. Most cities got the response they had wanted when they decided to promote downtown retail centers, and some succeeded far beyond their expectations.

Fear of Commerce

Downtown centers were quick to win popular acceptance; these were truly pavilions for the millions. Critical reactions, however, were mixed. Most journalists celebrated the results. The popular press, eager for a happy ending to its own depressing coverage of urban problems, seized on the opening of the downtown malls as evidence that the crisis was about over. And the business press, always pleased to find examples of entrepreneurial accomplishment, lionized James Rouse and applauded his projects as the long-awaited salvation of run-down cities.

Gurney Breckenfeld, writing in *Fortune,* argued that the Rouse markets came close to accomplishing what Jane Jacobs had urged in 1961 as an alternative to the earlier urban renewal plans: "The underlying concept . . . fits almost everywhere: a *close-grained* diversity of land uses is what makes urban projects flourish."[4] Breckenfeld recognized the commercial purpose of Rouse's projects, but this was commercialism with an artistic flair: "Their pulling power depends on an intricate blend of light-hearted good taste and restrained but canny design that makes visiting them fun. . . . Rouse's centers enliven commerce with artful showmanship. . . . They recapture the timeless delights to be found in the marketplace, the historic reason for cities." Commercial priorities were no problem as long as developers and architects handled them with restraint. At Harborplace the design was "self-effacing" but it was enhanced by interior details "honed . . . to near perfection": tilework, brass, signs, colors, plants, and the aromas of sausage, bread, chocolate, spices, and cheese. The atmosphere was "refreshingly honest" in part because Rouse avoided many tasteless shopping center cliches such as Muzak, fountains, plastic plants, and "gimcrack fakery to evoke nostalgia" in the form of hitching posts, fish netting, or stable lamps. The result, according to Breckenfeld, was "an exquisite gem" and an environment that was "warm, human, exciting," as Rouse himself had described it.[5]

At one stroke downtown malls brought into the heart of the city three things that intellectuals hated: commercialism, suburbia, and mass culture. They were a tempting target. Architecture critics had largely ignored suburban shopping malls, considering them unworthy of serious reviews. These professionals took a closer look when retail projects moved downtown, but they were skeptical.

One of the most thoughtful and fair-minded critics, Ada Louise Huxtable, described her reactions to the first phase of Faneuil Hall Marketplace. She had loved the old Quincy Market when it was a run-down produce terminal, and she was delighted that Boston had found a way to save it from the bulldozer. Its restoration, she felt, was "one of the stellar features of Boston's exemplary downtown renewal, a remarkably sensitive synthesis of new and old." Yet she was disappointed with the way the building had changed. "Why," she asked, "did I spend my first hour in the restored market awash in nostalgia for old produce stalls, old wooden beams, old narrow stairs, chaotic pushcarts and the kind of honest shabbiness that is the antithesis of chic?" She felt sympathy for another visitor who wanted to know, "Where the hell are the vegetables?" At the same time she understood why the building had to change in order to survive. Remodeling was expensive, and to pay for it the market would have to attract an affluent and sophisticated public. The vegetables were still there, as well as flowers, meat, oysters, and ethnic foods, but now they were in "elite, cleaned-up, skillfully merchandised settings." Although the changes were necessary and the solutions appropriate, she observed that "every 'appropriate' solution kills the old buildings a little bit at the same time that it keeps them alive." And yet she had to admit that the new market was fun: "After that first sad hour, I had a wonderful time."[6]

Calvin Trillin, author of "U.S. Journal" for the *New Yorker*, also deplored and enjoyed commercialism at the same time. On his visit to the renovated waterfronts of Boston and a few other cities, he found himself annoyed at their slick, commercial, look-alike decor. He worried that "at the present rate of brick-exposing and paint-stripping and beam-uncovering, all the old warehouses in all port cities will someday be thoroughly renovated as shopping areas that feature gourmet kitchen-supply shops and purveyors of hardwood toys and restaurants with names like The Purple Endive." In an essay subtitled "Thoughts Brought on by Prolonged Exposure to Exposed Brick," he wondered how the owners of exposed brick/hanging-plant/butcher-block decor restaurants across the country all discovered the same novelties at the same time. How, for instance, did they get the word to serve bloody marys in goblets with celery stalks in them and special sandwiches with the same write-ups in the menus? While pondering this question at a waterfront restaurant in Portland, Maine, he wrote, "My thoughts were interrupted by the realization that I had rather enjoyed the special sandwich at The Seamen's Club, and I don't really mind a celery stalk in my Bloody Mary."

Cute restaurant names bothered him, and he wanted to pass a law against naming them for vegetables or animals with unnatural colors: "The Blue Strawberry would be out, which would be a pity, since I had a spectacular meal in a restaurant by that name in Portsmouth." When he went to Boston, he found that sophisticates considered Quincy Market "a Disneyland model of a market rather than a market" and were slightly embarrassed to be seen there. Trillin shared their preference for more authentic market stalls and family-run restaurants, but before he could escape to the outside world, he found himself fascinated by a tomato slicer that reminded him of one he saw when he was a boy. For Trillin the merchandising strategy of the new marketplaces was too contrived and too controlled—but he still fell for it.[7]

One of the disturbing signs of commercialism was the transfer of suburban retailing formats to the cities. Critics were quick to emphasize the mismatch. David Morton, writing in *Progressive Architecture*, called the suburban shopping mall "a building type antithetical to the urban experience." Explaining the point further, Roberta Brandes Gratz argued that malls damage downtown by interrupting or destroying the key element that knits them together: the city street. "Malls," she wrote, "have no streets." What they have are limited pedestrian passages connecting parking lots and store entrances, but leading nowhere beyond the mall. Streets, in contrast, "link all the mixed functions of a city" while malls separate and divide activities. A mall could help revitalize downtown only if it is "modestly woven into the city fabric and its basic street system—letting the pedestrian in as easily as out, and creating no dead walls."[8]

Reviews of individual retail projects applied these same standards. Allen Freeman in the *American Institute of Architects Journal* characterized three mixed-use developments in downtown Atlanta as an "introverted trio . . . dramatic in themselves, . . . remote from one another and aloof from the everyday life of the street." Freeman understood that they turned away from the street in order to avoid subjecting customers to the rest of the city. A suburban visitor, he wrote, could drive into the garage, "escalate to work or play and leave by car without experiencing the rest of downtown."[9]

Critics looked for evidence of integration when they evaluated downtown malls. A well-known historic prototype soon became the measuring rod: the Galleria Vittorio Emanuele II in Milan, completed in 1878 and serving as the heart of the city for generations of Milanese and admiring visitors. The main walkway through the Galleria connects two lively downtown squares, while the cross axis links two secondary streets. Where the Galleria borders major streets, it has shop fronts on those streets and a handsome arcade over the sidewalk. David Morton called it "the antithesis of the monolithic shopping fortress that we know, and . . . perhaps the most important model for what shopping malls can be as they move to inner city."[10]

Critics who expected downtown retail centers to be designed with sensitivity to their surroundings were asking for something reasonable. When city governments moved beyond their earlier role as regulators and began to share decisions with developers, they had more power to make the new retail centers fit their surroundings. City negotiators who were determined to make their new projects work as part of downtown began to insist on designs that would serve this purpose. As a result those critics who were looking for well-integrated plans soon began to find them.

Morton was impressed with the Gallery at Market East in Philadelphia. This project had the suburban advantages of on-site parking, underground truck access, and unified architectural treatment, plus a vertical layout that was distinctly urban and matched surrounding buildings. Morton described the outside of the structure as a sharp contrast to the blank exterior of suburban malls: "vast glazed walls open onto the streets wherever possible, to bring their animation inside. This is not a sealed fortress of smart boutiques." He also noted the Gallery's exceptional connections to downtown pedestrian traffic, with direct access from the shopping complex to subway lines and a new commuter rail station.[11]

Two California projects also won critical recognition for their adaptations to downtown. A review of Santa Monica Place credited this downtown Rouse project with breaking away from the usual suburban "dumbbell plan" and opening the interior galleria to the street on all four sides. Despite this improvement, the reviewer found the arrangement less than successful because the department stores still turned their backs to the street.

Plaza Pasadena attracted favorable notice for a design appropriate to its downtown setting. Its key features were the monumental arched passage through one end of the mall that connected public buildings on either side, and the street-front stores that reinforced adjoining retail frontages. These elements were largely responsible for earning the project a *Progressive Architecture* award in 1979. Reviewer John Morris Dixon recognized Plaza Pasadena as a break with the suburban prototype: "Altogether, Plaza Pasadena represents a kind of landmark in contextual sensitivity. . . . Such limited victories are rare and worth examining."[12]

Such victories as the special design features of Plaza Pasadena came about largely because of joint public-private sponsorship. Dixon recognized that the design decisions he admired were costly ones, undertaken as a result of pressure from city officials. The critics who wrote about Santa Monica Place and the Gallery at Market East also understood that new public-private relationships had not only made these projects possible in the first place but had also pushed developers and their architects to fit them into the surrounding city. The Gallery in particular began as a proposal of the Philadelphia city planning commission in the 1950s, with planning director Edmund Bacon and his staff working out its most important integrating features long before the Rouse Company arrived on the scene.

Artificial Environments

The cities had the leverage to get the kinds of projects they wanted, and some were reshaping the suburban mall prototype into a distinctive downtown product. Where they were successful, they won critical as well as popular recognition. But there were limits to how far cities and developers could get away from the suburban standard and still draw a mass market. Although retail centers could go from horizontal to vertical and tie their public spaces into adjoining streets, they still had to remain sheltered places, managed with care, and intentionally different from ordinary shopping streets. This protected environment was basic to the success of shopping centers in suburbia, and when the cities turned to mall developers to revive downtown retailing, they were placing their bets on the suburban strategy.

By the 1970s middle-class people were avoiding downtown not only because they no longer lived nearby but also because years of decline had left it shabby and unsightly, with porno districts and skid rows pressing on its edges. Crime was an overwhelming concern, and shoppers worried about their safety downtown. A leading specialist in urban affairs, Ira S. Lowry of the Rand Corporation, had this to say about central cities in the late 1970s: "The quality of urban life has deteriorated. Interracial tensions periodically erupt in mob violence. Roving gangs of adolescents terrorize peaceable citizens. Muggings, burglaries, rape, and vandalism are commonplace. Drug abuse is widespread. Public schools are patrolled by guards, but classrooms are nonetheless vandalized, students robbed, and teachers beaten. . . . Unoccupied buildings are stripped and burned. Neighborhood retailers close their shops after a series of armed robberies or a night of looting. Public streets are littered and potholed. The sites of demolished buildings are piled high with rat-infested rubbish."[13]

While Lowry's comments had more to do with poor neighborhoods than with the heart of the city, similar images of mean and dangerous streets kept people away from downtown. Developers knew they had to overcome fear of the city in order to attract tenants and shoppers, and the self-contained mall was a logical way to do it. Even developers who took pains to work their projects into the downtown fabric still controlled them with great care; once inside, shoppers knew they were in a protected setting. Faneuil Hall Marketplace, for instance, has no barriers at its edges. Boston streets run right into the pedestrian paths within the project, and these in turn have no enclosures over them. Yet the difference from the street is striking. Within the Marketplace, all the lights work, the benches are in good repair, and the cobblestones are clean to Disney standards. On nearby streets the grime builds up on the pavement, and the wind blowing from the harbor stirs up a swirl of litter. City police make an occasional appearance on nearby streets, but within the project a dozen private security guards on duty at the same time establish a noticeable presence.

Critics questioned the results of this strategy to give the public a carefully sheltered, controlled environment for shopping. Inevitably it gave the new retail centers an artificial look. Developer management of the tenant mix reinforced a sense of stagecraft by restricting the range of stores to those that were most profitable and then controlling their signs and displays for the sake of uniformity. The new downtown centers look less spontaneous than traditional city streets with their blend of low- and high-rent stores and their profusion of signs and displays ranging from blatant salesmanship to understated elegance.

Suzanne Stephens wrote in *Progressive Architecture:* "Both of the inner-city shopping mall types—recycled buildings or new enclosed skylit galleries—reflect a strong element of escapism. The culture of consumption has always focused on this motif. But the tendency toward ersatz nostalgia on one hand, and controlled, filtered worlds on the other, pushes escapism over the edge into banality."[14] Although Stephens was not opposed to inventing mysterious, exciting environments, she found the drive for commercial success destructive of creative surprises. In the retail centers that made use of historic structures, the problem was "very predictable shops or restaurants; success breeds ever closer imitations of 'the successful.' " Newly built centers, on the other hand, used "the same controlled packaged formulas of the suburban counterparts to represent inside an idealized version of the street outside." Either way, she found little surprise or mystery. Further, she doubted whether commercial activity was compatible with good design: "Is the consuming public too preoccupied with eating popovers to notice the historic buildings anyway?"

Highbrows and Lowbrows

When architecture critics discuss retail projects, the conversation easily turns elitist. In 1981 the editors of *Progressive Architecture* sat down to reflect on three Rouse Company projects: Faneuil Hall, Harborplace, and South Street Seaport in New York. James A. Murphy started with a patronizing gesture: "I feel we should try our best to view these three Rouse developments as would their tenants and the public. Despite my own lack of interest in giant chocolate-chip cookies, plant carts, and pizza slices, they obviously have their constituency."[15] Suzanne Stephens, in the same vein, found the customers themselves creating a synthetic atmosphere: "Seeing hordes of people trooping through old buildings munching on popovers *doesn't* seem much different from an amusement park ambience."

Nory Miller attributed the carnival atmosphere to the projects more than the people: "These are places that, by their very nature, turn everyone into a tourist, native or not. They are isolated, self-conscious, and organized for entertainment. What they most remind me of is Atlantic City's boardwalk with a touch of Disneyland." Miller found the attempts at authenticity and local character unconvincing and considered Faneuil Hall "close to having a terminal case of the 'cutes.' " None of the projects had the genuine local flavor of such neighborhoods as Boston's North End or New York's SoHo, or of farmers' markets. The stores did not sell items that were truly local, while "the fast food puts fried rice next to souvlaki, coke with everything."

Stephens maintained that people do have a craving for authenticity, but what they get at Faneuil Hall and Harborplace are imitations. Even the marketing strategy built around unusual fast foods struck her as phony: "Unlike souvenir shops, gourmet foods look like a 'class' operation, while still having 'mass' appeal." And the interior decor was both unoriginal and damaging to the genuine merits of the original Faneuil Hall buildings: "Jazzy colorful banners, antique signs, craftsy interiors, turn-of-the-century type furnishings, and globe lights, canopies, and skylights all now belong to a basic renovation vocabulary for retail/restaurant use. . . . Although Faneuil Hall Market has more architectural character per square foot than most old buildings waiting to be preserved, it is difficult to see the walls of the central market for all the glass canopies."

The editors took accurate aim at market features that were less original and less authentic than they seemed, but the question remained whether these were shabby tricks or defensible compromises. Only one of the critics talked about the positive functions of these artificial environments. John Dixon argued that they offer their tenants solid advantages unavailable in more authentic parts of downtown: "Management promises ample, well-maintained pedestrian space, a complementary mix of tenants, and promotion to attract customers. Alternative locations, . . . with no management or publicity, draw fewer visitors of all kinds."

Dixon went beyond economic considerations to argue that Faneuil Hall Marketplace paid a debt to architectural history by preserving a landmark group of buildings in a sensitive way: "An important physical legacy was given a commercial use that fits its form and location." Robert Campbell, architecture critic of the *Boston Globe,* objected to the highbrow brush-off of downtown malls. Like other critics he used Faneuil Hall as a springboard for his comments, but he came to its defense. He summed up the indictment this way: it is only for tourists, and only white, middle-class ones at that; it is a boardwalk of ticky-tacky boutiques, a cliché of preservation-style architecture, a cynical fantasy of urban life, a Disneyland for grown-ups. He conceded that the marketplace has an "undeniably thin, staged quality." It is, he wrote, "a quick fix, an upper of urbanity that lifts your blood sugar and then lets you down, leaving you thirsting for more." All these criticisms have some truth in them, he wrote, "but the truths are small compared to the achievement."[16]

To highlight the achievement, Campbell tried to explain why the market is appealing in spite of its weaknesses. He argued that the public was warming up to cities and that Faneuil Hall Marketplace suited a time of change in popular taste. It was, he wrote, "a halfway house for people from the car culture who are trying to learn to love cities again." It coped with people's anxieties by giving them a place that was not dirty, confusing, dangerous, or frightening. The market was their "bright, gay, safe city."

The artificiality of Faneuil Hall, in Campbell's view, results from its halfway-house function. It is "an impersonation of a kind of urban life that no longer exists in most of America" and "a theatrical presentation of street life." It represents "a stage we have to go through as we begin cautiously, self-consciously to re-enact the urban culture we abandoned." Despite these elements of impersonation, Campbell maintained that the marketplace was no fake: "It's as real as it could be and still survive. And it will always retain some element of theater, because all good cities do."

Critics who scorned the downtown markets often put them down by comparing them to Disneyland. Campbell offered another comparison that was equally appropriate but not disparaging. The parks of Frederick Law Olmsted, widely regarded as masterpieces of civic design, "created idealized, quite artificial rural settings for the residents of the sprawling Victorian cities who yearned for their lost contact with nature." Downtown markets do something similar by providing an idealized city for people who have lost touch with urbanity. Their synthetic character does not make them unworthy or laughable.

The Olmsted parks are an interesting parallel, but a more direct forerunner of the downtown mall was the nineteenth-century shopping arcade, which began as a straightforward commercial response to troublesome city streets and eventually won lasting recognition as an achievement of civic design. One wonders how the critics who admire the Milan Galleria today would have reviewed it when it was new. They could easily have rejected it as a sheltered, phony environment that cut people off from the more authentic experience of life in the streets. What could be more artificial than the Galleria with its triumphal Roman arch for an entrance, a dome as wide as St. Peter's, intricate marble pavements, allegorical frescoes, and statues of famous Italians? With the passage of time, however, this and other arcades gradually became part of the city around them; critics looking back do not judge them by the hard standards they apply to new and unseasoned projects.

Robert Campbell senses a special quality in the way people regard downtown malls: "More than anything else, the marketplace is simply the place to go in Boston, the place to be. Perhaps each generation creates a kind of mythic building type for itself. What the skyscrapers were to New York in the '30s, the market is today, not only in Boston but in other cities: the place where the god of the city has taken up residence for the moment. . . . Each became the architectural myth of a particular time."

The market replaced the skyscraper not only as a symbol but also as a vision of what downtown should be like. The skyscraper, as Campbell put it, "was vertical, romantic, silent, aspiring, lonely and pointed to the future." Similar towers were among the hallmarks of the urban renewal era, rising from land swept bare of older buildings and surrounded by open space that allowed people to admire their clean lines from a distance. The marketplace, in contrast, "is horizontal, practical, talky, social, connective and a link with the past." It presents an alternative to the clean sweep, a return to the traditional forms and functions of cities.

The popular success of Faneuil Hall Marketplace was an instant demonstration that old streets, low buildings, and snug spaces filled with action could draw shoppers and create dollar value. These results made the downtown marketplace a practical model for rebuilding cities. But was the model flawed by commercial motives, as most architecture critics maintained? Commercialism did pose problems, yet in many cities developers learned to adapt their projects to urban surroundings and to merge high-powered merchandising with good design. Although the critics scored a few points, they did not make a compelling case against the city strategy of tying private interests to public purposes. If anything, the public-private combinations promoted better solutions to problems by giving city negotiators a chance to send unsatisfactory plans back to the drawing board.

Once-elegant market structures outlived their usefulness by the early 1900s, when delivery trucks jammed the narrow streets and merchants began to leave: South Market (Faneuil Hall Markets), early twentieth century. *Boston Redevelopment Authority.*

South Market after renovation: the congested street now a pedestrian space, and the structure restored to its original profile. Faneuil Hall Marketplace.

Quincy Market pre-renovation with old loading docks and basement awash at high tide. Faneuil Hall Markets. *Rotch Visual Collection, MIT.*

The new Quincy Market at night. Faneuil Hall Marketplace.

Quincy Market with remaining merchants prior to renovation. Faneuil Hall Markets. *Boston Redevelopment Authority.*

Quincy Market: the main arcade decorated for Christmas. Faneuil Hall Marketplace.

Quincy Market: new rotunda with old business signs. Faneuil Hall Marketplace.

Opening-day ceremonies, 1976: James Rouse at microphone, Mayor
Kevin White to right behind architect Ben Thompson. Faneuil Hall Marketplace.
Boston Redevelopment Authority.

Celebrating a success: Mayor Kevin White working the opening-day crowd. Faneuil
Hall Marketplace. *Boston Redevelopment Authority.*

(*top*) Ripe for clearance: a porno district in the heart of downtown San Diego. *The Hahn Co.*

(*bottom*) Opening-day credits, 1985: from left to right, Hahn Company president John Gilchrist and chairman Ernest Hahn, Senator (former mayor) Pete Wilson. Horton Plaza. *Centre City Development Corporation.*

Borrowing images: touches of Siena and Venice mixed with contemporary architecture. Horton Plaza. *The Hahn Co.*

Accommodating crowds in a setting that follows no known prototype. Horton Plaza.

Downtown malls attract young people in disproportionate numbers. Horton Plaza. *Centre City Development Corporation.*

The maze-like pathways of Horton Plaza against a backdrop of office towers whose taxes paid for redevelopment. *Centre City Development Corporation.*

11   Privatizing the City

While critics worked over the architecture of downtown shopping malls, very few people raised questions about the deals that made these projects possible. The new style of negotiated development was out of line with long-held notions of fairness in government, but public-private ventures were an idea whose time had come, and entrepreneurs in local government found plenty of support by the 1970s. Soon their own successes downtown gave further legitimacy to a growing trend in public policy.

Events of the 1960s and early 1970s had shaken people's faith in the capacity of government to deal with the nation's problems. The Vietnam War and the Watergate scandals revealed deception and incompetence. The Johnson administration made big promises to end poverty and eliminate racial inequality but proved unable to quiet the raging discontent of the country's cities by any means short of sending in armed troops. Before long both political leaders and academic evaluators were ridiculing federal efforts as little more than throwing money at problems, and opinion polls revealed an explosion of anti-government feeling. Proposals to bring private industry more fully into public programs made sense. City officials had their own reasons for turning to business firms for help: they were facing revenue problems and anticipating cutbacks in federal aid. As they began to work more closely with downtown developers, they found almost no opposition. And as they started to act in a more entrepreneurial style, even professional organizations of public officials were ready to endorse deal making.

By 1976 the National Association of Housing and Redevelopment Officials was publishing articles in praise of public-private partnerships, calling them "essential" for urban vitality. The National League of Cities put its stamp of approval on public-private dealing when it ran an enthusiastic article by Mayor Schaefer of Baltimore, one of the leading practitioners of the art. "Today," Schaefer wrote, "the public and private sectors are each acting more like the other used to act, and public/private 'deals,' publicly arrived at, have gained respectability."[1]

Encouraging private enterprise to solve public problems was one of the big ideas for government policy in the 1970s. Charles Schultze, chairman of President Carter's Council of Economic Advisors, picked up and elaborated on this point of view in his influential book, *The Public Use of Private Interest.* He described a growing need for public influence over normally private business decisions—for example, when uncertainties about the future prevented even well-established firms from investing in socially desirable ventures. Mayors and business coalitions could have interpreted their problem of attracting developers into the city exactly this way.

Schultze and other policy experts deplored the usual American solution to problems of this kind, which was to take decisions away from private business and transfer them to the "command-and-control techniques of government bureaucracy." Bureaucrats would try to control business behavior through regulation, but often neither their imagination nor their directions were up to the task. As regulation spread through the economy in the early 1970s, it generated widespread dissatisfaction. By the late 1970s the thrust was to try money incentives, such as tax credits for historic preservation, as alternatives to regulation. City entrepreneurship and public-private partnerships were part of this new tack in public policy.

President Carter embraced this strategy as a cornerstone of his policy to help cities. According to his 1978 report on the subject, "National urban policy must reflect a strong and effective partnership between the public and private sector." The reasons were clear: "Federal, state and local funds, no matter how plentiful, will not be enough to solve our urban problems. The private sector must help. Only it can provide the capital needed for rebuilding and growing; only it can carry out the large-scale development programs necessary to provide healthy local economies."[2]

The Carter administration not only helped to legitimize these arrangements but promoted them aggressively through its UDAG program, which provided federal money to close financing gaps for projects that combined city and private funding. Federal staff taught inexperienced local officials how to use public funds as leverage for private investment, how to negotiate with project sponsors for repayment of UDAG awards to reinvest in other ventures, and how to bargain for a share of the profits. Between 1978 and mid-1982 Washington approved more than 1,300 UDAG projects with federal commitments totaling $2.2 billion. Increasingly the cities acted as revenue-seeking investors rather than governments making grants. The proportion of project agreements that provided for city recapture of public funds went from 30 percent in 1978 to 90 percent in 1984, and many included provisions for profit sharing.

Republicans as well as Democrats liked public-private partnerships. President Reagan continued the UDAG program and created the White House Office on Private Sector Initiatives, a presidential task force, and an advisory council to promote this policy. His task force identified city development projects as a form of "investment partnership" that could overcome the limits of government. It noted with great approval "the shift from urban renewal bulldozer and antipoverty campaigns of the '60s to limited, tightly negotiated urban development agreements between the public and private sectors in the early 1980s." And its chairman called for a blending of two great American traditions: entrepreneurship and civic spirit.[3]

In the political rhetoric of the 1980s enthusiasm for public-private partnerships was almost unbounded. The Reagan administration proposed joint undertakings with commercial sponsors for everything from the funding of NASA space missions to the restoration of Ellis Island. And even the guardians of professionalism in local government were ready to throw in their lot with the entrepreneurs and deal makers. By 1983 the International City Management Association was introducing its members to the practical advantages of public-private negotiation in its widely respected publications, one of them titled *The Entrepreneur in Local Government*.

Cities that entered into close relationships with shopping center developers did not do it on the basis of political rhetoric. They did what they had to in order to build the malls they wanted. But by the time their projects were in midstream, the newly supportive climate of opinion was helpful. It allowed elected officials to take credit for bold initiatives that critics might have called backroom deals. It gave successful public sector entrepreneurs applause in professional circles rather than raised eyebrows and cold shoulders. And it gave the developers special standing among their colleagues for spotting opportunities that others missed and for doing projects genuinely different from the suburban prototype. This supportive climate generated political backing for the UDAG program, an important source of funds for many downtown projects.

For the cities, sharing decisions or undertaking joint developments proved far more successful than the divided-control strategy of urban renewal. The high failure rate among renewal projects suggests that if the cities had continued to operate according to the federal manual, many would still be trying to explain to angry voters why, after much trouble and expense, they had not found a developer for the rubble-filled site downtown. The new projects were not only completed, they were built in less time than the fifteen-year average for urban renewal projects. Further, because city officials had a seat at the negotiating table throughout the development period, they were able to get many features that they wanted but could not have anticipated at the time they transferred the land. A cost-saving option for the cities would have been to leave retail development entirely in the hands of private firms. But if cities had waited for developers to act on their own, most of them would still be waiting.

Running Risks: Burbank, St. Paul, Detroit

Public-private combinations won political acceptance, produced the projects that city officials wanted, and promised financial returns on city investments. Risk sharing was in fashion, and soon profit sharing as well. By the 1980s many cities were bargaining for a percentage of project income on top of their returns from tax collections or lease payments.

Although the track record is good so far, the risks are great for cities as well as developers. Projects still face lethal threats before construction begins. The commitments of developers and anchor tenants can change at a moment's notice. Rising interest rates, higher construction costs, and tax revisions can wipe out the most carefully calculated deals. If the project fails to materialize, the city is likely to be deeper in the hole than the developer because it pays the up-front costs of land assembly and site improvements. In San Diego, for example, up to the time of groundbreaking, the city had invested $22 million in Horton Plaza and the developer some $7 million.

Burbank, California, learned the hard way that risk taking for public-private ventures is more than a slogan. Starting in the late 1970s city officials worked on a plan for a downtown shopping mall.

They selected Ernest Hahn as developer and in 1983 signed a development agreement that required him to line up at least three anchor department stores. By mid-1984 he had firm commitments from four stores to participate in the project, three of the stores reserving their right to withdraw if others withdrew. Burbank then floated a bond issue and assembled the necessary land, laying out some $40 million by August 1986. Then a merger of two department store chains, the May Company and Associated Dry Goods, put one of the anchors under new management. The new owners promptly decided to pull their store out of the Burbank venture, and the interlocking commitments suddenly fell apart.

Hahn was unable to hold the other anchors together or to replace the one that left, and he began to discuss a termination of his agreement. Burbank was in a bind. The development agreement did not give Hahn the right to withdraw unilaterally, and the city could have brought a lawsuit rather than agree to a termination. Yet Hahn's good-faith effort to keep the deal together might have swayed a jury in his favor, and a lawsuit under the circumstances would certainly discourage any other developer from working with Burbank. It was the sort of crisis any city could face with a public-private project.

The only good news was that the Walt Disney Company expressed interest in developing the site for a retail and entertainment complex. Hahn and Burbank agreed to terminate their agreement in March 1987, and Hahn forfeited his deposit of $1 million. Burbank was still at least $39 million in the hole, however, with no firm offer from a developer to replace Hahn. A year later Disney dropped out of the picture when its projections showed a return on investment below its corporate threshold. Another entertainment firm, MCA, showed interest in taking over the area, and with luck Burbank may salvage enough to pay off its bondholders.

Aborted projects are not the only risk cities face; they can also lose their investment if a project fails to turn a profit. St. Paul and its port authority put up $25.8 million in loans for Galtier Plaza, an office-shopping-housing complex built in a warehouse district next to downtown. Plagued by cost overruns and construction delays, it opened in 1985 largely unfinished and vacant. By the spring of 1987 it was still unfinished and deeply in debt. The major lender, Chemical Bank of New York, took it over from the developer, promised to finish it, and negotiated a deal to save the city's investment. Early in 1988, however, Chemical Bank gave up its effort to complete the project and put it up for sale.

The city's chance of recovering its investment depended on the sale price since Chemical had first claim on the proceeds. In the summer of 1988 local real estate analysts anticipated a low sales price, with possible losses of as much as $17 million for the city and its port authority, and the project still unfinished. Chemical Bank found a buyer in early 1989 and negotiated a deal that left the city $9 million in the hole. "It's just delightful," said Mayor Latimer, relieved to cut his losses.

Downtown projects are also risky for developers. Few have been outstanding commercial successes, and several have had serious problems. The high cost of developing and operating downtown malls takes a large bite out of rental income, and city subsidies are not great enough to equalize the net returns with those of large suburban centers. Most developers described their in-town earnings as "acceptable" or "promising for the future." Only the owner of the Glendale Galleria, Thomas Schriber, called his project "a home run." Without solid data on the performance of these centers, the best source of information is a knowledgeable insider. Albert Sussman, who spent twenty-eight years as executive vice-president of the International Council of Shopping Centers, said in 1987 that very few developments were producing profitable returns on the tremendous equities invested in them. These are risky and demanding projects, according to Sussman, because "the rules for success in downtown . . . allow hardly any margin for error." To succeed in the city, a developer needs an unusual combination of location, design, tenant mix, and excitement. Many have mastered the suburban formula for shopping malls, but there are few rules of thumb that work in cities.

The limited profitability of most in-town centers reflects a continuing weakness of downtown retail demand. Even the lively shopping complexes that opened after 1970 failed to reverse the long-term decline of downtown retail sales. Between 1977 and 1982 the central business district of almost every major city recorded absolute losses in retail sales, after current dollars were adjusted for inflation. The only possible evidence of a turnaround is that some cities—including Baltimore, Boston, Cleveland, St. Paul, and Washington—lost sales at a slower rate from 1977 to 1982 than they had during the previous five years. Only in a few retail categories did some central business districts increase their share of metropolitan-area sales between 1977 and 1982. Baltimore, Los Angeles, and New Orleans made small gains in their share of area-wide retail food sales, and Baltimore and St. Louis had small increases in their share of sales at eating and drinking places. At least through 1982 downtown retailing was still an uphill struggle demanding an extra measure of ingenuity to lure people away from their suburban shopping habit. For all the innovation and excitement that the downtown malls offer, people still shop mostly in the suburbs.

Even projects with limited profits can still pull in enough people to give the cities most of what they want, and so far city officials have been more pleased with the results than the developers. But if profit margins are small and delayed, the high hopes that entrepreneurial cities attach to profit-sharing will prove unrealistic. Sussman concluded that "financial partners in these ventures almost always will have to wait a long time . . . before there can be profits to share."

Several downtown malls have lost money, and at least two—the Renaissance Center in Detroit and the Herald Center in New York—have gone into default. The Renaissance Center has become the prototype of a troubled downtown mall, a lesson in what can go wrong. This complex of four office towers, a retail mall, and a gleaming seventy-three-story hotel opened with great fanfare in 1977 and went into default in 1983 after its sponsors had already lost $140 million on it. At the time it defaulted, most of the office space was rented, but at rents too low to cover operating costs, and 40 percent of the retail space was vacant.

Renaissance Center was not the work of a profit-seeking developer and an entrepreneurial city government. It was basically a civic gesture by Henry Ford II, conceived a few years after the disastrous 1967 riots. Determined to help his community by providing what he called "a catalyst for the development of downtown," Ford hired architect John Portman to draw up plans for a showpiece on the Detroit riverfront. Using political and economic clout, he then persuaded the heads of fifty large corporations, including other giant auto manufacturers and tire producers, to join him in putting up $155 million in equity capital. Other executives described him as "very persuasive," and some suggested that the official symbol for Renaissance Center should be a twisted arm. Although he argued that the project was economically sound and would in time turn a profit, that was not a prime consideration. "No one was counting on a return," according to Richard Calmes, a vice-president of American Motors. "Everyone knew it was a corporate commitment to a social goal." Ford and his associates lined up financing for the $357 million venture with no funds from the city.

Downtown Detroit was not a promising location. The suburbs dominated both the office and retail markets of metropolitan Detroit, so attracting office tenants and middle-class shoppers was bound to be hard. The location and design of the center compounded these problems. It is half a mile from the heart of downtown, cut off from it by wide roads and railroad tracks. Portman's plan called for pedestrian bridges to link the center to downtown, but these were never built. Instead Portman's design stands as a symbol of isolation: an extreme case of a self-contained, inward-facing complex, surrounded by fortress-like two-story walls covering the heating and ventilating equipment.

Its forbidding appearance from the street may have been intended to make suburbanites feel secure from muggers, and the near invisibility of street-level entrances suggests that the only way to arrive is by car. Once inside, visitors can enjoy such unusual features as a six-story atrium, a half-acre reflecting pool, and five levels of aerial walkways. But many people find the circular retail layout confusing, and there is little doubt that experienced shopping center developers would have done it differently. James Rouse visited it a few months after the opening and concluded that "by everything I know this can't possibly succeed." It was, he said, "terribly complicated . . . , difficult to find your way around, extremely difficult for people to reach from the outside, largely confined in its market to the hotel and the office buildings, which are not enough to support as much retail space as they had. Just very badly planned." If there is a simple moral to the Renaissance Center story, it is that a partnership based on private sector commercialism plus public sector entrepreneurship has better prospects than one based on private sector commitment to philanthropy. Detroit would have benefited from the involvement of a retail developer who knew how to draw a crowd and city officials who wanted a new project for downtown.

Setup for Scandal

Besides posing financial risks, joint ventures can easily put public officials in conflict with accepted standards for government behavior. The deals cities make favor some developers with more help than others. Each project has its own rationale, and there are no formulas for setting a proper level of public assistance. In the public-private projects for which we have information, the public share of development costs ranged from 3 percent to 83 percent. If the first retail developer in a city faces a totally untested market and the second comes on the scene after anchor stores and mall tenants are eager to rent downtown space, should both have the same help from the city? What is fair and equitable is far from clear.

Can the city serve as both a partner and a regulator at the same time? If it has a financial stake in a project and stands to earn a share of the profits, will it investigate the project's impact on traffic and neighborhoods with the same care it applies to proposals from strangers?

Accountability can also prove troublesome. Hammering out development agreements that are long and complex even by real estate standards requires meeting behind closed doors. Eventually, when local government has to give formal approval, the press and the city council will learn about the bargains that were struck. But alternatives dropped along the way seldom come to light, and few people understand the deal well enough to take an informed position: the city, after all, is usually trading current costs against future returns that are necessarily uncertain. Besides, the deal that reaches the members of the city council is a fully negotiated agreement that they cannot take apart and amend piece by piece, so they have a choice of either rubber-stamping it or looking like enemies of progress. When Horton Plaza came up for council approval after seven years of work, swing voter Lucy Killea decided at the last minute to support it with the explanation that "I certainly wouldn't want everything to come to a halt, because we've been waiting too long." Is this accountability?

To find a developer, city officials usually issue an invitation for proposals and get back two or three worth considering. They generally select one and proceed to negotiate a detailed agreement. On the basis of what the city promises to contribute, the development company makes its final proposal of what it will build and what it will pay. In most cases later events lead the city to change its agreement and to allow the developer to revise his plans as well. When competitors who were not chosen discover the changes, they might well complain that city government has arbitrarily switched the terms on which it made its selection in the first place. Is this a fair selection procedure?

The argument that public financing for a project is unfair to business competitors has led to at least one court case. The owner of a hotel in Fort Wayne, Indiana, charged that the city's use of room tax revenues collected from his hotel to help develop a competing one was a taking of private property for other than public purposes and that it violated equal protection because it favored one hotel owner over another. A federal district court, however, ruled that the subsidy was reasonably related to a public purpose—economic development—and was not a violation of equal protection.

Only a few features of public-private negotiations actually proved troublesome politically. Opponents of Plaza Pasadena charged that the city's review process never gave the public or the planning commission a chance to consider alternatives to the plan put forward by the redevelopment authority. In St. Paul downtown property owners were furious with the city for agreeing to collect special taxes from them to pay maintenance costs for Town Square, which many regarded as a competitor. And in San Diego preservationists criticized the city for agreeing to a plan for Horton Plaza that destroyed several historic buildings. Aside from Pasadena, the projects we studied in detail were remarkably noncontroversial, and the opposition that did surface was seldom directed at behind-the-scenes deal making.

The recent selection of a developer to rebuild the site of New York City's Coliseum at Columbus Circle, however, illustrates the potential for scandal in these negotiations. Chairman Steven Sanders of the state legislature's Committee on Oversight, Analysis, and Investigation charged that the city reached a decision based on "unfair," secret negotiations and "bid manipulation and collusion." The city selected Boston Properties even though its original bid of $353 million for the land was far below that of a competitor. According to Sanders, city negotiators offered Boston Properties the project if it would raise its bid by $100 million to meet the competition. This firm had two and a half weeks to negotiate a new offer, while the original high bidder was given only four days to respond. Eventually Boston Properties won with a bid of $455 million. City finance commissioner Abraham Biderman, who headed the selection committee, claimed it had no legal obligation to sell to the highest bidder and found Boston Properties best qualified because it had lined up the investment house of Salomon Brothers as prime tenant. Having decided on a developer, the committee then tried to get a higher price for the property. This was a procedure that gave city officials great flexibility but opened them to charges of favoritism.

Does the general lack of controversy mean that public-private arrangements are meeting high standards for accountability and fairness? Not necessarily. It probably means that during the 1970s and early 1980s, the public was more concerned to see projects built than it was to have uniform procedures and equal chances for all competitors. The earlier system of divided control over urban renewal projects produced uniform rules by the volume but not enough results on the ground. By the 1970s the voting public had more reason to worry about economic development. The steady rise of personal income since World War II ground to a halt in the inflation and recession after the 1973 oil boycott. Families that wanted a middle-class life-style had to work harder than ever to get it, and even with millions of married women taking jobs, family income still declined by 6 percent in real dollars from 1973 to 1984. Mayors and council members felt voter pressure to hold the line on taxes and to work on projects that would produce jobs and revenue. Given these priorities, results were more important than fairness and accountability.

The current drive for development results does not mean that the public will tolerate outright corruption in public-private dealings. In such fields as defense contracting, environmental cleanups, and labor relations, evidence of misconduct continues to be harmful politically and leads to the firing and prosecution of top officials. Critics of public-private projects have been keeping watchful eyes on downtown deal making in the hopes of finding wrongdoing. It is natural enough to expect some in situations that require municipal staff to make decisions on multimillion dollar projects. To the credit of local officials and the developers, however, even while exposés of other graft made national news, we found no serious charges of development-related scandal in any of the cities we studied.

A look at public-private relations in the defense industry helps to put city development procedures in perspective. Defense procurement scandals have been widespread. The Department of Defense inspector general reported in 1985 that federal officials had recommended prosecution or administrative action for no fewer than 17,000 cases of misconduct during the past two and one-half years. Many of the largest defense contractors were involved. Rockwell International pleaded guilty to 20 counts of fraud; General Electric pleaded guilty to 108 counts of falsifying time cards; the Sperry Corporation pleaded guilty to charges of making false statements; the Pentagon refused to accept 4,700 kinds of microcircuits which it claimed Texas Instruments had failed to test properly; and Grumman Aircraft charged the navy $649 apiece for ashtrays (leading an exasperated secretary of defense to tell a press conference that he recommended using mayonnaise jars for ashtrays).

Critics of defense contracting blame these troubles in large part on a lack of competition that gives individual contractors great leverage when they strike bargains with federal officials and on the revolving door that allows retired military officers to work for the same companies they used to supervise. Both the lack of competition and the revolving door could also prove troublesome when cities deal with developers. City officials who wanted downtown malls usually found very few companies willing and qualified to build them. Still, officials bargained hard, and when they made concessions, they usually got something in return. The deals were seldom one-sided and often advantageous to the city. Once into negotiations, developers usually became committed to a project and were willing to compromise. Recall James Rouse's battle to avoid losing the Faneuil Hall project and his promise to report to the mayor personally in order to get it. Also public sector negotiators may have been effective because city hall is a good training ground for bargaining and they wanted professional recognition for a job well done.

The revolving door is a great temptation for city development officials whose skills have greater value for private industry than they do for most government bureaucracies. After holding senior redevelopment positions at a young age, they may find themselves with no place further to go in government. Meanwhile what they have learned about politics makes them attractive to developers who work with the city. Several public sector entrepreneurs have already left government to set up consulting offices, practice real estate law, or develop property.

When Anthony Gliedman resigned as New York's commissioner of housing preservation and development in 1986 and announced he was going to work for developer Donald Trump, city hall reporters responded with a "collective catching of breath" audible in the press room. In this case there was no question of a private firm rewarding a public official for past favors. Gliedman had earlier turned down a tax abatement for Trump Tower, and Trump both sued him and singled him out for a personal attack. (Later an appellate court ruled in favor of the abatement for Trump.) Further, New York has stricter controls than most other cities over its officials' activities after they leave public service. The city charter requires them to avoid working on matters directly related to their city jobs for three years after they leave and to avoid private work that could be "adverse" to the city for eight years. Even with safeguards in place, this kind of turnabout poses a threat to the city's ability to manage future negotiations fairly. As columnist Neal Peirce pointed out, Trump will have access to truly expert advice on "which officials to call, or what donation for a subway station, homeless shelter or political campaign might grease the skids for city-development decisions he wants."[4]

So far the cities that have had cooperative relationships with developers seem to have escaped serious trouble. Their record is good not only in comparison with the scandal-ridden defense industry but in comparison with any municipal government function. Yet the potential for scandal is so great that city officials should set up countermeasures in advance, such as requiring more uniform negotiating procedures, arranging for independent analyses of developer agreements, and tightening the restrictions on former officials who want to do business with the city.

How Public Is a Mall?

Out of the public-private negotiations came projects that gave private firms control over public places. The new retail centers were public places and private businesses at the same time. City officials were interested in both the public and the private functions since they wanted to bring large numbers of people back to downtown and also wanted to have a taxpaying, job-creating asset.

City negotiators and developers agreed that a privately controlled project, designed for the crowd, would serve their purposes. If the developer drew up plans that focused too narrowly on private purposes, city officials raised objections and pressed for changes. Usually the developers and their architects were responsive, so that completed projects strengthened downtown, rang up sales, and created public places under private management.

Private spaces began to function as city streets. They are not city streets, however; they are almost always owned, maintained, policed, heated, cooled, and controlled by private companies. The public does not have the same rights of access, since the owners set the hours and days when they are open. Sometimes, as in Pasadena, the city has negotiated agreements to keep certain passageways open to the public even when the rest of the complex is closed.

But project managers can keep people away from their public areas without actually closing them. Cincinnati had a running conflict with the Galbreath Company, developer of the Fountain Square South project, over the use of its 10,000-square-foot atrium. When the city agreed to invest some $21 million in this office-hotel-retail complex, the mayor and other top officials envisioned the atrium as a lively extension of Fountain Square, a busy outdoor meeting place across the street. The city, according to its development officer, wanted "an indoor living room—it was looking for the kind of activity of a Faneuil Hall or Harborplace in Baltimore." But the developer kept the atrium almost empty, with no sitting areas or food stands and few decorations. David Niland, an architect on the city's design review board, called it "the most vapid interior space that supposedly has civic overtones that I've ever seen in this country or elsewhere."

The developer apparently had a more limited purpose in mind for the atrium: to serve as a passageway for customers going to the 460-room Westin Hotel and specialty shops, not a playground for the public at large. According to the company's director of development and construction, "At no time did we ever advance to the city that it would be a big public place to sit. We were presenting it as an exciting place to pass through, but not a place to sit." Mayor Thomas Brush put it differently: "Along the way, we lost the public atrium. I think from the outset the tenants really didn't want the public in there unless they were going for a specific business. I think they didn't want it for security reasons."

Ultimately the issue is one of private control. The project architect, John Hagmann, defended the use of the atrium as strictly a company decision. "It is," he said, "still private property—to which there's a consensus that there be public access. The ways in which the space is used fall to the discretion of the ownership and of the hotel management." And Mayor Brush learned about the private nature of enclosed public spaces. In negotiating the next downtown public-private project, he said, "What we've tried to do . . . after learning our lesson from Westin, is to stay involved and insist on changes we want carried out. But it's difficult since we're not contractor nor owner."[5]

The privatization of public space has led to conflicts over the use of shopping malls for political activity. When the streets of downtown were filled with shoppers, they were the favorite places for politicians to meet voters, make a speech, circulate leaflets, or collect signatures for petitions. When shoppers moved off the streets and into suburban shopping malls, however, they were going from public to private property. Inevitably the rules changed.

Mall owners take different positions on what they will or will not allow, with many deciding on the basis of whether they think an activity will please or annoy their customers. Most readily allow community groups to use the mall for such inoffensive purposes as selling Girl Scout cookies, raffling cars for local charities, or organizing the Red Cross blood drive. Politicians soon discovered that malls are ideal for speeches or hand shaking, and while some mall owners are happy to have them drop in, others keep them out. Civil libertarians who took note that the malls were the new Main Streets of suburbia saw a threat to free speech in any attempt to restrict political activities, but during the early days of regional shopping malls, few people thought the matter was urgent enough for a serious challenge.

The political activism of the Vietnam War changed all that. Developers had successfully marketed an image of the shopping mall as a new downtown—not just a collection of stores but a meeting place for the community. Now war protesters put them to the test by asking to use their public spaces for rallies and demonstrations. Since there were few downtown malls at the time, the issue came to a head in suburbia. There developers had worked hard to create a relaxed atmosphere for family shopping with tasteful landscaping, subdued lighting, gurgling fountains, and piped music. Strident protests against a grim war would be about as helpful to this atmosphere as a child molester in Disneyland.

Shopping center operators had good cause to worry. On four consecutive Saturdays during the 1969 Christmas season, hundreds of teenagers gathered at the Northland mall outside Detroit to protest the war. Once demonstrators and counterdemonstrators had fist fights, smashed windows, and set off a smoke bomb. A large police force from several cities kept the other Saturday demonstrations under control but according to the manager "didn't seem to do much for the shoppers' sense of security." That holiday season so critical to retailers was no commercial success at Northland.

Many other mall owners decided to keep protesters out, while others let them in only if they promised to follow strict codes of behavior. Some were furious with any suggestion that their malls were as public as the streets they had replaced. "If our centers are public property," one developer fumed, "let the public police our malls, light our parking lots, shovel the snow and collect the garbage."

Antiwar protesters blocked from handing out leaflets in a mall in

Portland, Oregon, turned to the federal courts for relief, arguing that their right to speak in public places extended to private places serving a public purpose. If shopping malls had been built around streets that were truly public, rather than the Main Streets of public relations imagery, there would have been no contest. Justice Owen Roberts had written in a 1939 Supreme Court decision: "Wherever the title of streets and parks may rest, they have immemorially been held in trust for the use of the public and, time out of mind, have been used for purposes of assembly, communicating thoughts between citizens, and discussing public questions. Such use of the streets and public places has from ancient times been a part of the privileges, immunities, rights, and liberties of citizens."[6]

The Portland case eventually went to the U.S. Supreme Court, which ruled in 1972 that the protestors did not have a right to use the mall. The court opinion cited the lack of connection between the antiwar protest and the business activities inside the mall, as well as the availability of other ways for the group to take its message to the public, including handing out leaflets on the sidewalk outside. The court held that the shopping center was not a public place and that property did not lose its private character simply because the public was invited in.

While antiwar protests faded as an issue, political candidates were prepared to go to court to establish their right to campaign at malls. In a Massachusetts case, five-term congressman Michael Harrington testified that meeting people at shopping malls was one of the most effective ways for a candidate to establish voter recognition and political identity. The State Supreme Judicial Court noted in its *Batchelder* opinion that the shopping center in question was the most favorable place in the entire district for getting voter signatures, more so than canvassing the downtowns of nearby communities or going from door to door in residential neighborhoods. The Massachusetts Court first defined the issue at stake as access to the ballot rather than the broader exercise of free speech and then upheld the right of a candidate to solicit signatures at the shopping mall. As far as free speech was concerned, the court conceded that there are reasonable alternatives to the use of a shopping mall: "Ideas and views can be transmitted through the press, by door-to-door distributions, or through the mail, without personal contact." Yet collecting signatures for nomination was different: "A person needing signatures for ballot access requires personal contact with voters. He or she cannot reasonably obtain them in any other way." The court also took note that the shopping mall is the inheritor of traditional downtown functions: "Shopping malls . . . function in many parts of this State much as the 'downtown' area of a municipality did in earlier years."[7]

The U.S. Supreme Court in 1980 upheld a California decision giving access to political petitioners under a state constitutional guarantee of free speech, opening the way for state courts to decide cases on the basis of their own constitutions. State court decisions in both Washington and Massachusetts allow access to shopping malls for the circulation of petitions and nominating papers, as do several local court rulings in other states. Supreme courts in Connecticut, Michigan, New York, North Carolina, Pennsylvania, and Wisconsin, on the other hand, have held that shopping malls are private places whose owners can keep out petitioners and pamphleteers.

Even the decisions most favorable to political activity leave the malls far less open than public streets. They mainly protect the rights of political candidates to collect signatures for nomination, and secondarily protect the right of people to circulate petitions to government. They do not help groups that want to petition newspapers or corporations or that want to sponsor speeches or demonstrations. Further, mall managers can insist on advance notice and can limit signature collectors to certain hours and places, such as a small table somewhere in the mall. Managers can restrict the way petitioners operate by, for example, preventing them from using lights or loudspeakers or walking up to shoppers to ask for their signatures.

Court rulings aside, mall owners do let a variety of civic and political groups use their public areas, but they are selective. According to a 1986 survey of large shopping malls, nine of ten let in charitable and community organizations such as the United Way and Boy and Girl Scouts, and nearly two of three admitted some political organizations such as the major parties and the League of Women Voters. But less than half allowed petitioning, and only about one out of three let in groups taking positions on controversial issues such as abortion or nuclear disarmament. Less than one of three allowed political candidates to campaign, and some of these restricted campaigning to a single "meet the candidates night" or a walk-through without placards.

The main argument against allowing organized activities is that shoppers do not want them. As Gary Doyle, vice-president of the Taubman Company put it, "In an environment that you spend a lot of time and energy—not to mention money—designing to be non-disruptive, it's contradictory to let these groups in. Our studies show that customers don't like being intercepted."[8]

With the opening of city malls, the issue of political access began to move downtown. Only the lull in activism during the 1980s kept downtown centers from confronting the same pressures that suburban malls had faced during the Vietnam era. A 1986 episode at Horton Plaza, however, illustrates the conflicts that probably lie ahead. Playing for Real Theatre, a group opposed to U.S. policy in Central America, asked for permission to stage a ten-minute play depicting the bombing of El Salvador. Horton Plaza's manager turned them down but offered to let them collect signatures for a petition and pass out leaflets from a cart in the mall. This was the standard procedure for political petitioning, used by a dozen other political groups at Horton Plaza.

Playing for Real Theatre had no interest in this limited form of political expression. A few weeks later a San Diego police detective passed along a tip that the street theater group planned to enter Horton Plaza to create a disturbance that would publicize their cause, possibly by resorting to violence. Plaza management went to court and got a restraining order and then a preliminary injunction to prevent the group from staging a political play in the retail mall but allowing them to circulate a petition under management rules.

The theater group contested this injunction but lost their case on appeal. The appellate court pointed to several reasons for upholding the injunction: it allowed other forms of political expression in Horton Plaza; the retail center had no suitable staging area for a play; there was no evidence that Horton Plaza had displaced other public forums or that other suitable places were unavailable; and government help in building Horton Plaza did not necessarily give the retail center a more public purpose than any other shopping area. The court drew a distinction between suburban and downtown shopping centers. In the suburbs a shopping center often becomes the only place where enough people gather on foot to create a forum for political expression, while Horton Plaza has no monopoly on pedestrian traffic in downtown San Diego. Indeed the court took note of Horton Plaza park next to the retail center and questioned why the street theater group could not perform there with equal effectiveness.

On city streets, meanwhile, politicians and protesters are still free to work the crowd on the spur of the moment, without advance permission from anyone, and to go beyond collecting signatures: to carry posters, hand out leaflets, collect contributions, put on skits, and pose for television cameras. The variations and limits of court rulings, and the many restrictions of mall owners, mean that privatizing downtown has made it less of a political forum. Shopping centers are not as open as city streets. This is undeniably part of their appeal, but at the same time the public has traded some rights of political expression for quiet Saturdays at the mall.

Whether the trade is a good one depends on the city. If downtown has other places where crowds gather on public streets, there may be no need to use a shopping mall for political purposes. But if the streets and parks are empty most of the time and a downtown mall is the major crowd collector, restricting access to it deprives the city of a forum for ideas. City officials do have a chance to share decisions on political activity in downtown malls: when they negotiate the terms of their assistance to the developer, they can and should pin down appropriate public rights for the use of the common area.

Security at a Price

Enclosing downtown activity within private territory also brings both gains and losses in crime control. Mall owners rely on private guards for security, with city police as emergency backup. They have compelling reasons to protect customers since nothing can ruin the reputation of a mall faster than well-publicized crimes. And with private guards, they also have the resources for protection. The owners can exercise a degree of control over their security staff far exceeding a mayor's control over city police. Mall managers can station and schedule their guards however they want, changing assignments without interference from police associations or political cronies. They can enlarge or reduce the force as they wish, subject only to complaints from mall tenants who pay for security as an add-on to their rents.

Private employers of security guards can operate with so few restrictions that some specialists believe privatization in itself goes a long way toward improving security. One expert who argues this way is Chief Anthony Bouza of Minneapolis, a former Bronx commander for the New York City Police: "Any private enterprise could come into the City of New York . . . and police it better, for hundreds of millions of dollars less. All you have to do is work the police eight hours a day, forty hours a week, which would be a revolution."[9]

A common tactic in downtown malls is to open with an extra-large security force to discourage criminals and then cut the staff gradually if there are no signs of trouble. During an early saturation period, mall guards may gather conspicuously around people who look troublesome to let them know they are under surveillance. Security guards commonly patrol parking garages as well as the mall itself. In addition mall managers and tenants are concerned to keep parking areas well lit. Some malls make use of closed-circuit TV to monitor the parking areas, with the monitors intentionally noticeable in order to reassure shoppers and warn criminals. The security force in Plaza Pasadena patrols the garages quietly on bicycles in order to avoid signaling their approach.

All these precautions help make the public feel secure, but how secure they actually are is hard to know. Some shopping center executives take the position that a mall is like a small city, and crime is unavoidable. Security forces and safety measures can deter crime at the margin, they argue, but even well-managed malls have had assaults, rapes, and murders. The best security, in their view, is to have a large number of people in the mall.

The total environment of a shopping center gives the public good reasons for feeling safer there than on downtown streets. Malls have better lighting, a steadier flow of people, and fewer hiding places and escape routes for muggers. To the extent that crowds prevent crime, they have the crowds. To the extent that visible police officers discourage crime, they have those too. In-town shopping centers, according to a 1985 survey, usually have about three security officers on duty in the common area and parking lots, with more during peak periods. Nearly all wear uniforms and carry radios and handcuffs. In addition, many large stores have their own guards. On most downtown streets the only police presence is an occasional patrol car.

Yet putting security in the hands of private guards under the control of mall management raises controversial issues. First, civil liberty advocates point out that guards working on private property can operate outside the legal limits imposed on police. Unlike the police, they are under no obligation to tell suspects about their constitutional rights or to avoid random searches, since the courts have ruled that these protections are meant to restrain government but not private firms. In a New York case security guards at Bloomingdales did not tell a suspect that he had a right to remain silent, asked him to sign a statement admitting that he had stolen shirts, and assured him they would not prosecute. Store executives then decided to press charges and used his statement as evidence to convict him. The New York Court of Appeals found the store's actions to be legal.

Private guards can also exclude visitors who are not criminals but whose presence might disturb shoppers. Security officers find polite ways to hustle drunks off the property quickly and firmly, and the absence of shabbily dressed visitors in downtown malls suggests that guards have found ways of keeping street people outside as well. The Pike Place Market is exceptional in opening its doors to panhandlers, drifters, and winos.

Private security forces do not have the same priorities as public police. Their main concern is not to bring criminals to trial but to protect the interests of the firms that hire them. Sometimes these objectives are in conflict. Private guards may underreport crime out of concern to protect a mall's reputation for safety. Guards who investigate crimes may focus more on fixing weaknesses in company security than on finding and prosecuting criminals. Even when companies do identify criminals, they may try to get their money back without reporting the crime. When a Calgary bank caught a customer who had stolen $14,000 from its automatic tellers, the bank's officers tried to persuade him to sign for the money as a loan. Only after he refused did they call the police.

Privatizing the policing of downtown may lead to violations of the normal rights of some suspects while letting others go free, depending on the whims of the companies involved. When retailers set law enforcement priorities, there is also a danger of shortchanging the public. Although mall owners have every reason to worry about crimes of violence that could ruin their reputation, the major stores in downtown malls have serious concerns about shoplifting and employee dishonesty. If business priorities come first, these stores could concentrate their guards in high-price selling areas and near cash registers rather than in parking garages and other dead spaces.

The eagerness of city officials to solve downtown security problems through privatization in spite of these potential problems is a telling comment on the failure of government to make public places safe and attractive. New York, for example, turned to a private sector strategy for taking Bryant Park back from the drug dealers and shady characters who dominated it for years. Earlier efforts to reclaim this once-popular spot behind the New York Public Library included setting up book and flower stalls, a box office for discount tickets to music events, and a series of live concerts in the park. Yet the crowds never stayed long enough to make it safe, and the drug dealers and derelicts were back after dark. In 1983 the city shocked public park supporters by proposing to lease the entire grounds to a private, nonprofit corporation and to use part of it for a two-level pavilion housing a 1,000-seat restaurant. Its bright lights and concentrated activity were intended to make the park a safe place to visit. The plan was to raise development funds for the restaurant and park improvements from the city, the restaurant owner, and private foundations. Funds for maintenance, a chronic problem while the city was in charge, were to come out of restaurant profits, contributions from the city and the nonprofit corporation, and the proceeds of a special tax on surrounding businesses.

When civic groups raised objections to private control of this public area, park officials backed away from their offer to lease the entire grounds and decided to lease only the restaurant site. They still proposed to put the Bryant Park Corporation in charge of day-to-day management of the entire area but with the municipal Parks Department keeping supervisory responsibility.

This elaborate public-private plan, with a restaurant serving as both a magnet to bring people back and a profit center to fund park maintenance, was another version of the privatization of downtown space. Issues of private control proved less disturbing to city officials and the public than run-down, unsafe areas that they wanted to reclaim for the average citizen.

The Chaining of Main Street

The public use of private interest for revitalizing cities subjected a key part of downtown to the discipline of suburban malls. City officials who wanted to see crowds of shoppers welcomed that discipline, but people who favored local, independent storekeepers worried that it might squeeze them out. Although mall developers valued independent stores and often made special efforts to include them, national chains dominated the shopping center business. In the suburban prototypes two-thirds or more of mall tenants were usually part of national chains. These stores had excellent credit ratings and strong staying power in the event that the first few years in a new mall were unprofitable, and the investors who financed malls insisted on having a large number of them.

Over the years developers built close working relationships with the chain stores, and when they leased space in a downtown retail center, it was natural for them to turn to some of their most reliable tenants. Those who tried to break the pattern by recruiting independent merchants, in the style of the Rouse Company at Faneuil Hall, had to cope with nervous lenders. And even the Rouse Company, which specialized in finding locally based, independent tenants, rented to large numbers of chain stores in such downtown projects as the Philadelphia Gallery.

Neither custom nor financing, however, fully explained why shopping centers relied so heavily on national chains. An important part of the story was the weakness of existing downtown stores. The typical independent merchant was undercapitalized, operating from deteriorated facilities, and unable to get financing for renovation or expansion. To survive the lean years before downtown began to attract new investment, many had switched their line of merchandise to serve low-income customers. They were highly vulnerable to new competition and unable to reorganize for operating in a modern retail center.

The Hahn Company tried repeatedly to find independent merchants who could move into its new malls, recognizing that the independents were often more innovative and energetic than chain store managers. A mall location has tremendous advantages for a small store. "A local merchant doing a volume of $150,000," according to Hahn, "doesn't realize he can do five or six hundred thousand in a mall. He knows he is paying one dollar a square foot for rent, instead of $20 in a mall. But in a mall he can operate in a smaller space, with lower utility costs, and with twenty times the number of people walking by his store every day." Still, operating in a mall usually means opening seven days a week, handling several times the volume of merchandise, and following the rules of the management—in short, living a different life.

Few local merchants were both willing and able to make these changes. Land clearance for Plaza Pasadena displaced 166 established businesses, but only 11 showed interest in moving into the new shopping center, and a lone shoe store was the only one that actually did move in. Most of the firms relocated to other inexpensive buildings in and around Pasadena, where rents on Colorado Boulevard were one-fourth the cost of space in Plaza Pasadena. The shift to a shopping mall cost more than they could afford.

As chain stores replaced independent merchants, critics mourned the loss of local character. Yet this was an unavoidable outcome of the decision to use shopping centers to bring back downtown activity. Shopping centers, whether suburban or in-town, live by serving the vast middle of the market. They require a high sales volume in order to make productive use of their high-cost space. City officials eager for downtown shoppers cannot also keep all the low-productivity stores in place. To do so would not bring back the shoppers, nor would it pay for the private space intended for public use.

The public-private combinations produced a certain style of project that developers found manageable and profitable. Modern merchandising was an essential part of their strategy. Even when developers found independent merchants capable of switching to high-volume operations, such as the food stands at Faneuil Hall Marketplace, these businesses changed so much in the process that they no longer seemed as authentic as they once were. The problem, though, is that when they were "authentic," downtown was depressed.

The public-private strategy meant privatizing important downtown functions and following commercial rules. On the whole these changes produced the results that city officials and the public at large seemed to want, but they also brought some unpleasant surprises. It is too early for decisive judgments, and we lack the historic perspective that now frames the urban renewal era. Still, there are tensions between public and business interests that have to be weighed in the balance against the power of commercial projects to revitalize downtown.

Retail centers that draw visitors by the millions must do more for people than sell merchandise in a pleasant way. One of the principles guiding the rebuilding of cities, according to critics of redevelopment policy, was to reestablish "middle-class control." If bringing territory under middle-class control meant establishing places that conformed to conventional standards of behavior and appearance, this was very clearly one of the functions of downtown shopping malls. Not only the middle class but large numbers of people at all income levels shared an interest in making their city safe, hospitable, and orderly. Still reeling from a time when criminals terrorized whole neighborhoods, activists across the political spectrum turned to violence, and media commentators called almost any form of deviant behavior an alternative life-style, the public was more than ready for safe, controlled environments.

In San Diego reestablishing middle-class control meant taking Horton Plaza back from pornography merchants and skid row barkeepers, clearing out their customers, and building an imaginative, comfortable, safe place to visit. In St. Paul it meant replacing the rubble of superhole with a symbol of progress and a weather-tight park. In every city building a downtown retail center satisfied middle-class values by setting up secure, well-maintained, protected areas where a family could have a good time shopping and where teenagers could hang out safely. Suburbanites who had avoided downtown for years were comfortable with the standards of public behavior they found in shopping malls. Working-class people who strived to live decently and to keep their children out of trouble were also pleased to have a cleaner, safer city—one plausible reason why minority neighborhoods in most cities supported downtown redevelopment and voted for mayors who made a feature of it.

Aside from putting part of downtown under social control, the retail centers satisfied popular taste by building physical environments that had an agreeable, user-friendly character, in sharp contrast to the austere towers and abstract shapes of new office buildings. During the 1970s poking fun at modern architecture became culturally respectable. By 1981 Tom Wolfe's *From Bauhaus to Our House* gave eloquent voice to a long-simmering popular dislike of the coldness and severity of contemporary highbrow buildings. Britain's Prince Charles carried on the royal family's tradition of speaking up for middle-class values when he told the architectural profession what he thought of an avant-garde addition planned for the National Gallery of Art in Trafalgar Square. Charles compared the proposed design to "a monstrous carbuncle on the face of a much-loved and elegant friend." "For far too long," he went on, ". . . some planners and architects have consistently ignored the feelings and wishes of ordinary people. It is important in human terms to respect old buildings, street plans and traditional scales, and at the same time not to feel guilty about a preference for facades, ornaments and soft materials."[1] Widespread endorsement of this position confirmed a turn of taste not only in Britain but also in other countries where compulsive modernism had become a bore.

Downtown shopping malls played to this popular reaction by preserving landmarks, building comfortable and lively spaces for buying and selling, and incorporating long-standing department stores within new centers. Even projects built from scratch usually avoided the hard, bare surfaces of nearby office buildings. St. Paul planners highlighted generous landscaping and sculptured fountains at Town Square, Plaza Pasadena topped its archways with scenic murals, and Horton Plaza offered a fantasy land of color and decoration. These centers stood out not only against the rest of downtown but even against suburban malls. *Shopping mall* was no longer the right term for them, and they came to be known increasingly as downtown malls, retail centers, or marketplaces. For middle-class people accustomed to suburban shopping, the downtown marketplaces were different enough to be exciting but familiar enough to make them feel comfortable.

Uses of Commercialism

The retail centers combined civic improvement with commercialism, a combination that disdainful critics rejected out of hand. Without business sponsorship, however, most cities could never have afforded to build or maintain anything like these places. To get the projects, city officials had to come to terms with private profit as the driving force. The director of community development in St. Louis summed up the city's new attitude as, "It's O.K. to make money; profit is O.K." But they also had to make sure that investor interests did not override the city's objectives. The controversy over Fountain Square South in Cincinnati is an example of this conflict, with the developer unwilling to operate a meeting place for citizens at large. In the main, though, retail developers were searching for ways to draw a crowd and were eager to organize their malls for just this purpose.

City officials who wanted to humanize downtown recognized commercial enterprise as more than a way to pay the bills; it was an essential ingredient for bringing people together. Schooled in the principles of suburban malls, developers knew how to make shopping a pleasure instead of a chore. Visitors came to see what was in the stores, and for a few dollars they could enjoy a snack or buy something. Retailing worked so well as a focus of activity that city planners wanted plenty of it to brighten downtown. In the 1960s the light-and-air school of planners tried to improve downtown by encouraging developers to build open plazas and small parks alongside their office towers. In most cities, however, these public spaces attracted few visitors. By the 1970s the street-life school of planners relied on organized activities to bring people together, and they encouraged developers to line their ground floors and interior atriums with retail shops. New York drew on the street-life approach when it turned to a restaurant to rescue Bryant Park from the drug pushers.

In Boston design competitions for the large public space at Copley Square held twenty years apart reveal how closely civic purposes had come together with commercial ones. In 1966 the city-sponsored competition for Copley Square included this guideline: "Commercial activities within the square, such as restaurants, news stands, etc., are not desired." By 1984 the guideline was: "The availability of food and beverage attracts people. . . . The provision of food and beverage should be accommodated . . . around open-air tables sheltered by umbrellas or trees." The 1984 competition also called for a farmers' market and street vendors. The perspective shifted from a 1966 requirement to submit aerial views of the square to a 1984 request for street-level drawings showing Copley Square as a person would see it on the ground. In 1966 the city's redevelopment authority ran the whole show, but by 1984 nearby hotels and businesses supplied much of the initiative and were lining up to pay maintenance costs for the revamped square.

The intent of the new city strategy was to humanize downtown and make it safe by mixing public spaces with private businesses. A bonus was that the private sector would share the bill. Contrary to what the architecture critics wrote, a long list of buildings from earlier times showed that commercial projects could produce distinguished civic places; the great railroad terminals of American cities, the Milan Galleria, and Rockefeller Center were outstanding precedents.

Taming Times Square and Bryant Park

As attractive as the commercial-civic blend is, it has drawbacks. Profit-seeking developers normally build enterprises that serve the middle-class but drive out whatever is left of businesses serving the working class. In most cities this has not been an issue recently, but an unlikely project brought it to life in New York. The project was to rebuild Forty-second Street between Times Square and Eighth Avenue, a combat zone that makes San Diego's porno area look quaint by comparison. By the 1970s it had become a marketplace for drugs, a pickup spot for male and transvestite prostitutes, a hangout for muggers and pickpockets, and home to fourteen porno shops, thirteen cheap movie theaters, and various fast food and drink places. This street recorded more than twice as many criminal complaints as any other in the Times Square area, with drug offenses, grand larceny, robbery, and assault topping the list. The Forty-second Street project proposed to convert nine movie houses into performing arts theaters and to replace almost everything else with four office towers, a wholesale mart, a 550-room hotel, and a new retail complex.

The only public outcry to save this block came from people who worried that its criminal activities might drift into nearby residential neighborhoods. Two sociologists who studied the area asked a sample of New Yorkers to rank it among a dozen entertainment sections of Manhattan. To nobody's surprise it ranked at the bottom, but these researchers nevertheless put forward a two-part case for saving it. It is, they wrote, "a place where the laws of conventional society are suspended, where people come to seek adventure, to take risks in dealing in the fast life." Because this "night frontier" has value for certain groups in society, they were sorry to see it close, and they lamented the passing of "an exciting period of urban adventure."

The other part of their case rested on the functions of this area for ordinary working people. The streets around Times Square used to have pool halls, game rooms, and gyms where men could relax with friends. There were also inexpensive places for entertainment: cafeterias, grills with steam tables, low-cost movies, and jazz clubs. The atmosphere was downscale, even honky-tonk, but it was safe and clean. In an upscale Times Square, they asked, "Where will we find the New Yorkers without American Express cards and the lively cultural institutions these people once sustained?"[2]

The loss of downscale entertainment places is a valid issue for cities that are becoming relentlessly upscale. But in Times Square as in San Diego, the districts of innocent working-class fun gave way long ago to adult bookstores, sleazy bars, and the drug trade, with only some inexpensive movie houses surviving from earlier days. The sociologists who defended Times Square conceded that the "clean, well-lighted places of the downscale groups" were no more than memories. But while profit-based development is not actually destroying working-class institutions, neither is it replacing them. Blending commercial and civic purposes does wonders for the middle class but leaves little room for people with flatter wallets and plainer tastes.

Downtown marketplaces gave the public safe, attractive environments, but the commercial strategy of enclosing public spaces also took people off streets that were already half-deserted. Meanwhile developers of other downtown projects were creating more public places under private management, often with city help: atriums in hotels and office buildings, skyways, underground concourses, and interior plazas within mixed-use complexes. Cities that revitalized their downtowns were building a network of enclosed, climate-controlled areas separate from the street system. Design critics grumbled that these were artificial environments, but the public seemed to like them.

A handful of critics, most notably William H. Whyte, attacked the private enclosures as "the fortressing of America"—circling the wagons in a misguided attempt at security that would only discourage the pedestrian traffic necessary for real security. Whether security was real or illusory, visitors came in large enough numbers to drown out the critics. City officials who wanted to avoid walling off the new public spaces from the rest of downtown had to prod developers to tie their grand enclosures into nearby streets, but some cities discovered the issue too late to act on it.

Plans to commercialize public space occasionally ran into political opposition. New York's proposal to take Bryant Park back from drug dealers by building a restaurant in it and putting a nonprofit group in charge of park management moved slowly. After three years of inconclusive meetings and negotiations, restaurateur Warner LeRoy rolled up his winning proposal and left for a trip to Hawaii. Andrew Heiskell, who chaired the nonprofit corporation as well as the adjacent New York Public Library, attributed LeRoy's withdrawal to frustration with the long series of community groups, boards, and commissions that had to approve the project: "It tests the patience of any man, woman, child or animal."

Getting approval was hard because the restaurant was caught in a crossfire between some groups that opposed private management of public parks and others that considered the plan a last-ditch measure to make the park safe and usable. Heiskell's corporation met fifteen times with the influential Parks Council, a civic organization that objected to a large restaurant in the park because "we wanted to make sure it didn't become a private garden, a private enclave." Heiskell described the objectors as "interested mainly in survival of trees more than survival of parks or whether or not the park is run by pushers." After years of sheltering the drug trade, the trees in question, he added, were a sorry lot. Privatizing a park is like privatizing public streets: both trade away some governmental control in exchange for a promise of greater security and better maintenance. In most cities, privatizing public spaces was noncontroversial, perhaps because street users did not have the same watchdog organizations as park users. In New York four years of controversy and regulatory reviews finally led to a compromise plan for a smaller restaurant in the park.

Except for an occasional skirmish like the one at Bryant Park, the drive to reestablish middle-class control over unsafe and unsightly downtown areas was usually strong enough to shoulder aside other considerations. Marketplaces had few political problems because they made a clear contribution to this overriding purpose. Yet the problems that came to light from organizing downtown around commercial enclaves merit attention even without a public outcry.

School for Management

The building of marketplaces made another type of contribution by improving the capacity of cities to manage downtown development.

These projects operated on the same public-private principle that had led to long delays and disappointing results in the urban renewal program. But by the 1970s a new approach was producing completed retail centers faster and with much greater awareness of what would appeal to the public.

In cities that took over urban renewal sites, the time from naming a developer to celebrating opening day was reasonably short. Boston chose the Rouse Company to develop Faneuil Hall in 1973; the central Quincy Market opened in 1976 and the North and South Markets at one-year intervals afterward. St. Paul settled on Oxford Properties and Radisson Hotels in 1975; five years later Town Square was open. Seattle set up the Preservation and Development Authority to develop the historic core of Pike Place Market in 1973; the main market structures reopened between 1976 and 1978. The average urban renewal project stretched out over some sixteen or seventeen years: twelve years to get to the point of turning land over to a developer, plus another four or five for the developer to finish it. Cities operating outside the federal renewal program were able to shorten this timetable. Plaza Pasadena went from start to finish in ten years and Horton Plaza in thirteen.

One factor that made a difference was growing developer interest in downtown. The slowdown of mall building in suburbia during the 1970s prompted a few developers to think seriously about the cities, where office expansion was already under way and middle-income people were rediscovering old neighborhoods. The oil crisis that began in 1973 threatened to make suburban living more expensive and suggested that downtown office workers might live in the city. These were all plausible reasons for taking another look at downtown, but they were not compelling, especially with crime still keeping people away and local fiscal crises undermining the quality of city services.

An unexpected combination of events in the 1970s—including long lines at the gas pumps and a spurt of growth in service businesses looking for office space—gave the cities a better roll of the dice than they had seen in some time. One good roll was not enough to win, however. To make the most of this opportunity for rebuilding downtown, city officials first had to resolve problems that had frustrated their efforts for the past twenty years.

One of the most serious obstacles was their own inability to manage development projects that involved the private sector. Not only was the record of accomplishment poor in urban renewal but in an entire family of government programs that tried to use private business to achieve public objectives. A classic example was the ambitious public works program that the federal Economic Development Administration organized in 1965 to create jobs for unemployed workers in Oakland, California. It included plans for an airport hangar, marine terminal, industrial park, and business loans, all intended to attract 3,000 private sector jobs for the hard-core unemployed. The fanfare announcing this program in 1965 made national news, but five years later, the aircraft hangar, which was supposed to provide more than half the promised jobs, was still not built and the industrial park had created 30 jobs instead of an anticipated 420.

Political scientists Jeffrey Pressman and Aaron Wildavsky monitored Oakland's experience closely and chalked up its problems to the maze of decisions necessary to carry out the various projects. They estimated conservatively that the Oakland program depended on favorable action at seventy major decision points involving dozens of clearances by a wide range of public officials and business executives. A training program for airline mechanics, for instance, needed approval by no fewer than nine federal, state, and local organizations. Unless all the decision makers happened to be in agreement and shared a sense of great urgency, the chances of getting this program going were close to zero.

Since bureaucratic complexity was unlikely to go away, these researchers and others recommended making programs simpler and more direct. This was certainly good advice, but there was no way cities could accept very much of it and still build downtown retail centers. These projects had to have many independent decision makers because that is the nature of shopping centers. They had to be complicated because a location in the heart of downtown would touch the interests of scores of nearby property owners and the jurisdictions of a dozen or more public agencies.

Deciding to build retail centers meant that cities could not avoid complexity. Some of the projects they put together must be among the most complicated real estate deals ever attempted. Milwaukee's Grand Avenue, for example, consisted of six historic buildings connected by a series of new skyways and shopping arcades and served by two new and two old parking garages. The tangle of property interests and legal agreements alone is so knotted that it took two years just to work out title insurance for the center. According to the underwriter in charge, "I have been involved in this business 35 years and I have never seen a title this involved and probably never will again."

The opening of a hundred downtown retail centers since 1970 is evidence that cities found ways to break earlier development deadlocks and learned how to operate. These projects did not survive because of their simplicity. They survived mainly because negotiation worked better for city officials than the command-and-control tactics of urban renewal. By negotiating early with developers, city staff discovered ways of making projects feasible. Faced with unexpected crises, both sides were willing to find mutually acceptable solutions. Through repeated contact, developers learned enough about city troubles to pull their plans in line with local politics, while city negotiators learned enough about development to tune their proposals to the developer's bottom line.

The new negotiating style also gave city officials a chance to keep an eye on the final details of a project. Oakland government agencies lost influence over project decisions once they committed the money. One of the results was that companies used their subsidies to buy the latest equipment, which then reduced their need for the workers they had promised to hire. To cope with this problem Pressman and Wildavsky recommended payment on performance, that is, not writing government checks until a project had done what it was supposed to do. Payment on performance was impractical for the retail centers, since the financing gap that cities were closing usually demanded money up-front. But city officials accomplished the same purpose by establishing a right to share major decisions that gave them strong cards to hold through opening day or beyond.

Negotiated development turned out to be a major safeguard for city officials when they relied on commercial enterprises to rebuild downtown. It allowed public staff to watch the developers and keep projects on track, minimizing the risks of incomplete or abandoned ventures. Further, it gave public negotiators opportunities to challenge decisions they considered unwise or inappropriate.

The thrust of government policy toward the public use of private interest in the 1970s raised questions about whether private profit would be the dominant consideration, crowding out legitimate issues of public concern. But we found no private takeovers of downtown negotiations; instead both sides used the bargaining opportunity to extend their influence. Developers certainly shaped the terms of the deals that cities offered them. But at the same time city negotiators politicized decisions that used to belong to the private sector.

Once city officials became coinvestors who had to be consulted throughout the development process, they had a voice in traditionally private decisions. First, they enlarged their control over project design and operation well beyond what conventional land use and building regulations allowed. Then they invaded developers' sacred financial turf by bargaining for a share of the profits. Further, since they operated from an open agenda, they were free to raise politically important issues. When some cities gave high priority to jobs for local residents, they were able to bargain successfully over hiring practices as well. The new methods of project management, in short, gave cities a place at the bargaining table that they could use to promote the public interest.

The Hiding Hand

While improving the management of downtown projects, city officials were also sharpening their political skills. They defused anti-renewal protests by finding sites that did not threaten homes. When budget cuts endangered their Washington lifeline, they did what they could with funds remaining in old federal programs and moved to capture new ones such as UDAG. To supplement or replace federal money, they brokered contributions from the private sector and issued bonds backed by their own future property tax revenues. As direct federal aids disappeared, they switched to indirect ones by taking advantage of federal tax exemption on municipal borrowings. They used ingenious sale-leaseback arrangements to raise revenue, as in Seattle and San Diego, and they turned falling interest rates to their advantage by refinancing earlier bond issues.

These financing techniques followed a strategy established earlier in the urban renewal program: pay for projects with off-budget funds. When a project needs current tax dollars, it has to compete with other demands for the limited cash that can be wrung out of local taxpayers. Before city council members reach a decision, they usually weigh the cost against other uses of the money. But as far as most local officials are concerned, federal dollars are manna from heaven, and any project they underwrite is essentially costless.

As the federal pipeline dried up, cities used other methods of financing to do a similar end-run around normal budget reviews.

Bond issues based on tax increments or parking revenues, unlike general obligation bonds, do not have to go on the ballot for voter approval. The city council has to authorize these bonds, but since they take nothing from current tax receipts, they escape the hard looks and cold calculations reserved for cash outlays. They are close cousins of the special authority bonds that finance bridges and tunnels out of future tolls, quietly collecting and spending public money while avoiding the political struggle over annual budgets.

Off-budget financing was one of the keys to the success of downtown revitalization. From the beginning it made the high cost of redevelopment a manageable issue in city politics by presenting the bill to someone other than the average taxpayer. After Washington cut renewal funds loose from specific projects in 1974 and encouraged each city to set its own community development priorities, mayors faced strong pressures to scatter their money across the city in order to do something for every district. Off-budget financing came to the rescue once more; it helped the mayors to continue pouring resources into expensive projects by diffusing their cost over time and removing them from the annual competition for community development funds. The retail centers had political appeal partly because they promised community-wide benefits and partly because their costs were unclear and not due until sometime in the future.

Is off-budget financing anything more than a trick to make projects look good by concealing their full costs? Spreading costs to tomorrow's taxpayers has some justification since these are long-lasting projects with delayed payoffs. But off-budget financing has another function: it is a way of coping with the short time horizon of city politics. In the normal course of events city governments would do very little for the sake of future benefits. "Long-term," as defined by an aide to Chicago's legendary Mayor Richard Daley, "means next Monday." The federal government contributed generously to urban renewal precisely in order to give mayors a way to rebuild cities without losing the support of normal voters impatient for results. Once the renewal program was dead, development officials invented other ways of coping with pressures to spend for immediate needs only. Off-budget financing, in addition to saving their own jobs, helped them build projects that were risky but had long-term value.

Governments commonly back development projects without appreciating their true cost and risk, yet many projects do succeed in spite of unexpected problems. Economist Albert Hirschman, who noticed this pattern in developing countries, recognized it as a general principle of human behavior and gave it a name: the hiding hand. The people who planned economic development projects, he found, usually did not know in advance all the troubles that would threaten their enterprise. If they had known, they would have scrapped their plans because the problems were too formidable. Yet when crises did emerge, they managed to come up with creative ideas that not only rescued the projects but even improved on the original plans. They failed to anticipate problems, but they also underrated their ability to solve them. Hirschman argued that since most people underestimate their own creativity, they would never start projects that they were actually capable of doing unless they minimized the difficulties. The hiding hand is a beneficial principle that tricks people into meeting new challenges by keeping future problems out of sight.

Developers and promoters must have discovered this principle before Hirschman because he noticed how skillful they were at making difficult projects look attractive to decision makers. In the case of downtown shopping malls, the original promoters were usually public officials with a vision of distant success that glossed over problems along the way. The planners who made a commitment to save the Faneuil Hall markets without knowing how to do it, to clear superhole in St. Paul far in advance of redevelopment prospects, and to restore Horton Plaza as the commercial center of San Diego were either following the hiding hand or were using it to lead others. Ernest Hahn recognized the principle when Horton Plaza finally opened in 1985: "If you knew at the beginning that it was going to be as complicated as it turned out," he said, "you'd probably be disillusioned. . . . If you had to measure the worth against the dollar return, we probably wouldn't have started."

Pushing public development costs off the annual budget is one way of making hard, expensive projects inviting. It not only counters political pressures for short-term results but compensates for everyone's failure to recognize the creativity of such problem solvers as White-Rouse-Thompson or Trimble-Hahn-Jerde. To the extent that off-budget financing and other hiding hand methods gave cities a chance to build complex projects for the sake of future benefits, they are important contributions to managing development.

These methods sometimes grate against conventional beliefs about the proper way to conduct public business. One school of thought holds that taxing and spending decisions ought to be clear and open so that the voters and their representatives will know what they are paying and what they are getting for their money. Public finance in practice seems increasingly at odds with this principle. After studying the way cities raised revenue in the 1960s, political scientist Arnold Meltsner observed: "One of the great arts of the tax game is to design revenue sources so that people will not know that they are paying taxes. Taxes should not be seen nor felt, only paid."[3]

Government officials playing the tax game since then have learned how to make bond issues vanish from the ballot. In recent years as little as 15 percent of bonded debt has gone directly before the voters. Meanwhile, the family of off-budget tax and spending programs has grown large, including government-funded retirement systems, federal loans and loan guarantees, tax write-offs, public authority projects, and public sector leasing. Downtown planners joined a growing trend when they found ways to shield their own ventures from budget reviews and voter approval.

The results are troublesome to people who value accountability based on the informed consent of the governed. One critic has characterized "quiet spending programs" in terms that get to the heart of commercial-civic ventures: "They . . . spend large amounts of public resources with low levels of scrutiny. They avoid competition with other programs. They are financially complicated . . . ; costs and expenses are often obscured. They spend public resources but try to avoid the pinch of payment."[4]

Tax-increment financing, one of the leading downtown strategies, does all these so well that it sometimes makes projects irresistible. The Citizens League, a Minneapolis civic organization, recently studied Minnesota experience and found cities locking up startling amounts of future revenue in downtown tax-increment districts. Property taxes committed this way to pay for development costs grew from $437,000 collected in 1974 to $56 million collected by 1984. In the Minneapolis–St. Paul area many cities tied up 7 percent or more of their property tax base through tax-increment financing, with several mayors devoting half or more of their time to real estate projects.

Since tax-increment income does not come out of a fixed budget, cities can commit it to one project after another without ever having to make a choice among competing plans. The Citizens League worried that without a budget ceiling or a competition for public funds, city officials would waste money on development projects that were neither productive nor deserving. Since the public cost could be spread thin over repayment periods as long as twenty-five years, the league believed city officials would have too little motivation to drive a hard bargain with developers. Further, it warned that the large profits real estate firms stand to make out of public investments will tempt them to use campaign contributions or job promises to get what they want.

These dangers are real and not hard to recognize. Downtown entrepreneurs have put together a project-producing machine that works a little too well for comfort. Its success has a way of blinding people to the damage it can do if it turns into a flimflam for making weak projects look good. There has been little organized opposition to downtown retail centers and even less to potential dangers posed by commercial-civic enterprise, off-budget financing, and negotiated development. The Minneapolis report is no protest, but it is a sign of emerging awareness that the new style of redevelopment still has rough edges.

Selling Columbus Circle

Public-private deals in New York have raised more jarring questions about what the city's entrepreneurial skills are doing to the public interest. In New York the issue is whether the city walks away from its regulatory responsibility when it has a big financial stake in a project. Critics argue that when city negotiators invite bids for publicly owned Manhattan sites, they encourage recklessly oversized buildings in order to get top dollar for the land. As zoning restraints fall and megabuildings rise far above earlier skyscrapers, Ada Louise Huxtable has concluded: "The city is wide open. Greed has never been so chic. The public interest has never been so passé."[5]

The project that crystallized this issue was redevelopment of the Coliseum site at Columbus Circle, which triggered a flap over bidding procedures. City negotiators stretched the zoning regulations to the limit and then added a 20 percent bonus in exchange for requiring the developer to renovate a nearby subway station. With the bonus the building limit was up to 2.7 million square feet of floor space, more than in the Empire State Building. The terms of the bidding invitation—clear about size but vague on design guidelines—told developers that "the city cared about nothing except the money," reported Robert Campbell after checking with the architect of the winning proposal. (Even the earlier controversy over bidding procedures had revealed that city negotiators gave top priority to the financial qualifications of the developer and the sale price for the land.) Both the architect and the developer told Campbell they would have been happy to produce a building half this size but gave the city what it wanted. Their plans for a complicated structure with fifty-eight- and sixty-eight-story towers housing a shopping galleria, office space, and luxury apartments struck Campbell as "a craggy mountain range of granite and glass." In Huxtable's view, the city was "selling itself to the highest bidder."

The Municipal Art Society, the New York chapter of the American Planning Association, the Parks Council, and other project opponents brought a lawsuit in June 1987 to try to stop the project, arguing that the city's environmental review gave inadequate attention to the traffic congestion, loss of daylight, and deterioration of air quality that would result from this enormous building. In an area as clogged as midtown Manhattan, these were serious issues. Yet the dimensions of the structure were not the most telling objection. New Yorkers had taken earlier outsized projects in their stride, including Rockefeller Center with more than twice as much space and the World Trade Center with nearly four times as much. Whether the proposed building would be appropriate for this part of town is still an open question. Campbell maintained that the designers fit the building into its surroundings and moderated the effects of its vast bulk. The basic problem was that the city's commitment to a top-value project prevented it from making a fair judgment about size. The city dropped out as a referee enforcing the rules of the development game; after pocketing the price for the land, it began to run interference for the developer.

Critics were most disturbed that the city had gone into the real estate business. Campbell wrote, "Nothing . . . distinguished the city in this situation from a rapacious private developer." Preservation advocate Brendan Gill called the project an outrage because of its effect on Central Park across the street and then added: "What's worse, it wasn't a developer manipulating the laws, it was the city itself misusing its own power." The community board responsible for reviewing the project found itself up against city officials who promoted the project like a developer, only more so. The board chairman called the city "the worst developer we have faced." Speaking of the development company, he reported that "Boston Properties has bent over backward to work with us on problems with the Coliseum, but the city has tried to bulldoze it through." One critic with outstanding qualifications was Robert Caro, whose biography of Robert Moses, *The Power Broker,* is the classic study of big-city development politics. "What we are seeing here," said Caro, "is a total abdication of the moral responsibility of government."[6]

Project opponents won their lawsuit in December 1987 when the state supreme court found that the city had acted improperly in negotiating a sale price for the land based on a zoning change to be made by municipal agencies: "Government may not place itself in the position of reaping a cash premium because one of its agencies bestows a zoning benefit on a developer," the decision stated. "Zoning benefits are not cash items."

By that time the project was coming apart for other reasons as well. Opponents recruited celebrities including Jacqueline Onassis, Henry Kissinger, Bill Moyers, and Paul Newman to lend their names to fund raising, a media campaign, and demonstrations against the office towers. Then the financial services firm of Salomon Brothers, prime tenant and joint partner in the venture, withdrew in the wake of the October 1987 stock market crash. Boston Properties hired a new architect and started negotiating a scaled-down plan with Mayor Koch. If the city was going to change its specifications to a smaller building, however, comptroller Harrison Goldin argued that other developers—including the fifteen who had lost out earlier—should have a chance to make fresh proposals. One of the earlier competitors, Samuel LeFrak, accused the city of not playing fair and threatened a lawsuit.

City officials reinforced the doubts raised by their Coliseum performance when they refused to disclose the details of developer proposals for another public site at South Ferry. City hall endorsement of both projects even before the official zoning review raised further misgivings about public-private development in New York. "The city has become a development partner rather than the public's advocate," charged city councillor Ruth W. Messinger. Former council president Carol Bellamy argued that public-private projects undercut the ability of city planning staff to do their job: "With these joint ventures, the professional staffers know how the Mayor feels about a project. It's difficult for them to raise objections." City negotiators improve deals by insisting that developers build public improvements as part of their projects, such as the subway renovation at Columbus Circle. But Messinger and other critics questioned the value of tying these benefits to the projects: "Maybe the subway station that needs improvement most is in Brooklyn."

The New York experience warns of potential danger when government plunges too deeply into real estate development. If the city acts like a developer, who will look after the public interest? The dawning awareness of this danger could mark the end of a honeymoon for the pioneering methods of doing downtown projects. That same warning would have been in order earlier, but from the 1970s through the mid-1980s the public was more concerned with results than with process, and the results were generally positive. Redevelopment planners were able to define a public interest that suited their own needs. Their overriding concern was to get projects built with a minimum of delay—a reasonable concern when the Ghost of Renewal Projects Past still haunted city officials and threatened to bury their careers in a tomb of rubble. They defined the public interest also as bringing the middle class back to downtown, creating focal points of activity, humanizing the city, and stimulating economic activity. These were the same purposes the mayors and their business allies presented to a generally approving public.

This prevailing version of the public interest, however, was vague on questions of procedure. Entrepreneurial officials gave little consideration to issues of accountability, uniform regulatory treatment, or fairness to competitors and in fact were ready to cut corners on these matters for the sake of building their projects. Making efficient use of public funds was an important concern, though, and city negotiators often bargained hard to hold down costs and bring in financial returns on their investment.

There is little evidence that redevelopment officials were out of touch with what the public wanted. The drive to reestablish middle-class control over unsafe and unsightly downtown areas continues to be a strong force in city politics. Mayors recognize it by emphasizing the public benefits of building desirable projects downtown, and the few dissenters do not usually swing much political weight. When earlier downtown development was uprooting neighborhoods and driving small firms out of business, protest leaders put forward a view of the public interest that emphasized fairness and consultation with citizens on development decisions. These protests eventually carried the day, but once new mayors learned to build projects that were less damaging and more popular they were able to revive the earlier emphasis on results rather than process.

   Although this notion of the public interest keeps quiet about issues
of procedure and uniformity, it has not produced widespread abuses.
Critics in New York have raised appropriate issues for attention, but
few fears about the dangers of city entrepreneurship have materi-
alized so far. Cutting special deals with some retail developers but not
with others, for example, proved to have almost no effect in reducing
competition. When cities began to promote retail projects, developers
were hardly clamoring to build them downtown, so offering help to
one firm did not exclude others. And by helping a single developer
test an uncertain market, most cities increased the choices available to
consumers. The opening of the first retail center in a city gave the
public a new shopping option downtown, and if the first center was
successful, others began to follow. In Boston, for instance, Faneuil
Hall Marketplace helped establish the feasibility of downtown shopping, encouraging reinvestment along the old Washington Street retail row (Downtown Crossing and Lafayette Place), as well as the
development of Copley Place in the Back Bay and Marketplace Center
next to the original Faneuil Hall project. Minneapolis, New York,
Pittsburgh, and San Francisco are among other cities that have had
added more than a single downtown retail center since the early
1970s.
   On the other hand, it is likely that the easy politics of off-budget
financing led some cities to give developers more help than they
needed. The most sophisticated cities hired skilled staff or consultants to check developers' figures and to determine a level of help that
would be fair but not excessive. But extreme differences among cities
in the public share of development costs—from 3 percent to 83 percent—probably mean that less sophisticated communities either
overpaid or agreed to projects with such poor earning prospects that
they needed exceptional subsidies.
   On balance the mistakes that cities made in negotiating these projects were small in comparison with their achievements. In most
places opponents were unable to find enough ammunition to organize people against downtown development projects. Yet the public
interest keeps changing. As downtown projects restore a measure of
order, security, and economic progress to the center of the city, new
political leaders may win a mandate to overhaul the management of
public-private ventures. The Minneapolis and New York critiques
could be early signals of the next turn of the wheel—one that will

define the public interest in terms of clearer accountability, more uniform rules for developers, and fuller representation of resident interests in whatever negotiations are necessary.

The methods of development pioneered by downtown shopping malls are not for all time. They are a strong and useful set of procedures, but they need more work.

13   Downtown Malls and the City Agenda

A shopping mall, new office towers, a convention center, an atrium hotel, a restored historic neighborhood. These are the civic agenda for downtown development in the last third of the twentieth century, a trophy collection that mayors want. Add a domed stadium, aquarium, or cleaned-up waterfront to suit the circumstances, and you have the essential equipment for a first-class American city.

The showpieces on this list are useful as well as trendy. They help a city keep up with its competitors while also meeting some local need such as getting rid of an eyesore, saving a landmark, or creating a civic symbol. Although the projects rarely result from systematic forethought, they often fit together surprisingly well. Most serve a common function: restoring downtown as a center of economic activity.

Baltimore illustrates the way a retail center links into a chain of projects spanning the decades. Its new downtown became an instant success with the opening of Harborplace in 1980, but that success was thirty years in the making. Shoreline improvements around the Inner Harbor—a new bulkhead, landfill, marina, piers, public parks, and promenades—date from a bond issue voted in 1948. Other projects that remade the core of Baltimore in stages include the 33-acre Charles Center office complex built in the 1960s; the Maryland Science Center, World Trade Center, and Convention Center in the 1970s; and the National Aquarium and Hyatt Regency Hotel that opened within a year after Harborplace. This was a costly series of projects, with the public sector bill alone totaling more than $200 million. And although each has its special history, they feed off each other.

The downtown agenda was more than a grab-bag of pet projects because of the steady interest of elected officials and business executives in strengthening the downtown economy. Business coalitions especially had a large stake in revitalizing the city center, and their support was usually crucial for launching any large project. In deciding which projects to push, they usually threw their weight behind those that served an economic development purpose.

Downtown retail centers were part of this total agenda, adding a fresh acrobatic act to a three-ring circus in the making. They thrilled the crowds, but their long-run impact at the box office is hard to separate from the rest of the show.

Corporate Territory

What are the collective functions of the downtown projects that cities worked so hard to build? To the extent that cities had a strategy, it was to make downtown efficient for business firms and attractive to visitors and middle-class residents. Critics called this thrust the corporate-center strategy. Richard Child Hill studied Detroit, pinned this label on its recent development priorities, and argued that the same logic has been shaping most large American cities: "Overall investment priorities are to transform this aging industrial city into the modern corporate image: a financial, administrative, and professional services center . . . ; a research and development site for new growth industries . . . ; an emphasis upon recommercialization rather than reindustrialization; and an orientation toward luxury consumption that is appealing to young corporate managers, educated professionals, convention goers, and the tourist trade."[1]

Many elements of the new downtowns fall into place as part of the contemporary office economy. The office buildings deliver space for company headquarters and for corporate services ranging from law firms and consultants to copy shops and lunch counters. Downtown hotels and restaurants take care of business visitors. The convention center brings trade shows and industry meetings, producing more patrons for hotels, theaters, and shopping malls. Some of the executives and professionals want to live in the city and can afford to renovate interesting old houses; once settled in town they help support theaters, museums, and retail shops.

The connections among these developments do not mean that city officials anticipated how they would fit together and then planned them. Baltimore did make comprehensive plans for several large chunks of downtown, but most other cities took their opportunities as they saw them, one by one. Detroit's former city planning director, resigning after six years in the job, spoke openly about the decision process: "Planning in Detroit is the mayor's phone number. He deals with development on an ad hoc basis." In New York planning is so chaotic that the city opened its huge Javits Convention Center with no parking garage, no connection to the subway system, and no zoning for hotel construction in the vicinity. This erratic operating style left officials free to choose projects related to the office economy, but a string of one-shot decisions hardly adds up to an organized corporate center strategy.

The rebuilding of downtown also changed the kind of work people could find there. Deindustrialization came to the cities long before the country at large worried about the loss of manufacturing. Office doors were opening for the educated while industrial lofts and warehouses were closing their doors on blue-collar workers. Jobs created by the office economy raised questions about who would benefit from the new downtown. Hill argued that "for Detroit's less advantaged workers, the Renaissance means trading a former possibility for blue-collar jobs at decent wages for the future probability of scarce, low-paying, dead-end service work." He envisioned the Detroit Renaissance as "a Golden Arch surrounded by deteriorating and impoverished workers' neighborhoods."[2]

There were some dissenters from the chorus of approval over Baltimore. Reporter Michael C. D. Macdonald contended that to build the "bistros and boutiques of Harborplace" was simply to "graft on an array of cute shops to a troubled factory town." A visitor from Britain's Manchester *Guardian* called the Inner Harbor development "gold fillings in a mouthful of decay." These critics were right to question how helpful the new downtowns would be for disadvantaged city residents, but when they faulted city government for rebuilding downtown inappropriately, they failed to recognize how few options the mayors had.

When the cities made their first plans to rescue downtown, economic and technological changes were already destroying their industrial base. In the early 1950s manufacturing dominated the city economy, supplying more jobs than services, wholesaling, and retailing combined. By the mid-1950s, however, industrialists were racing to the suburbs, and downtown manufacturing started its long decline.

There was little the cities could do to hold on to industry. Assembly-line production cut short the useful life of their cramped multistory factories. Long, low industrial plants were better suited to the new technologies for handling materials. Also, as trucking replaced railroad freight, manufacturers wanted sites with good highway access. The suburbs had plenty of land for horizontal building layouts, off-street loading docks, and parking for workers. In the cities assembling large enough sites for industry meant buying small parcels from separate owners, dealing with holdouts who asked high prices, and then tearing down existing buildings. Comparable sites were likely to cost twenty to thirty times more in a city than in a suburb.

The civic leaders and public officials who drew up renewal plans in the 1950s did not consider manufacturing important for the downtown of the future. Still, many cities did use some of their renewal money to clear land for industry. They discovered that the process was slow, costly, and unproductive. Economist Raymond Vernon concluded as early as 1962 that city efforts and subsidies were "not swift enough or flexible enough or generous enough to match the offerings of private land on the outskirts." Nearly twenty years later another researcher looked back at the efforts cities had made and confirmed Vernon's judgment: the long lead time needed to get the site, the restrictions city governments imposed on new development, and their inexperience at marketing land contributed to a poor track record. Manufacturers had failed to turn up, and cities ended by selling the land for warehouses or service businesses.

Manufacturers had solid business reasons for moving to the suburbs, reasons city officials were powerless to change. If there was no practical way to keep manufacturing in town, the mayors had to figure out what sort of economic activity could take its place. Saving downtown was so far removed from traditional city functions— paving streets, managing parks, policing neighborhoods—that most mayors hardly knew where to begin. When they saw possibilities for promoting individual projects, they were ready to try almost anything. If the rebuilding of downtown gave too much emphasis to high-skill office jobs, that result came more from a process of discovering what worked than from any deliberate policy.

While city officials were still casting a wide net for feasible projects, Vernon's monumental New York Metropolitan Region Study in the 1950s identified the kinds of businesses that stood to gain most from a downtown location. The largest group of firms still rooted to downtown were those whose executives wanted face-to-face contact with other people: lawyers who had to talk with clients and partners, bankers who had to negotiate with borrowers, corporate officers who had to meet with experts in taxes or bonds or product design. Their need to be in touch with others often and quickly led them to locate in the heart of the city, where the business specialists had clustered for mutual convenience. These communication-oriented firms employed perhaps one-fifth of an urban area's labor force and formed the critical downtown concentration most likely to resist the lure of the suburbs.

Some specialized manufacturers also operated best from in-city locations because they needed fast access to subcontractors and suppliers, short delivery times to customers, or face-to-face contact with any of those. Printers, for example, had to meet with customers to go over layout and then had to deliver the finished product on a tight schedule. Manufacturers of high-fashion clothing had to be able to see the fabrics, buttons, and buckles they were going to buy and had to keep up with the latest information to find out which designs and colors were selling. Mass producers of standardized clothing might operate successfully from small towns in low-wage regions, but the fashion industry had to be in the big city.

This diagnosis—publicized through books, conferences, and speeches—meant that the central city was a promising location for a large number of offices and a small number of manufacturers. With office work expanding nationally, it was the best prospect for downtown since the office elite wanted to be not only in the central city but in its main business district. Vernon recognized that routine office operations such as data processing were likely to move to the suburbs, but even if cities captured a smaller share of office growth than in the past, he expected their number of office jobs to increase. "At the very center of such cities," he wrote in 1959, ". . . there is every reason to expect continued vitality." Yet the vitality he predicted was based primarily on the elite functions of skilled executives and the specialists they hired. His forecast implied fewer downtown jobs for the less skilled people who used to work in the industrial lofts, factories, and freight terminals.

250 Empire State Buildings

When the cities moved downtown planning from the drafting board to the bulldozer, they tried many kinds of projects. In the 1950s and 1960s about one-third of urban renewal land in big cities was earmarked for apartments, one-third for commercial and industrial developments, and one-fourth for government buildings. Among the commercial ventures office complexes were prominent; Gateway Center in Pittsburgh, Charles Center in Baltimore, the Mile High Center in Denver, and Prudential Center in Boston were some of the largest and best-known office projects. Although office buildings were more feasible than most other possibilities for downtown, these were not easy projects. City governments gave many kinds of help, including buying and clearing land, building parking garages, selling sites below cost, and giving tax abatements. Sometimes this help was not enough because the demand for first-class office space was too uncertain. In Pittsburgh Richard King Mellon had to lean personally on local executives before they made advance commitments to lease space in the new buildings.

Encouraged by this sort of help, venturesome developers began to put up speculative office buildings in downtowns that had seen little or no commercial construction since the 1920s. When tenants rented space in a reasonable time, these early projects demonstrated more effectively than any economic study that office buildings could succeed downtown. They made it easier for the cities to sell land for offices in later projects, and they even persuaded some developers to put up buildings without city help. In Baltimore, for example, a company that lost the competition for an office tower in Charles Center decided to buy land across the street and build one on its own. Both towers leased up quickly.

City attempts to promote office development were well timed to meet an unprecedented surge of office demand in the national economy. The trend started when corporations that were pouring out consumer products during the boom years of the 1950s needed more and more people to handle administration, product development, research, marketing, and finance. White-collar jobs in manufacturing firms began a steady climb from 20 percent of total employment in the 1940s to almost 40 percent by the 1980s.

Corporations searching for wider markets not only took on more administrative staff but also set up headquarters and branch offices in big cities, close to their financial advisers, lawyers, and consultants. The firms supplying these producer services in turn grew larger to meet the needs of the new corporate offices, as well as a rising consumer demand for similar services. The number of jobs in finance, insurance, and business and professional services jumped from

3 million in the mid-1950s to more than 11 million by the early 1980s. In addition, the growth of government and nonprofit agencies added to the demand for office space. Service jobs in total (counting government and nonprofit jobs) increased from 57 percent of U.S. employment in 1947 to 71 percent in 1982. Manufacturing meanwhile slipped from 32 percent to 22 percent of the total.

The rise of a service economy concentrated job growth in occupations well suited to downtown. It was not surprising, then, that cities threw their energies into getting office work; it was the growth sector of the economy and one of very few fields where they might rival the suburbs. As far as manufacturing jobs were concerned, the cities found it so hard to compete for industry against their own suburbs in the 1950s and 1960s that there was little point in trying to compete against Taiwan or Korea by the 1970s and 1980s.

City strategies began to pay off when office buildings broke ground in one downtown after another. Earlier New York had dominated the nation's office development, producing half the space built in all the downtowns of the thirty largest metropolitan areas in the 1950s. By the 1960s downtown office construction spread to all regions of the country as eight cities each built more than 4 million square feet and New York's share slipped to one-third of the total. The spread continued after 1970 as Chicago, Washington, Houston, San Francisco, Dallas, Los Angeles, Boston, and Denver became leading producers of downtown office space and cut New York's share to 29 percent in the 1970s and 17 percent by the early 1980s.

While the list of major office centers grew longer, the pace of construction accelerated. During the 1960s the thirty largest metropolitan areas added more than twice as much office space to downtown as they had built in the 1950s, and in the 1970s they developed one and one-half times as much as in the 1960s. Then a construction boom without parallel produced more downtown office space from 1980 to 1984 than during the entire decade of the 1970s. From the 1960s through 1984 1,325 office buildings were built or started in the downtowns of the thirty largest urban areas, supplying almost 550 million square feet of floor space—the equivalent of 250 new Empire State Buildings.

Putting this record into historic perspective is hard because of inadequate data, but what was built since 1960 is almost certainly greater than the total amount of downtown office space these cities had accumulated from all the years of construction before 1960. It is not all a net increase of office space, however, because some new buildings replaced older ones, nor is it all filled with businesses, because the tail-end of the construction boom in the early 1980s left some cities with buildings that will not be fully rented for several more years at current absorption rates. Still it was clear that the cities had found a big downtown winner in office construction.

In individual cities the changes were startling. During the 1970s alone Denver more than doubled its downtown office space, and Atlanta, Detroit, Houston, Newark, Pittsburgh, and Seattle had increases of more than 50 percent. Many downtowns dead to development since the 1920s suddenly sprang to life. San Francisco had only one major new office building between 1930 and 1958, but the next twenty years brought no fewer than fifty-two new office towers to downtown. Boston added only a single office tower from the 1930s through the 1950s, but sixty office buildings between 1965 and 1987 gave it a new skyline. Kevin White, the mayor who presided over the transformation of downtown Boston, saw office construction move from a slow and uncertain start to what he called a real estate "feeding frenzy" by the time he left office in 1984.

The achievement of the cities was not so much capturing a larger slice of office development as it was holding on to a steady share. In the late 1950s the downtown districts of the thirty largest metropolitan areas had just over 20 percent of the nation's office space. During the 1960s they kept pace with the rest of the country by getting about 20 percent of new office construction. Later their share edged up by perhaps one percentage point in the 1970s and then may have reached 25 percent during the office boom of 1980–1984. Keeping up with the national trend was an accomplishment when central cities were falling behind in almost every other way. And during a time of explosive suburban office growth, holding a steady share close to 20 percent was enough to give the rebuilding of downtown a secure economic base.

Once the real estate market was well established, city governments were able to cut back their support for new office buildings. By the 1970s developers were putting up office buildings on small sites in established office districts rather than in large clearance areas. Cities continued to be supportive by granting requests for rezoning and street changes, and in some cases by striking tax deals, but land write-downs and public works construction were not needed as often.

Lodgings and Lobbies

Dr. Samuel Johnson, reflecting on the pleasures of public houses in eighteenth-century London, commented that "there is nothing which has yet been contrived by man, by which so much happiness is produced as by a good tavern or inn." Big-city hotels inherited a tradition of dispensing hospitality and good cheer, making downtown an attractive place for business as well as social life. During the suburban buildup of the 1950s and 1960s, however, the hotel industry followed the rush away from the city. Developers built new motels along interstate highways, near airports, or close to suburban business centers, and they built them with swimming pools, parking, air conditioning, and gleaming bathrooms. The typical downtown was left with a sorry collection of worn-out hotels trading on whatever charm survived from their better days.

Although critics said the new motels were sterile and lacked character, the New Yorker's Calvin Trillin spoke up for travelers when he speculated that the critics had never "spent many nights on the sagging beds next to the hissing pipes of the old commercial-traveler hotels the new motels replaced." Trillin went on: "I was always delighted to find out that the town I was to visit had horrified its historical society by tearing down the very hotel Grover Cleveland had once eaten lunch in—replacing it with a plastic and cinder-block motel that could be used by a passing intellectual as an example of cookie-cutter mass production and could be used by a passing Travelling Person to get a decent night's sleep and an operating shower."[3]

Companies that settled into the new downtown offices soon wanted modern hotels nearby where they could put up out-of-town clients and business colleagues in comfort. When the cities organized downtown renewal projects, they began to include new hotels, as in Town Square and next to Horton Plaza. Downtown hotels took several forms: the midsized commercial hotel for business travelers, the large hotel with special facilities for conventions, and the small luxury hotel for well-heeled tourists and top executives. Beyond these functions the downtown hotel soon became a civic showpiece and a badge of achievement.

When architect-developer John Portman opened the first of his Hyatt Regency Hotels as part of Atlanta's Peachtree Center in 1967, he introduced a design that made every city want one. Time described his hotels as "razzle-dazzle fantasy buildings full of gadgets (glass-enclosed elevators) and gimmicks (multistory lobbies garnished with trees, fountains and cafes). . . . They are known in the trade as 'Jesus Christ' hotels: when visitors walk in for the first time, their eyes bulge and they gasp 'Je-sus Chee-rist.' '"[4]

For a combination of economic reasons, prestige, and simply the search for feasible projects, the cities launched a hotel boom that echoed their office thrust. During the 1960s hotel construction added an average of 4,000 rooms a year to the downtowns of the thirty-eight largest metropolitan areas; between 1970 and 1982 the rate increased to more than 5,400 new rooms a year. New York, Chicago, Washington, New Orleans, and Atlanta each added more than 7,000 hotel rooms from 1960 through 1982, and Boston, Philadelphia, San Francisco, Seattle, and St. Louis were among the dozen cities that added more than 3,000 rooms.

One signal of how eager city governments were to get new hotels, and how willing to spend public money to do it, was the way they used the UDAG program. With few guidelines from Washington, the cities had wide discretion in the types of projects they could propose, and hotels were first on many wish lists. When federal officials approved the first fifty awards in 1978, nearly one-third turned out to be hotels or hotel–convention center complexes. Neighborhood groups were outraged, and critics lampooned UDAG as "the greatest hotel-building program in history." Secretary of Housing and Urban Development Patricia Harris defended hotels as good sources of jobs for low-income people but eventually agreed to use different priorities for future awards no matter how much the mayors wanted hotels.

Once the hotel market was tested and proved, government help was less important. With office construction booming and convention centers planned, the demand for hotels was strong enough to convince the large chains that downtown was ripe. The thirty-eight largest urban areas built 319 downtown hotels with 110,000 rooms between 1960 and 1982. From 1973 to 1983 alone, the supply of convention-quality downtown hotel rooms more than doubled in Atlanta, Boston, Indianapolis, Philadelphia, Phoenix, Portland, St. Paul, San Antonio, Seattle, and Washington.

After offices, hotels generated the next largest volume of downtown construction. Portman hotels with their flashy atriums spread from Atlanta to Chicago, Los Angeles, and San Francisco, inspiring dozens of other cities and developers to create dazzling public spaces. Many hotels are clustered with office buildings and stores to form large mixed-use complexes. Of some 130 downtown mixed-use projects built between 1970 and 1985, more than seven of ten contained at least one hotel. In this kind of setting hotels expanded the enclosed network of off-street territory with concourses and lobbies designed to attract not only overnight guests but also the public at large. The reception area of the Radisson Hotel in St. Paul, for example, serves as an extension of Town Square and the four skyways that meet there.

A few hotels exploited special locations, including the Marriott Long Wharf in Boston whose shiplike interior and popular bars and restaurants bring crowds to the waterfront. Some recreated elegant settings of the past in restored buildings, such as the Olympic Four Seasons in Seattle and the Willard Hotel in Washington. The Helmsley Palace Hotel in New York incorporated Villard Houses, an architectural gem from the 1880s, within a new tower. Architecture critic Paul Goldberger called the contemporary tower a "cheap-looking box" but considered the renovated interiors of Villard Houses "without a doubt, the finest public rooms of any hotel in New York."[5]

Conventioneers

Offices and hotels together set the stage for a remarkable feature of American life, the convention. Conventions bring people together to share information about a business or profession, check out new products and listen to sales pitches, or socialize over common interests in anything from cats to religion. These meetings must satisfy widespread desires, for their number tripled from 1975 to the early 1980s. By 1983 some 48 million delegates attended more than 90,000 meetings in the United States. Convention delegates are an upscale group in terms of education, occupation, and income. They spend $300 to $400 per delegate per trip on lodgings, food, and other local goods and services. In total, local spending by conventioneers amounted to about $20 billion by 1984.

Mayors hungry for revenues, jobs, and projects found convention centers mouth watering. The trade shows and sales gatherings they pulled in could promote local business and fill hotels and restaurants. Rapid growth in the number and size of conventions created demands for exhibition and meeting space that went far beyond what the big hotels could offer and even beyond the capacity of exhibition halls built as recently as the 1950s. Sensing their opportunity city governments raced to expand old convention centers and to build new ones. A few cities that made an early start at rebuilding downtown—such as Cleveland, Detroit, and Minneapolis—produced spacious convention centers in the 1960s. But the big push came with the construction of more than 100 convention centers after 1970. In 1970 only 15 cities could handle a trade show for 20,000 people; by 1985 some 150 cities were equipped for it. Among those that built downtown convention centers with 100,000 square feet or more were Baltimore, Buffalo, Denver, Los Angeles, Milwaukee, New York, Philadelphia, and Pittsburgh. Many other cities, including Boston, Chicago, and Indianapolis, made major additions to centers built earlier. In 1982 Georgia issued bonds to enlarge a center in Atlanta that had opened only six years before but, according to its director, was "literally booked solid through the year 2000."

Unlike office buildings or hotels, however, convention centers almost never make a profit, no matter how many bookings they get. "Losing money is our way of life," according to the manager of a successful Illinois center. Their problem is competition: center managers are so eager to land conventions that they undercut each other by charging prices too low to cover development and operating costs. The purpose of a center, from the point of view of city officials, is not to turn a profit but to bring prosperous, fun-seeking conventioneers to town. Convention centers are on the development agenda as loss leaders whose red ink should be wiped away by jobs and earnings in downtown hotels, restaurants, and stores. Since most jobs in these establishments do not demand much training or experience, convention centers may do more for disadvantaged city residents than new office buildings. Further, trade shows usually hire local people to set up displays and staff the exhibit halls. And convention visitors produce revenue for local government by paying sales and hotel taxes.

Cities that want convention centers have to find a way to pay for them. Subsidizing a developer is not a workable approach unless the city is prepared to underwrite operating losses as well as development costs. In their search for funds, cities drew on many special revenue sources. Chicago issued general obligation bonds to expand its gigantic McCormick Place in 1978, servicing the debt with proceeds from the state cigarette tax. New York's new convention center is financed through a $375 million bond issue for which the state will make debt service payments, with a backup guarantee from tolls collected by the Triborough Bridge and Tunnel Authority. Income from the center goes toward meeting operating expenses, and even under this arrangement the first-year projection was for a $6 million deficit. San Francisco used a hotel room tax to service both the debt and operating expenses of its Moscone Center. Washington, D.C., used revenues from hotel and business income taxes to pay for the site for its new center, and to build the center it borrowed $77.3 million from the U.S. Treasury to be repaid out of general funds.

The cities took risks of many kinds when they financed these centers. Construction cost overruns were not unusual (the New Orleans Superdome won voter approval as a bond issue for $30 million but eventually cost $163 million, and the budget for New York's Javits Center grew from $375 million to $486 million). Although most city officials were knowledgeable enough to anticipate losses, the deficits were sometimes greater than they expected. Five years after opening a new center, Buffalo found itself attracting only half the visitors predicted in its feasibility studies.

Despite the risks and the intense competition, many big cities attracted heavy convention traffic, and officials laid claim to economic and job benefits that outweighed their deficits. Smaller cities were less likely to keep their halls busy. Among the top thirty cities for convention bookings are such downtown achievers as San Francisco, Chicago, New York, Atlanta, Detroit, Boston, and Philadelphia. Although downtown redevelopment based on office expansion did not necessarily make a convention center succeed, it certainly helped. The strong showing of some cities in the convention trade, the lure of large and growing delegate spending, plus an itch to compete made the convention center a favorite in the new downtown.

The Gentry Come to Town

Another part of the downtown development agenda that clicked into place alongside downtown offices and shopping malls was the revival of in-town living for the well-off. Luxury housing was an early fixture of urban renewal, but most projects of the 1950s and 1960s moved slowly and had only slight success. Not until after the clearance strategy ground to a halt did a noticeable number of well-heeled people begin to resettle in cities. Instead of moving into new apartment towers, they were finding older homes in neighborhoods that had survived the bulldozer.

Most of the newcomers were young, white, professionals or man-

agers. The residents they replaced were typically older, lower income, and more likely to belong to minority groups. To journalistic
observers, this was the long-awaited arrival of the gentry, and
gentrification became the catchword. For city officials who had tried
for years to bring in what James Q. Wilson called "a tax-paying,
culture-loving, free-spending middle class," it was a dream come
true.

Renovated houses in long-neglected parts of the city attracted
much attention in the 1970s. As Victorian style came back into fashion, young professionals were soon cruising the littered streets in
their BMWs and pounding the broken pavements with their Gucci
shoes, searching for brownstones to buy. The visibility of these new
urban pioneers added the word *yuppie* to the language and led trend
watchers to exaggerate the dimensions of what was happening. By
the beginning of 1979 *Harper's, Newsweek,* and the *New York Times
Magazine* took note of how the new elite group was reviving in-town
neighborhoods and declared that the urban crisis was over.

Researchers who studied gentrification had a different perspective.
By 1977 almost all of the thirty largest cities had neighborhood reinvestment, but declining neighborhoods greatly outnumbered those
enjoying a revival. Renovation was centered in some one hundred
neighborhoods and involved less than one-half of 1 percent of the
houses in these cities. An investigation of the changing racial makeup
of census districts within three miles of downtown, as well as of
neighborhoods known for gentrification, confirmed that the net effects were small. Although case studies showed that gentrification
usually replaced black residents with white ones, close-in neighborhoods continued to lose whites and gain blacks in eight of ten cities
between 1970 and 1980. Further contrary to impressionistic accounts,
there was little evidence of the widely heralded back-to-the-city
movement. Most of the renovators were first-time home buyers who
were moving from rental apartments in the city. People like them a
few years earlier, however, would have bought their first homes in
the suburbs.

Although the revitalization of inner neighborhoods amounted to
less than met the eye, it was still important for the cities. It marked a
turnaround in long-established trends and brought a new group of
affluent residents within reach of the city assessor and close enough
to downtown to help support its theaters, restaurants, concert halls,
and shopping.

Was this movement, with its displacement of the poor by the

wealthy, part of a deliberate city strategy? As with most other development trends, it resulted largely from outside circumstances, but the cities pushed it along. Its origins were mainly in life-style changes among the large postwar generation that came of age during the 1970s. Many two-worker families valued the convenience of living in the city, and many shared the new taste for Victorian ornamentation and craftsmanship that contrasted sharply with suburban homes. Nearly three-fourths of the structures in revitalizing neighborhoods surveyed in 1977 were at least seventy-five years old.

Housing market conditions also worked in favor of the cities. Suburban home prices escalated to record levels in the 1970s, making the cost of older city houses a bargain in comparison. Even after the renovation bills, a home in an old neighborhood was a good value, and the number of families buying existing homes rather than new ones doubled between 1970 and 1978.

A critical factor, moreover, was one that the cities helped to create: a concentration of office and professional jobs nearby. Families in gentrifying neighborhoods ranked closeness to jobs as one of the main reasons for moving there. When geographer Brian Berry analyzed cities where house prices and quality were favorable to gentrification, he found that the ones where gentrification actually took hold had much higher rates of downtown office growth than the others.

Beyond their stimulus to downtown office development, city governments took other steps to encourage gentrification. A few organized urban renewal projects to improve rather than bulldoze older neighborhoods. Society Hill in Philadelphia and the South End in Boston were early examples of gentrification supported by renewal projects. Many cities used federal community development funds to fix up streets and parks in neighborhoods where revitalization was under way; others made tax-lien properties available at nominal cost to "homesteaders" who promised to renovate them; still others ran promotional campaigns boosting certain neighborhoods as good places to buy homes. A number of cities leaned on local financial institutions to make home loans in areas that were formerly "redlined" for avoidance by loan officers, and by 1977 thirty-eight cities took part in demonstration programs organized by the Federal Home Loan Bank Board to encourage mortgage lending in old neighborhoods.

In the highly regulated real estate markets of central cities, hardly any new trend gets under way without government involvement.

When sociologist Sharon Zukin studied the remarkable growth of studios and apartments carved out of old industrial lofts in Manhattan, she found the busy hand of government. First, the state legislature legitimized the movement by amending the building code to allow artists to live and work in industrial or commercial space. Then it helped expand the market by broadening the definition of artists and put a city agency in charge of certifying eligibility. Soon the criteria included "commitment to art" as a substitute for an occupation in the arts. Then the city rezoned one area after another to authorize conversions of manufacturing space into studios and living quarters, including the well-known TriBeCa area near the financial district, where loft living was permitted even without studios or artists. Later the city stimulated the trend by offering tax breaks to developers who converted entire industrial buildings to apartments.

The combination of a new life-style and a taste for industrial architecture, plus favorable economics and supportive regulation, made loft living a large-scale movement in New York. The number of people living in converted lofts went from a few thousand in the early 1960s to some 50,000 by the late 1970s, with still more living in whole industrial buildings converted into apartments. The same trend, on a much smaller scale, got under way in the warehouses and industrial buildings of Boston, Chicago, Cleveland, Philadelphia, Pittsburgh, St. Paul, and even Los Angeles, while building inspectors winked at illegal residents, and city officials offered tax benefits to developers.

Encouraging middle- and upper-income people to live in the city was one of the earliest aims of downtown revitalization. When reinvestment in old neighborhoods turned out to be a practical way to make it happen, city governments did what they could to help; fashionable housing would not only strengthen the tax base but could attract creative, entrepreneurial people to keep the service economy growing. Downtown business coalitions were usually in favor, since a good in-town neighborhood was a valuable living option for executives and professionals. For both officials and citizens who worried about downtown, bringing in residents promised to make the streets livelier and safer on a twenty-four hour basis.

Stagecraft

Rebuilding the city was not enough; it was equally important to spread the word about the rebuilding. Big-city mayors who were promoting office buildings, hotels, convention centers, and restored neighborhoods got busy marketing their cities to real estate investors, business executives, convention planners, and home buyers. City governments acted more and more like press agents hyping an image and selling a product. They coined slogans and advertised them to the world. After New York established itself as the Big Apple, Minneapolis promoters countered with the Mini-Apple. They put together multimedia presentations—split-screen slide shows and videotapes with musical sound tracks—and took them to conventions around the country.

They also organized road shows. Pittsburgh hosted a luncheon at New York's Helmsley Palace to give a message to media producers and corporate executives: "Pittsburgh is no longer Steel City." Mayor Richard Caliguiri and a prestige brigade of local notables—President Richard Cyert of Carnegie-Mellon University, actress Barbara Feldon, and other home-town stars of television, sports, and business—told their audience that Pittsburgh had become a world-class city with clean air, green trees, safe streets, a temperate climate, a vibrant economy, and $5 billion in private downtown construction in just seven years. After screening a film, *Pittsburgh Renaissance*, a television executive asked rhetorically, "Where was the first combined liver and heart transplant operation?" and delivered an emphatic answer: "Pittsburgh, two weeks ago. Nobody ever talks about that."[6]

The cities staged events designed to draw crowds and get into the media: street fairs, ethnic fairs, film fairs, book fairs, world's fairs, marathons, Grand Prix auto races, arts-in-the-parks festivals, jazz festivals, winterfests and summerfests, New Year's and Chinese New Year's parades, and celebrations of anything else that could be celebrated.

New York gave a spectacular birthday party for the Brooklyn Bridge centennial in May 1983. It featured a ticker-tape parade over the great bridge from Brooklyn and through the Manhattan financial district, with brass bands, horse-drawn carriages, costumed marchers, an elephant from the Big Apple Circus, the Budweiser Clydesdale horses, and Mayor Koch in a Brooklyn Dodgers baseball cap. The gala continued with street fairs, roof parties, boat rides, and a harbor-craft flotilla. The Brooklyn Philharmonic played music into the night, including a piano concerto, "Keys to the City," commissioned for the occasion, and the famous Grucci family put on a $200,000 fireworks display. The Centennial Commission organized events throughout the summer and into the fall, spending a budget of $2.8 million. The celebration filled not only the streets but the national airwaves and the press. Anyone alive in the United States at the time had to be cut off from the rest of the world to avoid hearing about the Brooklyn Bridge.

Promotion no longer ended at the water's edge. Mayors increasingly took trade missions abroad to speak for local businesses and to bring new companies to town. Mayor Andrew Young of Atlanta, capitalizing on his earlier experience as United Nations ambassador, earned a special reputation for extended duty overseas. The mayors of Philadelphia, New Orleans, Syracuse, and Albuquerque among other cities took steps to open foreign markets, including setting up trade development agencies and establishing tariff-free foreign trade zones for storing and assembling imported products.

Most of these promotions did not spend much city money. Preparing film and slide shows, hosting media people, and even taking a mission to China are minor items in a big-city budget. Staging festivals runs into more money, but business contributions usually cover the costs. Large corporations took care of most of the Brooklyn Bridge extravaganza and in return got their names attached to the various shows. Whether promotional efforts are for boosterism or for economic development, they do not seem to trouble the taxpayers, and they may broadcast an image of the community that residents appreciate.

When cities got into construction projects for promotional purposes, boosterism came at a higher cost. Knoxville sponsored a world's fair on the edge of downtown in 1982 largely in the hope that it would launch some $200 million in downtown development. The city floated more than $30 million in bond issues; it spent $44 million in federal redevelopment grants, $225 million in federal highway funds, and millions of its own to improve downtown and beef up the police department to handle the crowds. City officials intended to get their money back by selling the fair site as prime development land and collecting property taxes from it. Although the fair drew 11 million visitors, it failed to generate the "decade of development" that the mayor had promised. Within two years developer interest in downtown was dead, the fair site was almost deserted, the federal government had dumped its $21 million U.S. Pavilion for $1, and the city was left owing its lenders $57 million. The next mayor announced that property taxes were going up to help pay off the debt.

Big League Ambitions

Of all the items on the current development agenda, sports stadiums best illustrate the uneasy mix of image building, boosterism, and economic purpose that keep city governments hustling. Cities all over the country have been competing to get or hold big league sports teams. They pour huge sums into building or renovating stadiums, which they then lease at bargain prices. (Many stadiums are outside the congested business district, but among the cities that have used them to fill holes in and around downtown are Indianapolis, Minneapolis, New Orleans, Pittsburgh, St. Louis, and Seattle.) To justify the cost, mayors predict economic benefits while arguing in the same breath that a city cannot achieve true greatness without professional sports. Mayor Federico Peña told a national television audience that his campaign to bring major league baseball to Denver is "an investment decision" and "a business opportunity" that would generate "a terrific $75-million economic impact." But after a break in the conversation, he came back with the other half of the argument: "I think any great city in this country has to have a major-league baseball team. It's just part of the American tradition."[7]

Mayor Coleman Young of Detroit laid off city workers and cut services to cope with a fiscal crisis in the mid-1970s, but he used a $5 million federal grant and a $25 million revenue bond issue to fix up Tiger Stadium so that he could sign the Detroit Tigers to a thirty-year lease. "Make no mistake about it," Young maintained, "if the Tigers had left Detroit, it would have been the death knell for the city." Baseball was not only a morale builder but also a money maker: "The very fact that they drew more than 2½ million people into the city has an obvious economic impact."[8]

While Denver and Detroit may have to struggle with image problems, New Yorkers should have no need for professional sports to prop up their status. Mayor Abe Beame must have felt differently though. Even as New York was heading toward bankruptcy in the early 1970s, his administration bought Yankee Stadium from the Yankees for $12 million and signed the team to a thirty-year lease by promising to bring the old ballpark up to competitive standards. The agreement called for reconstruction that would make it "equivalent in all respects with the best features of the new stadia at Pittsburgh, Philadelphia and Cincinnati." One financial analyst described the city's position as "like Rome agreeing to renovate the Colosseum incorporating the best features of the New Orleans Superdrome." What it meant in practice was that the city met the Yankees' demands for very high standards and spent $61.5 million on the renovation.

The lease called for the Yankees to pay rent as a percentage of their gross receipts from admissions and concessions but allowed them to deduct all maintenance costs from the rent. The Yankees, to nobody's surprise, have been maintaining the stadium in mint condition, using almost all the rent the city would otherwise collect. In 1976 their gross receipts were close to $12 million, and the city's rent percentage according to the lease was 10 percent minus maintenance costs. After deducting for maintenance, the team billed the city for "negative rent"—which the city refused to pay. In 1977 they grossed $13.4 million and paid only $171,000 in rent. By the early 1980s maintenance costs were regularly outstripping the rent, and the city made annual payments to the Yankees for taking care of the stadium. As of 1987 the city was trying to cap the amount of negative rent it would pay while making plans to invest $10 million more in new luxury boxes and to cosponsor $60 million worth of parking and road improvements. The price tag of image building is high for the city, but the Yankees enjoy an image of strength and self-reliance even while they demand handouts for champions.

Stadiums and the teams that use them supply only a handful of local jobs for ticket sellers, groundkeepers, hot dog vendors, and parking lot attendants. Unlike convention centers, they do not normally bring in tourists who stay for several days and use their credit cards at local hotels, restaurants, and stores. City governments take in mainly admission taxes and contributions to stadium rents. Offsetting these benefits are the costs to the city of renovating or building stadiums, operating them, and leasing them below cost. Competing for a limited number of big league franchises, cities vie to offer the most generous deals. The freedom an established team has to move to a more profitable location drives a further wedge into the city's already weak bargaining power. When the Oakland Raiders not only broke National Football League rules by moving to Los Angeles but also won $50 million in a lawsuit challenging the NFL's right to control team location, they made the threat of moving all the more credible.

The economic impacts of major league sports have never been studied systematically, but a good analysis of Baltimore showed an unsteady pattern of gains and losses even under conditions that were exceptionally favorable for city hall. From 1977 through 1983 two major league teams—the Colts and the Orioles—were paying rent to use the same municipal stadium, and the city's outlays were essentially limited to maintenance and utility costs for the ballpark plus overtime pay for police assigned to work at games. Maryland paid for almost all improvements to the stadium during this period. The city spent more than it collected from baseball and football in three of the seven years, collected more than it spent in another three, and just about broke even one year. For the seven-year period, the city earned a net "profit" of just over $1 million. During these years, however, the state's commitment for capital improvements was $5 million. If Baltimore had paid for renovations, as many other cities do, the profit would have turned into a $4 million net loss.

No reasonable expectation of financial benefit could possibly explain why city officials are ready to spend whatever it takes to bring in sports teams. The symbolic value of being in the "big leagues," and the inclination of mayors to promote anything that might be popular, are far more likely explanations. "If you ask people what the great cities in America are," said Mayor William Hudnut of Indianapolis, "I'll bet 99 out of 100 cite an NFL city."

The mixture of sports with politics made the stadium itself into a symbol of civic achievement, encouraging cities to outdo one another in the elegance of their structures. A Chicago architect called the contemporary sports palace "the civic icon of the late 20th century . . . the equivalent of a cathedral, proof in the citizens' minds that they're world-class cities."[9] In place of the old ballpark, sports boosters now want multipurpose, all-weather stadiums with retractable domes. And they want corporate luxury boxes garnished with television monitors, padded furniture, and all the other trimmings of the executive suite—perhaps the ultimate in privatization of public space.

Even the technological problems of domed arenas have not discouraged their promoters. Stadium architects trying to avoid the cavelike atmosphere created by early concrete domes turned next to fabric roofs held up by air pressure. At the Hoosierdome in Indianapolis, the pressurized interior worked against city attempts to attract and hold onto sports fans. When the desired crowds came pouring in through several open doors at once, the roof drooped like a cold soufflé, and when a single door opened during a game, 45-mile-an-hour winds popped loyal fans out through the exit like champagne corks.

Beyond angling for sports franchises, mayors were scanning the horizon for other projects to draw visitors and please voters. Performing arts theaters, concert halls, and art museums sprouted in one downtown after another. Success anywhere spawned imitations. Waterfront aquariums in Boston and Baltimore sparked a follow-the-leader trend when their attendance figures and admission fees spoke with undeniable eloquence. Baltimore's aquarium was the state's top tourist attraction of 1984, adding an estimated 3,000 jobs and $88 million to the economy. Fish turned out to have genuinely popular appeal: Chicago's aquarium, open since 1930, set a record in 1985 with 900,000 visitors, while Boston's attendance peaked at over a million in the same year. By 1986 Baltimore and Chicago were working on expansions, and the list of cities with new aquariums planned or under way ranged from seaports such as Boston, Norfolk, and New Orleans to landlocked Dallas, Denver, and Kansas City.

While mayors often draw inspiration from competing cities, they also like to build promotional projects that trade on the special character of their own communities. A seemingly endless variety of museums celebrates pioneering days or industrial history or local arts. Halls of fame exhibit memorabilia of everything from sports to country music. Many of these institutions do entertain visitors, but some serve mainly as symbols of a desperate struggle for recognition. The depressed industrial city of Rome, New York, recently pushed out the frontier of booster creativity when it pried $150,000 loose from the state legislature to complete work on its New York State Museum of Cheese. Rome claims to be the home of America's first cheese factory and, as Mayor Carl Eilenberg promised, "We intend to milk this for all it's worth."

The pursuit of crowd pleasers, coming on top of the attempt to reconstruct a central city economy, illustrates the variety of motives that entered into decisions to build downtown shopping malls. Although the malls were risky ventures by most standards, on a spectrum of projects ranging from office complexes to cheese museums city officials had to give them a high rating.

Logic in the Patchwork

The city record on downtown revitalization includes examples of fluff, of groping for direction, of grasping at almost any opportunity to bring in outside resources. But it also reveals a thread of economic and developmental rationality running through the downtown agenda. To call the composite of projects a corporate center strategy is to dignify it beyond the reality of piecemeal, trial-and-error decisions. But the national economy was changing in a way that favored office work and corporate services as the new core of downtown. And the logic of city development produced a series of ventures that were feasible because they were anchored in some way to the jobs and businesses that were growing downtown.

There was also another logic at work: the logic of local politics. For most mayors it meant that projects had to produce visible community-wide benefits. Jobs and business growth counted heavily in political terms, but they were not enough. City administrations also needed brick-and-mortar symbols to demonstrate their accomplishments. Office towers, elegant hotels, and large convention centers served this purpose well, and if they could not be completed within a mayor's term, then artists' renderings, display models, groundbreakings, and ribbon cuttings created political credit along the way. The mayors wanted projects with broad popular appeal, places that the voting public would visit. Festivals, fairs, and celebrations were right for this purpose, and big league sports were even better. Beyond a certain point, city initiatives had a way of edging into unfocused image building and boosterism, but most of what the cities did in the 1970s and 1980s was calculated to appeal to large numbers of their people. This concern to please the public at large a was big change from the elitism of the 1950s, when downtown leaders were building projects for narrow groups of users.

Both political and economic logic led to the downtown retail centers. When we asked mayors why they had decided to push these projects, they kept economic considerations far in the background. The reasons they gave included to make downtown a place for entertainment and visiting as well as for work, to have street life in the evenings and on weekends, to get rid of eyesores that the shopping malls would replace, to preserve landmarks, and to demonstrate the city's competence to manage development. Creating jobs and raising tax revenues were secondary considerations when they came up at all, and the casual record keeping we found with respect to retail jobs and tax collections reinforces the impression that once a project was built, city officials had little interest in documenting these particular results.

The economic logic came from other quarters. Business leaders saw a new shopping mall as a way to enhance the value of their own property, a place where their employees might shop or have lunch, entertainment for out-of-town visitors, and a spur to conventions and tourism that might help their firms. Above all they saw it as a catalyst for further downtown development. Within city hall some key people also backed retail projects on economic grounds. In St. Paul both the director of the city's Department of Planning and Economic Development and the head of the port authority believed Town Square would have enormous value in promoting other downtown investment.

The retail centers produced results that fit the political logic behind them. What they did for economic development is hard to establish. Beyond the construction and retail jobs they created, they were clearly helpful, yet their economic impacts have hardly been measured, and the most important ones never can be measured. Most cities that sponsored shopping malls were doing so much else simultaneously that there is no way to know how important the malls in themselves were for downtown development.

Faneuil Hall Marketplace, for example, is surrounded by new buildings and by historic structures renovated for condominiums, stores, and offices. But the city was putting ambitious plans for its waterfront area into effect long before the market was redone, and developers were already beginning to operate there. With the exception of two new hotels flanking the marketplace, there is no reason to believe it is directly responsible for other projects. By bringing huge crowds into town and by demonstrating that investors could earn a profit, however, it certainly accelerated development. Samuel Mintz, an architect long active in the area and designer of one of the two adjoining hotels, recalls the galvanizing effect of Quincy Market's opening: "Suddenly Boston was hot, and property values in the waterfront area doubled."

Replacing derelict buildings with a jewel of historic preservation also made the few blocks around Faneuil Hall especially desirable for development. From 1977 through 1985 office rents and land prices increased notably faster near the marketplace than in the rest of downtown. Real estate consultants who analyzed the changes estimated that the marketplace boosted nearby land prices by 20–25 percent and office rents by 5–15 percent over the general downtown increase.

Faneuil Hall Marketplace made its greatest impact when the rest of downtown was still in the doldrums. From 1970 through 1976 while the marketplace was under development, real estate sales prices climbed 13 percent in real dollars within the five adjacent blocks, while they dropped 16 percent in the rest of a forty-block study area. By the time the marketplace was open, the start of an office boom drove prices up ten times faster in the nearby financial district than in the market neighborhood from 1977 to 1979. As development spread across central downtown, property values grew at the same rate near the market and in the rest of the area extending into the financial district.

In other cities there is also evidence that the retail centers promoted economic development beyond the payrolls and taxes they added. Mayor Latimer and Gary Stout reported that Oxford Properties' commitment to the Town Square project helped persuade other investors to build in downtown St. Paul. Gerald Trimble, redevelopment director while Plaza Pasadena was built, cited executives who considered the retail center an important factor in their decision to build nearby. Once Plaza Pasadena brought large number of shoppers downtown, other developers began to renovate shops nearby while larger stores planned a higher-income mall for another part of downtown.

Some retail centers had impacts on downtown development that their backers never intended. Seattle's development-minded business community and the pro-growth political establishment in the late 1960s wanted to tear down the Pike Place Market to make way for office buildings. Architectural preservationists and other citizen groups rallied to save it not because they wanted economic development but because they loved the old farmers' market. Economic development was never an issue in the campaign to save Pike Place; it was the major rationale for proposals to destroy it.

Ironically the renovated public market is now one of the prime tourist sights in Seattle, producing business for hotels, restaurants, and stores. In addition the market has had a noticeable impact on downtown development. Apartment, office, and commercial complexes form a ring around it, representing some $230 million in investment and in many cases advertising closeness to the market as a feature to attract tenants. In short, the architectural preservationists turned out to be more in tune with emerging public taste than the hard-headed economic thinkers of the time.

The development of San Diego's Horton Plaza had the most direct connection to other downtown projects. From the outset Hahn and several department store heads insisted on a city commitment to develop several thousand houses or apartments downtown plus a convention center and hotels as a requirement for their retail center. Mayor Pete Wilson and other San Diego officials were more than willing to go along since these conditions were entirely in line with their own ambitions for downtown. The city might have sponsored these projects at some future time, but Horton Plaza was the catalyst. A year after the opening, Trimble reported strong interest from developers who wanted to build in the long-neglected area around it. Horton Plaza, he observed, had convinced them that the city is serious about revitalizing its once-decaying urban core.

In Boston, St. Paul, Seattle, Pasadena, San Diego, and other cities, developers started many new projects while the retail centers were under way or soon after their completion. Their timing suggests the strong possibility of a cause-and-effect relationship, and knowledgeable observers in these cities claim that the retail projects were important contributors to other development. More than that cannot be said with any certainty.

The downtown shopping malls were well suited to a time of transition in the recovery of downtown. They made a start at bringing people back to the city and helped attract tourists, conventioneers, and business visitors. They made in-town living more attractive. By changing the development signals, they stimulated at least some other construction and possibly a great deal. They gave the cities new and interesting places to visit, plus some unusual shopping opportunities. To ask for much more is to have very high expectations indeed. And to expect definitive evidence of the results is like asking for scientific proof of what the Eiffel Tower has done for Paris.

The city agenda for downtown had a rough underlying logic that encouraged economic growth. Faced with suburban competition and fiscal strains, city governments managed to ride the coattails of an emerging service economy and to bring their plans into line with it. Creative officials were able to reconcile the demands of politics and economics by finding projects that were both popular and functional. While the development agenda had its underside of puffery and faddishness, it went a long way toward reviving downtown as a business center.

In the process of rebuilding downtown, city government transformed itself. The recent agenda is important not only for what it built but for what it said about the commitment of city officials. It sent a message to developers, business people, and the public that local officials were taking greater responsibility for the economic well-being of the city.

For mayors and council members to act as civic boosters promoting real estate development is nothing new, but now they do it with a difference. Before World War II city development projects were limited to such clearly municipal functions as building streets, parks, schools, libraries, police stations, and firehouses. These were the public works that served a resident population, and city officials scattered them through the neighborhoods where people lived. The more recent agenda crosses the old barrier between public and private development by using public power and money to promote office buildings, hotels, convention centers, shopping malls, stadiums, and more. Now the projects are located away from places where most people live, concentrated instead in a downtown of corporate offices, business visitors, suburban commuters, and tourists.

This agenda, a forceful response to the postwar urban condition, was probably the only response that could have worked. In blurring the line between public and private, it mirrored the new public-private combinations for managing development and the trend toward privatization of public space. Making the once-rigid boundary easier for both sides to cross was a major contributor to downtown development. But the results raised legitimate questions about whether the new downtowns were as helpful to average city residents as they were to business.

After thirty years of rebuilding, most big cities had new downtowns by the 1980s. Gone were the manufacturing districts of the 1950s, the working harborside warehouses, the freight terminals, some of the once-thriving department stores and specialty shops, and most working-class neighborhoods. Gone too were the rubble fields of the 1960s, when the wrecking crews were finished but the builders nowhere in sight. The new centers featured a cluster of office towers mixed with new hotels and civic buildings, freeways pumping heavy traffic to the edge of downtown, modern housing complexes, a shopping mall, some renovated office buildings and warehouses, many new restaurants, and at least one restored Victorian neighborhood.

These changes were visible enough to counteract the negative image of big cities in perpetual crisis. Even a public that clearly preferred to live in suburbs or small towns recognized that cities had advantages as well as problems. By 1978 half the respondents in a national survey considered large cities best for job opportunities, health care, colleges and universities, culture, public transportation, and restaurants and movies.

Less visible, but equally important to city residents, were changes in the workplace. Far fewer workers had production jobs, and many more were in service, professional, or government occupations. In metropolitan Cleveland, where two of every three workers in the 1940s had manufacturing jobs, the figure was down to one of three by the 1980s. In industrial Pittsburgh, where the last of the blast furnaces closed in 1980, manufacturing jobs dropped from half the area's total to less than one-fifth while downtown acquired the nation's third-largest concentration of Fortune 500 corporate headquarters. Core cities that used to rumble with industry turned into silent office canyons. In 1953 half the workers in Philadelphia had production jobs, whole only one of ten was in information processing and other high-skill services; by 1980 half were in these services and only one of four in production. White-collar cities of the 1950s kept breeding more office jobs. Boston, with one-fifth of its jobs in information and high-skill services as early as 1953, had more than half in these lines of work by 1980. Even the skyscraper citadel of New York still had four of every ten workers in manufacturing or construction in 1953 but less than one out of four by 1980.

But the cities' cultivation of an office economy did not go far enough to reduce poverty and unemployment for their residents. Most large cities of the Northeast and Midwest lost manufacturing jobs faster than they gained white-collar work, leaving them with fewer jobs overall. At the end of the 1970s the central cities of metropolitan areas continued to have higher unemployment rates than the rest of the nation and as of 1979 were worse off relative to the suburbs than they had been in 1970. City families earned lower incomes, with the median down by 4 percent in constant dollars from 1969 to 1978, in contrast to a 5 percent increase for suburban families. The number of people living in poverty remained unchanged in the central cities while it went down in the rest of the country.

Even in cities where the office boom was strongest, resident unemployment and poverty grew worse after 1970. The ten cities that led the nation in downtown office development from 1950 through 1984 had higher unemployment in 1982 than in 1970. Nine of these ten also had higher proportions of people with poverty-level incomes in 1979 than in 1969. From 1979 through 1985 the poverty population in the nation's central cities grew from 16 percent to 19 percent of the total. New York and Chicago, the top two in office construction, had as many as one person of four living in poverty in 1985.

Researchers who make comparisons among cities usually use a composite index to rate economic well-being. One index based on unemployment, the proportion of people in poverty, and changes in real income between 1970 and 1980 shows Atlanta, Baltimore, New York, and Philadelphia—all among the heavy hitters in downtown development—slipping from better conditions in 1970 to join the ten worst-off cities in the country by 1980. If downtown revitalization was a renaissance, it was still no protector of city people.

One reason that downtown growth made only a small dent in poverty and unemployment among city residents is that commuters filled many of the white-collar jobs. Suburbanites held more than half the professional, technical, and managerial jobs in Boston, Detroit, and San Francisco in 1980 and more than one-third in many other big cities. In the new downtown office buildings, commuters held about 60 percent of the jobs in San Francisco and 70 percent in Boston.

Boston and San Francisco are not typical, but they do illustrate why downtown expansion disappointed some city residents. A flourishing office district turned Boston into more of a commuter city between 1970 and 1980, with the resident share of city-wide jobs dropping from 36 to 33 percent and then climbing back a notch to 34 percent by 1986. In San Francisco office growth created some 166,000 new jobs between 1965 and 1980. Yet during that same period the total number of employed San Francisco residents dropped by almost 18,000, leading city planner Chester Hartman to conclude: "It is indisputable that office growth has not provided net employment benefits for the city's residents."[1]

There is no simple explanation for who works where in a modern urban area, but a few trends are worth noting. While downtown jobs were changing, so were city populations. They were changing in opposite directions. The jobs were increasingly for men and women who were good at speaking, writing, and managing and for technical experts in law, finance, computers, and other specialties needed to run businesses. Even as the work became more demanding, the best educated and most skilled workers continued to leave the cities, while less educated minority groups and immigrants increased their numbers. The central city became more and more the home of people with too little education and experience for high-skill service jobs. Those were not the only jobs, however. The new offices also needed people to run the copy machines, answer the phones, and operate the word processors. City workers had better chances of getting into these lower-paying office occupations.

The rebuilding of downtown brought other kinds of businesses with more jobs for city residents. Hotels, restaurants, and retail stores had a greater share of entry-level jobs and generally hired a higher proportion of workers from the city. In Boston city residents landed 40 percent of the jobs in newly built retail stores and half the jobs in new hotels. In Baltimore 40 percent of the permanent jobs at Harborplace went to minority workers.

Indicting City Hall

With new downtowns rising while low incomes and unemployment continued for city residents, it was easy to blame city hall for promoting the wrong kind of development. Academic researchers, slow to discover the extent of downtown development and grudging in their recognition of any merit in it, saw little social value in the growth of corporate headquarters and business services. They accused cities of selling out resident interests in order to do what was good for business.

Norman Krumholz of Cleveland State University, formerly the city's planning director, argued that the alleged successes in city development "have for the past thirty years, worked to enhance and expand the institutional, cultural, and downtown areas of many cities. Sometimes these projects added new taxes to the dwindling coffers of their cities. But these projects have done little or nothing for the poverty, joblessness, and declining neighborhoods of poor and working-class central-city residents."[2] Desmond Smith, writing about the information-based economy of New York, saw it leading mainly to "the rise of a super-rich mercantile class at the expense of the disadvantaged. New York, after a hundred or so years as the melting pot, has entered the age of the Uncommon Man. The common man has virtually no future in the brave new city. White-collar, high-technology jobs are no help in the unskilled poor."[3]

But the cities did not arrange the national economy, and they were not responsible for changing its base from manufacturing to services. Nor did city governments create the racism that kept minority groups from equal access to education, business, and good jobs. Underlying much of the criticism of city development was a dispute about the nature of the urban problem. During the 1960s and early 1970s the news media and many public officials agreed that it was basically a problem of improving living conditions for poor people and minority groups concentrated in the cities. Before that the press and city officials had defined the urban problem as the decline of downtown and the flight of the middle class to the suburbs. And in the mid-1970s, when New York and several other big cities teetered at the edge of bankruptcy, opinion leaders redefined the urban problem as finding a way for city government to stay solvent.

The most severe criticism came from writers who continued to think of the urban problem as the condition of the poor. From their point of view city governments had betrayed the commitments they made in the 1960s to end poverty and racism. There is some truth in this critique, but it is a partial truth. Cities in the postwar era never had the capacity on their own to invest a meaningful level of resources in education, housing, job training, or community services to meet the needs of the poor. They made their commitments in response to strong federal leadership and with an understanding that Washington would foot most of the bill. Politics is the art of the possible, and a strategy focused on improving poverty neighborhoods no longer made sense after the Nixon and Ford administrations began to put the brakes on federal aid to cities.

Federal contributions to state and local spending did not actually turn down until midway through the Carter administration, but the handwriting was on the wall by the early 1970s. Both Congress and the White House showed less interest in helping the mayors, though the fiscal problems of older cities grew worse during the post-1973 inflation and recessions. Hard pressed to keep costs down, raise additional taxes, or increase bonded debt, cities struggled to stay solvent. Several—including New York, Boston, Cleveland, and Philadelphia—reached the brink of default and bankruptcy. Many more made deep cuts in public services but continued to bear heavy tax burdens. When President Ford refused to help New York out of its fiscal crisis in 1975, one of the most memorable headlines of the decade told mayors across the country what they could expect from Washington: "Ford to City: Drop Dead," read the front page of the *Daily News.*

Faced with rising fiscal strains at home and growing indifference in Washington, city governments could not possibly find a solution to the problem of urban poverty. Following the rule of politics that "if there is no solution, there is no problem," the mayors redefined the urban problem. They turned back to their earlier ambition to rebuild downtown; for this problem there were solutions within their grasp. To get those solutions they revived several features of earlier days: involving downtown business interests in setting redevelopment priorities, favoring construction projects over public services, searching for projects that would trigger more development, and emphasizing projects that interested the broad middle class more than the poor.

Once city governments returned to their downtown agenda, promoting office growth was the most practical strategy for them. Chasing after manufacturing while production jobs were in nationwide decline would have been a prescription for failure. Cleveland's attempt to follow this strategy is instructive. In the late 1970s the city spent more than $1.2 million to assist an inner-city industrial park that promised jobs for hundreds living in nearby public housing projects. Two new firms—a mattress factory and a bakery—and two existing plants that expanded with city help eventually hired a grand total of eight people from the neighborhood, three of them for short-term openings.

Manufacturing Myths: New York and Pittsburgh

Suppose a production center strategy did succed: How many more jobs would it create for the city's poor? A close look at workers and jobs in New York City raises serious doubts about manufacturing as a solution to the problems of unskilled city dwellers. In hiring, manufacturers and office managers are not as different as the critics assume. True to the stereotype, 37 percent of the workers in New York's manufacturing firms had less than a high school education in 1980, compared with 14 percent of workers in finance, insurance, real estate, and business and professional services. But contrary to the stereotype, manufacturers also hired a large number of suburban workers. Commuters held 23 percent of all manufacturing jobs, as against 20 percent of office jobs, and at every education level their share of jobs was higher in manufacturing than in office and service firms.

Analyzing the distribution of jobs by education level, moreover, explains how New York's increasing concentration of office work was actually able to expand opportunities for people who never finished high school. Between 1970 and 1980 New York lost about 100,000 manufacturing jobs but added about 300,000 office and service jobs. If the education level of workers in these fields as of 1980 was representative of the entire decade, then the manufacturing decline eliminated some 37,000 jobs for high school dropouts while office growth during the same years added 42,000 jobs for dropouts. These same changes did much more for college graduates, producing a net increase of about 100,000 jobs for them, but for dropouts at least the supply of jobs more than held steady. At the same time, since office firms were more likely than manufacturers to hire city residents, the change from production to office work gave residents at all education levels an edge over commuters.

Nothing short of massive growth in manufacturing would resolve the job and income problems of high school dropouts, and massive manufacturing growth in the heart of the city is unrealistic. Calculations for New York, where 16 percent of 1980 jobs were in manufacturing, show that even a doubling of this share (with proportional cuts in all other lines of work) would raise the proportion of jobs for dropouts only from 22 percent to 25 percent.

Further, the allegedly one-sided economy of New York, where two of every three jobs are concentrated in the office stronghold of Manhattan, employed as high a proportion of dropouts in 1980 as the national economy. The argument that the corporate center job mix is responsible for city unemployment and poverty rests on shaky ground. Since this prototypical city of high-skill services hires as many dropouts, proportionally, as the country at large, city development policies can hardly be faulted for shortchanging the unskilled. New York's high poverty and unemployment rates in 1980 did not result from an exceptionally small share of jobs for dropouts but from an exceptionally large proportion of dropouts in the population—40 percent, compared with 35 percent in all central cities and 28 percent in all suburbs. Other big cities troubled by economic distress in spite of their downtown revival also lagged behind national education levels, with the proportion of dropouts in Baltimore, Cleveland, Philadelphia, and St. Louis even higher than in New York.

Critics of downtown development fail to recognize how many jobs are still open to people with little education. Office establishments hire a combination of unskilled, semiskilled, and highly skilled employees. Half the jobs in Manhattan financial firms, for example, go to some 250,000 secretaries, stenographers, and clerks. In an analysis of labor requirements in nine of the largest cities, sociologist John Kasarda classified industries as entry level when their mean employee education level was fewer than twelve years and knowledge intensive when their mean education level was more than fourteen years. Since every one of these cities has had major downtown office development in recent years, it is not surprising that jobs in entry-level industries declined in seven of the nine between 1970 and 1980. What is surprising is that even after this decline, the nine cities in 1980 still had three times as many jobs in entry-level industries as in knowledge-intensive ones.

Recent experience in Pittsburgh gives no grounds for handwringing over the service economy. Between 1977 and 1982 the Pittsburgh area had heavy industrial losses that wiped out close to 15 percent of manufacturing jobs. While production work was in decline, however, professional and personal services were growing almost enough to make up for it so that overall employment dropped by less than 4 percent. The decline was concentrated in high-paying manufacturing jobs, while the growth was concentrated in professional services, where 1977 earnings averaged little more than half as much. If wage levels had remained the same after 1977, the people of Pittsburgh would have taken deep cuts in income.

What happened instead is that as the service sector grew larger, its wage levels and working hours also increased. As more Pittsburgh workers moved into service occupations, average earnings overall climbed 6 percent in real dollars from 1977 to 1982. At worst the transformation of the area's economy could have slowed the rate of increase in earnings, but the total payroll still increased. There were unquestionably income losses for laid-off production workers, but at the same time enough people were leaving manufacturing voluntarily to create nearly three times as many vacancies as there were layoffs. Economist Louis Jacobson, who did the study, concluded that it is possible for communities to maintain high pay levels while they shift from manufacturing to services. In addition, even at a time of exceptional decline, normal turnover made it possible for displaced manufacturing workers to find jobs similar to the ones they lost. The record in Pittsburgh as in New York shows the service economy to be troublesome enough to make its critics believable but not so troublesome as to make them right.

In New York and Boston typical office jobs pay about as much as manufacturing work. (Comparisons have to be inexact because wage and salary data usually ignore fringe benefits and fail to report the number of weeks people actually work in a year.) Administrative support staff in New York, consisting mainly of clerical workers, had salaries averaging $10,700 in 1980, while semiskilled factory and transportation operatives, fabricators, and laborers made $10,200. In Boston general office clerks did as well as assemblers and fabricators in 1985–1986, and typists in service firms earned as much as stock clerks in industry. In moderate-skill occupations word-processing typists made as much as precision textile, apparel, and furniture workers; legal secretaries did as well as precision printing workers; and sales agents for service firms had higher pay than sheet-metal workers or drafters.

Wage differences in the country at large favor manufacturing over service jobs but not for all occupations and not by wide margins. The bedrock blue-collar occupations of operatives, assemblers, and inspectors, for example, had median weekly earnings of $287 in 1985 in comparison with $286 for administrative support and clerical workers. As many as 30 percent of administrative support and clerical workers earned less than $7,400 a year (in 1986 dollars), compared with 26 percent of operatives and 23 percent of transport workers and material movers. And at the upper end only 5 percent of administrative support workers earned more than $29,600, compared with 10 percent of operatives and 15 percent of transport workers and material movers. The large blue-collar occupation of laborers, however, lagged far behind administrative support workers, with 51 percent earning less than $7,400 a year and only 3 percent more than $29,600.

The advantages of blue-collar work are probably greater than wage differences indicate since fringe benefits tend to be more generous and employees tend to work more hours per year in manufacturing than in service firms. If cities could capture a greater share of manufacturing, they would be better off in several respects. A broader-based economy would make them less vulnerable to downturns in finance and other cyclical fields; a wider variety of jobs would help residents who have a hard time fitting into offices; and even marginally higher earnings in manufacturing would improve opportunities for low-income workers. Yet the differences between blue-collar and white-collar work are not great enough to explain the persistence and recent increase of urban poverty. Critics who lay heavy blame on the job mix created by corporate center development have based their case more on stereotypes than on data.

There are at least three explanations for why strong downtown economies have not done more for city residents. One is that low-income people fail to learn about office job openings for which they are qualified or could be qualified with minimal training. If they have no friends or relatives working downtown, they miss the informal contacts that most people use to find work; and company recruiters have a habit of avoiding inner-city neighborhoods. Acting on this theory, a number of cities have tried to change the job recruitment and training practices of downtown firms.

Another explanation is that many city residents lack the education to function well in either a factory or an office. The exceptionally high proportion of high school dropouts among city residents lends support to this explanation. So too does the experience of many companies with city recruits who cannot read or do basic arithmetic. A New York bank, for example, tried to recruit tellers without requiring a high school diploma but found that barely half the applicants were able to pass an examination geared to the eighth-grade level. Similarly the New York Telephone Company discovered in 1987 that only 16 percent of city applicants could pass its entry-level examinations for jobs ranging from telephone operator to service representative. This second explanation has prompted both cities and employers to try to improve school performance and student attendance.

Still another explanation is that many of the poor in central cities are not in the job market at all. In New York almost four of five women who headed poverty families in 1980, and nearly half the men, were neither working nor looking for work. Of these people who were not in the labor force, 75 percent of the women and 60 percent of the men had either never worked or had last worked more than five years ago. If the downtown economy expanded enough to create a severe labor shortage, rising wages for ordinary jobs might pull some people off the streets or off welfare. Driving up wages through extra-full employment, however, is probably beyond the power of even the most ambitious mayors, and city officials usually look to the states and the federal government to help the long-term unemployed.

Is Development Unfair?

Even aside from the jobs issue, critics indicted cities for promoting downtown development by taking from the poor to give to the rich. City governments in the 1970s acted with unexpected harshness, and nowhere was the turnabout clearer than in New York. Earlier New York had been especially generous in supporting welfare, housing, and health care for the poor, but after the fiscal crisis of 1975 it was a different city. Political leaders put aside their social commitments and concentrated instead on making the economy grow. "The main job of government," declared newly elected Mayor Ed Koch in 1978, "is to create a climate in which private business can expand in the city to provide jobs and profit. It's not the function of government to create jobs on the public payroll."[4] If that meant creating profit opportunities for the business sector while cutting spending for everyone else, mayors were willing to play Scrooge for a time.

New York cut the municipal work force by 25 percent, laying off police officers, firefighters, teachers, and city hospital nurses. City officials froze pay levels for public employees and welfare grants for the poor while double-digit inflation devastated family budgets. But they found money for what they wanted. In the late 1970s, according to one analysis, city outlays that were intended to stimulate private development, such as transportation and utility improvements, increased by 72 percent while those intended for redistributing income to the poor grew by only 20 percent. The projects that moved ahead included a $1.1 billion sewage treatment plant in northern Manhattan, the first section of a $5 billion tunnel to bring drinking water into the city, a new subway tunnel linking Manhattan and Queens, and the $486 million Javits convention center.

One of the largest developments of the time was Battery Park City, 92 acres of office towers and apartment buildings sited on landfill in lower Manhattan. An early plan called for subsidizing one-third of the 14,000 apartments for the poor and one-third for middle-income families. A revised plan, based on new priorities in 1979, gave the subsidies to the office buildings instead (in the form of tax abatements) and changed the housing into 14,000 luxury apartments. When Battery Park City opened in 1985, a reporter asked Manfred Ohrenstein, the liberal minority leader of the state senate, why the project had changed. "What happened was the fiscal crisis," Ohrenstein explained. "Economic reality intruded."

Eager to push development, city government gave tax breaks to all sorts of projects with little regard for social purpose or need for subsidy. A conspicuous example was the glittering Trump Tower on Fifth Avenue, with its million-dollar condos and peach-colored marble atrium circled by six levels of some of the most costly retail space in America—all subsidized with $100 million worth of tax abatements. The city gave $7.2 million in tax abatements for IBM's new headquarters and $42 million for AT&T's, and it kept tax assessments far below current market values for choice commercial buildings. Official policy is to assess commercial property at 60 percent of fair market value. The Pan Am Building, however, which sold for $400 million in 1980, carried an assessed value of less than 25 percent of what it brought on the market, and the Manufacturers Hanover Trust building, sold for $161 million in 1981, had an assessment of less than 20 percent of its sale price. When Rockefeller Center offered common stock to the public for the first time in 1985, its management commissioned an independent appraisal, which valued the original 12-acre complex at $1.6 billion, yet the center's assessed value was only 22 percent of the appraisal figure. Economist Robert Lekachman summarized the city's response to the fiscal crisis this way: "The deal was that, for the average person and certain minorities, services were going to get a lot worse. Meanwhile, the city became a developer's paradise."[5] Critics attacked the new policies as unfair, while supporters pointed to the benefits of the construction boom in New York and to the net increase of more than 200,000 private sector jobs in the city from 1977 to 1985.

New York was in step with most other cities. Others that laid off public employees in the late 1970s included Chicago, Cleveland, Detroit, Minneapolis, and Philadelphia. Mayor Coleman Young of Detroit went a step further by inviting citizens to donate trees, benches, and playground equipment to his deficit-ridden city and to volunteer as recreation workers and even armed police auxiliaries. Researcher Richard Child Hill, writing of Young's do-it-yourself government, complained that "since enormous tax subsidies are going to private corporations, voluntary civic enterprise . . . amounts to the exploitation of collective concern for private advantage."[6]

The critics had good arguments. Mayors were trimming budgets by sacrificing public employees and the residents who needed them to protect their neighborhoods, teach their kids, and care for their health. After this selective belt tightening, city officials used the savings to create profit opportunities for developers. When the new office economy finally emerged downtown, it did more for the elite than for the common people. From a moralistic point of view, the brand of downtown development most cities practiced was unfair, one-sided, and regressive. It was "welfare for the rich," according to one opponent, while another complained bitterly, "What we get out of it is a beautiful skyline."

Where Is the Opposition?

If the moralistic view of winners and losers were the only way to look at downtown development, then outraged victims, especially minority groups and the poor, should have been fighting to stop projects while self-interested business and professional groups were mobilizing to build them. Some researchers thought the rebuilding of downtown was a class struggle along these battle lines. "Current urban programs," according to Susan Fainstein and Norman Fainstein, ". . . reflect the dominance of the business class over the life of the city." Sociologist Joe R. Feagin described urban real estate development as a war between the special interests and the masses. "Class conflict," he wrote, "—developers and their allies versus citizens—has long been part of city dynamics. On the one side we have the progressive city councils and urban grass-roots peoples' movements opposing unbridled growth and development. On the other side we have the class of profit-oriented developers, bankers, landowners, and industrial executives who buy, sell, and develop land and buildings in cities just like they do with other for-profit commodities."[7]

Yet the evidence is that political activists usually wanted only to make changes in the design or operation of a retail center; there was little outright opposition from any quarter and almost none from low-income or minority groups. Opponents of Plaza Pasadena, for example, were mainly well-educated professional people critical of the size and cost of the center. The redevelopment authority, aware that an earlier renewal project had stirred up resentment by disrupting a black community, took care to consult with black groups and persuaded them that a downtown retail center would benefit nearby minority neighborhoods.

Black and Hispanic residents in San Diego were concentrated in areas south and east of downtown, far from most new shopping centers north of the city. They wanted better shopping, as well as the jobs Horton Plaza would produce, and they spoke in support of the project from the beginning. The opponents were not grass-roots radicals but ideological conservatives who opposed the use of eminent domain and other city assistance for private ventures, plus middle-class preservationists who wanted to change the plan to save more historic buildings.

The major opposition to Town Square in St. Paul came from owners of downtown commercial property. In Seattle groups from the far left to the far right supported the movement to save Pike Place Market, with the downtown business establishment leading the campaign to replace it with an urban renewal project. In Boston there was no serious opposition to Faneuil Hall Marketplace, and in Baltimore black voters and the city at large endorsed Harborplace in a bond referendum.

The growing sophistication of city officials in handling the politics of development was a fundamental reason for the lack of organized opposition in the 1970s. Urban renewal and highway construction had left a legacy of fierce local resistance to redevelopment. They dealt with it by locating projects on small, strategic sites rather than trying to rebuild entire districts. They chose land away from residential neighborhoods and wherever possible worked in areas that most people were willing to write off—underused waterfront and warehouse districts or civic eyesores such as porno districts. The image of grass-roots activists fighting off the bulldozer is mostly a remnant of old renewal and highway controversies with little relevance to recent projects.

Removing the threat of neighborhood clearance took the steam out of protest movements. The unfairness of cutting city services while rewarding developers was a less compelling issue, and both the public at large and minority groups valued the creation of more downtown jobs. Even the low-skill, low-pay jobs that some critics labeled dead-end and menial were useful to many people. Hotel and restaurant work helped minority communities struggling with chronic youth unemployment by giving young people a chance to get off the streets and onto a payroll. Because offices hire a wide variety of employees with different levels of education and experience, low-income groups also had a real stake in the main downtown growth industries. One of the highest-growth fields, finance and business services, added some 154,000 jobs to New York City between 1977 and 1984; only one-third of these new jobs were in high-status professional, technical, and managerial categories, while half were clerical and one-sixth were blue collar and service.

Because of this mix of occupations, most groups in the city stood to benefit from expansion of the downtown office economy. When New York's economic recovery got under way in the late 1970s, blacks and other racial minorities increased their job totals even faster than the rest of the city. From 1977 through 1982 their employment was up by 20 percent, with nearly six of every ten new jobs in white-collar fields. Hispanic workers increased their employment by 15 percent during these years, with virtually all the gains in white-collar jobs.

Blacks are about as well represented as other New Yorkers in the leading growth sectors of business and professional services, finance, insurance, and real estate; 25 percent of all employed blacks and 26 percent of all employed New Yorkers worked in these fields in 1980. Hispanics are nearly as well represented, with 20 percent in the same lines of work. In Chicago, Cleveland, Detroit, Philadelphia, and Washington, the proportion of blacks working in finance, insurance, and real estate in 1985 was within two percentage points of the proportion of whites. None of this is to say that blacks and Hispanics do as well as whites in getting the top office jobs, nor does it justify cutting services to them in order to subsidize developers, but it does place them squarely among the people who work in the heart of the new downtown economy. Their incomes depend on the prosperity of corporate offices. In New York nearly three times as many blacks work in the corporate headquarters–corporate service sectors as in manufacturing.

With the old stereotypes in mind, opponents of downtown revitalization who expected minorities to join them were in for a surprise. Even in New York, where Mayor Koch hardly made minority economic participation a theme of his administration, blacks and Hispanics gave strong support at the polls to a government that promoted and subsidized private sector job growth. After Koch's landslide reelection in 1985, one critic from the left conceded that it was time to rethink his own position: "In a city whose employment base . . . is shifting faster than anywhere else in the country from manufacturing to corporate services, the assumption that 'left-out' minorities are 'progressive' or oppositional foundered on Koch's 38 percent showing among blacks (close to black candidate Farrell's 40 percent) and Koch's 70 percent showing among Hispanics. The returns from minority neighborhoods . . . confirmed that upwardly aspiring minority voters, from the church-going working poor to home-owning professionals, accept the disciplines of the new corporate dispensation whose master teacher Koch has become. Most of those struggling to start small service firms or make it through the technical schools and community colleges have little problem with almost anything the mayor says or does."[8]

While voting has more than a single dimension—and New York's development policies undoubtedly attracted much support for other reasons—the new downtown economy should have helped the mayor at the polls because it created good jobs at a variety of skill levels. In addition, it improved the city's finances enough to restore service cuts of the mid-1970s. Increases in city hiring after 1980 brought total municipal employment back above its high point of 1974 to a record peak by 1987. And as the economy recovered, the city dusted off earlier plans to tap Battery Park City Authority revenues for subsidizing housing. In December 1987 Mayor Koch and Governor Mario Cuomo agreed to set aside enough of the authority's future rental income to pay back a $1 billion bond issue for low- and middle-income apartments in other parts of the city.

Bargaining for Downtown Jobs: Baltimore and Boston

Some city governments, having invested so heavily in the new down-towns, tried to do more for their residents than wish them luck at landing a job. The same face-to-face negotiations that got projects built showed city officials a way to bargain over jobs for residents and openings for local businesses. They had learned through experience that developers would cut deals many different ways in order to make a project work. There was no right or wrong way; almost any way that promised a reasonable return could be acceptable, and de-velopers were even willing to share that return with the city as part of a deal.

The public-private negotiating agenda proved to be open to new items. Many cities insisted on provisions for hiring minority contrac-tors for construction work on downtown projects, and a few bar-gained over permanent jobs and business options for city residents. Mayor Coleman Young of Detroit stood out in this respect. Presiding over a mostly black city plagued by problems of industrial decline, Young followed a typical strategy of cutting city services while promoting the growth of the private economy—but he did it with a difference. He and his business allies worked openly to develop a black professional and managerial class and to encourage black entrepreneurs.

Young increased the proportion of city jobs going to blacks, partic-ularly in administrative and professional slots. Detroit's purchasing department invited minority entrepreneurs to review city needs for products and services. An official preference system gave bidding advantages to small businesses owned by "disadvantaged persons" and to local firms over outside ones. And all companies that bid on city contracts, applied for tax abatements, or took part in city eco-nomic development projects had to meet strict affirmative action hir-ing standards.

Oakland, California, was another industrial city that gave local resi-dents a direct stake in downtown development. With several new office buildings, a Hyatt Regency Hotel and Convention Center, and a retail and entertainment district at Jack London Square, the city staged its comeback. Mayor Lionel Wilson used public-private negoti-ations to manage projects, including putting together a consortium of thirty local corporations to acquire majority ownership of the new hotel. The city council set a series of contracting and hiring targets for all publicly assisted projects, including 26 percent of all construction expenditures to go to minority firms and 50 percent of the construction workforce to be minorities. The city arranged for neighborhood-based development corporations to acquire equity shares in publicly assisted projects, including the hotel and a downtown office building. Kansas City, Missouri, among others, required set-asides for minority contractors and equity shares for minority-owned corporations in several development projects.

These strategies are reminiscent of the way political machines eighty years ago used the city payroll and contracts to get jobs for immigrants. Civil service laws and competitive bidding requirements have changed the rules of the game, but development negotiations have opened fresh opportunities for cities to influence private business decisions on jobs and contracts. In the case of Harborplace, a coalition of black contractors and religious leaders made an issue of economic benefits during the campaign for a bond issue to finance the project. The Rouse Company, eager for voter support in the black community, made a series of public commitments to affirmative action in construction contracts, construction jobs, permanent jobs, and tenant selection. "We had to win a referendum," explained James Rouse. ". . . If the black community had not supported Harborplace, it would have been defeated. . . . That meant we had to talk about . . . the employment of black people and . . . bringing black businesses into Harborplace."[9]

The Rouse Company set targets of 10 percent of total contract value for minority contractors, 25 percent minority participation in construction jobs, 50 percent minority participation in Harborplace jobs under the control of the Rouse Company, assistance to minorities in finding jobs with businesses in the project, and a special effort to find and help minority merchants for Harborplace. The company exceeded its targets for minority contractors, construction workers, and permanent jobs, and 22 of the original 128 businesses in the project were minority owned. Rouse conceded readily, however, that his good will alone would not have produced these results. Asked whether he thought outside pressure was important in promoting minority economic development, he answered that "it takes pressure; it takes endless, endless, endless pressure." As for whether business is willing to make the commitment without pressure, he had this to say: "I think business may be willing to but I think it won't. Business is busy. It is occupied by all kinds of deadlines and demands and budgets, and all kinds of things that are occupying you enormously in the completion of a task."[10]

The pressure in Baltimore came from an unusual requirement for voter approval of the Harborplace bond issue. In Boston, public-private negotiations over the Copley Place project produced similar results. When the Urban Investment and Development Company (UIDC) proposed to develop a retail-hotel-office complex over a Massachusetts Turnpike interchange, state officials responsible for the site set up a citizen committee to review the plans and negotiate for an acceptable project. To reduce the risk of public controversy, Governor Michael Dukakis involved resident groups early.

The Copley Place site is on the edge of downtown, near low-income and minority neighborhoods. The new project was going to be a large workplace with an estimated 6,300 permanent employees, of whom 3,300 would be newly hired and 3,000 would be office staff transferred from other locations. Citizen negotiators were quick to focus attention on hiring to fill the new jobs. A resident task force proposed hiring goals of 50 percent of the permanent jobs for Boston residents, 50 percent for women, and 30 percent for minorities. Since residential neighborhoods close to the project contained 17.2 percent of the city's labor force, they proposed a target of 17.2 percent of the permanent jobs for people living within that area. In addition, they proposed that UIDC set aside retail space for minority and community-owned businesses at below-market rents.

This was a tall order. It would have a direct impact on the developer's ability to find hotels and retail tenants for the project since they would be subject to special hiring commitments. Nevertheless, UIDC accepted these terms among others as part of a deal written into its lease agreement with the Turnpike Authority. It agreed to provide 15,000–20,000 square feet of community-oriented retail space at reduced rents, to set up a recruitment and referral office for affirmative action hiring, and to work with a city-state-resident committee at helping project businesses meet the goals. To make relations with its tenants more manageable, the development company insisted on applying the hiring goals to the entire work force rather than to each individual business and agreed to encourage rather than require tenants to give advance notice of future job vacancies.

There was still more to come. When UIDC and the city decided to apply for UDAG funds for the project, the federal Department of Housing and Urban Development added further targets specifying percentages of low- and moderate-income workers. Later agreements with the city required UIDC to sponsor job fairs and meetings, produce tenant handbooks describing the hiring commitments, fund programs for preemployment and skill training, and give the city advance notice of those job vacancies for which its own management had direct hiring responsibility. Eventually UIDC laid out more than $700,000 for special recruitment and training programs.

With these understandings in place, city government and neighborhood residents acted on James Rouse's point that pressure is necessary to get the development company's attention. The city set up a new agency to enforce hiring agreements on government-funded projects. This agency, as well as the state-city-citizen liaison committee, kept close watch on hiring procedures and results. Governor Dukakis and Mayor White maintained contact with UIDC executives, and White met personally with the managers of the Marriott and Westin hotels to impress on them that good relations with the city would depend heavily on their hiring performance. A group of community organizations filed a complaint with the Department of Housing and Urban Development charging faulty administration of the agreement, and then led protest marches outside Copley Place. Mayor White held back a UDAG payment to UIDC until he got more specific commitments to job action. And the liaison committee insisted on holding face-to-face meetings with retail tenants to browbeat them into meeting hiring targets.

By late 1984 Copley Place firms had hired 3,100 new permanent employees for hotel, retail, or property management positions; 62 percent were Boston residents, 35 percent were minority, 50 percent were women, 26 percent lived in the impact area, and 83 percent fell within the low- to moderate-income category. Although individual employers did not meet all the goals, collectively the project met or exceeded them. Employment figures for other hotels and department stores in Boston show that the two Copley Place hotels and the Neiman-Marcus department store were in line with industry-wide staffing practices in most categories but hired significantly higher proportions of minority employees, particularly in better-paying managerial and professional hotel jobs.

Just as local officials negotiated to increase their control over the makeup and design of downtown projects, so Massachusetts officials used their bargaining power to take far more control of job hiring than they could have through ordinary procedures. That Copley

Place netted more than 1,900 new jobs for city residents, of whom nearly 1,100 were minority workers, was no small accomplishment.

San Diego officials made similar use of their position as investors in Horton Plaza to get jobs for city residents. Mayor Roger Hedgecock turned to the Private Industry Council of San Diego County, a training and placement organization, to find jobs for low-income and unemployed San Diegans in Horton Plaza and other city-assisted development projects. The council then served as the main employment office for Horton Plaza. By March 1986 store openings created nearly 1,000 new jobs, and the council filled half of them. Of the people placed by the council, seven of every ten were minority workers and six of ten came from high-unemployment, low-income neighborhoods targeted for recruitment.

Slowing the Pace

With downtown work diverse and expanding and with public-private negotiation widely accepted as a way to influence hiring decisions, cities are in a position to do more for their residents when they strike future deals. The momentum of downtown development may well be slower, however, as the exceptional conditions of the early 1980s lose some of their power.

The engine driving most downtown projects has been office growth. While office construction first flourished and then boomed across the country, the downtowns of large cities managed to hold onto their share of a large and growing pie. But the labor force will grow much more slowly in the 1990s—a delayed result of the downturn in birthrates after the mid-1960s—and labor shortages will cut back the growth of new jobs. Taking these and other factors into account and allowing for the large supply of offices standing vacant in 1985, David Birch of MIT projected less than half as much office construction between 1985 and 1995 as there was between 1975 and 1985. A few metropolitan areas, such as Baltimore, Detroit, New York, and Washington, may continue to build about as many offices as they did from 1975 to 1985, but others such as St. Louis, San Diego, Denver, and Los Angeles could drop to one-third or less of recent levels.

Whether downtown can maintain its share of new construction is also a question, since the suburban land supply, labor force, and transportation systems continue to prove highly attractive to office firms. Another trend limiting downtown office development is the transfer of routine office operations from in-town locations to cheaper back offices in the suburbs or beyond, such as Citicorp's recent decision to put a Manhattan-style office tower across the river in Queens. More is involved than a search for cheaper sites. As companies put in computer systems for handling large amounts of clerical work, they have less need for the unskilled city work force. Between 1970 and 1980 the elimination of file clerks and messengers wiped out 20,000 jobs for young people in New York's banks, insurance firms, and telephone, gas, and electric companies. The jobs that remain demand higher levels of skill. Companies move their back offices to the suburbs not only to lower their operating costs but also to find skilled clerical and technical workers and to get close to community colleges that train them. In the process of moving, according to economist Thierry Noyelle, they leave behind minority women who were advancing through the clerical ranks and replace them with white women from the suburbs. Contrary to the critics of corporate center development, it is not the arrival of office jobs downtown that hurts minorities but their departure.

Increasing international competition may also undercut downtown office development. Just as manufacturing proved vulnerable to overseas competitors in the past, so financial and corporate services could by vulnerable in the future. Some large firms are already moving their computer programming and systems development from downtown not only to the suburbs but also to selected third world countries with large numbers of college graduates. "The model of the footloose assembly plant . . . moving from California or New York to Thailand or Hong Kong," according to Noyelle, ". . . is no longer the proper model to understand worldwide competition in tomorrow's service economy. Rather, it is the model of . . . software work being contracted out to firms in India."[11]

Cities have been able to borrow their share of project development costs at below-market rates because the interest they paid on their bond issues was exempt from federal income tax. Thanks to federal help in the form of uncollected taxes, they managed to cut their interest costs by about one-third in comparison with taxable bonds of similar quality. The Tax Reform Act of 1986 struck a blow to public-private projects by restricting tax exemption for state and local bond issues that assist private businesses. It ruled out tax-exempt bonds for

sports stadiums, convention centers, industrial parks, and most parking garages. Redevelopment bonds are in a special category; they
may be eligible for tax exemption but only for narrow purposes and
within dollar limits assigned to each state.

A city that wants to use tax-exempt bonds for redevelopment will
have to designate blighted areas that meet federal as well as state
rules, including new federal requirements for the size and maximum
number of project areas. The city will not be able to use tax-exempt
bond proceeds to put up new buildings or enlarge existing ones or to
build parking facilities unless they service clearly governmental activities. Spending for streets, public spaces, and utilities poses no problems, but cities can no longer use tax-exempt funds for mall
components such as the enclosed park in Town Square.

The 1986 law established state ceilings that will bite deeply into
current volumes of tax-exempt borrowing. If the new rules had been
in force in 1984, California would have had to cut its state and local
bond issues by $3.2 billion, Pennsylvania by $1.1 billion, Minnesota
by $896 million, and New York by $633 million. City officials who in
the past were able to float tax-exempt redevelopment bonds with a
minimum of red tape may instead have to apply for state approval in
competition with bond proposals for a wide range of other activities,
including housing, gas and electric systems, water and sewer projects, mass transit, and student loans. Competing for a fixed allocation
could in principle deal with some of the weaknesses of off-budget
financing by encouraging a more deliberate public choice of the most
promising projects. But state officials rather than local ones will be
making the decisions, and whether they will base them on the merits
of projects or on giving each group its turn at the public trough
remains to be seen.

Several results are predictable. First, city finance officers and their
bond underwriters will arrange project borrowings to make the most
of loopholes in the 1986 law. After exhausting these possibilities, city
officials will either have to cope with the delays and frustrations
of state and federal reviews in order to issue tax-exempt bonds or
will have to pay higher interest on taxable bonds or loans from the
developer.

At the same time the UDAG program that helped finance one of
every two downtown malls from 1978 through 1985 is coming to an
end. From 1968 through 1984 UDAG funding averaged some $600
million a year, but by 1986 the budget was down to $350 million, and

in 1987 HUD Secretary Samuel Pierce called for the elimination of the program. Congress in 1988 voted to eliminate funding for the next fiscal year, leaving only a small balance in the pipeline. The shrinking or disappearance of UDAG awards, together with restrictions on tax-exempt borrowings, will raise the cost of public-private development projects and make their financing harder.

Even as big-city mayors were winning elections by rebuilding downtown, their projects rubbed some citizens the wrong way. Office towers and other commercial buildings disrupted familiar streets and became disturbing symbols of corporate wealth and power. For many years the dissenters were neither strong enough nor well enough organized to have much practical effect, but by the mid-1980s they were finding allies and winning at least a few battles to rein in downtown development.

Some features of downtown development that might have generated opposition—such as the privatization of public space or the weak accountability of off-budget financing—did not move many political activists. The discontents that surfaced over the years were more ideological and therefore less open to compromise. Many downtown critics found no social value in real estate development. Forgetting that people live and work in new buildings, they contended that the only benefits went to rich, influential developers.

Another ideological perspective was that of critics who railed against the loss of office buildings from the 1920s and deplored the larger towers that replaced them. Their argument, as Ada Louise Huxtable described it in her account of the World Trade Center controversy in New York, was that "flat-topped behemoths will destroy the beauty of the romantically spired Lower Manhattan skyline." This point of view is both shallow and shopworn. "The hue and cry," she wrote, "equals that raised at the time those spires were built. They were attacked then as barbaric, oversized wreckers of scale and sunlight. . . . The responsible intellectual community refused to forgive the design sins of those early skyscraper builders with their decorative curtain-wall classicism, fancy-dress Gothic, 'senseless' spires and Halicarnassus water towers for another forty years. This is the skyline the same intellectual community now wants to protect." Huxtable faulted these critics for embalming a skyline, rejecting new construction technology, and dodging the more practical issues of how new buildings relate to "the needs, functions and uses of the city at ground level."[12]

In time the ideological critics made common cause with people who had more tangible grievances, including the ground-level impact of buildings. Commuters found traffic to new downtown offices clogging local streets and overcrowding mass transportation. Middle-income families found rising real estate values and executive demand for in-city living pushing housing costs out of their reach. With citizen groups pressing these and other complaints, San Francisco in 1980 began requiring developers of major downtown office buildings to put up housing or contribute to a housing trust fund. Boston followed with similar requirements in 1983. At about the same time Seattle and Miami began asking developers to underwrite housing in exchange for zoning bonuses that permitted extra office construction. In 1981 San Francisco also imposed a charge on downtown office developers to pay for improvements to the municipal transit system. These measures were intended more to extract community benefits from office growth than to stop projects, but they were also signs of growing skepticism about the desirability of downtown development.

San Francisco gave a stronger signal of political change in 1986. After turning down ballot proposals for limiting downtown growth four times since 1971, the voters approved a 1986 zoning initiative that clamped a tight lid on the main office district. It cut the height, size, and number of new buildings permitted under the city's official downtown plan and set an annual ceiling of 475,000 square feet of new office space, equivalent to just one big-city office building of average size each year. Sue Hestor, a veteran activist of the anti-growth movement and one of the leaders of the 1986 campaign, explained the vote partly as a reaction to high rents and traffic tie-ups and partly as a protest against developers. "People have been told," she said, "that all this growth . . . is good for them, good for jobs and the city's economy. But I think they realized that they've been sold a bill of goods, that they don't benefit, that the profits are taken out by the developers and the costs are borne by the residents."[13]

In contrast to San Franciso, which had a long history of opposition to growth, Los Angeles generally welcomed and even enshrined development. Yet in 1986 Los Angeles voters endorsed an initiative cutting by half the amount of commercial construction allowed in most parts of the city. The Los Angeles vote was no protest against downtown projects, since it specifically exempted downtown from the new restrictions, but it was one more sign of voter uneasiness with office and retail expansion. City council member Marvin Braude, an author of the initiative, interpreted the two-to-one margin of victory as a dramatic turnaround: "People no longer want the destiny of the city determined by large developers and their lobbyists."

California often leads the way in political fashions, as it did with the environmental movement and the taxpayer revolt of the 1970s. When both San Francisco and Los Angeles have second thoughts about city development at the same time, trend watchers are bound to take notice. But as far as rebuilding downtown is concerned, even if this political reversal should spread eastward it is not as devastating as the earlier freeway and renewal protests. It could add fresh complications to downtown projects, requiring mayors and business leaders to make more careful choices and to conduct negotiations in ways that will make the public more comfortable. And it could rule out some voter-antagonizing projects, whether valuable or not, that might have slipped through a few years ago.

The Mall Business

While the politics and public financing of downtown growth were becoming more difficult, the business climate for retail development was improving. Downtown malls had been a gamble for developers. Even with city help, large equity investments and company reputations were on the line. In most cities the gamble paid off, and downtown earned back its reputation as a viable place for retailing.

How profitable the centers are is hard to determine. The first question has to be: profitable for whom? City government, mortgage lenders, developers, merchants, and equity investors all have different perspectives. For the financial institutions that backed these malls, the record is more than satisfactory, TIAA and others netted risk premiums by lending for early downtown malls, and virtually every project did well enough to meet its debt service obligations. With any pattern of widespread problems, mortgage lenders would have redlined downtown projects. Instead the number of lenders grew in the 1980s, and more national institutions—life insurance companies, pension funds, commercial banks—financed downtown malls than in the 1970s. As these organizations lined up to participate, they whittled away the earlier risk premium to the point that TIAA had to look elsewhere for the combination of risk and return it wanted.

For developers, profitability is more open to question. The conventional industry benchmark is still sales per square foot of retail space—an indicator of how much rent tenants can pay and how much the property is worth. By this measure downtown retail centers have done as well as the top suburban malls. For thirty-three downtown centers, median sales per square foot in 1987 were $272, compared with medians of $157 and $179 for regional and superregional suburban malls; only the top 10 percent of suburban malls reported sales figures higher than the ones downtown.

High sales, however, are not the same as high profits. Downtown malls are costly to build and costly to run, so debt service and operating expenses can eat up the rental revenue generated by high sales. Specialty marketplaces patterned on the Faneuil Hall model often ring up phenomenal sales but still have problems. Their public areas must be very large to handle the crowds, and these areas are expensive to build, maintain, and operate. The high volume of food they sell produces huge amounts of garbage to haul away and monumental cleaning bills. Their promotional budgets are exceptionally high because they depend heavily on attracting tourists. Although developers do their best to pass all these operating costs through to the tenants, there are limits to how much the tenants can absorb. This cost structure helps explain why the Rouse Company lost money on its market at South Street Seaport in New York in 1987 in spite of a record-breaking sales figure of $560 per square foot. With 12 million visitors a year, this project was undoubtedly more of a moneymaker for the city, the merchants, and the lender than it was for the developer.

Developers learned how to make downtown ventures more productive. Recent centers had much higher sales than earlier ones. Of thirty-three downtown centers, median sales per square foot for those built between 1981 and 1985 were more than one and one-half times higher than for those built ten years earlier. And the number of new specialty centers opening across the country dropped by 75 percent from 1984 to 1988. In the spring of 1988 even the Rouse Company, which had a worldwide reputation for its specialty marketplaces, announced plans to stop building them in the future. And James Rouse's Enterprise Foundation, which developed small specialty marketplaces in order to generate funds for philanthropic activities, concluded that the concept worked poorly away from big cities and gave up its role as manager of ailing projects in Toledo; Flint, Michigan; and Richmond, Virginia.

The shakeout of specialty centers is a sign that developers are becoming more selective in the way they plan their city projects, but they are not withdrawing. The Rouse Company will diversify its repertoire but has several more downtown centers in progress and intends to keep looking for big-city opportunities. The Hahn Company opened a new center in Minneapolis in 1987 and in 1988 had projects under way in downtown Sacramento and New York City. UIDC, developer of Water Tower Place in Chicago and Copley Place in Boston, opened a new center at 900 North Michigan Avenue in Chicago in 1988 and had plans for another opposite the Marshall Field store. The Enterprise Foundation is working in the heart of Philadelphia. Many developers, national and local, entered downtown for the first time in the 1980s. Among them were three of the country's largest mall builders, long known for their explicit avoidance of downtown: Edward J. DeBartolo opened a center in San Antonio, Melvin Simon opened centers in Indianapolis and St. Louis and announced another in New York, and A. Alfred Taubman started construction in downtown Columbus, Ohio.

These developers looked at factors beyond sales per square foot. UIDC vice-president Norman Elkin focused on long-term value when he reviewed the performance of Water Tower Place and Copley Place in 1988. Sales and rentals had increased steadily, so that leases signed in 1988 were for rents five times higher than at the opening of Water Tower in 1976 and three times higher than at the opening of Copley Place in 1983. As the value of a property appreciates, developers can refinance it at current value to reduce their equity investment, sometimes taking out more equity than they ever put in. Or they can sell it at a profit. Comparing downtown with suburban performance, Elkin reported greater and faster appreciation at Water Tower and Copley than at the company's suburban malls. Moreover, the retail sections of these mixed-use complexes had outperformed the rest, with 1988 sales per square foot of $510 at Water Tower Place and $442 at Copley. Both projects would have been profitable if the company had built nothing but the retail malls and parking; in addition, the shopping areas helped fill the offices, hotels, and apartments. As for the future, Elkin believed downtown had become easier to build in than suburbia: government was supportive, financing was more readily available, and neither lenders nor retailers were afraid of downtown any more.

The Hahn Company had a similar experience. Both Plaza Pasadena and Horton Plaza were appreciating rapidly in value as of the end of

1988, John Gilchrist reported, though his firm was not yet earning a satisfactory return on Horton Plaza. For Gilchrist as well, downtown was no longer a difficult place to work. If a project was sound, financing was readily available with no risk premium. Tenants were available too. The most difficult resource was an anchor department store but not because of the earlier reluctance to go downtown; as a result of the many mergers and takeovers of department store chains, most stores were consolidating instead of expanding.

For developers downtown was neither the wasteland of the late 1960s nor the fresh promise of the late 1970s. It had become more neutral, a location to be considered on its merits, and more integrated into the mainstream of finance and development. Developers were in the business of building a destination for shopping, and the record had shown it could be in downtown, at the edge of downtown, or in the suburbs. Lenders were prepared to lend, specialty stores were ready to pay high rents, and department stores that wanted to expand were willing to go to the city. By the late 1980s the playing field was level. After thirty years, that was an achievement.

Do Cities Learn?

In the improved development climate, neither the office downturn, nor the tighter strings on public finance, nor the colder political climate are life threatening to downtown. Cities faced much harder challenges in the past and dealt with them by experimenting and taking risks. As a former alderman in St. Louis put it, "There's an advantage to being in desperate shape. What it does it force radical action."

The latest cracks in the downtown facade came at the end of an unusual stage in the rebuilding of cities. The 1970s turned into an unexpected golden era; a sustained office boom, federal financing without bureaucratic interference, and local political support for public-private projects created a remarkable time of opportunity. An age of regulation gave way to an age of enterprise. Entrepreneurs in city government and maverick real estate developers plunged in with technical skill, creativity, and money. Predictable changes will demand new solutions, but neither cities nor developers are starting out empty-handed. By now most cities have the basic equipment to attract development: a new office district, good hotels and restaurants, a shopping mall, a convention center, a historic neighborhood or two.

They have projects that keep downtown competitive as a place for business, as well as ornaments that make it enjoyable for the public. As important, they have proof that downtown is no longer a graveyard of ambitious plans. Further, the public and private entrepreneurs who built these projects have polished a set of skills that nobody knew a few years earlier.

The downtown retail centers are products of these new skills, but their roots go back to the 1950s when political coalitions first organized to rebuild downtown. Development strategies have come a long way since then: from bulldozing whole neighborhoods to practicing microsurgery; from compulsive modernization to preserving a sense of the past; from designing office and apartment complexes for isolation to creating attractions that draw the crowds; from pushing city solutions on developers to solving problems through negotiation; from raiding federal highway and renewal budgets to packaging local and private sector funds.

Skeptics explain these changes by granting that government sometimes acts correctly but only after exhausting all the alternatives. It is true that civic leaders had to learn by trial and error that sanitizing the city led to disaster, but once political opposition forced that lesson on them, they were quick to find better strategies. Contrary to the well-worn image of public sector inertia, city officials were energetic and flexible in changing the projects they did and the ways they did them. Unlike the typecast bureaucrat, hundreds of agency heads and staff members were eager to try new ideas, resourceful in solving problems, and willing to take risks.

The new methods for managing downtown development were almost as much of an achievement as the rebuilding itself. Public-private negotiations from the earliest stages of a project gave developers a chance to use their talent for attracting a mass market, and it gave city negotiators a chance to press for whatever was important to them. For developers negotiation was already a way of life. "It is easier by far to deal with the city of Baltimore," observed James Rouse, "than it is to deal with a department store." Face-to-face negotiations gave both sides a forum for settling differences without threats or lawsuits. Their conflicts, in fact, often led to better projects by prodding developers to depart from their standard model.

Deal making for downtown projects was in line with the 1970s idea that financial incentives could get private interests to serve public purposes. This approach led both cities and developers to cross the boundary that used to separate public from private responsibilities. Developers ended up owning and managing public spaces, an arrangement that produced conflicting claims over public rights of access and political expression. City officials in turn ended up with a major voice in decisions that used to be private, including details of design, management, and the uses of rental income.

Development negotiations were flexible enough to cover preferential hiring of low-income and minority residents. The few cities that brought this issue to the bargaining table discovered that they could get workable agreements, and their success should inspire more job compacts in the future. Further, cities are in a position to make room at the table for local groups that have important stakes in the outcome, such as the neighborhood organizations that pressed for hiring commitments at Copley Place. Stretching the agenda and adding more negotiators are not steps to be taken casually because there is a danger that too heavy an agenda or too large a delegation will, like the tug of war over Bryant Park, test the patience of "any man, woman, child or animal." But cities have shown great skill in making adjustments without sliding back into the old implementation deadlocks. Fast learning and shrewd management may not be able to solve every problem, but they can handle at least a few more at the margin.

Public-private deal making was critical for the rebuilding of downtown. Among its monuments are the new retail centers, which required the fullest public-private interaction and incorporated thirty years of practice. Joan Didion described the shopping malls of her youth, built in the heyday of suburban optimism and confidence, as "pyramids to progress."[14] The downtown retail centers of the 1970s and 1980s are more like triumphal arches marking the survival of inner cities that almost everyone had given up for dead. The arches may be premature because survival is not the same as triumph, but they mark a turning point that brought the middle class back to town, added a glow to specialized office districts, and turned downtown into a resource that can make life better for city people.

Notes

Chapter 1

1. William Fulton, "The Robin Hood of Real Estate," *Planning* 51 (May 1985), p. 6.

2. Martha Weinman Lear, "A Master Builder Sites a Shopping Mall," *New York Times Magazine*, August 12, 1973, pp. 82, 84.

3. Kolloff, cited by Johann Friedrich Geist, *Arcades: The History of a Building Type* (Cambridge, Mass.: MIT Press, 1983), p. 67.

4. From *A Tramp Abroad*, quoted in Geist, *Arcades*, p. 392.

5. Lewis Mumford, *The City in History* (New York: Harcourt, Brace, 1961), p. 439.

Chapter 2

1. This and the following quotations are from Wilfred Owen, *Cities in the Motor Age* (New York: Viking Press, 1959), which reports on the proceedings of the Connecticut General Conference.

2. U.S. National Commission on Urban Problems, *Building the American City: Report to the Congress and the President of the United States* (Washington, D.C.: Government Printing Office, 1968), p. 154.

3. Section 110, Housing Act of 1949, 42 U.S.C., 1441.

4. Miles Lord, chief judge, Ninth Federal District Court, Minneapolis, transcript of remarks to U.S. Justice Department Condemnation Seminar, Virginia Beach, October 30, 1979.

5. Charles Abrams, *The City Is the Frontier* (New York: Harper & Row, 1965), p. 135.

6. Robert A. Caro, *The Power Broker* (New York: Vintage Books, 1975), p. 848.

7. Ibid., pp. 880, 882.

8. Basil G. Zimmer, *Rebuilding Cities: The Effects of Displacement and Relocation on Small Business* (Chicago: Quadrangle Books, 1964), pp. 61, 62.

9. "Cities: The Renaissance," *Time*, March 23, 1962, p. 19.

Chapter 3

1. Daniel P. Moynihan, "Policy vs. Program in the '70's," *Public Interest*, no. 20 (Summer 1970), 94.

2. U.S. Department of Commerce, Bureau of Public Roads, *America's Lifelines: Federal Aid for Highways* (Washington, D.C.: Government Printing Office,

1962), p. 11, cited by Kenneth R. Geiser, Jr., "Urban Transportation Decision Making: Political Processes of Urban Freeway Controversies" (Cambridge, Mass.: MIT Department of Urban Studies and Planning/Urban Systems Laboratory, June 1970), p. 2.

3. Norman V. Watson, acting assistant secretary for renewal and housing management, Department of Housing and Urban Development, "Urban Renewal and the Relocation Process" (remarks prepared for delivery at the Conference of the National Association of Housing and Redevelopment Officials, Sun Valley, Idaho, September 24, 1970).

4. Lewis Mumford, *The Highway and the City* (New York: Harcourt, Brace, 1963), p. 234.

5. John Kenneth Galbraith, *The Affluent Society* (1958; Harmondsworth, Middlesex: Penguin Books, 1962), p. 249.

6. Committee for Economic Development, *Public-Private Partnership: An Opportunity for Urban Communities* (New York: Committee for Economic Development Research and Policy Committee, 1982), p. 1.

7. William Lilley III, "Cities and Suburbs: Herman Death Ends an Era," *National Journal*, September 18, 1971, p. 1939.

8. Jeanne R. Lowe, *Cities in a Race with Time* (New York: Vintage Books, 1968), p. 162.

9. Roy Lubove, *Twentieth-Century Pittsburgh* (New York: John Wiley, 1969), pp. 139–140.

10. Jane Jacobs, *The Death and Life of Great American Cities* (New York: Random House, 1961), p. 4.

11. Edward M. Wood, Jr., Sidney N. Brower, and Margaret W. Latimer, "Planners' People," *Journal of the American Institute of Planners* 32 (July 1966), 228–234.

Chapter 4

1. Harris W. Willingham, "Shopping Centers in the Urban Renewal Program," in International Council of Shopping Centers 1959 Annual Convention *Proceedings* (New York: International Council of Shopping Centers, 1960), p. 136.

2. Victor Gruen, *Centers for the Urban Environment: Survival of the Cities* (New York: Van Nostrand Reinhold Company, 1973), pp. 22–27.

3. Kay Miller, "Southdale's Perpetual Spring," *Minneapolis Star and Tribune Sunday Magazine*, September 28, 1986, p. 12.

4. Lear, "Master Builder," p. 12.

5. Grady Clay, "What Makes a Good Square Good?" in Editors of Fortune, *The Exploding Metropolis* (Garden City, N.Y.: Doubleday, 1958), p. 172.

6. "Supercity," *Architectural Forum* 136 (April 1972), 30.

7. Allied Stores Corporation, *1963 Annual Report*, pp. 6–8.

8. "Convention '72 Report: Small Center Needs Draw Top Interest at Convention," *Shopping Center World* 2 (July 1972), 46.

9. "Convention '73 Report," *Shopping Center World* 3 (April 1973), 32, 37.

10. Ernest W. Hahn, "Concerns of Our Industry" (address to the International Council of Shopping Centers Conference, Miami Beach, May 8, 1972).

11. "Downtown Malls Debated," *Chain Store Age Executive* (May 1977), 56.

12. Gurney Breckenfeld, " 'Downtown' Has Fled to the Suburbs," *Fortune* 86 (October 1976), 162.

Chapter 5

1. U.S. National Advisory Commission on Civil Disorders, *Report* (Washington, D.C.: Government Printing Office, 1968), "Summary," p. 10.

2. Kenneth E. Boulding, "The City as an International System," *Daedalus* 97 (Fall 1968), 1118.

Chapter 9

1. Downtown Seattle Association, *Annual Report: 1978* (Seattle, 1978).

2. Donald Canty, "San Diego Gets an Exuberant New Downtown Development," *Architecture* 74 (November 1985), 16.

3. "Horton Plaza: The Urban Festival Opens August 9," special report by *San Diego Home/Garden Magazine* in cooperation with Ernest W. Hahn, Inc. and the Centre City Development Corporation, 1985.

4. Robert Lindsey, "San Diego Builds a Village Just to Shop In," *New York Times*, August 17, 1985, p. 48.

5. Sam Hall Kaplan, "Horton Plaza: Hope, Hype," *Los Angeles Times*, August 18, 1985, Real Estate p. 1; Paul Goldberger, "Freewheeling Fantasy in San Diego," *New York Times*, March 19, 1986, p. A12.

6. Canty, "San Diego Gets," p. 16.

7. Robert Guenther, "Horton Plaza May Introduce Shopping Centers' New Look," *Wall Street Journal*, June 26, 1985, p. 29.

Chapter 10

1. "A City Revival?" *Newsweek*, January 15, 1979, pp. 28–35.

2. Craig Claiborne, "A Yeasty Plateau," *New York Times Magazine*, December 9, 1984, pp. 131–132.

3. Calvin Trillin, "U.S. Journal: New England," *New Yorker*, May 16, 1977, p. 101.

4. Gurney Breckenfeld, "Jim Rouse Shows How to Give Downtown Retailing New Life," *Fortune*, April 10, 1978, p. 91.

5. Gurney Breckenfeld, "The Rouse Show Goes National," *Fortune*, July 27, 1981, pp. 48–54.

6. Ada Louise Huxtable, "Why You Always Win and Lose In Urban Renewal," *New York Times*, September 19, 1976, p. 34D.

7. Trillin, "U.S. Journal."

8. David Morton, "Shopping Goes to Town," *Progressive Architecture* 62 (July 1981), 81; Roberta Brandes Gratz, "Downtown Devitalized," *Progressive Architecture* 62 (July 1981), 82.

9. Allen Freeman, "Introverted Trio of MXD's Dominates Atlanta's New Downtown," *American Institute of Architects Journal* 66 (September 1977), 34–37.

10. Morton, "Shopping Goes to Town."

11. David Morton, "Suburban Shopping Downtown?" *Progressive Architecture* 59 (December 1978), 64.

12. John Morris Dixon, "Procession in Pasadena," *Progressive Architecture* 62 (July 1981), 94, 97.

13. Ira S. Lowry, "The Dismal Future of Central Cities," in Arthur P. Solomon, ed., *The Prospective City* (Cambridge, Mass.: MIT Press, 1980), pp. 161–162.

14. Suzanne Stephens, "Introversion and the Urban Context," *Progressive Architecture* 59 (December 1978), 53.

15. "Roundtable on Rouse," *Progressive Architecture* 62 (July 1981), 100.

16. Robert Campbell, "Evaluation: Boston's 'Upper of Urbanity,' " *American Institute of Architects Journal* 70 (June 1981), 24–31.

Chapter 11

1. William Donald Schaefer, "Public/Private Partnership: Views and Its Future," in *City Economic Development* (Washington, D.C.: National League of Cities, January 15, 1979), p. 6.

2. U.S. President, *National Urban Policy Report: 1978* (Washington, D.C.: U.S. Department of Housing and Urban Development, 1978), p. 121.

3. U.S. President, Task Force on Private Initiatives, *Investing in America* (Washington, D.C.: Government Printing Office, 1983), pp. 5, 7.

4. Joyce Purnick, "Three More High City Officials Resign as Shake-up Con-

tinues," *New York Times*, February 27, 1986, p. B1; Neal R. Peirce, "The Ethics of Revolving-doorism," *Boston Globe*, June 23, 1986, p. 16.

5. "Cincinnati Critics Assert Public Atrium Is 'Vapid' and Lacking in Amenities," *New York Times*, January 2, 1983, p. 18.

6. Hague v. CIO, 307 U.S. 496 (1939), cited by Howard Ball, "Careless Justice," *Polity* 11 (Winter 1978), 208.

7. Donald P. Batchelder v. Allied Stores International, Inc., 388 Mass. 83 (1983).

8. Margaret Hunter, "Malls Broadly Allow Access, Survey Shows," *Shopping Centers Today* (June 1986), 1.

9. Martin Tolchin, "Private Guards Get New Role in Public Law Enforcement," *New York Times*, November 29, 1985, p. A1.

Chapter 12

1. Robert Campbell, "Applying Old Ideas to New Buildings," *Boston Globe*, December 12, 1984, p. A36.

2. William Kornblum and Vernon Boggs, "Redevelopment and the Night Frontier," *City Almanac* 18 (Summer 1985), 16–18.

3. Arnold J. Meltsner, *The Politics of City Revenue* (Berkeley: University of California Press, 1971), p. 38.

4. Herman Leonard, *Checks Unbalanced: The Quiet Side of Government Spending* (New York: Basic Books, 1986), p. 15.

5. Ada Louise Huxtable, "Creeping Gigantism in Manhattan," *New York Times*, March 22, 1987, p. 2H.

6. Jane Gross, "Two Big West Side Projects Fuel Anti-Development Sentiment," *New York Times*, November 29, 1987, p. 1.

Chapter 13

1. Richard Child Hill, "Crisis in the Motor City," in Susan S. Fainstein, Norman I. Fainstein, Richard Child Hill, Dennis Judd, and Michael Peter Smith, *Restructuring the City* (New York: Longman, 1983), p. 105.

2. Hill, "Crisis in the Motor City," p. 117.

3. Calvin Trillin, "U.S. Journal: Atlanta," *New Yorker*, March 29, 1976, p. 105.

4. "Downtown Is Looking Up," *Time*, July 5, 1976, p. 61.

5. Paul Goldberger, *On the Rise* (New York: Penguin Books, 1985), p. 266.

6. "Pittsburgh Gives a Luncheon to Try Out Its New Image," *New York Times*, February 28, 1984, p. B1.

7. "The MacNeil/Lehrer News Hour," Public Broadcasting Network, July 11, 1984, transcript.

8. Peter Gammons, "World Series Is Civic Pride," *Boston Globe*, October 8, 1984, p. 27.

9. Hal Lancaster, "Stadium Projects Are Proliferating Amid Debate over Benefit to Cities," *Wall Street Journal*, March 20, 1987, p. 37.

Chapter 14

1. Chester Hartman, *The Transformation of San Francisco* (Totowa, N.J.: Rowman & Allanheld, 1984), p. 262.

2. Norman Krumholz, "Recovery of Cities: An Alternate View," in Paul R. Porter and David C. Sweet, eds., *Rebuilding America's Cities* (New Brunswick, N.J.: Rutgers Center for Urban Policy Research, 1984), p. 174.

3. Desmond Smith, "Info City," *New York*, February 9, 1981, cited by Michael C. D. Macdonald, *America's Cities* (New York: Simon and Schuster, 1984), p. 365.

4. Cited by Fainstein et al., *Restructuring the City*, p. 252.

5. Martin Gottlieb, "A Decade after the Cutbacks, New York Is a Different City," *New York Times*, June 30, 1985, p. 1.

6. Hill, "Crisis in the Motor City," pp. 111–112.

7. Joe R. Feagin, *The Urban Real Estate Game* (Englewood Cliffs, N.J.: Prentice-Hall, 1983), p. 2.

8. Jim Sleeper, "Koch's Victory and a Transformed New York," *Boston Globe*, September 17, 1985, p. 19.

9. U.S. Commission on Civil Rights, *Urban Minority Economic Development: Hearing Held in Baltimore, Maryland, November 17–18, 1981*, testimony of James W. Rouse, p. 259.

10. U.S. Commission on Civil Rights, *Urban Minority Economic Development*, pp. 256–257.

11. Thierry J. Noyelle, *New Technologies and Services* (College Park, Md.: University of Maryland Institute for Urban Studies, 1985), p. 25.

12. Ada Louise Huxtable, *Will They Ever Finish Bruckner Boulevard?* (New York: Macmillan, 1971), pp. 27–29.

13. Robert Lindsey, "California Voters Calling Halt to Uncontrolled City Growth," *New York Times*, November 15, 1986, p. 1.

14. Joan Didion, "On the Mall," in *The White Album* (New York: Pocket Books, 1980), p. 179.

Sources

Following is a list of works we used for our research. The material is organized into twelve subjects, followed by notes on the case studies and a list of people interviewed.

List of Abbreviations

AF	Architectural Forum
AR	Architectural Review
BG	Boston Globe
BW	Business Week
ICSC	International Council of Shopping Centers
NYT	New York Times
PA	Progressive Architecture
SCW	Shopping Center World
UL	Urban Land
ULI	Urban Land Institute
WSJ	Wall Street Journal

1 Shopping Centers

Growth and Evolution

Although researchers have paid little attention to the suburban shopping center, there is a vast amount of source material in the fields of business, architecture, and development. Our research on shopping centers began with the development of the suburban prototype. We relied on numerous articles from architectural and business journals, which chronicled in greater detail than now imaginable the birth of what was considered a revolutionizing trend for retailing. See "Markets in the Meadows," *AF* 90 (March 1949), 114–118; "Suburban Retail Districts," *AF* 93 (August 1950), 106–121; C. B. Palmer, "The Shopping Center Goes to the Shopper," *NYT Magazine,* November 29, 1953, pp. 14–15; Dero A. Saunders, "Department Stores: Race for the Suburbs," *Fortune* 44 (December 1951), 98–102; "Planned Postwar Shopping Centers Come Big," *BW*, no. 1206 (October 1952), 124–126; and Art Zuckerman, "America's Shopping Center Revolution," *Dun's Review and Modern Industry* 71 (May 1958), 36–37. Of particular interest for its engaging hot-off-the-press account from the fashion industry's viewpoint are the newspaper columns of Samuel Feinberg collected in *What Makes Shopping Centers Tick* (New York: Fairchild Publications, 1960).

If, in retrospect, the shopping center seems the ideal location for suburban department stores, it was not so apparent in the early days; retail executives had to be persuaded of its merits. Sources on the reluctance of department stores are referenced below under RETAILING—Department Stores. On why shopping centers were especially good for department stores, see "Planned Growth for Retailing," *Stores* 38 (January 1956), 9–12, written by B. Earl Puckett, a top executive of Allied Stores, one of the earliest developers of planned shopping centers.

Nowhere is the growth of shopping centers fully documented. The industry's march across suburbia is the subject of an early academic piece by Yehoshua S. Cohen, *Diffusion of an Innovation in an Urban System: The Spread of Planned Regional Shopping Centers in the United States 1949–1968*, University of Chicago, Department of Geography, Research Paper No. 140 (1972). Most of the story, however, comes from anecdotes and developers' recollections. See Ernest W. Hahn, "Ernie Hahn Speaks Out: I—On What Went Wrong in Center Development; II—For Variable Rate Loans for Regionals," *SCW* 4 (December 1975), 9–12; "Interview, Edwin N. Homer: The Industry Has Made a Positive Shift," *SCW* 8 (December 1978), 17–21; "Interview, Leonard L. Farber: 'I Never Had the Wildest Dreams,' " *SCW* 8 (March 1978), 97–98; "Interview: Edwin N. Homer," *SCW* 8 (December 1978), 17–21; and "Are Center Go-Go Years Over?" *Chain Store Age Executive Edition* (May 1977), 52–55.

An important source of information on all aspects of shopping centers is the industry trade group, ICSC. ICSC's archival library in New York contains an invaluable collection of materials dating from their earliest meetings in the late 1950s; especially interesting for what developers considered problems of development are the conference programs and keynote addresses.

In 1966 the industry started to take account of its growth in a systematic fashion. Data on the number and types of shopping centers cited in the text come from the biennial surveys reported, first in *Chain Store Age*: S. O. Kaylin, "A Profile of the Shopping Center Industry," 112 (May 1966), E16–E22; and subsequently in various issues of *SCW*. We made use of S. O. Kaylin, "SCW Industry Survey Shows 16,114 Centers in U.S., Canada, Selling $163 Billion Yearly," *SCW* 3 (January 1975), 19–21. On the production record between 1971 and 1976 noted in the text, data come from: Ernest W. Hahn, Inc., *Annual Report: 1972, 1973, 1974, 1975;* "Charting MSA's 20 Years of Development," *Developments at Melvin Simon & Associates, Inc.* 9 (Winter 1981), 10; Rouse Company, *Annual Report: 1981;* and information from Edward DeBartolo Company and the Taubman Company, January 1988.

Our search for what city planners had to say about the changing commercial landscape in the suburbs turned up little. Two exceptions are: Brian J. L. Berry, "A Critique of Contemporary Planning for Business Centers," *Land Economics* 35 (November 1959), 306–312; and Edgar M. Horwood, "Public Policy and the Outlying Shopping Center," *Journal of the American Institute of Planners* 24 (1958), 215–222. For a contemporary and personal commentary on malls and their pervasiveness across the landscape, see William Severini Kowinski, *The Malling of America: An Inside Look at the Great Consumer Paradise* (New York: William Morrow and Company, 1985).

Changing Rules—Environmental and Regulatory Constraints

After the initial burst of mall building in the 1960s, shopping center developers confronted growing legal and environmental challenges. An important source for a complete presentation of these problems is Steven J. Eagle, "Shopping Center Control: The Developer Besieged," *Journal of Urban Law* 51 (1974), 585–647. Although the challenges actually did little to diminish what turned out to be a record-breaking production of malls during the 1970s, developers were increasingly anxious about the shifting regulatory environment in which they operated, and their concerns were evident in numerous trade journal articles and at industry conferences. See "Are Center Go-Go Years Over?" *Chain Store Age Executive Edition* (May 1977), 52–55; Harry Newman, "The Shape of the Future" (address to ICSC Conference, Miami Beach, 1970, ICSC archival files); "Convention '72 Report: Small Center Needs Draw Top Interest at Convention," *SCW* 2 (July 1972), 34–40; "Real Estate Conference: Builders Worry over Ecology, Lack of Land," *SCW* 2 (November 1972), 41–44; "Convention '73 Report: Concern for Environment, Return to Downtown, Major Issues at Convention," *SCW* 3 (July 1973), 26; and "Convention '74 Report: Enviro Scare Behind, Uncertain Future Ahead, ICSC Holds Biggest Convention Ever," *SCW* 4 (July 1974), 36–38.

The federal Environmental Protection Agency's proposed regulations on auto emissions and trip generation were of particular concern. See "ICSC's Sussman Sees Centers Fighting 'War for Survival' Because of Ecology Laws," *SCW* 3 (December 1973), 14–15; "SCW's Editorial Advisory Board Speaks Out on Energy and Ecology," *SCW* 4 (September 1974), 13–17; "Needless Cost, Frustration Laid to Furor over Environment," *SCW* 3 (April 1973), 24; and "Convention '73 Report."

A few years later the Carter administration issued an executive order for energy conservation that appeared threatening, initially. We reviewed articles by policy analysts and industry people in *Shopping Centers: U.S.A.*, edited by George Sternlieb and James W. Hughes (New Brunswick, N.J.: Rutgers Center for Urban Policy Research, 1981). See the White House statement, "Community Conservation Guidance," pp. 83–88; Marshall Kaplan, "Community Conservation Guidance: A Promising Initiative," pp. 71–82; and Albert Sussman, "Community Conservation Guidelines: A Failure," pp. 63–70. A useful overview article in the same book is George Sternlieb and James W. Hughes, "Introduction: The Uncertain Future of Shopping Centers," pp. 11–16.

For a discussion of the broader context in which these environmental issues were played out within the development industry, see Bernard J. Frieden, *The Environmental Protection Hustle* (Cambridge, Mass.: MIT Press, 1979).

The Move to Downtown

The record of public and private efforts to revive downtown retailing begins with the pedestrian malls of the late 1950s and early 1960s. An early article by Shirley F. Weiss, "The Downtown Mall Experiment," *Journal of the American Institute of Planners* 30 (February 1964), 66–73, is useful for its reporting on the extent of street closings by the early 1960s. More recent reports are: Margaret S. Wirtenberg, "Downtown Pedestrian Malls," in Sternlieb and Hughes, *Shopping Centers: U.S.A.*, pp. 229–236; "Main Streets Girding to Do Battle with the Suburban Shopping Mall," *NYT*, March 1, 1985, p. B1; and Glen Weisbrod and Henry O. Pollakowski, "Effects of Downtown Improvement Projects on Retail Activity," *Journal of the American Planning Association* 50 (Spring 1984), 148–161. Although problems were apparent after several years, the reports on their failure and abandonment did not come until much later. The sources we made use of are: Laurie M. Grossman, "City Pedestrian Mall Fails to Fulfill Promise of Revitalizing Downtown," *WSJ*, June 17, 1987, p. 29; and Marty Carlock, "Some Cities Walk Away from Pedestrian Malls," *BG*, September 5, 1987, p. 37.

The earliest efforts to transplant the suburban prototype are covered briefly in the following articles: Lathrop Douglass, "Revitalizing Downtown Shopping Centers," *AR* 46 (July 1969), 136–145; S. O. Kaylin, "Fort Lauderdale's Rebirth May Set Pattern for Cities," *SCW* 2 (May 1972), 50–53; "Centers Play Key Role in Revitalizing Central Cities," *SCW* 2 (March 1972), 19–33; and "Suburban Malls Go Downtown," *BW*, November 10, 1973, pp. 90–94. Another commentary, written by a long-time observer of business trends, Gurney Breckenfeld, is noteworthy for its negative assessment of the potential for downtown malls as of the mid-1970s: " 'Downtown' Has Fled to the Suburbs," *Fortune* 86 (October 1976), 80–87.

For developers' and retailers' views of the potential for downtown malls, we made use of the following published sources: Ernest W. Hahn, "Concerns of Our Industry" (address to ICSC Conference, Miami Beach, May 8, 1972, ICSC archival files); A. Alfred Taubman, "The Third Generation—Urban Centers," *SCW* 3 (January 1973), 5; "Why Developers and Retailers Are Taking Hard Looks at Downtown Shopping Centers," *Chain Store Age Executive Edition* (May 1967), E38–E41; "Suburban Malls Go Downtown," *BW*, November 10, 1973, pp. 90–94; and "Downtown Malls Debated," *Chain Store Age Executive* (May 1977), 56–57. Our most revealing sources on this topic were interviews with Ernest Hahn and executives of his firm and with James Rouse.

After the immediate success of Faneuil Hall Marketplace, downtown retailing was more widely reported by business and industry presses. See Howard Rudnisky, "A Battle No Longer One-sided," *Fortune*, September 17, 1979, pp. 129–135; Isadore Barmash, "Retailers Gaining Confidence in Changing

Downtowns," *National Mall Monitor* 9 (September–October 1979), 27–30; and Gurney Breckenfeld, "The Rouse Show Goes National," *Fortune,* July 27, 1981, pp. 48–54. In addition, a monograph by ULI staff provided important secondary source material on centers across the country: J. Thomas Black, Libby Howland, and Stuart L. Rogel, *Downtown Retail Development: Conditions for Success and Project Profiles* (Washington, D.C.: ULI, 1983).

One of the most interesting stories connecting retailing with architectural form is the history of arcades in Europe as a prototype for today's downtown malls. The definitive source on this is Johann Friedrich Geist, *Arcades: The History of a Building Type* (Cambridge, Mass.: MIT Press, 1983), pp. 59–90.

The Mall as More Than Shopping

There is little to go by on this topic other than journalistic accounts: for example, "Shopping Centers Grow into Shopping Cities," *BW,* September 4, 1971, pp. 34–38. For an idea that shoppers wanted noncommercial activities such as libraries and teen centers located in the mall: *U.S. News and World Report,* June 18, 1973, pp. 43–46; also see Eric Peterson, "Shopping Centers: The Role Centers Must Play," *SCW* 5 (July 1976), 10–13.

The social function of malls has been cited widely but little studied. For a general descriptive discussion, see Jerry Jacobs, *The Mall: An Attempted Escape from Everyday Life* (Prospect Heights, Ill.: Waveland Press, 1984); Martin B. Millison, "Teenage Behavior in Shopping Centers" (ICSC, 1976); Nathan Cobb, "There's Nothing to Do, So We Come Here," *BG,* February 27, 1985, pp. 57–58; Seth S. King, "Suburban 'Downtowns': The Shopping Centers," in L. H. Masotti and J. K. Hadden, eds., *Suburbia in Transition* (New York: Viewpoints, 1974); Ray Richards, "Malls Become More Than Place to Shop," *BG,* June 7, 1985, p. 17; Leland L. Nicholls and Robert S. Jones, "Leisure in the Marketplace," *Parks and Recreation* (December 1976), 8–11; and CBS News, "After the Dream Comes True," broadcast transcript, CBS TV, August 4, 1982.

Of particular note is a social commentary capturing the spirit and symbolism of mall development written by Joan Didion as an informal recollection: "On the Mall," in her book *The White Album* (New York: Pocket Books, 1980), pp. 179–185.

Building and Operating Shopping Centers

The primary text detailing the process of development and presenting case studies of representative centers is published by the ULI and updated regularly. We made use of J. Ross McKeever and Nathaniel M. Griffin, *Shopping Center Development Handbook* (Washington, D.C.: ULI, 1977). Other informative sources are: Roy P. Drachman, "Chain Store Leasing in Shopping Centers," *UL,* 18 (February 1959), 6–9; Daniel S. Levy, "ABC's of Shopping Center Leases," *Real Estate Review* 1 (Spring 1971), 12–16; John Robert Foster, "The Effect of Shopping Center Financing on the Opportunity for Occupancy by Independent Retailers, *Southern Journal of Business* 2 (1967), 25–40; and Joseph Barry Mason and Charles Thomas Moore, "A Note on Interchange Location Practices by Developers of Major Retail Centers," *Land Economics* 48 (May 1972), 187. From the earliest days of the industry, parking standards commanded particular attention; see ULI, *Parking Requirements for Shopping Centers*, Technical Bulletin 53 (1965).

Writing for a broad audience, Martha Weinman Lear captures the essence of the process by describing the methods and views of the industry's largest developer, Edward DeBartolo, in "A Master Builder Sites a Shopping Mall," *NYT Magazine*, August 12, 1973, pp. 12–13.

Specialty Centers as a New Prototype

Ten years after the opening of San Francisco's pioneering projects Ghirardelli Square and the Cannery, one of the top retail journals recognized the trend: "Innovative Centers Launched Downtown Trend," *Chain Store Age Executive Edition* (May 1974), E29–E32. The new type of center commanded much attention after the successful opening of Faneuil Hall. See ARCHITECTURAL CRITICISM. From a market and retailing perspective, the specialty center concept is discussed fully by Nina Gruen in "Gestalt Magnetism or What Is Special about Specialty Shopping Centers?" *UL* 37 (January 1978), 3–9. Also, "Appendix E, Specialty or Theme Centers," *Dollars and Cents of Shopping Centers 1978* (Washington, D.C.: ULI, 1978).

The growth of festival centers in the Minneapolis–St. Paul area is the subject of two interesting articles by Judith A. Martin: "If Baseball Can't Save Cities Anymore, What Can a Festival Market Do?," *Journal of Cultural Geography* (Fall–Winter 1985), 33–46; and "Beyond the Malling of America: The Rise of Twin Cities Festival Markets," *CURA Reporter* 15 (May 1985), published by the University of Minnesota Center for Urban and Regional Affairs, pp. 1–6.

2 Retailing

Department Stores

The rise of the big department stores that dominated downtown in the late nineteenth century is vividly discussed in several well-noted historical accounts of city life. See Gunther Barth, *City People* (New York: Oxford University Press, 1982), chap. 4; Daniel J. Boorstin, *The Americans: The Democratic Experience* (New York: Vintage Books, 1974), chap. 10; and Lewis Mumford, *The City in History* (New York: Harcourt, Brace, 1961), pp. 434–439. Stories about the fun of shopping in the grand department stores are in Robert Hendrickson, *The Grand Emporiums* (New York: Stein and Day, 1980), and Leon Harris, *Merchant Princes* (New York: Berkley Books, 1979).

The postwar decline of downtown flagship stores marked a turning point in retailing history. The earliest and most influential piece of research on the declining profits of big stores is George Sternlieb, *The Future of the Downtown Department Store* (Cambridge, Mass.: MIT–Harvard Joint Center for Urban Studies, 1962). Addressing city planners who were thinking about the redevelopment of central business districts, Sternlieb presented his conclusions in "The Future of Retailing in the Downtown Core," *Journal of the American Institute of Planners* 29 (May 1963). For information on retail sales, we also relied on the influential study by Raymond Vernon, *The Changing Economic Function of the Central City* (New York: Committee for Economic Development, 1959); data in John C. Bollens and Henry J. Schmandt, *The Metropolis* (New York: Harper & Row, 1965); and Jeanne R. Lowe, *Cities in a Race with Time* (New York: Vintage Books, 1968), pp. 379–380, 414–415.

To trace department stores' suburban expansion strategy and move out of downtown, we reviewed annual reports for the largest department store chains—the May Co., Allied Stores, Broadway-Hale Stores, Federated Department Stores, and Montgomery Ward—for 1960 through 1974. A good source of information on the current state of the industry is Barry Bluestone, Patricia Hanna, Sarah Kuhn, and Laura Moore, *The Retail Revolution: Market Transformation, Investment, and Labor in the Modern Department Store* (Boston: Auburn House, 1981).

Several maverick department stores were among the pioneering developers of shopping centers. Entrepreneurs quickly took over the field, yet several chains such as Allied Stores, May Co., Dayton Hudson, and Sears actively continued to develop malls. For sources on the numbers of malls owned by department stores, see Larry Smith, "Department Store Trends in the Development of Shopping Centers," *UL* 11 (March 1952), 1, 3–6; and Suzanne Klein, "Department Stores as Developers: 150 Shopping Malls, 140 Million Square Feet, 40 Million Feet Planned," *SCW* 5 (December 1976), 17–19.

The explosive growth of regional malls could not have taken place without the endorsement of department stores. Initially, however, they were reluctant players, skeptical of moving beyond downtown and uncertain about joining forces with other retailers. See Dero A. Saunders, "Department Stores: Race for the Suburbs," *Fortune* 44 (December 1951), 98–102; and Robert H. Armstrong, "Branch Store Policies," *UL* 13 (September 1954), 1, 3–6. On Sears's pioneering move beyond downtown in the 1920s, see Alfred D. Chandler, Jr., *Strategy and Structure: Chapters in the History of the Industrial Enterprise* (Cambridge: MIT Press, 1962), pp. 235–240.

When department stores first moved to the suburbs in the 1920s with small, upscale stores, executives were plagued with problems. See J. Edward Davidson, "Postwar Merchandising Problems," *Journal of Retailing* 19 (October 1943), 67–73; Fabian Linden, "The Business of Department Stores," Technical Paper No. 7 (New York: National Industrial Conference Board, 1959); and Edward Benjamin Weiss, *Selling to and through the "New" Department Store* (New York: Funk & Wagnalls Co. in association with Printers' Ink Publishing Co., 1948), pp. 11–33.

Intense competition among retailers played an important role in pushing department stores toward the suburbs and into shopping centers. A speech by retailing's leading scholar of the period, Malcolm P. McNair, "Department

Stores on Uneasy Street," for the National Retail Dry Goods Association in New York, January 12, 1953, provides a succinct statement of the threat. Other sources we made use of are: Malcolm P. McNair, *The American Department Store, 1920–1960: A Performance Analysis Based on the Harvard Reports*, Bureau of Business Research Bulletin No. 166 (Boston: Harvard University Graduate School of Business, 1962); and Robert David Entenberg, *The Changing Competitive Position of Department Stores in the United States by Merchandise Lines*, rev. ed. (Pittsburgh: University of Pittsburgh Press, 1961).

Much of what is known about the relationship between developers and department stores is industry lore; there is little written material. We relied heavily on interviews with developers: Ernest W. Hahn, John Gilchrist, Jr., William Doyle, of the Hahn Company; Ronald Hahn; and James W. Rouse; lenders: Carol Nichols; as well as others in the industry: Albert Sussman, A. Jerry Keyser, Jerome Lipp, and Gerald Trimble. The three-way alliance of developers, department stores, and lenders is frequently cited by all parties as a useful set of checks and balances on uneconomic projects. For an early statement, see Leonard L. Farber, "Some Disturbing Trends in Shopping Center Development" (speech at ICSC Conference, Dallas, April 9, 1962, ICSC archival files).

A primary source of information on the power relationships between department stores and developers, in particular, their role as gatekeepers of shopping centers, comes from the Federal Trade Commission's antitrust proceedings against big stores in the early 1970s. For an overview, see Judy Gardner, "Consumer Report/FTC Seeks Wider Impact in Antitrust Work, Puts New Emphasis on Planning," *National Journal*, July 15, 1972, pp. 1151–1159. For a full discussion of the legal issues, see "Notes: The Antitrust Implications of Restrictive Covenants in Shopping Center Leases," *Harvard Law Review* 86 (1972–1973), 1201–1249. We also reviewed consent decrees for Federated Department Stores, Gimbel Brothers, Inc., Sears, Roebuck and Co., and complaints in the matter of Tysons Corner Regional Shopping Center, and the Rouse Co., in the authors' files. For industry views on the subject we made use of "Discounters . . . in Malls???? Question Flares as FTC Cites Tysons Corners," *Chain Store Age Executive Edition* (September 1971), E58-60; and "Round-Table Pinpoints: New Directions for Shopping Center Industry," *SCW* 3 (May 1973), 115.

Competition between Small Business and Shopping Centers

The bias against independent retailers was an issue from the early days of the industry's development. See U.S. Congress, Senate Subcommittee of the Select Committee on Small Business, *Hearings on Shopping Centers—1959*, 86th Cong., 1st sess., April 28, 29, 1959; and Victor Gruen, "Relocating Small Businesses in Large Shopping Centers: Why Isn't It Being Done?" *Journal of Housing* 16 (July–August 1959), 237–238. For a current reference on the topic, see Glen Weisbrod, "Can Ma and Pa Compete Downtown?" *UL* 42 (February 1983), 20–23.

Trends in Retail Sales

Data on retail sales for the nation, selected metropolitan areas, and central business districts come from U.S. Bureau of the Census retail trade surveys. There is a substantial lag in publication, but it remains the singular source for detailed data tabulations. We made use of *Census of Retail Trade: Major Retail Centers, 1972* (Washington, D.C.: Government Printing Office, 1976); *Census of Retail Trade: Major Retail Centers, 1976* (Washington, D.C.: Government Printing Office, 1980); and *Census of Retail Trade Geographic Area Series, 1982* (Washington, D.C.: Government Printing Office, 1984). An analysis of the potential for retail development downtown is presented in ULI, *Revitalizing Downtown Retailing: Trends and Opportunities* (Washington, D.C.: U.S. Department of Housing and Urban Development, April 1983), pp. 5–13.

Downtown Malls

Concepts: The first notion was to transplant the suburban model. See references under SHOPPING CENTERS—The Move to Downtown. By the early 1980s there were a number of different models for downtown malls. See Frank H. Spink, Jr., "Downtown Malls: Prospects, Designs, Constraints," in *Shopping Centers: U.S.A.* ed. George Sternlieb and James W. Hughes (New Brunswick, N.J.: Rutgers Centers for Urban Policy Research, 1981), pp. 203–218; J. Thomas Black, Libby Howland, and Stuart L. Rogel, *Downtown Retail Development: Conditions for Success and Project Profiles* (Washington, D.C.: ULI, 1983); and Gurney Breckenfeld, "Jim Rouse Shows How to Give Downtown Retailing New Life," *Fortune,* April 10, 1978, pp. 85–91.

Politics: No published literature covers the politics of building malls downtown. The case studies we developed for our own curriculum purposes were designed to fill the gap, and they are used at several schools across the country. The sources and interviews we relied on for those accounts are listed under CASE STUDIES.

Implementation Issues: Our project-specific case studies also detail the problems and conflicts accompanying the development of downtown retail centers. We relied on interviews with industry experts. We also made use of reports on individual centers from ULI's Project Reference File listed under PROJECTS; and Dave Hollis, "Downtown Lessons: The Primer Is Slowly Being Written," *National Mall Monitor* 9 (September–October 1979), 57.

A general treatment of the problems of implementing complex policy-driven programs is in Jeffrey L. Pressman and Aaron B. Wildavsky's classic, *Implementation* (Berkeley, Calif.: University of California Press, 1973). For a comment on how programs can be made to work, see Martin A. Levin and Barbara Ferman, *The Political Hand* (New York: Pergamon Press, 1985).

Design and Character: See SHOPPING CENTERS—The Move to Downtown and ARCHITECTURAL CRITICISM.

Performance: Information on the performance of downtown centers was difficult to gather in any systematic fashion. Data on profits are hard to come by, and the need to account for costs on a uniform basis for centers under different ownership makes the task especially complex. We relied heavily on interviews with knowledgeable people in the field: Norman Elkin, John Gilchrist, Jr., Martin Millspaugh, A. Jerry Keyser, Thomas Schriber, and Albert Sussman.

In addition, using sales per square foot as a basis for measuring performance, we collected information on a sample of downtown centers from figures compiled by the National Research Bureau and published in *Shopping Center Directory 1989—29th Edition* (Chicago: Automated Marketing Systems, 1988); for the industry at large, data come from the 1987 edition of *Dollars and Cents of Shopping Centers,* published by the ULI. Other useful articles we drew on are: Peter D. Leibowitz, "The Preliminary Track Record," in George Sternlieb and James W. Hughes, *Shopping Centers: U.S.A.* (New Brunswick, N.J.: Rutgers Center for Urban Policy Research, 1981), pp. 219–227; and Albert Sussman, "Shopping Centers—Yesterday, Today, and Tomorrow," *Real Estate Finance Journal* 3 (Summer 1987), 56–60.

The performance of festival malls has attracted much attention. Informative articles on the problems facing several centers are: Robert Guskind and Neal R. Peirce, "Faltering Festivals," *National Journal,* September 17, 1988, pp. 2307–2311; Andrew L. Yarrow, "Seaport: Sprightly at 200, Mature at 5," *NYT,* August 19, 1988, p. C10; plus a series of articles in the December 1988 issue of *Shopping Centers Today:* Margaret Hunter, "Festivals: Is the Party Over?" p. 1; Margaret Hunter, "Why Festival Centers Have Problems," p. 10; "Pioneer James Rouse Looks Overseas for New Projects," p. 9; and "Fewer Festivals Being Developed," p. 10. An estimate of the money loss from some Rouse Company festival centers is reported in Goldman Sachs Investment Research, *The Rouse Company,* prepared by Robert C. Adler, December 30, 1988, p. 3.

For information on the failures, we drew on news accounts of the problems. On Herald Center, see Isadore Barmash, "Herald Center: More Troubles," *NYT,* March 24, 1987, p. D1. On Renaissance Center, see "Downtown Is Looking Up," *Time,* July 5, 1976, pp. 54–62; "Detroit's Downtown Gets a Tonic," *BW,* August 9, 1976, p. 52; "Detroit's Big Renaissance Center Project Put into Default on $200 Million Mortgage," *WSJ,* January 12, 1983, p. 56; "Towering Debts," *Time,* January 24, 1983, p. 63; Susan Dentzer with Richard Manning, "Hard Times for the 'Ren Cen,' " *Newsweek,* January 24, 1983, p. 58; and G. Bruce Knecht, "Renaissance Center: Ford's Costly and Failing Bid to Revive Detroit," *NYT,* July 3, 1983, sect. 3, pp. 4–5. We also made use of information collected for a paper prepared by John Robertson for our MIT seminar on methods of downtown development, May 1984.

3 The Urban Crisis

History of Downtown

Several very good sources listed under RETAILING describe the rise of the big-city department stores.

Postwar Decline

There is an enormous literature on the decline of cities. The definitive analysis of how cities and suburbs were changing in the postwar period is the monumental New York Metropolitan Region Study, directed by Raymond Vernon. The nine published volumes resulting from this study are a gold mine of insight into the economic, social, and political forces remaking American cities in the middle of the century. We drew particularly on the first volume, Edgar M. Hoover and Raymond Vernon, *Anatomy of a Metropolis* (Cambridge, Mass.: Harvard University Press, 1959), and the summary volume, Raymond Vernon, *Metropolis 1985* (Cambridge, Mass.: Harvard University Press, 1960). These ideas were incorporated in Raymond Vernon, *The Changing Economic Function of the Central City* (New York: Committee for Economic Development, 1959).

Other works we drew on are: Robert C. Weaver, *Dilemmas of Urban America* (Cambridge, Mass.: Harvard University Press, 1965); Anthony Downs, *Urban Problems and Prospects* (Chicago: Markham, 1970); Jeanne R. Lowe, *Cities in a Race with Time* (New York: Vintage Books, 1968); and Charles Abrams, *The City Is the Frontier* (New York: Harper & Row, 1965).

Data on the number of people going downtown in the 1950s came from John R. Meyer, John F. Kain, and Martin Wohl, *The Urban Transportation Problem* (Cambridge, Mass.: Harvard University Press, 1965), pp. 35–37. On the proportion of property taxes coming from central business districts, see Committee for Economic Development, *Guiding Metropolitan Growth* (New York: CED, 1960); and Charles Abrams, *The Language of Cities* (New York: Viking Press, 1971).

For an economist's statement of the flight to the suburbs, see John F. Kain, "The Distribution and Movement of Jobs and Industry," in James Q. Wilson, ed., *The Metropolitan Enigma* (Garden City, N.Y.: Doubleday Anchor, 1970). For data on housing vacancies and population migration, see Bernard J. Frieden, *The Future of Old Neighborhoods* (Cambridge, Mass.: MIT Press, 1964), pp. 13, 20. And on institutional racism in city housing markets, see Lynne B. Sagalyn, "Mortgage Lending in Older Urban Neighborhoods: Lessons from Past Experience," *Annals of the American Academy of Political and Social Science* 465 (January 1983), 98–108.

The elite's view of the problem draws heavily upon the Connecticut General conference proceedings reported in Wilfred Owen, *Cities in the Motor Age* (New York: Viking Press, 1959), and Raymond Vernon's insightful analysis in *The Myth and Reality of Our Urban Problems* (Cambridge, Mass.: MIT–Harvard

Joint Center for Urban Studies, 1962). His argument is developed more fully in the text of the Stafford Little Lectures he presented in 1961, included in the same book. Also see John Kenneth Galbraith, *The Affluent Society* (1958; Harmondsworth, Middlesex: Penguin Books, 1962).

On city planners' response with large-scale plans for downtown, see Clyde E. Browning, "Recent Studies of Central Business Districts," *Journal of the American Institute of Planners* 27 (February 1961), 82–87; and on the types of people who appeared in sketches of the new projects, Edward M. Wood, Jr., Sidney N. Brower, and Margaret W. Latimer, "Planners' People," *Journal of the American Institute of Planners* 32 (July 1966), 228–234.

What Role for Cities?

For general commentary during the urban renewal era, see "The City: Under the Knife, or All for Their Own Good," *Time*, November 6, 1964, pp. 60–75; Robert Moses, "Are Cities Dead?" *Atlantic* 209 (January 1962); Victor Gruen, *The Heart of Our Cities* (New York: Simon and Schuster, 1964); and Edmund K. Faltermayer, "What It Takes to Make Great Cities," *Fortune* 75 (January 1967), 118–123, 146–151.

With the worsening of urban conditions and the failures of the urban renewal strategy, critics again reexamined the city's function. For pessimistic conclusions, see George Sternlieb, "The City as Sandbox," *Public Interest*, no. 25 (Fall 1971), 14–21; and Kenneth E. Boulding, "The City as an International System," *Daedalus* 97 (Fall 1968), 1111–1123. Another source that examines the role of the city and contains a valuable collection of essays on urban conditions as of the 1970s is Arthur P. Solomon, ed., *The Prospective City* (Cambridge, Mass.: MIT Press, 1980); in particular, see Ira S. Lowry, "The Dismal Future of Central Cities," pp. 161–203; J. Thomas Black, "The Changing Economic Role of Central Cities and Suburbs," pp. 80–123; Franklin J. James, "The Revitalization of Older Urban Housing and Neighborhoods," pp. 130–160; and Roger W. Schmenner, "Industrial Location and Urban Public Management," pp. 446–468.

In the late 1970s the press reported that the urban crisis appeared to be at a turning point. See, in particular, T. D. Allman, "The Urban Crisis Leaves Town," *Harper's* 257 (December 1978), 41–56; Blake Fleetwood, "The New Elite and an Urban Renaissance," *NYT Magazine*, January 14, 1979, pp. 16–33; and "A City Revival?" *Newsweek*, January 15, 1979, pp. 28–35.

Downtown Comeback

For assessments written in the urban renewal era from the 1940s to the early 1970s, see "Cities: The Renaissance," *Time*, March 23, 1962, pp. 16–20; and Morton Hoffman, "The Outlook for Downtown Housing," *Journal of the American Institute of Planners* 27 (February 1961), 43–55. During this period the widespread popularity of street closings was generally taken as a symbol of a hoped-for comeback; for references, see SHOPPING CENTERS—The Move to Downtown."

For the 1970s and 1980s see "Downtown Is Looking Up," *Time,* July 5, 1976, p. 61; "Cities Are Fun!" *Time,* August 24, 1981, pp. 42–53; E. R. Shipp, "Rebound from Long Decline Is Seen in St. Louis" *NYT,* February 2, 1985; and George James, "A Faded Summer Place with Hopes of Revival, *NYT,* May 26, 1986, p. 21.

A number of nationwide trends cast new light on cities' traditional attributes. On gourmet food, see Craig Claiborne, "A Yeasty Plateau," *NYT Magazine,* December 9, 1984, pp. 131–132. For commentaries on how other changes in consumer tastes worked to cities' advantage, see Jane Davison, "Bringing Life to the Market," *NYT Magazine,* October 10, 1976, pp. 74–78; and Calvin Trillin, "U.S. Journal: New England," *New Yorker,* May 16, 1977, pp. 101–107. On historic preservation, see David Listokin, *Living Cities: Report of the Twentieth Century Fund Task Force on Urban Preservation Policies* (New York: Priority Press, 1985). On the popular dislike of coldness and severity in modern architecture, see the short, engaging essay by Tom Wolfe, *From Bauhaus to Our House* (New York: Pocket Books, 1982).

For information on the baby boom's coming of age, we drew on a number of sources. Population data come from Louise B. Russell, *The Baby Boom Generation and the Economy* (Washington, D.C.: Brookings Institution, 1982). Also see Landon Y. Jones, *Great Expectations: America and the Baby Boom Generation* (New York: Ballantine Books, 1980), chap. 17; and Frank S. Levy and Richard C. Michel, "The Economic Future of the Baby Boom," research report (Washington, D.C.: Urban Institute, 1985).

To document the role of gentrification in the revival of cities, we relied on the following sources: Phillip Clay, *Neighborhood Renewal* (Lexington, Mass.: Lexington Books, 1979); Daphne Spain, "A Gentrification Scorecard," cited by June Manning Thomas, "Redevelopment and Redistribution," in Paul R. Porter and David C. Sweet, eds., *Rebuilding America's Cities* (New Brunswick, N.J.: Rutgers Center for Urban Policy Research, 1984), pp. 143–159; Franklin J. James, "The Revitalization of Older Urban Housing and Neighborhoods," in Arthur P. Solomon, *The Prospective City* (Cambridge, Mass.: MIT Press, 1980); and Brian J. L. Berry, "Islands of Renewal in Seas of Decay," in Paul E. Peterson, ed., *The New Urban Reality* (Washington, D.C.: Brookings Institution, 1985), pp. 69–96. For a review of changes in the residential character of the Society Hill section of Pittsburgh, see Michael H. Schill and Richard P. Nathan, *Revitalizing America's Cities* (Albany: State University of New York Press, 1983).

On the conversion of warehouse space to residential lofts, see Sharon Zukin, *Loft Living* (Baltimore: Johns Hopkins Press, 1982); Seth H. Lubove, "Following New York's Lead, Other Cities Are Turning Industrial Space into Lofts," *WSJ,* February 4, 1986, p. 33; and Suzanne Slesin, "Downtown Los Angeles: The New Settlers," *NYT,* April 12, 1984, p. C1. And on city officials' favorable attitude toward housing, we made use of an interview with former Seattle mayor Wes Uhlman; comments by Harvey I. Sloane, mayor of Louisville, Urban Land Institute Conference, Phoenix, October 11, 1985; and M.

Leanne Lachman and Robert E. Miller, "Downtown Housing—Where the Action Is," *Real Estate Report* (Real Estate Research Corporation) 14 (Second Quarter, 1985), 1–3.

Federal Government Reports on the Condition of Cities

Two seminal reports by government experts on the problems of cities were published in the late 1960s: U.S. National Advisory Commission on Civil Disorders, *Report* (Washington, D.C.: Government Printing Office, 1968); and *Building the American City: Report to the Congress and the President of the United States* (Washington, D.C.: Government Printing Office, 1969) by President Johnson's National Commission on Urban Problems, a report rich in data as well as observations.

Beginning in 1978 the U.S. president's office began issuing an annual report on urban conditions; we used *National Urban Policy Report: 1978* (Washington, D.C.: U.S. Department of Housing and Urban Development, 1978); U.S. Department of Housing and Urban Development, *The President's Urban Policy Report: 1980;* and U.S. President, *National Urban Policy Report: 1984* (Washington, D.C.: U.S. Department of Housing and Urban Development, 1984).

Public Opinion on Cities and City Life

Joseph Zikmund II, "Do Suburbanites Use the Central City?" *American Institute of Planners Journal* 37 (May 1971), 192–195; Gallup Opinion Index, Report No. 110, "Analysis: Managed Growth" (August 1974); and U.S. Department of Housing and Urban Development, *The 1978 HUD Survey on the Quality of Community Life* (Washington, D.C.: U.S. Department of Housing and Urban Development, 1978). Also, see poll data reported in Seymour Martin Lipset and William Schneider, *The Confidence Gap* (New York: Free Press, 1983).

Continuing Problems in the 1980s

Data on poverty and unemployment of central city residents come from Vincent P. Barabba's study, "The Demographic Future of the Cities of America," in Herrington J. Bryce, ed., *Cities and Firms* (Lexington, Mass.: Lexington Books, 1980), pp. 3–45; U.S. Bureau of the Census, *County and City Data Book 1972* (Washington, D.C.: U.S. Government Printing Office, 1973), table 6; *County and City Data Book, 1983*, table C; and *State and Metropolitan Area Data Book, 1986*, table B. Poverty figures for 1985 were supplied by Sheldon Danziger, University of Wisconsin Institute for Research on Poverty, from the 1986 Current Population Survey tapes. Data on median family income are from U.S. Office of the President, *Economic Report of the President* (Washington, D.C.: Government Printing Office, 1986), p. 286.

Data on commuter shares of central city employment from U.S. Census of

1980 are reported in Samuel M. Ehrenhalt (New York regional commissioner of labor statistics), "Growth in the New York City Economy: Problems and Promise" (paper presented to Eighteenth Annual Institute on Challenges of the Changing Economy of New York City, New York City Council on Economic Education, May 8, 1985). Similar information for Boston is from 1981 surveys reported in Boston Redevelopment Authority, *Boston Tomorrow: Background on Development* (Boston: Boston Redevelopment Authority, n.d.), table IX-5; and "Resident Workers Share of Boston Jobs," Boston Redevelopment Authority Research Department (February 1987).

For the ranking of cities on a composite index of economic well-being, we referred to a report by the National Urban Policy Advisory Committee, *Urban America 1984: A Report Card*, prepared for U.S. Congress Joint Economic Committee, Subcommittee on Investment, Jobs, and Prices (1984).

4 Urban Renewal and Highway Programs

Urban Renewal

History and Origin: See Marc A. Weiss, "The Origins and Legacy of Urban Renewal," in J. Paul Mitchell, ed., *Federal Housing Policy and Programs* (New Brunswick, N.J.: Rutgers Center for Urban Policy Research, 1985), pp. 153–276; and Ashley A. Foard and Hilbert Fefferman, "Federal Urban Renewal Legislation," in James Q. Wilson, *Urban Renewal: The Record and the Controversy* (Cambridge, Mass.: MIT Press, 1966), pp. 71–125.

The view that clearance was the only solution to the problems of cities is laid out by Louis Mumford in *From the Ground Up* (New York: Harcourt Brace Jovanovich, 1956), pp. 226–229; and Owen, *Cities in the Motor Age,* pp. 26, 47, 72, cited under THE URBAN CRISIS. For a description of the shift to rehabilitation strategy, in particular, the Boston experience, see Langley C. Keyes, Jr., *The Rehabilitation Planning Game* (Cambridge, Mass.: MIT Press, 1969). The programmatic shift to housing for low- and moderate-income households is in Section 512, Housing and Urban Development Act of 1968, P.L. 90-448; and evidence of change is documented by Heywood T. Sanders, "Urban Renewal and the Revitalized City," in Donald B. Rosenthal, ed., *Urban Revitalization* (Beverly Hills and London: Sage Publications, 1980), pp. 103–126.

"Blight" was defined by Section 110 of the Housing Act of 1949, 42 U.S.C. 1441. The legal requirements, however, turned out to have little practical effect. For an insightful analysis of "the blight that's right," see Charles Abrams, *The City Is the Frontier* (New York: Harper & Row, 1965). The program's economic logic was also guided by the prisoners' dilemma paradigm. This argument about neighborhood effects on individual decisions to improve properties is explained in Otto A. Davis and Andrew B. Whinston, "The Economics of Urban Renewal," in James Q. Wilson, *Urban Renewal: The Record and the Controversy* (Cambridge, Mass.: MIT Press, 1966), pp. 50–67.

Implementation Problems: Many of the earliest and best essays detailing the problems of carrying out the program's mandate are contained in Wilson, *Urban Renewal.* We made use of Harold Kaplan, "Urban Renewal in Newark," pp. 233–258; James Q. Wilson, "Planning and Politics: Citizen Participation in Urban Renewal," pp. 407–421; and Wilton S. Sogg and Warren Wertheimer, "Legal and Governmental Issues in Urban Renewal," pp. 126–188.

On the "rubble" problem, see Roger Montgomery, "Improving the Design Process in Urban Renewal," pp. 452–484, in Wilson, *Urban Renewal;* Morton Hoffman, "The Outlook for Downtown Housing," *Journal of the American Institute of Planners* 27 (February 1961), 43–55; and Heywood T. Sanders, "The Politics of City Redevelopment" (Ph.D. diss., Harvard University, 1977). Some of the reasoning leading to projects designed for isolation is evident in Morton Hoffman, "The Outlook for Downtown Housing," *Journal of the American Institute of Planners* 27 (February 1961), 43–55, in particular, p. 51. The telling speech in which the developer's role was characterized as an accessory after the fact was delivered by Harris E. Willingham, "Shopping Centers in the Urban Renewal Program," at the International Council of Shopping Centers 1959 Annual Convention, *Proceedings* (New York: ICSC, 1960), pp. 133–136.

All of the program's many implementation problems—the bureaucratic delays, rubble-filled lots, displacement troubles—as well as its progress and achievements, were cataloged in the report of President Johnson's Commission on Urban Problems, *Building the American City* (Washington, D.C.: Government Printing Office, 1969), chap. 6.

Displacement and Relocation: A primary source on this issue is a report by the U.S. Advisory Commission on Intergovernmental Relations, *Relocation: Unequal Treatment of People and Businesses Displaced by Government* (Washington, D.C.: Advisory Commission on Intergovernmental Relations, 1965). Other studies of the impact of displacement and the inability of households to move into better housing are summarized in Chester Hartman, "Relocation: Illusory Promises and No Relief," *Virginia Law Review* 57 (1971), 745–817. For figures on relocation assistance for households and businesses, see Bernard J. Frieden, *Metropolitan America: Challenge to Federalism* (Washington, D.C.: Advisory Commission on Intergovernmental Relations, 1966), p. 76.

A number of works describe the anguish and loss of displacement: Marc Fried, "Grieving for a Lost Home: Psychological Costs of Relocation," in James Q. Wilson, ed., *Urban Renewal* (Cambridge, Mass.: MIT Press, 1966), pp. 359–379; Marc Fried and Peggy Gleicher, "Some Sources of Residential Satisfaction in an Urban 'Slum,' " *Journal of the American Institute of Planners* 27 (November 1961), 305–315; and Daniel Thursz, *Where Are They Now?* (Washington, D.C.: Health and Welfare Council of the National Capital Area, 1966), pp. 100–101. The Fried articles report on Boston's West End project; Thursz's study is of the South West project in Washington, D.C.

Information on the business experience is from Basil G. Zimmer, *Rebuilding Cities: The Effects of Displacement and Relocation on Small Business* (Chicago:

Quadrangle Books, 1964); and U.S. Advisory Commission on Intergovernmental Relations, *Relocation*, pp. 52–58.

On the cover-up of displacement, see Edgar S. Cahn, Timothy Eichenberg, and Roberta V. Romberg, *The Legal Lawbreakers* (Washington, D.C.: Citizens Advocate Center, 1970; Richard T. LeGates, "Can The Federal Welfare Bureaucracies Control Their Programs: The Case of HUD and Urban Renewal," Working Paper No. 172 (Berkeley: University of California, Institute of Urban and Regional Development, May 1972); and Chester Hartman, "The Housing of Relocated Families," in Wilson, ed., *Urban Renewal*, pp. 293–335. For the speech in which HUD acknowledged the cover-up, see Norman V. Watson, acting assistant secretary for renewal and housing management, Department of Housing and Urban Development, "Urban Renewal and the Relocation Process" (remarks prepared for delivery at the Conference of the National Association of Housing and Redevelopment Officials, Sun Valley, Idaho, September 24, 1970).

Revolts and Protest: The illustrative case of the bulldozing of Los Angeles's Mexican-American community of Boyle Heights is drawn from Rodolofo F. Acuña, *A Community under Siege*, Los Angeles Chicano Studies Research Center Monograph 11 (Los Angeles: University of California, 1984), pp. 57–58, 65, 126. The story of the West Village (Manhattan) controversy is from Jeanne R. Lowe, *Cities in a Race with Time* (New York: Vintage Books, 1968), pp. 98–103; and J. Clarence Davies III, *Neighborhood Groups and Urban Renewal* (New York: Columbia University Press, 1966), pp. 72–109.

An explanation of urban renewal's contribution to the 1960s urban rioting can be found in U.S. National Advisory Commission on Civil Disorders, *Report* (Washington, D.C.: Government Printing Office, 1968), pp. 80–83. For general references on federal support for resident control of government programs in their neighborhoods, see U.S. Advisory Commission on Intergovernmental Relations, *Intergovernmental Relations in the Poverty Program* (Washington, D.C.: Advisory Commission on Intergovernmental Relations, 1966), esp. p. 28; John G. Wofford, "The Politics of Local Responsibility: Administration of the Community Action Program—1964–1966," in James L. Sundquist, ed., *On Fighting Poverty* (New York: Basic Books, 1969), pp. 70–102; and Daniel P. Moynihan, *Maximum Feasible Misunderstanding* (New York: Free Press, 1969).

Critique and Evaluation: The critical literature on the failures of urban renewal is extensive. The classic in the field is Jane Jacobs's searing critique, *The Death and Life of Great American Cities* (New York: Random House, 1961). One of the earliest and strongest indictments of the program was Martin Anderson's book, *The Federal Bulldozer* (Cambridge, Mass.: MIT Press, 1964). Also see Lawrence M. Friedman, *Government and Slum Housing* (Chicago: Rand McNally, 1968); Sanders, "Urban Renewal and the Revitalized City," in *Urban Revitalization;* and William Michelson, "Most People Don't Want What Architects Want," *Trans-Action* 5 (July–August 1968), 37–43.

For an account of the Nixon administration's actions to merge urban renewal into a community development block grant, see Bernard J. Frieden and Marshall Kaplan, *The Politics of Neglect* (Cambridge, Mass.: MIT Press, 1975), chaps. 9–11. Also, William J. Stull, "From Urban Renewal to CDBG: Community Development in Nine Cities," in C. F. Sirmans, ed., *Research in Real Estate* (Greenwich, Conn.: JAI Press, 1982), vol. 2, with a tally on urban renewal costs on p. 185.

Highway Program Takeover

Highway Politics and the Growth of Urban Freeways: The discussion of the federal aid highway system draws heavily from Gary T. Schwartz's definitive article, "Urban Freeways and the Interstate System," *Southern California Law Review* 49 (March 1976), 406–513.

Use for Slum Clearance: James W. Follin, "Coordination of Urban Renewal with the Urban Highway Program Offers Major Economies in Cost and Time," *UL* 15 (December 1956), 3–6; and S. G. Johndroe, Jr., "Effective Examination," in Southwestern Legal Foundation, *Proceedings of the Eighth Institute on Eminent Domain* (Dallas: Southwestern Legal Foundation, 1967), p. 85.

Racial Factors in Highway Routes: Schwartz, "Urban Freeways and the Interstate System"; and Miles Lord, chief judge, Ninth Federal District Court, Minneapolis, transcript of remarks to U.S. Justice Department Condemnation Seminar, Virginia Beach, October 30, 1979.

Opposition and Protests: General references on the subject are Alan Lupo, Frank Colcord, and Edmund P. Fowler, *Rites of Way* (Boston: Little, Brown, 1971); Grady Clay, "The Competitors," manuscript prepared for the MIT–Harvard Joint Center for Urban Studies, August 10, 1962, chap. 3; Alan A. Altshuler and Robert W. Curry, "The Changing Environment of Urban Development Policy—Shared Power or Shared Impotence?" *Urban Law Annual* 10 (1975), 3–41; and Daniel P. Moynihan, "Policy vs. Program in the '70's," *Public Interest*, no. 20 (Summer 1970), 90–100. The discussion of how opposition groups conducted their campaigns is based on Kenneth R. Geiser, Jr., "Urban Transportation Decision Making: Political Processes of Urban Freeway Controversies" (Cambridge, Mass.: MIT Department of Urban Studies and Planning/Urban Systems Laboratory, June 1970), pp. 365–422.

The attack on highway building as "pyramid building with a vengeance" by Lewis Mumford comes from his book, *The Highway and the City* (New York: Harcourt, Brace, 1963). Also see A. Q. Mowbray, *Road to Ruin* (Philadelphia: Lippincott, 1969). Books attacking highways noted in text and other critical works are cited by Gary T. Schwartz, "Urban Freeways and the Interstate System," *Southern California Law Review,* 49 (March 1976), 406–513, p. 410.

Record of Construction and Cost: See Schwartz, "Urban Freeways and the Interstate System," pp. 428, 442, 443, 444, 487; and Alan A. Altshuler with James

R. Womack and John R. Pucher, *The Urban Transportation System* (Cambridge, Mass.: MIT Press, 1979), pp. 34–35, 340–341. Data on the money spent on highways and urban routes were supplied by C. L. Shufflebarger, chief, Interstate Management Branch, U.S. Department of Transportation, June 3, 1987. On the costs of dislocation of the highway and urban renewal programs, see Anthony Downs, *Urban Problems and Prospects* (Chicago: Markham, 1970), pp. 218–219.

5 Business and Cities

Urban Renewal Era (1940s–1970s): The Role of Business Coalitions

For a discussion of the role of real estate interests in the shaping of the initial urban renewal legislation, see Marc A. Weiss, "The Origins and Legacy of Urban Renewal," in J. Paul Mitchell, ed., *Federal Housing Policy and Programs* (New Brunswick, N.J.: Rutgers Center for Urban Policy Research, 1985), pp. 153–276. Accounts of the influence of local business groups in particular cities can be found in Heywood Sanders's doctoral thesis and Raymond Wolfinger's account of New Haven, both cited under CITY DEVELOPMENT POLITICS AND POLICY. Also see Timothy K. Barnekov and Daniel Rich, "Privatism and Urban Development: An Analysis of the Organized Influence of Local Business Elites," *Urban Affairs Quarterly* 12 (June 1977), 431–460, for a more theoretical interpretation by political scientists.

Evolution of Public-Private Partnerships

One of the best articles describing the long-term development of cooperative efforts is Shelby Stewman and Joel Tarr's case study of Pittsburgh, "Four Decades of Public-Private Partnerships in Pittsburgh," in R. Scott Fosler and Renee A. Berger, eds., *Public-Private Partnerships in American Cities* (Lexington, Mass.: Lexington Books, 1982), pp. 59–128.

During the Carter administration, the public-private policy initiative was articulated in the *National Urban Policy Report: 1978* (Washington, D.C.: U.S. Department of Housing and Urban Development, 1978); and later it was endorsed by the Reagan administration. See U.S. President, *National Urban Policy Report: 1984* (Washington, D.C.: U.S. Department of Housing and Urban Development, 1984), and the report of Reagan's Task Force on Private Initiatives, *Investing in America* (Washington, D.C.: Government Printing Office, 1983).

On the origins of Carter's UDAG program, which provided financial support for public-private projects, see U.S. Department of Housing and Urban Development, *The President's National Urban Policy Report: 1980* (Washington, D.C.: 1980); Susan S. Jacobs and Elizabeth A. Roistacher, "The Urban Impacts of HUD's Urban Development Action Grant Program," in Norman Glickman, ed., *The Urban Impacts of Federal Policies* (Baltimore: John Hopkins Press, 1980), pp. 335–363. On the uses of program funds, see U.S. Department of Housing and Urban Development, *Urban Development Action Grant Program: Second Annual Report* (Washington, D.C.: Department of Housing and Urban Development, 1980); and U.S. Department of Housing and Urban Development, *An Impact Evaluation of the Urban Development Action Grant Program* (Washington, D.C.: Government Printing Office, 1982). For additional sources, see FINANCING DOWNTOWN REDEVELOPMENT.

Negotiated Development and Deal-making Strategies

General works in this area include Robert Witherspoon, "Codevelopment: City Rebuilding by Business and Government," *Development Component Series* (Washington, D.C.: Urban Land Institute, 1982); John J. Kirlin and Anne M. Kirlin, *Public Choices—Private Resources: Financing Capital Infrastructure for California's Growth through Public-Private Bargaining* (Sacramento: California Tax Foundation, 1982); and Rachelle L. Levitt and John J. Kirlin, eds., *Managing Development through Public/Private Negotiations* (Washington, D.C.: ULI and the American Bar Association, 1985). Also we have drawn on notes and papers from our participation in a year-long seminar and concluding conference on Negotiated Development, sponsored by the Lincoln Institute for Land Policy during the 1985–1986 academic year in Cambridge, Massachusetts.

6 Public-Private Relationships

In City Development

The literature in this field owes much to the studies supported by the Committee for Economic Development, a business group with a long interest in the problems of cities. Two publications of particular note are: *Public-Private Partnerships in American Cities* (Lexington, Mass.: Lexington Books, 1982), a collection of case studies that describe public-private efforts in Atlanta, Baltimore, Chicago, Dallas, Minneapolis–St. Paul, Pittsburgh, and Portland, Oregon, edited by R. Scott Fosler and Renee A. Berger; and Committee for Economic Development, *Public-Private Partnership: An Opportunity for Urban Communities* (New York: Committee for Economic Development Research and Policy Committee, 1982).

Many articles describe how development partnerships work. Among the most informative are Nell Surber and Ralph Bolton, "Fountain Square South: Public/Private Partnership Works in Cincinnati," *UL* 41 (September 1982), 3–5; William Donald Schaefer, "Public/Private Partnership: Views and Its Future," in *City Economic Development* (Washington, D.C.: National League of Cities, January 15, 1979); and Joseph G. Madonna, "Public/Private Partnership for Downtown Development," *UL* 39 (February 1980), 12–19. For an analysis of different types of partnerships, see Susan E. Clarke and Michael J.

Rich, "Partnerships for Economic Development: The UDAG Experience," *Journal of Community Action* 1 (1982), 52–56.

The proceedings of two seminars on the topic sponsored by the MIT Center for Real Estate Development are collected in *Spring Seminars 1984: An Examination of Public/Private Issues in Real Estate Development* (Cambridge, Mass.: Center for Real Estate Development, 1984). Included are comments by former Mayor Kevin H. White, developers Daniel Rose and Ernest W. Hahn, and San Diego's public sector entrepreneur, Gerald M. Trimble.

One of the most useful discussions of the pragmatic issues confronting cities and developers entering into development partnerships is an unpublished paper by Sacramento redevelopment attorney, Joseph E. Coomes, Jr., "Problem Solving through Redevelopment Agreements" (prepared for Making Better Use of Urban Space, sponsored by the Lincoln Institute of Land Policy, February 11–12, 1983), authors' files.

The trend toward public-private combinations appeared in arenas other than city development. In reference to our discussion in the text, see John Noble Wilford, "NASA's Next Mission: Big Business in Space," *NYT Magazine*, September 18, 1983, p. 47; and Robert D. McFadden, "Private Help Sought for Restoring Ellis Island," *NYT*, December 12, 1981, p. 1.

Using public money to change the behavior of private enterprise was one of the big ideas for government policy in the 1970s. Charles Schultze, chairman of President Carter's Council of Economic Advisers, set forth a point of view that had been gathering strength for several years in his influential book, *The Public Use of Private Interest* (Washington, D.C.: Brookings Institution, 1977).

City Risk Taking

The practical advantages of public-private negotiation were endorsed by the International City Management Association in *The Entrepreneur in Local Government*, ed. Barbara H. Moore (Washington, D.C.: ICMA, 1983); and *Shaping the Local Economy*, ed. Cheryl A. Farr (Washington, D.C.: ICMA, 1984). City planning professionals also acknowledged the growing trend with articles on current practice in the American Planning Association's publication, *Planning*; in particular, see William Fulton, "On the Beach with the Progressives," 51 (January 1985), 4–9; Ana Arana, "Doing Deals: How California Communities Mix and Match Financing Techniques to Pay for New Development," 51 (February 1986), 30–33; and William Fulton, "The Profit Motive: Across the Country, Cities Are Becoming Real Estate Developers, and Planners Are Leading the Way," 53 (October 1987), 6–10. Also see Douglas R. Porter, "Deal Making in Dallas: A Primer for Public/Private Negotiations," *UL* 45 (February 1986), 10–13.

With increased deal making, more cities acquired a financial stake in projects through profit-sharing arrangements. For example, see Lawrence M. Fisher, "Cities Turn into Entrepreneurs," *NYT*, April 4, 1987, p. 33; David E. Dowall, "Public Land Development in the United States," *Journal of Real Estate Development* 2 (Winter 1987), 19–28; Robert Guenther, "Cities Getting

Part of Profits for Giving Aid to Developers," *WSJ*, September 29, 1982, p. 35; Neil A. Stone, "Using Real Estate Deals to Fill City Treasury," *UL* 45 (January 1986), 27–28; and Susan E. Clarke and Michael J. Rich, "Making Money Work: The New Urban Policy Arena," in *Research in Urban Policy* (Greenwich, Conn.: JAI Press, 1985), 1:101–115.

Information on the trend toward city profit sharing comes from our sample of thirty-nine projects, which is described under FINANCING DOWNTOWN RE-DEVELOPMENT. For an analysis of financial deal making for one city, see Lynne B. Sagalyn, "Measuring Financial Returns When the City Acts as an Investor: Boston and Faneuil Hall Marketplace" (paper presented at the annual meetings of the American Real Estate and Urban Economics Association, New York, December 30, 1987).

For cities that enter into public-private arrangements, there are financial risks. For our discussion of St. Paul's problems with Galtier Plaza, see Julie Ann Hoffman, "Galtier Plaza Refinancing Came in the Nick of Time," *St. Paul Press and Dispatch*, March 16, 1986, p. 1A; Anthony Neely, "Alpha Was Big Loser at Galtier Plaza," *Minneapolis–St. Paul City Business*, May 20, 1987, p. 1; Richard Meryhew, "Galtier Plaza Up for Sale," *Minneapolis Star Tribune*, February 6, 1988, p. 1A; Richard Meryhew, "Group is Closing in on Deal for Galtier," *Minneapolis Star Tribune*, July 2, 1988, p. 1A; and Richard Meryhew, "After Years of Turmoil, Galtier Plaza is Sold," *Minneapolis Star Tribune*, January 31, 1989, p. 1B. On the problems Burbank faced with the collapse of its downtown retail project, see Kathleen A. Hughes, "MCA May Develop Proposed Project Dropped by Disney," *WSJ*, April 14, 1988.

For general sources on entrepreneurship, we reviewed Eugene Lewis, *Toward a Theory of Bureaucratic Political Power* (Bloomington, Indiana: Indiana University Press, 1980); Jameson W. Doig and Erwin C. Hargrove, " 'Leadership' and Political Analysis," in *Leadership and Innovation*, ed. Jameson W. Doig and Erwin C. Hargrove (Baltimore: Johns Hopkins University Press, 1987); Howard H. Stevenson and David E. Gumpert, "The Heart of Entrepreneurship," *Harvard Business Review* (March–April 1985), 85–94; and Peter Drucker, *Innovation and Entrepreneurship: Practice and Principles* (New York: Harper & Row, 1985).

Also, see references under CITY DEVELOPMENT POLITICS AND POLICY—Mayors, Redevelopment Officials, City Negotiators.

Developers

For the profile of James Rouse, we drew on a personal interview, as well as the following published sources: William Fulton, "The Robin Hood of Real Estate," *Planning* 51 (May 1985), 4–10; "James Wilson Rouse," *Fortune*, March 23, 1981, p. 108; Gurney Breckenfeld, "Jim Rouse Shows How to Give Downtown Retailing New Life," *Fortune*, April 10, 1978, pp. 85–91; and "Cities Are Fun," *Time*, August 24, 1981, pp. 42, 53. From Rouse's published views, we reviewed "The Regional Shopping Center: Its Role in the Community It Serves" (prepared for the Seventh Urban Design Conference, Harvard Graduate School of Design, April 26, 1963, authors' files); "Must Shopping Centers Be Inhuman," *AF* 116 (June 1962), 105–108; and "You Must Take a Good Look at Your Responsibilities," *SCW* 5 (November 1976), 9–12.

For the profile of Ernest Hahn, we drew on a series of personal interviews, as well as interviews with long-time associates and staff, in particular, John Gilchrist, Jr., Ronald Hahn, Harry Newman, Jr., and Albert Sussman. We made use of "The Half Billion Dollar House That Hahn Built," *National Mall Monitor* 9 (May–June 1979), 45–52; and "Interview: Ernest Hahn: 'We'll Have Stable Growth . . . ,'" *SCW* 6 (February 1977), 13–16.

The comment on developers as masters of long-drawn-out negotiations is from Leonard L. Farber, "Shopping Centers in the 1960s" (address to ICSC Conference, San Francisco, May 2, 1960).

Conflicts of Interest

We cite a number of potentially troublesome conflicts. The primary court case on whether deal-by-deal city assistance is unfair to business competitors is *Lartnec v. Fort Wayne–Allen County Convention and Tourism Authority*, cited in *Land Use Digest* (ULI), November 15, 1985, p. 1.

As a prime illustration of the problems cities can encounter when they act as both regulator and developer, we draw on New York's handling of the disposition of the Coliseum site at Columbus Circle. We made use of the following newspaper and journal accounts that chronicled the controversy: Robert Lenzner, "N.Y. Legislator Attacks Contract Given Zuckerman," *BG*, September 25, 1986, p. 43; Alan Finder, "Salomon Threatens to Withdraw from Project on Columbus Circle," *NYT*, February 6, 1987, p. B3; Ada Louise Huxtable, "Creeping Gigantism in Manhattan," *NYT*, March 22, 1987, p. 2H; Robert Campbell, "New York: Quick Cash, Bad Planning," *BG*, September 8, 1987, p. 60; Albert Scardino, "They'll Take Manhattan," *NYT Magazine*, pt. 2, December 7, 1986, pp. 34–37; David W. Dunlap, "Suit Is Filed to Halt Towers at Coliseum Site," *NYT*, June 7, 1987, p. 39; Jane Gross, "Two Big West Side Projects Fuel Anti-Development Sentiment," *NYT*, November 29, 1987, p. 1; Thomas J. Lueck, "Judge in New York Strikes Down Sale of Coliseum Site," *NYT*, December 8, 1987, p. A1; Elizabeth Kolbert and Joyce Purnick, "For New York, Coliseum Setback and a Costly Victory," *NYT*, December 9, 1987, p. B1; John Taylor, "The Shadow: The Uproar over the Big Coliseum Project," *New York*, October 5, 1987, pp. 40–48; and Brendan Gill, "The Sky Line: On the Brink," *New Yorker*, November 9, 1987, pp. 113–126. In addition, we used the following *NYT* articles: Thomas J. Lueck, "Hundreds Protest Coliseum Tower Plan," October 19, 1987, p. B3; Thomas J. Lueck, "Brokerage Quits Coliseum Site Project," December 4, 1987, p. B1; Thomas J. Lueck, "Coliseum Developer to Revise Plans," December 5, 1987, p. 31; Paul Goldberger, "Coliseum Plan Will Get New Architect," December 16, 1987, p. B1; Joyce Purnick, "Why the Columbus Circle Plan is Shaky," December 17, 1987, p. B1.

On the subject of corruption and the revolving door syndrome in the defense industry, we made use of Richard Halloran, "The Trouble with Defense

Contractors," *NYT Magazine,* December 8, 1985, pp. 142–154; William Proxmire, "Cleaning Up Procurement: Why Military Contracting Is Corrupt," *NYT,* December 15, 1985, p. F3; and Mark Thompson, "GAO Study Indicates Pentagon-Industry Revolving Door," *BG,* August 31, 1986, p. 17. With regard to New York's experience, see Joyce Purnick, "Three More High City Officials Resign as Shake-up Continues," *NYT,* February 27, 1986, p. B1; and Neal R. Peirce, "The Ethics of Revolving-doorism," *BG,* June 23, 1986, p. 16.

Key issues surrounding the privatization of the city have to do with a blurring of distinctions between public and private activities. Our analysis of the change in downtown environments focuses on two trends: the use of open, common areas in private developments as public spaces and the private control of public spaces. For a good critical reaction to the movement of street-level activity indoors and to skyways, see William H. Whyte's commentary, "The Humble Street: Can It Survive?" *Historic Preservation* 32 (January–February 1980), 34–41. Also, for a city's disappointing result from a public-private understanding, see "Cincinnati Critics Assert Public Atrium Is 'Vapid' and Lacking in Amenities," *NYT,* January 2, 1983, p. 18.

Is the Mall a Public Place? For a discussion of the legal issues surrounding the question, the most informative source is Steven J. Eagle, "Shopping Center Control: The Developer Besieged," *Journal of Urban Law* 51 (1974), 585–647. The legal cases on public access and free speech in malls cited in the text are Hague v. CIO, 307 U.S. 496 (1939), and Lloyd Corp. v. Tanner, 407 U.S. 551 (1972), as cited by Howard Ball, "Careless Justice," *Polity* 11 (Winter 1978), 200–228; and Donald P. Batchelder v. Allied Stores International, Inc., 388 Mass. 83 (1983); Pruneyard Shopping Center v. Robins, 447 U.S. 74, 81 (1980).

Other sources covering the issue are Louis G. Redstone, *New Dimensions in Shopping Centers and Stores* (New York: McGraw-Hill, 1973); Jack H. Morris, "Shopping Centers: Main Street Moves to the Mall," *WSJ,* February 20, 1969; Robert Lindsey, "A Patchwork of Rulings on Free Speech at Malls," *NYT,* February 10, 1986, p. A12; David Margolick, "Albany High Court Lets Malls Restrict Leafleting," *NYT,* December 20, 1985, p. A1; Margaret Hunter, "Fighting Access," *Shopping Centers Today* (August 1987), 1; "Horton Plaza in Access Action," *Shopping Centers Today* (May 1987), 26; and Margaret Hunter, "Malls Broadly Allow Access, Survey Shows," *Shopping Centers Today* (June 1986), 1.

Information on the planned protest for Horton Plaza is from an interview with Mark Kruse, corporate counsel, Hahn Company, August 6, 1987; and decision on appeal, Horton Plaza Associates v. Playing for Real Theatre, 184 Cal. App. 3d 10 (1986).

Much of the material on public access and free speech in malls also covers issues of private control of public space. In addition, we made use of Martin Tolchin, "Private Guards Get New Role in Public Law Enforcement," *NYT,* November 29, 1985, p. A1; and Clifford D. Shearing and Philip C. Stenning, "Private Security: Implications for Social Control," *Social Problems* 30 (June 1983), 493–506. Data on private security forces in in-town malls come from a survey of fifty large shopping centers conducted by ICSC during the fall of 1985.

The discussion of the attempts to privatize the operation and maintenance of Bryant Park in Manhattan is drawn from a series of articles in the *New York Times:* Deirdre Carmody, "Vast Rebuilding of Bryant Park Planned," December 1, 1983, p. A1; Paul Goldberger, "The 'New' Bryant Park: A Plan of Pros and Cons," December 1, 1983, p. B2; Deirdre Carmody, "City Offers Legislation for Privately Run Restaurant in Bryant Park," May 27, 1984, p. 43; Deirdre Carmody, "Cafe Cluster in Plans for Bryant Park," April 21, 1986, p. 81; Sara Rimer, "Restaurateur Withdraws Proposal for Bryant Park," March 19, 1986, p. B1; and Deirdre Carmody, "Questions about Restaurant Stall Bryant Park Redesign," December 1, 1986, p. B2.

Additional references on the uses of commercialism and public spaces are Robert Campbell, "Copley Square Provides Rare Second Chance," *BG*, January 10, 1984, p. 30; William Kornblum and Vernon Boggs, "Redevelopment and the Night Frontier," *City Almanac* 18 (Summer 1985), 16–18; and Charlotte Curtis, "Fighting the Nation's Fortresses," *NYT*, March 11, 1986, p. C13.

7 Architectural Criticism

Uncovering critiques of shopping centers proved to be difficult. To architects who saw their role as stylists of beautiful buildings, the regional shopping center was too undistinguished to merit review. Until the mall moved downtown, critics generally ignored it. Most of the criticism, however, was implicit, tied to the suburb bashing of the 1950s and 1960s. See, for example, a review of Victor Gruen and Larry Smith's book, *Shopping Towns, U.S.A.*, by Sibyl Moholy-Nagy, "If Shopping Centers Must Be," *PA* 41 (September 1960), 204, 207. Also Serge Chermayeff, "The Shape of Privacy (1961)," and "Environmental Design and Change (1966)," in Richard Plunz, ed., *Design and the Public Good: Selected Writings 1930–1980 by Serge Chermayeff* (Cambridge: MIT Press, 1982), pp. 47–70; and Vincent Scully, "American's Architectural Nightmare: The Motorized Megalopolis," *Holiday* 39 (March 1966), 94–95, 142–143.

There were a few exceptions, critics who saw some attributes of the regional mall that could help downtown—Grady Clay, for example: "Plenty of Action: Suggestions for the City Square," *American Institute of Architects Journal* 30 (September 1958), 27–36; "What Makes a Good Square Good?" in Editors of Fortune, *The Exploding Metropolis* (Garden City, New York: Doubleday, 1958), pp. 166–172; and "Outside of the Mall Is Mistake, But Inside Is a Real Wonderland," *Courier-Journal* (Louisville), March 25, 1962. Also Jane Jacobs, in *Death and Life of American Cities*, comments objectively on regional centers; see pp. 162, 346–349. For a critical review of shopping centers written much later, on the twentieth anniversary of Southdale, see historian Neil Harris's analysis, "Spaced-Out at the Shopping Center," *New Republic*, December 13, 1975, pp. 23–26.

Once the mall moved downtown, architectural critics took notice. Articles covering the topic appeared in many of the professional journals; see Suzanne Stephens, "Introversion and the Urban Context," *PA* 59 (December 1978), 49–53; Roberta Brandes Gratz, "Downtown Devitalized," *PA* 62 (July 1981), 82; and Margaret F. Gaskie, "Shopping Centers," *Architectural Record* 170 (April 1982), 124–129. In "Shopping Goes to Town," *PA* 62 (July 1981), 81, David Morton writes about what downtown shopping centers can be if the Milan Galleria, and not the suburban transplant, is the model. Robert Campbell's article in the *Boston Globe*, "Applying Old Ideas to New Buildings," December 12, 1984, p. A36, provides a good commentary on design concepts behind the downtown centers.

As the first major festival center successfully attracting people downtown again, Faneuil Hall was reviewed by numerous critics. See Jane Davison, "Bringing Life to the Market," *NYT Magazine*, October 10, 1976, pp. 74–78; Ada Louise Huxtable, "Why You Always Win and Lose in Urban Renewal," *NYT*, September 19, 1976, p. 34D; Calvin Trillin, "U.S. Journal: New England," *New Yorker*, May 16, 1977, pp. 101–107; and Gurney Breckenfeld, "Jim Rouse Shows How to Give Downtown Retailing New Life," *Fortune*, April 10, 1978, pp. 84–91. One of the most insightful reviews was Robert Campbell's discussion of Faneuil Hall Marketplace as a halfway house for people learning to love cities again, "Evaluation: Boston's 'Upper of Urbanity,' " *American Institute of Architects Journal*, 70 (June 1981), 24–31.

Other festival centers built by Rouse were also covered by the national media and trade journals. "Roundtable on Rouse," *PA* 62 (July 1981), 100–106 presents a critique of Harborplace, South Street Seaport, and Faneuil Hall; also see Gurney Breckenfeld, "The Rouse Show Goes National," *Fortune*, July 27, 1981, pp. 48–54. A frequent commentator on cities, *New York Times* architectural critic Paul Goldberger comments briefly on Baltimore's Harborplace (and Detroit's Renaissance Center) in *On the Rise* (New York: Penguin Books, 1985).

When Horton Plaza opened, reviews could again be found in national as well as local newspapers. We used: Donald Canty, "San Diego Gets an Exuberant New Downtown Development," *Architecture* 74 (November 1985), 16; Robert Guenther, "Horton Plaza May Introduce Shopping Centers' New Look," *WSJ*, June 26, 1985, p. 29; Robert Lindsey, "New Life for San Diego's Downtown," *NYT*, April 27, 1985, p. 7; Robert Lindsey, "San Diego Builds a Village Just to Shop In," *NYT*, August 17, 1985, p. 48; Sam Hall Kaplan, "Horton Plaza: Hope, Hype," *Los Angeles Times*, August 18, 1985, Real Estate p. 1; Paul Goldberger, "Freewheeling Fantasy in San Diego," *NYT*, March 19, 1986, p. A12; Lori Weisberg, "Downtown's Pastel Emporium Is in the Pink," *San Diego Union*, August 10, 1986, p. 1; and "Horton Plaza Lures a Variety of Visitors," *San Diego Union*, August 10, 1986, p. 1.

Coverage of other downtown retail centers was much more selective. For Pike Place Market, we drew on Ann Satterthwaite's analysis, "The Rediscovery of Public Markets as Nuclei of Neighborhoods," *American Institute of Architects Journal* 66 (August 1977), 46–48; and Betty J. Ritter, "Magical Market Place: Seattle's Pike Place Market," *AF* 138 (April 1973), 58–63; and for Plaza

Pasadena, we used John Morris Dixon, "Procession in Pasadena," *PA* 62 (July 1981), 94–97.

For other cities mentioned in the text, see Allen Freeman, "Introverted Trio of MXD's Dominates Atlanta's New Downtown," *American Institute of Architects Journal* 66 (September 1977), 34–37. For Philadelphia's Gallery at Market Street East, see David Morton, "Suburban Shopping Downtown?" *PA* 59 (December 1978), 64–67; and Donald Canty, "Philadelphia's Giant Shopping Machine," *AF* 125 (November 1966), 34–42. For Rouse's regional-type center in Santa Monica, see Barbara Goldstein's review, "A Place in Santa Monica," *PA* 62 (July 1981), 84–89. On Chicago's Water Tower Place, see Robert J. Young, "The Malls at Water Tower Place," *AR* 162 (May 1977), 99–104; and Charles Hoyt, "The Seven Level Shopping Mall at Water Tower Place: A Try for a Revolutionary Thing," *AR* 159 (April 1976), 136–140. And on Baltimore's Harborplace, see David Morton, "A New Marketplace with the Vitality of an Old Landmark: Harborplace in Baltimore," *AR* 168 (May 1980), 100–105; and Grady Clay, "The Roving Eye: On Baltimore's Inner Harbor," *Landscape Architecture* 72 (June 1982), 48–53.

8 City Development Politics and Policy

Urban Renewal and Postrenewal Growth Politics

In researching the political background against which city development takes place, we relied on a number of works written by political scientists. One of the earliest and most in-depth studies of urban renewal politics that details the mayor's stake in the process and the role of business coalitions is Raymond E. Wolfinger's case study of New Haven, *The Politics of Progress* (Englewood Cliffs, N.J.: Prentice-Hall, 1974). Another book documenting redevelopment politics is *The Contested City* (Princeton: Princeton University Press, 1983) by John H. Mollenkopf. Focusing on Boston and San Francisco, Mollenkopf describes the conflicts between neighborhood groups and urban renewal administrators that led to the shift from bulldozer tactics to greater citizen participation. Also in this genre is Chester Hartman's *The Transformation of San Francisco* (Totawa, N.J.: Rowman and Allanheld, 1984), which gives a historical review critical of the rebuilding of downtown and account of the growing opposition movement. In the process of telling their stories, Hartman and Mollenkopf detail the downfall of an earlier command-and-control style of renewal personified by San Francisco's renewal chief, Justin Herman. Also see William Lilley III, "Cities and Suburbs: Herman Death Ends an Era," *National Journal*, September 18, 1971, p. 1939.

Another book that provided a valuable anthology of case studies of several cities, from a similarly critical view of growth coalitions and development politics, is *Restructuring the City: The Political Economy of Urban Redevelopment*, ed. Susan Fainstein, Norman Fainstein, Richard Child Hill, Dennis Judd, and Michael P. Smith (New York: Longman Press, 1983). Studies especially useful within that book are: "Crisis in the Motor City: The Politics of Economic

Development in Detroit," pp. 80–125, by Richard Child Hill, in which he defines and discusses the corporate center strategy (on this topic we also draw on "Detroit Gains a Plan and Loses Top Planner," *Planning* 51 [December 1985], 28); Michael P. Smith and Marlene Keller, "Managed Growth and the Politics of Uneven Development in New Orleans," pp. 126–166; Dennis R. Judd, "From Cowtown to Sunbelt: Boosterism and Economic Growth in Denver," pp. 167–201; and Susan S. Fainstein, Norman I. Fainstein, and P. Jefferson Armistead, "San Francisco: Urban Transformation and the Local State," pp. 202–244.

Mayors, Redevelopment Officials, City Negotiators

On the conflicts and cross-pressures big-city mayors faced governing cities in times of tight fiscal conditions and high social tension, see Douglas Yates's, *The Ungovernable City* (Cambridge, Mass.: MIT Press, 1977). For a first-hand account of their motives and strategies for supporting downtown redevelopment, we interviewed Mayors Kevin White (Boston), George Latimer (St. Paul), and Wes Uhlman (Seattle). Other sources on the national attention and future political rewards to mayors from completing successful downtown projects are: James Q. Wilson, "The Mayors vs. the Cities," *Public Interest*, no. 16 (Summer 1969), 25–37; "Latimer Wins Fifth Term by Landslide," *St. Paul Dispatch*, November 9, 1983, p. 1; "Baltimore Spurned a Trend," *BG*, September 20, 1983, p. 13; and "Cities Are Fun!" *Time*, August 24, 1981, pp. 42–53.

The strategies and operating styles of big-city renewal chiefs are described in a number of sources. In his manuscript, *The Competitors*, prepared for the MIT–Harvard Joint Center for Urban Studies, August 10, 1962, Grady Clay profiles San Francisco and Brookline, Massachusetts, in depth and comments in passing on many other cities as of 1960. On Robert Moses, the definitive source is Robert Caro, *The Power Broker* (New York: Knopf, 1974). Other sources include the already referenced works by Hartman and Mollenkopf on Justin Herman and Edward Logue; and Harold Kaplan's essay, "Urban Renewal in Newark," in James Q. Wilson, ed., *Urban Renewal: The Record and the Controversy* (Cambridge, Mass.: MIT Press, 1966), pp. 233–258.

Profiles of redevelopment officials and city negotiators are drawn from personal interviews with John Clise (Seattle), Gerald Trimble (Pasadena, San Diego), Gary Stout (St. Paul), and Stewart Forbes (Boston). In addition, we referred to newspaper articles and other documents from the case study materials.

City Policies for Service Sector Growth

Innumerable articles describe cities' attempts to attract industry. Specific illustrations in the text come from the following sources: on property tax incentives, Albert Scardino, "Trump Finds Big 'Bonus' on Fifth Avenue," *NYT*, February 8, 1986, p. 33; Goldman, Sachs and Co. and Shearson Lehman

Brothers Inc., *Rockefeller Center Properties, Inc.*, prospectus, September 12, 1985; Sam Verhavek, "Buildings Got Tax Breaks, But What Did City Receive?" *NYT*, May 24, 1987, p. 6E; interview with William Spong, Research Division, New York City Department of Finance, August 27, 1986. With reference to the change in priorities in New York occasioned by the fiscal crisis of the mid-1970s, see Martin Gottlieb, "A Decade after the Cutbacks, New York Is a Different City," *NYT*, June 30, 1985, p. 1; Martin Gottlieb, "Battery Project Reflects Changing City Priorities," *NYT*, October 18, 1985, p. B1. For a critical discussion of changing policies favoring the conversion of industrial space to loft housing in Manhattan, see *Loft Living* (Baltimore: Johns Hopkins Press, 1982), by Sharon Zukin.

Critical Views on Growth Politics

With the shift toward a service sector economy and the growth of office towers in downtowns across the country, the politics of redevelopment has come under increasing critical scrutiny. Some works are: Norman I. Fainstein and Susan Fainstein, "Economic Restructuring and the Politics of Land Use Planning in New York City," *Journal of the American Planning Association* 53 (September 1987), 237–248; Michael C. D. Macdonald's journalistic account of redevelopment, *America's Cities: A Report on the Myth of Urban Renaissance* (New York: Simon and Schuster, 1984); Norman Krumholz's informal comment, "Recovery of Cities: An Alternate View," in Paul Porter and David C. Sweet, *Rebuilding America's Cities: Roads to Recovery* (New Brunswick: Center for Urban Policy Research, 1984), pp. 173–190; and Joe R. Feagin's ideological attack on development in *The Urban Real Estate Game* (Englewood Cliffs, N.J.: Prentice-Hall, 1983).

The resistance-to-growth movement, as Ada Louise Huxtable pointed out in an essay in her book *Will They Ever Finish Bruckner Boulevard?* (New York: Macmillan, 1971), pp. 27–29, goes back to the 1920s when the intellectual community decried the first wave of city skyscrapers. As discussed in the last chapter of text, today's antigrowth movement is centered in California, with popular sentiment expressing itself in big-city growth-control moratoriums and linkage policies. See Robert Lindsey, "California Voters Calling Halt to Uncontrolled City Growth," *NYT*, November 15, 1986, p. 1; "Ballot Measures," *California Planning and Development Report* 1 (December 1986), 4; Gerald D. Adams, "A Last-Ditch Effort to Save Downtown San Francisco," *Planning* 50 (February 1984), 4–11; Robert Reinhold, "Growth in Los Angeles Poses Threat to Bradley," *NYT*, September 22, 1987, p. A16; Douglas Porter, ed., *Downtown Linkages* (Washington, D.C.: ULI, 1985).

Jobs and Redevelopment

A central part of the debate over the new downtowns revolves around the question of whether service sector employment growth is creating "good" or "bad" jobs. The issue has a sizable literature. Our sources on the character of downtown employment are: Aaron S. Gurwitz and G. Thomas Kingsley, *The Metropolitan Cleveland Economy* (Santa Monica, Calif.: Rand Corporation, 1982); Ruth Eckdish Knack, "Pittsburgh's Glitter and Gloom," *Planning* 51 (December 1985), 4–11; and John D. Kasarda, "Urban Change and Minority Opportunities," in Paul E. Peterson, *The New Urban Reality* (Washington, D.C.: Brookings Institution, 1985), pp. 33–68.

Information on jobs and education is from Daniel E. Chall, "New York City's 'Skills Mismatch,' " *Federal Reserve Bank of New York Quarterly Review* 10 (Spring 1985), 20–27. Data on Manhattan's share of New York jobs come from Samuel M. Ehrenhalt, "Growth in the New York City Economy: Problems and Promise" (paper presented to Eighteenth Annual Institute on Challenges of the Changing Economy of New York City, New York City Council on Economic Education, May 8, 1985); and Alexander Reid, "Growth in Finance Jobs Slackens in Manhattan," *NYT*, December 15, 1985, p. 59.

In discussing service sector job generation, we cite the record for selected cities where data on jobs, wage levels, and incomes have been analyzed by economic specialists. For Pittsburgh we consulted a study by Louis Jacobson, "Labor Mobility and Structural Change in Pittsburgh," *Journal of the American Planning Association* 53 (Autumn 1987), 438–448. For New York the data come from Samuel M. Ehrenhalt, "Insight and Outlook: The New York Experience as a Service Economy" (paper presented at Nineteenth Annual Institute on Challenges of the Changing Economy of New York City, May 14, 1986). For Boston we analyzed data from Massachusetts Division of Employment Security, Economic Research and Analysis Service, "Selected Occupational Wages in Manufacturing Industries" (May, June 1986), and "Selected Occupational Wages in Service Industries" (April, May 1987). Wage distribution data for 1985 were calculated by Bennett Harrison and Barry Bluestone based on *March, 1985 Current Population Survey*, reported in Harrison and Bluestone, *The Great U-Turn* (New York: Basic Books, 1988). Data on blacks in service sector jobs come from U.S. Department of Labor Bureau of Labor Statistics, *Geographic Profile of Employment and Unemployment 1985*, Bulletin 2266 (September 1986), table 25.

Newspaper accounts of the problems of recruiting qualified employees are by Elizabeth Neuffer, "Companies Cite Poor Skills in Entry-Level Applicants," *NYT*, July 4, 1987, p. 29, and Louis Uchitelle, "America's Army of Non-Workers," *NYT*, September 27, 1987, p. 1F.

The story of how cities have begun to negotiate for jobs for city residents draws on a number of sources. Mayor Coleman Young's active policy to bring Detroit's minority entrepreneurs into the bidding for city contracts is described in Richard C. Hill's article, "Crisis in the Motor City," in Susan Fainstein et al., *Restructuring the City* (New York: Longman Press, 1983). The description of Oakland's initiatives to give local residents a direct stake in downtown development comes from several sources: Robert Mier, "Job Generation as a Road to Recovery," in Paul Porter and David C. Sweet, *Rebuilding America's Cities* (New Brunswick, N.J.: Center for Urban Policy Research, 1984), pp. 160–172; Robert Lindsey, "Oakland 'Renaissance' Is One of Many in the West," *NYT*, November 17, 1985, p. 4E; Susan E. Clarke, "More Autonomous Policy Orientations: An Analytic Framework," in Clarence N. Stone and Heywood T. Sanders, eds., *The Politics of Urban Development* (Lawrence, Kansas: University Press of Kansas, 1987), pp. 105–124. In the case of Baltimore's initiatives for minority construction jobs and merchant positions at Harborplace, we drew on information from our interview with James Rouse; U.S. Commission on Civil Rights, *Urban Minority Economic Development: Hearing Held in Baltimore, Maryland, November 17–18, 1981*, testimony of James W. Rouse, pp. 256–257, 259; and U.S. Commission on Civil Rights, *Greater Baltimore Commitment* (Washington, D.C.: U.S. Commission on Civil Rights, 1983), pp. 56–57. Information on Copley Place comes from Keri Lung, "The Job Linkage Approach to Community Economic Development" (Master's thesis, MIT, June 1985). Information on San Diego's efforts was provided by Hal Scott, economic development coordinator, Private Industry Council, San Diego, California, March 13, 1986.

Hiding Hand Strategies

Political strategies to get downtown projects built relied heavily on techniques of off-budget financing, whose sources are referenced under FINANCING DOWNTOWN REDEVELOPMENT. Our discussion of a second critical factor, what development economist Albert Hirshman defined as the "hiding hand," draws on his insightful rendering of this concept in chapter 1 of his book, *Development Projects Observed* (Washington, D.C.: Brookings Institution, 1967). The example of Ernest Hahn's intuitive application of the principle is from Robert Showley, "Hahn's Perseverance Turned a Dream into Reality," *San Diego Union*, August 8, 1985, Downtown, p. 17.

9 Downtown Agenda

Offices

The competitive advantage of cities to hold and attract the types of service sector jobs that demand face-to-face communication was articulated by Raymond Vernon in his study of New York reported in *The Changing Economic Function of the Central City* (New York: Committee for Economic Development, 1959). A recent analysis of the problems of attracting manufacturing industry is Roger W. Schmenner, "Industrial Location and Urban Public Management," in Arthur P. Solomon, ed., *The Prospective City* (Cambridge, Mass.: MIT Press, 1980), pp. 446–448.

The term *corporate center strategy* comes from Richard Child Hill's analysis of Detroit's push to develop the office sector economy, "Crisis in the Motor City: The Politics of Economic Development in Detroit," in S. Fainstein et al., *Restructuring the City* (New York: Longman Press, 1983), pp. 80–125. Information on the growth of speculative office construction comes from several sources: Urban Investment and Development Co., "Downtown Office Construction in Major U.S. Cities" (Chicago: Urban Investment and Development Co., 1984); Urban Investment and Development Co., "Downtown Indicators Report: 1983" (Chicago: Urban Investment and Development Co., 1983); and William C. Wheaton and Raymond G. Torto, "The National Office Market, History and Future Prospects, III," Working Paper (MIT Center for Real Estate Development, January 1986). For estimates of the inventory of office space as of 1960, see Regina B. Armstrong, "National Trends in Office Construction, Employment and Headquarter Location in U.S. Metropolitan Areas," in P. W. Daniels, ed., *Spatial Patterns of Office Growth and Location* (New York: John Wiley, 1979), pp. 88–90. Also see John Avault and Mark Johnson, "A Survey of Commercial and Institutional Development in Boston's Neighborhoods 1975–1989, Part IV" (Boston: Boston Redevelopment Authority Policy Development and Research Department, April 1987).

Manufacturing employment estimates are from William C. Wheaton and Raymond G. Torto, "The National Office Market: History and Future Prospects, II" (Cambridge, Mass.: MIT Center for Real Estate Development, February 1985). The discussion of factors leading to increased office employment is based on Thomas J. Stanback, Jr. and Thierry J. Noyelle, *Cities in Transition* (Totowa, N.J.: Allanheld, Osmun, 1982), chap. 2; data on service employment are from Thierry J. Noyelle, *New Technologies and Services* (College Park, Md.: University of Maryland Institute for Urban Studies, 1985).

Future prospects for office construction are drawn from David Birch, *America's Office Needs: 1985–1995* (Cambridge, Mass.: MIT Center for Real Estate Development, 1986). Labor force projections are from George Sternlieb, *Patterns of Development* (New Brunswick, N.J.: Rutgers Center for Urban Policy Research, 1986), p. 236. Also see William C. Wheaton, "Population and Employment Decentralization in America's Major Metropolitan Areas: 1967–1983," Working Paper No. 4 (Cambridge, Mass.: MIT Center for Real Estate Development, November 1986).

For definitions and examples of different types of downtown hotels, see Laventhol and Horwath, *Hotel/Motel Development* (Washington, D.C.: ULI, 1984). For the numbers of new hotel rooms in selected cities, we referred to Urban Investment and Development Co., "Downtown Indicators Report: 1983" (Chicago: Urban Investment and Development Co., 1983), tables G-6, G-7, and *Gavel*, an annual listing of hotels by city for convention planners, tabulations from editions 1973 and 1984. We also made comparisons of the downtown hotel inventory over time by using AAA travel guides.

Convention Centers

A good source on the topic is Dennis R. Judd and Margaret Collins, "The Case of Tourism: Political Coalitions and Redevelopment in the Central Cities," in Gary A. Tobin, ed., *The Changing Structure of the City* (Beverly Hills, Calif.: Sage Publications, 1979), pp. 177–199. For information on typical dollar expenditures by tourists, we also drew from David Listokin, "The Convention Trade: A Competitive Economic Prize," *Real Estate Issues* 10 (Fall–Winter 1985), 43–46.

To build convention centers, cities had to find ways to pay for them, manage construction cost overruns, and answer the critics. Other sources on these issues are: "Convention Centers: Urban White Elephants?" *U.S. News and World Report*, August 30, 1982, pp. 61–62; Harold Henderson, "Meet Me in Peoria . . . Rockford . . . Danville," *Planning* 48 (November 1982), 16–17; Dave Ahearn,"Convention Center Boom Continues as Cities Try to Boost Local Economies," *Bond Buyer*, January 17, 1983, p. 1; and "Boston Convention Center: High Hopes and Critics," *NYT*, November 9, 1986, p. 50. Reference to the Louisiana Superdome is from Dan McGuinness, "Convention Centers: Too Much of a Good Thing?" *Planning* 48 (November 1982), 13–15; and for New York's Javits Center, Deirdre Carmody, "Center Chiefs Ponder Space, Inside and Out," *NYT*, March 3, 1986, p. B1.

Housing

For notes on sources on the gentrification trend and its importance to cities, see THE URBAN CRISIS—Downtown Comeback.

Stadiums

There has been little systematic study of cities and their drive for big league sports teams. A good analysis is Arthur T. Johnson, "Economic and Policy Implications of Hosting Sports Franchises: Lessons from Baltimore," Working Paper 4, Maryland Institute for Policy Analysis and Research (Catonsville, Md.: University of Maryland, Baltimore County, 1984). Also see Arthur T. Johnson, "Municipal Administration and the Sports Franchise Relocation Issue," *Public Administration Review* 43 (November–December 1983), 519–528.

For additional background material and current events, we relied on numerous newspaper or other media accounts. In particular, see "The MacNeil/ Lehrer News Hour," Public Broadcasting Network, July 11, 1984, transcript; Peter Gammons, "World Series Is Civic Pride," *BG*, October 8, 1984, p. 27; Julia Vitullo-Martin, "Econoclast—Yankee Stadium: A Good Principle Badly Implemented," *Fiscal Observer*, October 12, 1978, pp. 13–14; Sam Roberts, "City as Landlord: A Tenant Is Paid to Stay and Play," *NYT*, April 13, 1987, p. B1; James Galtuso, "Why Congress Is Out-of-Bounds If It Makes Rules for Football," *Backgrounder* (Heritage Foundation), July 9, 1985; and New York State Urban Development Corporation, "Sportsplex Recommends 20,000 Seat Open Air Sports Stadium for Buffalo," news release, June 5, 1984; also "U.D.C. Vote Backs Buffalo Stadium," *NYT*, December 20, 1985, p. B2.

On the symbolic importance of being in the "big leagues," see Hal Lancaster, "Tale of Two Cities: Why Football Mesmerizes Baltimore, Indianapolis," *WSJ*, January 14, 1986, p. 27; Ruth Eckdish Knack, "Stadiums: The Right Game Plan?" *Planning* 52 (September 1986), 6–11; Hal Lancaster, "Stadium Projects Are Proliferating amid Debate over Benefit to Cities," *WSJ*, March 20, 1987, p. 37; and Ben A. Franklin, "Battle over Plan for Baltimore Stadiums Takes on Epic Tone," *NYT*, June 21, 1987, p. 39. On the topic of design, see

Hal Lancaster, "Despite New Technologies, Design Problems Remain," *WSJ*, March 20, 1987, p. 37.

City Boosterism

Cities do much to promote their cause. For accounts of their wide-ranging activities, we made use of "Pittsburgh Gives a Luncheon to Try Out Its New Image," *NYT*, February 28, 1984, p. B1; Sara Rimer, "Of Cheese, Plant Closings and a City on a Comeback," *NYT*, November 13, 1986, p. B1; Deirdre Carmody, "Brooklyn Bridge Birthday Is Hometown Celebration," *NYT*, May 25, 1983, p. A1; "100th Birthday: A Glance Back," May 26, 1983, p. B3; and William Robbins, "Cities Going Where the Business Is," *NYT*, June 24, 1984, p. E3. Also, "Knoxville 1982 World's Fair: The Start of Something Big," *Weekly Bond Buyer*, March 8, 1982, p. 1; William E. Schmidt, "The Desolate Legacy of Knoxville's World's Fair," *NYT*, May 18, 1984, p. A10; and "The 1982 World's Fair Site in Knoxville, Tennessee," *Land Use Digest*, July 15, 1984, p. 3.

10 Financing Downtown Redevelopment

The Public Side

There is a short literature on the money behind downtown development but no systematic data on the sources of project financing. To research project financing, we relied on primary source materials for our case studies, as well as secondary materials to create our own data base. We collected data on the public share of total development cost, sources of public money, source of long-term mortgage financing, and the incidence of profit-sharing arrangements for a sample of thirty-nine downtown projects that included at least 50,000 square feet of retail space. (This group is part of the larger sample of seventy-five downtown retail projects for which we collected data on the roles of government, the size and character of the retail activity, as well as other descriptive information on the project. See PROJECTS for the list of projects.) For sixteen projects with profit-sharing arrangements, we followed up with telephone interviews on the status of revenues coming to cities.

The main sources for information on individual projects are: J. Thomas Black, Libby Howland, and Stuart L. Rogel, *Downtown Retail Development: Conditions for Success and Project Profiles* (Washington, D.C.: ULI, 1983); International Council of Shopping Centers, "Issues in Downtown Retail Development: An Overview of Recent Experience," Shopping Center Report (New York: ICSC, 1984); National Council for Urban Economic Development, *Coordinated Urban Economic Development: A Case Study Analysis* (Washington, D.C.: NCUED, 1978); ULI, *Joint Development: Making the Transit Connection Work* (Washington, D.C.: ULI, 1979), pp. 33–62; ULI, *Mixed-Use Development Projects in North America: Project Profiles* (Washington, D.C.: ULI, 1983); ULI, project reference files, selected issues, 1971–1986 (see listing under PROJECTS); Rachelle L. Levitt, ed., *Cities Reborn* (Washington, D.C.: ULI, 1987); selected articles in *UL* and *PA*; and authors' newspaper clip files supplemented by telephone inquiries.

A good descriptive piece on the range of tools cities can use to facilitate public-private development is Gary E. Stout and Joseph E. Vitt, "Public Incentives and Financing Techniques for Codevelopment," ULI Development Component Series (Washington, D.C.: ULI, 1982). Two other general sources on revenue financing proved to be helpful: Virginia L. Horler, *Guide to Public Debt Financing in California* (San Francisco: Rauscher Pierce Refsnes, 1982); and Philip J. Fischer, Ronald W. Forbes, and John E. Petersen, "Risk and Return in the Choice of Revenue Bond Financing," *Governmental Finance* (September 1980), 9–13.

On the role of UDAG money, see the references for BUSINESS AND CITIES— Evolution of Public-Private Relationships. Also see John R. Gist, "Urban Development Action Grants: Design and Implementation," in Donald B. Rosenthal, ed., *Urban Revitalization* (Beverly Hills: Sage Publications, 1980), vol. 18, Urban Affairs Annual Reviews, pp. 237–252; and "The UDAG Program," *UL* 44 (April 1985), 36–37.

Off-Budget Financing

A good, succinct description of the off-budget character of federal urban renewal financing is Charles Abrams, *The City is the Frontier* (New York: Harper Colophon, 1956), pp. 98–123. Also see Martin Anderson, *The Federal Bulldozer* (Cambridge, Mass.: MIT Press, 1964), chap. 8. For a study of the ways by which cities raised revenue in the 1960s, see Arnold J. Meltsner, *The Politics of City Revenue* (Berkeley: University of California Press, 1971).

For the 1970s and 1980s, tax-increment financing (TIF) was one of the most widely used off-budget techniques in public-private development deals. For a primer on states that have the necessary enabling legislation, see Jack R. Huddleston, "A Comparison of State Tax Increment Financing Law," *State Government* 55 (1982), 29–33. For a good description of how TIF works and an overview of its pros and cons, see Robert Sabatini, *Tax Increment Financing: Municipal Finance of Development, Redevelopment, and Rehabilitation* (Cambridge: Harvard Graduate School of Design, 1978).

We also relied on the expertise of Joseph Coomes and Gerald Trimble, who explained the intricate structures of public-private redevelopment financing. Especially valuable is a paper by Joseph E. Coomes, Jr., "Problem Solving through Redevelopment Agreements" (prepared for a conference titled Making Better Use of Urban Space, sponsored by the Lincoln Institute of Land Policy, February 11–12, 1983).

Two good pieces that take a critical look at TIF are: George Lefcoe, "When Governments Become Land Developers: Notes on the Public-Sector Experience in the Netherlands and California," Lincoln Institute for Land Policy Monograph No. 78-3 (Cambridge, Mass., 1978); and Jack Huddleston, "Variations in Development Subsidies under Tax Increment Financing," *Land Economics* 57 (August 1981), 373–384.

The problem of accountability is the central focus of a good book by Herman B. Leonard, which examines the many forms of off-budget financing, *Checks Unbalanced: The Quiet Side of Government Spending* (New York: Basic Books, 1986). Similar concerns at the municipal level are evident in a report sponsored by the Minneapolis Citizens League, "Accountability for the Development Dollar," prepared by Role of Cities in Real Estate Development Committee, Citizens League, Minneapolis, June 20, 1985.

With the passage of the 1986 Tax Reform Act, the use of TIF is likely to diminish. Our discussion of redevelopment financing in the future draws on John E. Petersen, "Tax-Exempts and Tax Reform: Assessing the Consequences of the Tax Reform Act of 1986 for the Municipal Securities Market" (Washington, D.C.: Government Finance Research Center, December 1986); John E. Petersen and Cathie G. Eitelberg, "The Tax Reform Act of 1986: Major Provisions Affecting the Tax-Exempt Securities Market" (Washington, D.C.: Government Finance Officers Association, 1986); and U.S. Congress, House Report 99-841, *Tax Reform Act of 1986: Conference Report to Accompany H.R. 3838*, 99th Cong., 2d sess., September 18, 1986.

The Private Side

To research the story behind the private financing of downtown development, we relied primarily on our case studies and interviews with Ernest W. Hahn, John Gilchrist, Jr., Randy Foxworthy, William Greenough, Carol Nichols, Jill Ker Conway, Bruce Hayden, and A. Jerry Keyser.

The problems Rouse experienced lining up construction financing for Faneuil Hall were typical of the times. Permanent financing was easier to come by only because Teachers Insurance and Annuity Association (TIAA) backed the pioneering downtown projects. In researching TIAA's role, we reviewed the pension fund's portfolio composition, level of mortgage investments, investment returns, and policy directions as revealed in its annual reports for selected years covering 1960–1987.

Other sources are: Martin Cleary, "Shopping Center: A Lender's Perspective," in *Shopping Centers: U.S.A.*, ed. George Sternlieb and James W. Hughes (New Brunswick, N.J.: Rutgers Center for Urban Policy Research, 1981); and George R. Puskar, "Regional Malls: A Preferred Institutional Investment," *Real Estate Finance Journal* 3 (Summer 1987), 77–83.

11 Cities

Baltimore

Grady Clay, "The Roving Eye: On Baltimore's Inner Harbor," *Landscape Architecture* 72 (November 1982), 48–53; Joseph Stellar, "A MXD Takes Off:

Baltimore's Inner Harbor," *UL* 41 (March 1982), 11–19; Katharine Lyall, "A Bicycle Built-for-Two: Public-Private Partnership in Baltimore," in R. Scott Fosler and Renee A. Berger, *Public-Private Partnership in American Cities* (Lexington, Mass.: Lexington Books, 1982), pp. 17–57; Dean Schwanke, Eric Smart, and Helen J. Kessler, "Looking at MXDs," *UL* 45 (December 1986), 20–25; U.S. Commission on Civil Rights, *Greater Baltimore Commitment* (Washington, D.C.: U.S. Commission on Civil Rights, 1983), pp. 56–57; "Baltimore Spurned a Trend," *BG*, September 20, 1983, p. 13; and Ben A. Franklin, "Battle over Plan for Baltimore Stadiums Takes on Epic Tone," *NYT*, June 21, 1987, p. 39.

Boston

Langley C. Keyes, *The Rehabilitation Planning Game* (Cambridge, Mass.: MIT Press, 1969); John H. Mollenkopf, *The Contested City* (Princeton: Princeton University Press, 1983); and Rachelle L. Levitt, *Cities Reborn* (Washington, D.C.: ULI, 1987), pp. 9–53.

"The 90 Million Dollar Development Plan," *City Record* (Boston), September 24, 1960, pp. 755–774; "The Livable City," *BG*, November 11, 1984; Joseph Giovanni, "Boston Waterfront: At 25, a Model Urban Renewal," *NYT*, September 21, 1986; Robert Campbell, "Copley Square Provides Rare Second Chance," *BG*, January 10, 1984, p. 30; "Boston Convention Center: High Hopes and Critics," *NYT*, November 9, 1986, p. 50; and Keri Lung, "The Job Linkage Approach to Community Economic Development" (Master's thesis, MIT, 1985).

John Avault and Mark Johnson, "A Survey of Development by Economic Sector, 1975–1989" (Boston: Boston Redevelopment Authority, April 1987); and Lewis Bolan, "Harborplace and Faneuil Hall Area Study," prepared for Jerry Schlichter, E. St. Louis, Illinois (Washington, D.C.: Leggatt McCall Advisors, July 29, 1985); Boston Redevelopment Authority, *Boston Tomorrow: Background on Development* (Boston: Boston Redevelopment Authority, n.d.); "Resident Workers Share of Boston Jobs" (Boston: Boston Redevelopment Authority Research Department, February 1987).

Los Angeles

Rodolofo F. Acuña, *A Community under Siege*, Monograph 11 (Los Angeles: University of California, Los Angeles Chicano Studies Research Center, 1984); Suzanne Slesin, "Downtown Los Angeles: The New Settlers," *NYT*, April 12, 1984, p. C1; Robert Reinhold, "Growth in Los Angeles Poses Threat to Bradley," *NYT*, September 22, 1987, p. A16.

New York

Raymond Vernon, *The Changing Economic Function of the Central City* (New York: Committee for Economic Development, 1959); Robert A. Caro, *The*

Power Broker (New York: Vintage, 1975); and Sharon Zukin, *Loft Living* (Baltimore: John Hopkins Press, 1982). On the West Village urban renewal controversy, see Jeanne R. Lowe, *Cities in a Race with Time* (New York: Vintage Books, 1968), pp. 98–103; and J. Clarence Davies III, *Neighborhood Groups and Urban Renewal* (New York: Columbia University Press, 1966), pp. 72–109.

Norman I. Fainstein and Susan Fainstein, "Economic Restructuring and the Politics of Land Use Planning in New York City," *Journal of the American Planning Association* 53 (September 1987), 237–248; Martin Gottlieb, "A Decade after the Cutbacks, New York Is a Different City," *NYT*, June 30, 1985, p. 1; Martin Gottlieb, "Battery Project Reflects Changing City Priorities," *NYT*, October 18, 1985, p. B1; Albert Scardino, "Trump Finds Big 'Bonus' on 5th Avenue," *NYT*, February 8, 1986, p. 33; Goldman, Sachs and Co. and Shearson Lehman Brothers Inc., *Rockefeller Center Properties, Inc.*, prospectus, September 12, 1985; Sam Verhavek, "Builders Got Tax Breaks, But What Did City Receive?" *NYT*, May 24, 1987, p. 6E; Jim Sleeper, "Koch's Victory and a Transformed New York," *BG*, September 17, 1985, p. 19; Jeffrey Schmalz, "New York Reaches Accord on Housing," *NYT*, December 27, 1987, p. 1; Charlotte Curtis, "Fighting the Nation's Fortresses," *NYT*, March 11, 1986, p. C13; Alan Finder, "New Peak Is Reported in New York Employees," *NYT*, December 11, 1987, p. 80; Joyce Purnick, "Three More High City Officials Resign as Shake-up Continues," *NYT*, February 27, 1986, p. B1; and Neal R. Peirce, "The Ethics of Revolving-doorism," *BG*, June 23, 1986, p. 16.

Deirdre Carmody, "Center Chiefs Ponder Space, Inside and Out," *NYT*, March 3, 1986, p. B1; Julia Vitullo-Martin, "Econoclast—Yankee Stadium: A Good Principle Badly Implemented," *Fiscal Observer*, October 12, 1978, pp. 13–14; Sam Roberts, "City as Landlord: A Tenant Is Paid to Stay and Play," *NYT*, April 13, 1987, p. B1; Deirdre Carmody, "Brooklyn Bridge Birthday Is Hometown Celebration," *NYT*, May 25, 1983, p. A1; and "100th Birthday: A Glance Back," *NYT*, May 26, 1983, p. B3. Also see references on the Coliseum/Columbus Circle and Bryant Park under PUBLIC-PRIVATE RELATIONSHIPS—Conflicts of Interest.

Samuel M. Ehrenhalt (New York regional commissioner of labor statistics), "Growth in the New York City Economy: Problems and Promise" (paper presented to Eighteenth Annual Institute on Challenges of the Changing Economy of New York City, New York City Council on Economic Education, May 8, 1985); Samuel M. Ehrenhalt, "New York City's Labor Force: Change and Challenge," *City Almanac* 17 (December 1983), pp. 9–10; Samuel M. Ehrenhalt, "Insight and Outlook: The New York Experience as a Service Economy" (paper presented at Nineteenth Annual Institute on Challenges of the Changing Economy of New York City, May 14, 1986); Daniel E. Chall, "New York City's 'Skills Mismatch,' " *Federal Reserve Bank of New York Quarterly Review* 10 (Spring 1985), 20–27; Alexander Reid, "Growth in Finance Jobs Slackens in Manhattan," *NYT*, December 15, 1985, p. 59; and Matthew Drennan, "Economy," in Charles Brecher and Raymond D. Horton, eds., *Setting Municipal Priorities: 1982* (New York: Russell Sage Foundation, 1984), pp. 55–88.

Pittsburgh

Roy Lubove, *Twentieth-Century Pittsburgh* (New York: John Wiley, 1969); Shelby Stewman and Joel A. Tarr, "Four Decades of Public-Private Partnerships in Pittsburgh," in R. Scott Fosler and Renee A. Berger, *Public-Private Partnerships in American Cities* (New York: Committee for Economic Development Research and Policy Committee, 1982), pp. 59–127; Rachelle L. Levitt, *Cities Reborn* (Washington, D.C.: ULI, 1987), pp. 106–146.

Louis Jacobson, "Labor Mobility and Structural Change in Pittsburgh," *Journal of the American Planning Association* 53 (Autumn 1987), 438–448; Ruth Eckdish Knack, "Pittsburgh's Glitter and Gloom," *Planning* 51 (December 1985), 4–11; and "Pittsburgh Gives a Luncheon to Try Out Its New Image," *NYT*, February 28, 1984, p. B1.

San Francisco

Chester Hartman, *The Transformation of San Francisco* (Totawa, N.J.: Rowman and Allanheld, 1984); John H. Mollenkopf, *The Contested City* (Princeton: Princeton University Press, 1983). William Lilley III, "Cities and Suburbs: Herman Death Ends an Era," *National Journal*, September 18, 1971, p. 1939; Susan S. Fainstein, Norman I. Fainstein, and P. Jefferson Armistead, "San Francisco: Urban Transformation and the Local State," in Susan S. Fainstein, Norman I. Fainstein, Richard Child Hill, Dennis Judd, and Michael Peter Smith, *Restructuring the City: The Political Economy of Urban Redevelopment* (New York: Longman, 1983), pp. 202–244; and Gerald D. Adams, "A Last-Ditch Effort to Save Downtown San Francisco," *Planning* 50 (February 1984), 4–11; Grady Clay, "The Competitors" (manuscript prepared for the MIT–Harvard Joint Center for Urban Studies, August 10, 1962).

Other Cities

Atlanta: Calvin Trillin, "U.S. Journal: Atlanta," *New Yorker*, March 29, 1976, pp. 102–106.

Buffalo: New York State Urban Development Corporation, "Sportsplex Recommends 20,000 Seat Open Air Sports Stadium for Buffalo," news release, June 5, 1984; and "U.D.C. Vote Backs Buffalo Stadium," *NYT*, December 20, 1985, p. B2.

Burbank: Kathleen A. Hughes, "MCA May Develop Proposed Project Dropped by Disney," *WSJ*, April 14, 1988.

Cincinnati: Nell Surber and Ralph Bolton, "Fountain Square South: Public/Private Partnership Works in Cincinnati," *UL* 41 (September 1982), 3–5; and

"Cincinnati Critics Assert Public Atrium Is 'Vapid' and Lacking in Amenities," *NYT*, January 2, 1983, p. 18.

Columbus, Ohio: Joseph G. Madonna, "Public/Private Partnership for Downtown Development," *UL* 39 (February 1980), 12–19.

Dallas: Douglas R. Porter, "Deal Making in Dallas: A Primer for Public/Private Negotiations," *UL* 45 (February 1986), 10–13.

Denver: Dennis R. Judd, "From Cowtown to Sunbelt: Boosterism and Economic Growth in Denver," in S. Fainstein et al., *Restructuring the City* (New York: Longman, 1983), pp. 167–201.

Detroit: Richard C. Hill, "Crisis in the Motor City: The Politics of Economic Development in Detroit," in Fainstein et al., *Restructuring the City,* pp. 80–125; "Detroit Gains a Plan and Loses Top Planner," *Planning* 51 (December 1985), 28.

Indianapolis: Hal Lancaster, "Tale of Two Cities: Why Football Mesmerizes Baltimore, Indianapolis," *WSJ*, January 14, 1986, p. 27.

Knoxville: "Knoxville 1982 World's Fair: The Start of Something Big," *Weekly Bond Buyer*, March 8, 1982, p. 1; William E. Schmidt, "The Desolate Legacy of Knoxville's World's Fair," *NYT*, May 18, 1984, p. A10; and "The 1982 World's Fair Site in Knoxville, Tennessee," *Land Use Digest*, 17, July 15, 1984, p. 3.

Louisville: Rachelle L. Levitt, *Cities Reborn* (Washington, D.C.: ULI, 1987); pp. 56–104.

Newark: Harold Kaplan, "Urban Renewal in Newark," in James Q. Wilson, ed., *Urban Renewal: The Record and the Controversy* (Cambridge, Mass.: MIT Press, 1966), pp. 233–258.

New Haven: Raymond E. Wolfinger, *The Politics of Progress* (Englewood Cliffs, N.J.: Prentice-Hall, 1974); and Norman I. Fainstein and Susan Fainstein, "New Haven and the Limits of the Local State," in Fainstein et al., *Restructuring the City*, pp. 27–79.

New Orleans: Michael P. Smith and Marlene Keller, "Managed Growth and the Politics of Uneven Development in New Orleans," in Fainstein et al., *Restructuring the City,* pp. 126–166; and "Convention Centers: Too Much of a Good Thing?" *Planning* 48 (November 1982), 13–15.

Oakland: Robert Mier, "Job Generation as a Road to Recovery," in Paul R. Porter and David C. Sweet, *Rebuilding America's Cities: Roads to Recovery* (New

Brunswick: Center for Urban Policy Research, 1984), pp. 160–172; and Robert Lindsey, "Oakland 'Renaissance' Is One of Many in the West," *NYT*, November 17, 1985, p. 4E.

Santa Monica: William Fulton, "On the Beach with the Progressives," *Planning* 51 (January 1985), 4–9.

St. Louis: E. R. Shipp, "Rebound from Long Decline Is Seen in St. Louis," *NYT*, February 2, 1985; Rachelle L. Levitt, *Cities Reborn* (Washington, D.C.: ULI, 1987); pp. 149–203.

St. Paul: In addition to the material for the Town Square case study, "Latimer Wins Fifth Term by Landslide," *St. Paul Dispatch*, November 9, 1983, p. 1; and on Galtier Plaza, see PUBLIC-PRIVATE RELATIONSHIPS—City Risk Taking.

12 Downtown Projects

BAYSTATE WEST "Baystate West, Springfield, Ma.," ULI Project Reference File, vol. 2 (1972); David Mudgett, "Bringing Excitement Back to Baystate West," *UL* 42 (January 1983), 22–25.

CANAL PLACE Jane A. Brooks and Deborah H. Weeter, "Canal Place: A Clash of Values," *UL* 41 (July 1982), 3–9.

THE CANNERY "Innovative Centers Launched Downtown Trend," *Chain Store Age Executive Edition* (May 1974), E29–E32.

CENTRAL CITY MALL "Central City Mall, San Bernardino, Calif.," Urban Land Institute Project Reference File, vol. 3 (1973); "Nucleus of San Bernardino Redevelopment Is Its Mall," *SCW* 2 (March 1972), 22–26.

COLISEUM/COLUMBUS CIRCLE See references under PUBLIC-PRIVATE RELATIONSHIPS—Conflicts of Interest.

CROWN CENTER SHOPS "The Crown Center Shops, Kansas City, Kansas," ULI Project Reference File, vol. 4 (1974).

FANEUIL HALL MARKETPLACE See CASE STUDY references.

FOUNTAIN SQUARE SOUTH Nell Surber and Ralph Bolton, "Fountain Square South: Public/Private Partnership Works in Cincinnati," *UL* 41 (September 1982), 3–5.

THE GALLERY AT MARKET STREET EAST "The Gallery, Philadelphia, Pa.," ULI Project Reference File, vol. 8 (1978); ULI, *Joint Development: Making the Transit Connection Work* (Washington, D.C.: ULI, 1979), pp. 33–62; David Morton, "Suburban Shopping Downtown?" *PA* 59 (December 1978), 64–67; and Donald Canty, "Philadelphia's Giant Shopping Machine," *AF* 125 (November 1966), 34–42.

GALTIER PLAZA See references under PUBLIC-PRIVATE RELATIONSHIP—City Risk Taking.

GLENDALE GALLERIA Jim Stevens, "New Downtown Mall Is Put Together by Public/Private Team: Glendale Galleria, Part I," *SCW* 5 (October 1976), 22–25; Jim Stevens, "Project's Construction Convinces the Skeptics," *SCW* 5 (January 1977), p. 24; and "Case Study II: Galleria II," in "Issues in Downtown Retail Development: An Overview of Recent Experience," Shopping Center Report (New York: ICSC, 1984), pp. 16–18.

HARBORPLACE and THE INNER HARBOR David Morton, "A New Marketplace with the Vitality of an Old Landmark: Harborplace in Baltimore," *AR* 168 (May 1980), 100–105; Grady Clay, "The Roving Eye: On Baltimore's Inner Harbor," *Landscape Architecture* 72 (June 1982), 48–53; "Inner Harbor, Baltimore," in S. J. Pratter, ed., *Dollars from Design* (Washington, D.C.: National League of Cities, 1981), pp. 17–23; and "Case Study 19: Baltimore, Maryland Charles Center/Inner Harbor," in *Coordinated Urban Economic Development: A Case Study Analysis* (Washington, D.C.: National Council for Urban Economic Development, 1978).

HARTFORD CIVIC CENTER "Case Study 17: Hartford, Connecticut, Hartford Civic Center," in *Coordinated Urban Economic Development: A Case Study Analysis* (Washington, D.C.: National Council for Urban Economic Development, March 1978), pp. 201–211.

HERALD CENTER See RETAILING—Downtown Malls.

HORTON PLAZA See *Case Study* references.

HOUSTON GALLERIA "The Galleria, Houston, Texas," ULI Project Reference File, vol. 1 (1971); "Supercity," *AF* 136 (April 1972), 24–39.

GHIRARDELLI SQUARE "Innovative Centers Launched Downtown Trend," *Chain Store Age Executive Edition* (May 1974), E29–E32.

GRAND AVENUE "The Grand Avenue, Milwaukee, Wisconsin," ULI Project Reference File, vol. 13 (1983); and "Milwaukee's Grand Avenue: An Old Name—A New Look," *Guarantor* (November–December 1982), 2–5.

PIKE PLACE MARKET See CASE STUDY references.

PLAZA PASADENA See CASE STUDY references.

RENAISSANCE CENTER See RETAILING—Downtown Malls.

SANTA MONICA PLACE Barbara Goldstein, "A Place in Santa Monica," *PA* 62 (July 1981), 84–89.

SOUTHDALE Neil Harris, "Spaced-Out at the Shopping Center," *New Republic*, December 13, 1975, pp. 23–26.

ST. ANTHONY MAIN "St. Anthony Main, Minneapolis, Minnesota," ULI Project Reference File, vol. 11 (1981).

TABOR CENTER "Tabor Center, Denver, Colorado," ULI Project Reference File, vol. 17 (1987).

TOWN SQUARE See CASE STUDY references.

WATER TOWER PLACE "The Inside Story on Water Tower Place," *National Mall Monitor* (January–February 1977), 13–16; "Marketers Tell What's Behind the Selling of Water Tower Place," *SCW* 9 (May 1979), 44–46; Robert J. Young,

Selected City Marketplaces, 1971–1985

Name	Date opened	City	Type	New retail space*
Baystate West	1971	Springfield, Mass.	mixed use	204.7
Worcester Center	1971	Worcester, Mass.	mixed use	762.9
ARCO Plaza	1972	Los Angeles	mixed use	225.0
Central City Mall	1972	San Bernardino, Calif.	regional	958.3
Trolley Square	1972	Salt Lake City	specialty	249.7
Broadway Plaza	1973	Los Angeles	mixed use	383.2
IDS Center	1973	Minneapolis	mixed use	na
Courthouse Center	1973	Columbus, Ind.	regional	161.6
Crown Center Shops	1973	Kansas City	mixed use	355.0
ZCMI Center	1974	Salt Lake City	regional	750.0
Civic Center Mall	1975	Hartford, Conn.	mixed use	188.0
Pike Place Market	1976	Seattle	specialty	379.0
Water Tower Place	1976	Chicago	mixed use	668.0
Glendale Galleria	1976	Glendale, Calif.	regional	856.0
New Market at Head House	1976	Philadelphia	specialty	90.0
Fanueil Hall Marketplace	1976	Boston	specialty	219.0
Tandy Center Mall	1977	Fort Worth, Texas	mixed use	323.0
Market at Citicorp Center	1977	New York	mixed use	65.0
Lexington Center	1977	Lexington, Ky.	mixed use	62.0
Omni International	1977	Miami	regional	310.0
Gallery at Market East	1977	Philadelphia	regional	447.4
Hawthorne Plaza	1977	Hawthorne, Calif.	regional	836.3
Port Plaza Mall	1977	Green Bay, Wis.	regional	585.0
Renaissance Center	1977	Detroit	mixed use	340.0
Rainier Square	1978	Seattle	mixed use	87.2
City Center Square	1978	Kansas City	mixed use	75.0
Pier 39	1978	San Francisco	specialty	200.0
St. Anthony Main	1978	Minneapolis	specialty	95.5
The Shops/Station Square	1979	Pittsburgh	mixed use	145.0
The Atrium/Uncle Sam Mall	1979	Troy, N.Y.	specialty	160.0
Arcade Square	1980	Dayton, Ohio	mixed use	85.0

(continued)

Name	Date opened	City	Type	New retail space*
Town Square	1980	St. Paul	mixed use	220.9
Plaza of the Americas	1980	Dallas	mixed use	100.0
Santa Monica Place	1980	Santa Monica	regional	565.2
Plaza Pasadena	1980	Pasadena	regional	584.5
Galleria of White Plains	1980	White Plains, N.Y.	regional	885.0
Harborplace	1980	Baltimore	specialty	142.0
Albee Square Mall	1980	Brooklyn	specialty	156.0
Georgetown Park	1981	Washington, D.C.	specialty	206.0
Bourse	1981	Philadelphia	mixed use	102.0
Brightleaf Square	1981	Durham, N.C.	mixed use	82.8
Embarcadero Center	1982	San Francisco	mixed use	325.0
Louisville Galleria	1982	Louisville, Ky.	mixed use	284.0
Illinois Center	1982	Chicago	mixed use	350.0
Santa Rosa Mall	1982	Santa Rosa, Calif.	regional	711.0
Grand Avenue	1982	Milwaukee	regional	245.0
Long Beach Plaza	1982	Long Beach	regional	612.5
Rainbow Centre	1982	Niagara Falls	regional	220.0
Stamford Town Center	1982	Stamford, Conn.	regional	900.0
Market at Davol Square	1982	Providence, R.I.	specialty	63.0
Windmill Place	1982	Flint, Mich.	specialty	73.0
Pavilion/Old Post Office	1983	Washington, D.C.	mixed use	52.9
Charleston Tower Center	1983	Charleston, W. Va.	mixed use	905.8
Canal Place	1983	New Orleans	mixed use	260.0
Trump Tower	1983	New York	mixed use	160.0
Copley Place	1983	Boston	mixed use	368.0
One Oxford Center	1983	Pittsburgh	mixed use	80.0
Glendale Galleria II	1983	Glendale, Calif.	regional	509.2
Gallery II	1983	Philadelphia	regional	371.6
Wausau Center	1983	Wausau, Wis.	regional	410.3
Waterside	1983	Norfolk, Va.	specialty	78.7
South Street Seaport	1983	New York	specialty	253.0
Alexandria Torpedo Factory	1983	Alexandria, Va.	specialty	na

(continued)

Name	Date opened	City	Type	New retail space*
Tabor Center	1984	Denver	mixed use	116.8
Lafayette Place	1984	Boston	mixed use	300.0
Shops at National Center	1984	Washington, D.C.	mixed use	124.0
City Center	1984	Minneapolis	mixed use	455.0
Portside	1984	Toledo, Ohio	mixed use	60.0
Hyatt-Saks	1985	Cincinnati	mixed use	122.9
St. Louis Centre	1985	St. Louis	mixed use	350.0
Horton Plaza	1985	San Diego	regional	885.0
Tivoli	1985	Denver	specialty	170.0
St. Louis Union Station	1985	St. Louis	mixed use	159.0
Herald Center	1985	New York	specialty	130.0
Marketplace Center	1985	Boston	mixed use	66.0

*In thousands of square feet.

"The Malls at Water Tower Place," *AR* 162 (May 1977), 99–104; and Charles Hoyt, "The Seven Level Shopping Mall at Water Tower Place: A Try for a Revolutionary Thing," *AR* 159 (April 1976), 136–140.

Profiles of the following projects are in J. Thomas Black et al., *Downtown Retail Development: Conditions for Success and Project Profiles* (Washington, D.C.: ULI, 1983): ARCO Plaza, Baystate West, Broadway Plaza, Canal Place, Charleston Town Center, Eaton Centre, Faneuil Hall Marketplace, Gallery at Market Street East, Glendale Galleria, Grand Avenue, Harborplace, Horton Plaza, Lexington Center, Louisville Galleria, NCNB Plaza, Pike Place Market, Plaza of the Americas, Plaza Pasadena, Port Plaza Mall, Rainbow Centre, The Shops at Station Square, St. Louis Centre, Town Square, Water Tower Place.

Case Studies

Five case studies on downtown retail centers form the basis for our analysis of the problems and process of building retail centers downtown: Faneuil Hall Marketplace (Boston), Horton Plaza (San Diego), Plaza Pasadena (Pasadena, Calif.), Pike Place Market (Seattle), and Town Square (St. Paul). Working from a briefing guide we drafted, research assistants interviewed the main participants, reviewed project files, and drafted the cases. We then did follow-up interviews, circulated the draft cases among the principal actors, and made cross-checks on factual material with other sources. Most of the work was done between 1983 and 1985.

Many of the data come from public agency documents and memoranda and developer project files. These primary materials provided information on scheduling, design issues, negotiations, development costs, financing, and leasing. The public documents were especially important because they included development agreements spelling out the business terms. We also made use of secondary sources. In the notes below, we identify who worked on the cases and the people interviewed. We also note any additional material we used not cited in the case studies.

Faneuil Hall

The account of Faneuil Hall Marketplace is based on Jacques Gordon, "Faneuil Hall Marketplace: A Case Study," prepared for educational use, in authors' files. Sources include documents from the files of the Boston Redevelopment Authority and Faneuil Hall Marketplace, Inc., published articles and reports, and interviews of Benjamin Thompson, Stewart Forbes, Roy Williams, Norman Leventhal, James McLean, Alex Ganz, Sharon Cavanaugh, Edward Logue, Carol Todreas, Jeanne Alexander Woods, John Sayres, Kevin Lynch, and Mayor Kevin White. In follow-up work on the city's lease revenue payments, data were supplied by John Avault, BRA research economist, and on the terms of profit sharing by Paul L. McCann, executive assistant to the director, BRA.

Additional sources are Benjamin Thompson and Jane McC. Thompson, *Restoration of Faneuil Hall Marketplace: Comments on Historic, Architectural and Urban Issues* (brochure, August 1976); Stewart Forbes, BRA memorandum, February 6, 1974; Rouse Company Research Department, "Consumer Research: Faneuil Hall Marketplace" (1978?), survey undertaken October 1977; John Hubner, "All That Glitters Is Not Gold: How Rouse Rakes It in at Faneuil Hall Marketplace," *Real Paper*, March 31, 1979, pp. 14–19; Colin Campbell, "About Boston: Faneuil Hall Marketplace after Ten Years," *NYT*, August 16, 1986, p. 6; and "Marketplace Security Keeps the Grinch Away," *BG*, December 3, 1985, p. 25.

On the Faneuil Hall tenants' suit, see Joanne Lipman, "Angry Tenants Charge Rouse Co. with Unfair Practices in Its Malls," *WSJ*, June 18, 1984, p. 25; Bruce A. Mohl, "Faneuil Hall Lawsuit Ruled Class Action," *BG*, January 10, 1984, p. 52; Douglas M. Bailey, "Faneuil Hall Merchants Win $3M from Developer," *BG*, October 31, 1986, p. 73.

On the fiscal implications of redevelopment, see Lynne B. Sagalyn, "Measuring Financial Returns When the City Acts As an Investor" (paper presented to the American Real Estate and Urban Economics Association, December 30, 1987); this paper also documents the change in land values in downtown Boston. John Avault with Elizabeth Fitzpatrick, "An Overview of Factors Influencing Commercial Real Estate Values in Boston 1977–1990," Boston Redevelopment Authority Policy Development and Research Department, October 9, 1986; and Lewis Bolan, "Harborplace and Faneuil Hall Area Study," prepared for Jerry Schlichter, East St. Louis, Illinois (Washington, D.C.: Leggatt McCall Advisors, July 29, 1985.

Articles on the opening of Faneuil Hall Marketplace are Ken O. Botwright, "This Is Yours . . . Enjoy It," *BG*, August 27, 1976, p. 1; Margo Miller, "The Day the Marketplace Opened," *BG*, August 27, 1976, p. 23; James Hammond, "Historic Market Reopens," *Boston Evening Globe*, August 27, 1976, p. 1; John Kifner, "A 'New' 1826 Market Joins Boston's Downtown Revival," *NYT*, August 27, 1976, p. B1; Jane Davison, "Bringing Life to Market," *NYT Magazine*, October 10, 1976, pp. 74–78; and Gurney Breckenfeld, "Jim Rouse Shows How to Give Downtown Retailing New Life," *Fortune*, April 10, 1978, pp. 84–91. Also see ARCHITECTURAL CRITICISM.

Horton Plaza

The account of Horton Plaza, San Diego, is based on Jacques Gordon, "Horton Plaza, San Diego: A Case Study of Public-Private Development," MIT Center for Real Estate Development, Working Paper No. 2, December 1985. The case draws on documents from the Centre City Development Corporation, Planning Department of the City of San Diego, and Ernest W. Hahn, Inc., and interviews with Roy Potter, Angeles Leira, Gerald Trimble, John Gilchrist, Jr., Dan Felix, A. Jerry Keyser, Frank Alessi, Michael Stepner, David Allsbrook, Harry Evans, Mary Joralman, Carol Lindenmulder, Max Schmidt, James Spotts, and Scott Ashton.

Other sources are Christie Baxter, "Case Study: University Town Centre, San Diego," prepared as part of a series of case studies of downtown development directed by Bernard J. Frieden and Lynne B. Sagalyn, MIT Department of Urban Studies and Planning, April 1985; "Horton Plaza, San Diego, Ca.," ULI Project Reference File, vol. 16 (1986); "Horton Plaza: The Urban Festival Opens August 9," special report by *San Diego Home/Garden Magazine* in cooperation with Ernest W. Hahn, Inc., and the Centre City Development Corporation (1985); Ernest W. Hahn, Inc., "Horton Plaza: Summary of Tenant Design Criteria"; n.d.; "Horton Plaza Lures a Variety of Visitors," *San Diego Union*, August 10, 1986, p. 1; and Michael Krey, "City Seems Ready to Let Hahn Slide," *San Diego Daily Transcript*, April 9, 1987.

The architectural reviews we used are: Donald Canty, "San Diego Gets an Exuberant New Downtown Development," *Architecture* 74 (November 1985), 16; Robert Guenther, "Horton Plaza May Introduce Shopping Centers' New Look," *WSJ*, June 26, 1985, p. 29; Robert Lindsay, "New Life for San Diego's Downtown," *NYT*, April 27, 1985, p. 7; Robert Lindsey, "San Diego Builds a Village Just to Shop In," *NYT*, August 17, 1985, p. 48; Sam Hall Kaplan, "Horton Plaza: Hope, Hype," *Los Angeles Times*, August 18, 1985, Real Estate p. 1; Paul Goldberger, "Freewheeling Fantasy in San Diego," *NYT*, March 19, 1986, p. A12; and Lori Weisberg, "Downtown's Pastel Emporium Is in the Pink," *San Diego Union*, August 10, 1986, p. 1. Also see ARCHITECTURAL CRITICISM.

Pike Place Market

The account of the Pike Place Market is based on Nancy Fox, "Pike Place Market: A Case Study," prepared for educational uses, in authors' files. The case study drew on materials from files of the Pike Place Market Preservation and Development Authority, government documents, published reports, and interviews of John Clise, Harris Hoffman, Harriet Sherburne, Phyllis Lamphere, John Turnbull, Virginia Felton, James Mason, Alf Collins, Shirley Collins, Wes Uhlman, Tom Brunton, Bruce Lorig, Sally Gene Mahoney, and James Braman.

Other sources are Seattle Department of Community Development, "Survey of Merchants and Businesses in the Pike Place Urban Renewal Project" (August 1982); Clise letter and city council critique in City of Seattle, "Public Corporations in Seattle: A Survey Report to the Seattle City Council" (August 1981); Downtown Seattle Association, *Annual Report: 1978* (Seattle, 1978); Ann Satterthwaite, "The Rediscovery of Public Markets as Nuclei of Neighborhoods," *AIA Journal* 66 (August 1977), 46–48; and Betty J. Ritter, "Magical Market Place: Seattle's Pike Place Market," *AF* 138 (April 1973), 58–63.

Plaza Pasadena

The account of Plaza Pasadena is based on Lynne B. Sagalyn, "Case Study: Plaza Pasadena, Pasadena," prepared for educational uses, in authors' files. The case study draws on documents from the Pasadena Redevelopment Agency, City of Pasadena Planning Commission, Pasadena Community Development Commission, and Ernest W. Hahn Inc. and interviews with Paul Curran, William Doyle, John M. Gilchrist, Jr., Ernest W. Hahn, Ronald Hahn, A. Jerry Keyser, Jerome F. Lipp, Dale A. Nelson, Cornelius J. Pings, William C. Reynolds, Christopher Sutton, Gerald M. Trimble, and Randy Curruchi.

Other sources are Gerald M. Trimble, "Regrowth in Pasadena," *Urban Land* 36 (January 1977), 4–14; Pasadena Redevelopment Agency (Los Angeles County, California), "Official Statement Relating to $3,800,000 Downtown Development Project Series 1975 Notes," October 16, 1975; "Summary Report on the Conveyance and Lease of Property within the Downtown Redevelopment Project to H-CHH Associates by the Pasadena Redevelopment Agency," n.d.; John Morris Dixon, "Procession in Pasadena," *PA* 62 (July 1981), 94–97; and ULI, *Plaza Pasadena, Pasadena, California*, Project Reference File, vol. 12 (July-September 1982).

Town Square

The account of Town Square is based on Christie Baxter, "Case Study: Town Square, St. Paul," prepared for educational uses, in authors' files. Sources include documents from the files of the City of St. Paul and of the developer, Oxford Properties U.S. Ltd., and interviews with George W. Latimer; Robert F. Van Hoef, Douglas Foster, James T. Hart, Eugene Engelburt, Edward

Helfeld, Robert V. Hovelson, Lindley Deardorff, Philip Nason, Eugene Kraut, Gary E. Stout, Bruce Johnson, Stephen Wellington, James Bellus, Ronald Maddox, Weiming Lu, Peggy Reichert, Robert Davis, Barry Engin, Peggy Fedder, William Pierson, Daniel McCaffrey, and William Eiden.

Pedestrian traffic counts were made available by Barry Laskov, vice-president of retail marketing, Oxford Properties, November 16, 1983. Information on 1985 retail sales and department store reactions is from Wilma Randle, "Changes Affect Town Square," *St. Paul Pioneer Press and Dispatch,* April 27, 1986, p. 1D.

Interviews

(conducted by authors,* or by research associates)

Frank Alessi,* finance director, Centre City Development Corporation, San Diego; 1983.

David Allsbrook, project director for Horton Plaza, Centre City Development Corporation, San Diego; 1983.

Scott Ashton,* Horton Plaza project director for architect Jon Jerde; 1984.

James Bellus,* director, Department of Planning and Economic Development, St. Paul; 1984.

James Braman,* former director, Seattle Department of Community Development, 1983.

Tom Brunton,* Seattle Department of Community Development; 1983.

Sharon Cavanaugh, former leasing agent, Faneuil Hall Marketplace, Inc.; 1983.

Grady Clay,* former editor, *Landscape Architecture,* and former real estate editor, *Louisville Courier-Journal;* 1986.

John Clise,* director of Pike Place Market; 1983.

Alf Collins,* Seattle journalist; November 16, 1983.

Shirley Collins,* merchant in Pike Place Market; 1983.

Jill Ker Conway,* former president of Smith College and former trustee of the College Retirement Equities Fund; 1987.

Joseph E. Coomes,* redevelopment attorney, Sacramento, Calif.; 1984–1987.

Paul Curran,* project architect for Plaza Pasadena; 1985.

Randy Curruchi,* manager of Plaza Pasadena, Hahn Company; 1983.

Robert Davis, staff, Comprehensive Planning Department, Twin Cities Metropolitan Council; 1983.

Lindley Deardorff, former project manager of Town Square, Oxford Properties, U.S., Ltd.; 1983.

Scott Ditch,* director of public relations, Rouse Company; 1985.

William Doyle,* vice-president for predevelopment, Hahn Company; 1983.

William Eiden, former manager, Donaldsons Department Store, St. Paul; 1983.

Norman Elkin,* vice-president, JMB/Urban Development Co. (formerly Urban Investment and Development Co.); 1985–1988.

Eugene Engelburt, owner of St. Paul Book and Stationery Co.; 1983.

Barry Engin, former project manager for St. Paul Department of Parks; 1983.

Peggy Fedders, accountant, St. Paul Port Authority; 1984.

Daniel Felix,* vice-president redevelopment, Hahn Company; 1983.

Virginia Felton,* public relations director, Pike Place Market; 1983.

Stewart Forbes, former deputy director for development, Boston Redevelopment Authority; 1983.

Douglas Foster, former St. Paul Housing and Redevelopment Authority urban designer; 1983.

Randy Foxworthy,* executive vice-president, Melvin Simon & Associates, Inc.; 1987.

Alex Ganz, director of research, Boston Redevelopment Authority; 1982, 1983.

John M. Gilchrist, Jr.,* president of Hahn Company; 1983, 1984, 1987, 1988.

William Greenough,* past president and chairman of the board, Teachers Insurance and Annuity Association–College Retirement Equities Fund; 1987.

Ernest W. Hahn,* former chairman of the board and president of Hahn Company; 1983, 1985, 1987.

Ronald Hahn,* former vice-president, Hahn Company; 1983.

James T. Hart, former St. Paul Housing and Redevelopment Authority attorney; 1983.

Bruce Hayden,* chairman, Tolzmann & Associates, Inc., and former lending officer at Connecticut General and Life Insurance Co.; 1987.

Edward Helfeld, former executive director, St. Paul Housing and Redevelopment Authority; 1983.

Harris Hoffman,* director, Pike Place Market; 1983.

Robert V. Hovelson, vice-president, Oxford Properties, U.S., Ltd; 1983.

Bruce Johnson, vice-president, Donaldsons Department Store, St. Paul; 1983.

Mary Joralman,* president, Save Our Heritage Organization (SOHO); 1984.

A. Jerry Keyser,* president, Keyser Marston Associates, 1983, 1987, 1988.

Eugene Kraut,* vice-president, St. Paul Port Authority; 1983.

Phyllis Lamphere,* former city council member, Seattle; 1983.

George W. Latimer,* mayor of St. Paul; 1983.

Angeles Leira,* project planner, San Diego Planning Department; 1983, 1985.

Norman Leventhal, chairman and chief executive officer, Beacon Companies, Boston; 1983.

Carol Lindenmulder,* past president, Save Our Heritage Organization (SOHO); 1984.

Gary Lindstrom, former property manager of Town Square, Oxford Properties, U.S., Ltd.; 1983.

Jerome F. Lipp,* president, Carter Hawley Hale Properties, Inc.; 1983, 1985.

Edward Logue,* former director, Boston Redevelopment Authority; 1983, 1985.

Bruce Lorig,* developer in Pike Place Market area, Seattle; 1983.

Weiming Lu, director, Lowertown Redevelopment Corporation, St. Paul; 1983.

Kevin Lynch,* former consultant on planning on Boston's Government Center and Waterfront areas; 1983.

Ronald Maddox, former St. Paul city councillor and Building Owners and Managers Association member; 1983.

Sally Gene Mahoney,* Seattle journalist; 1983.

Daniel McCaffrey, vice-president for Retail Development, Oxford Properties, U.S., Ltd.; 1983.

James McLean,* general manager, Faneuil Hall Marketplace, Inc.; 1983.

Gerald Maier,* senior vice-president, Philadelphia Industrial Development Corporation; 1985.

Samuel Marasco,* general counsel, Hahn Company; 1983.

Amos Martin,* president, St. Paul Chamber of Commerce; 1983.

James Mason,* former project director, Pike Place Market; 1983.

Martin Millspaugh,* president, Enterprise International Development Co.; 1985, 1988.

Phillip Nason, former chairman of the board, First National Bank of St. Paul; 1983.

Dale Nelson,* project manager of Plaza Pasadena and Horton Plaza, Hahn Company; 1983.

Carol Nichols,* vice-president, Mortgage and Real Estate, Teachers Insurance and Annuity Association; 1987.

William Pierson, Department of Planning and Economic Development, St. Paul, construction manager for Town Square; 1983.

Cornelius J. Pings,* former president of the board, Pasadena Redevelopment Authority; 1983.

Matt Potter,* San Diego city planner active in opposition to Horton Plaza; 1984.

Roy Potter,* executive vice-president, San Diegans, Inc.; 1983.

Francine Rabinovitz,* principal, Hamilton-Rabinovitz, and professor, University of Southern California; 1983.

Peggy Reichert, deputy director of planning, Department of Planning and Economic Development, St. Paul; 1983.

William G. Reynolds,* executive director, Pasadena Community Development Commission; 1983.

James W. Rouse,* formerly chairman, Rouse Company, and chairman, Enterprise Foundation; 1985.

John Sayres, project director of Downtown Waterfront Renewal Area, Boston Redevelopment Authority; 1983.

Max Schmidt,* assistant vice-president, Centre City Development Corporation, San Diego; 1983.

Thomas Schriber,* president, Donahue-Schriber; 1987.

Harriet Sherburne,* former project director, Pike Place Market; 1983.

Chares E. Smith,* consultant to Rouse Company; 1989.

Charles H. Spaulding, partner, Spaulding & Slye; 1983.

William Spong,* staff, Research Division, New York City Department of Finance; 1986.

James Spotts,* former acting director of Centre City Development Corporation, San Diego; 1984.

Michael Stepner,* deputy director, San Diego City Planning Department; 1983, 1984.

Gary E. Stout, former director, Department of Planning and Economic Development, St. Paul; 1983.

Albert Sussman,* former executive director, International Council of Shopping Centers; 1985.

Christopher Sutton, opponent of Plaza Pasadena; 1983.

Poston Tanaka,* vice-president, finance, Hahn Company; 1983.

Benjamin Thompson,* architect for Faneuil Hall Marketplace; 1983.

Carol Todreas, former director of promotions for Faneuil Hall Marketplace, Inc.; 1983.

Gerald R. Trimble,* executive director, Centre City Development Corporation, San Diego, and former executive director, Pasadena Redevelopment Authority; 1983, 1984, 1985, 1987; in his role as consultant to Burbank; 1987.

John Turnbull,* coordinator of Pike Place Market Historical Commission; 1983.

Wes Uhlman,* former mayor of Seattle; 1983.

Robert F. Van Hoef,* vice-president, First National Bank, and former executive director of Metropolitan Improvement Committee and Operation 85; 1983.

Raymond Vernon,* professor, Kennedy School of Government, Harvard University; 1983.

Stephen Wellington, director, Department of Planning and Economic Development, St. Paul; 1983.

Kevin White,* former mayor of Boston; 1985.

Roy Williams, former project director, Faneuil Hall Marketplace, Inc.; 1983.

Jeanner Alexander Woods, assistant general manager for retailing, Faneuil Hall Marketplace, Inc.; 1983.

Index